The Theory and Reality of New Western International Intervention

Zhang Yunling   Zhou Hong

LIBER PUBLICATIONS INTERNATIONAL
London - Berlin - Istanbul - Santiago

This edition is an authorized translation from the Chinese language edition, published in cooperation with **Social Sciences Academic Press**, Beijing, China.

Published with financial support of the Innovation Program of the Chinese Academy of Social Sciences.

The Theory and Reality of New Western International Intervention
Editors: Zhang Yunling, Zhou Hong
Original Title: 西方新国际干预的理论与现实 / ISBN: 978-7-5097-3424-7
Copyright © Social Sciences Academic Press, 2012.
We thank Canut Intl. Publishers for their translation cooperation.

Liber Publications International.
33 Holmlea Rd.
Reading RG8 9EX
United Kingdom

Copyright © Liber Publications International, 2017
All rights reserved. No part of this book may be used or reproduced in any manner whatsoever without the written permission of the publishers.
ISBN: 978-605-9914-49-9
Printed in UK
Lightning Source Ltd. UK
Chapterhouse, Pitfield Kiln Farm
MK11 3LW
United Kingdom

Contents

Preface   i

Introduction   1
—Criticism on the Military Intervention against Libya
   Zhou Hong

Humanitarian Intervention and Its Constraints
— Criticism on the Military Intervention against Libya
   Shi Yinhong   17

Analysis of the Motives behind US Military Interventions in the Post-Cold War Era
   Qi Haixia   37

European Humanitarian Interventions after the Cold War:
—Theories, Policies and Practices
   Zhao Huaipu   63

A Discussion on the Means, Results and Influences of International Intervention Performed by Western Major Countries
— Taking the Middle East as an example
   Wang Jinglie   97

Coercive Diplomacy and the Issue of International Conflict Management
— Case Analysis of Iran Nuclear Crisis
   Zhou Shixin   **123**

The Evolution and Development of Judicial Intervention
— A Survey on the Practices of the International Court of Justice (ICJ)
   Song Jie   **143**

Principal Forms of Interventions by U.S. and
the Factors Behind Its Interventions
   Zhang Jiadong   **177**

Democratic Aid and International Interventions by the U.S.
   Liu Guozhu   **201**

On Western Neo-interventionism:
The Libya War and the "Libyan Model"
   Wang Lincong   **227**

The Military Intervention by EU in Libya
   Wu Xian   **247**

International Interventions and Governance in the Balkan Region
— Bosnia and Herzegovina Case
   Kong Tianping   **271**

External Religious Intervention:
The Case of Kosovo Conflict
   Zhang Yuan   **291**

Editor's Preface

As international interference incidents augment in many regions of the world, the issue of international interference came fore more prominently in the academy and international law researches. Currently, we can observe multifarious forms international interventions, and their impacts on the international developments are obvious and increasingly influential.

Since, international interventions take a myriad of forms in terms of their goals, methods employed and assume different properties, it is not easy to generalize them. Although, some international interventions can never be justified from the aspects of the law and international norms, it should be admitted that some international interventions have reasonable grounds, and play benign and constructive roles, and the latter are properly authorized by the UN Security Council, they prevent evil incidents, safeguard justice and peace, thus lives, security and rights of many people are guaranteed. This kind of intervention, most of the time, take peaceful forms, deploying peacekeeping troops to prevent violence from further escalation.

On the other hand, irrational interventions are viewed as ad hoc, counterproductive and illegitimate interventions, they are not authorized by the UN Security Council, or go beyond its authorization stipulations, thereby bypass the international law and institutions, and serve the narrow interests of certain states or groups, this type of interventions sometimes employ non-violent ways such as economic and political sanctions, embargoes and containment of a country, but mostly resort to military forces, heavy bombing and shelling and even overthrow the current regime, replace the government and promote their own allies ascending to power.

Looking from a rational historical view, the increasing demands for international intervention can be seen an important manifestation of human progress, because human beings share the same dwelling space——our earth——and mankind cannot stand idly by or stand aside when other humans are suffering and their lives are threatened, which require the interference of international aid and support.

But, if the illegitimate international interventions go rampant, then it will cause great harm, since such interventions, no matter under which holy banner, are bound to serve the selfish interests of a group of states or their strategic aims, whereas other nations and people become their victims. It also worth mentioning that international interventions by the major Western powers are increasingly spreading, and some states in collusion strive to use loopholes of UN authorizations, mislead the international community, and pressure the UN Security Council, to get approvals for interventions, and even we observe that some states bypass the UN and arbitrarily launch military operations targeting other countries and even attempt regime changes.

Western interventionists have invented and developed abundant concepts and theories to justify their intentions and actions. In this way they attempt to dress the irrational international intervention under a "reasonable" cloak. At the same time, such interventionism sides with the strong against the weak, consequently, weaker nations are put under double pressure, practically and theoretically, thus losers are victimized and demonized, acts of the strong and illegitimate are presented as "natural" rights, resulting in the logic of the strong: the survival of the strongest.

In order to develop a comprehensive and deeper understanding of the theories and practices of Western international interventions, in 2011 the Institute of International Studies attached to CASS has launched a topical research and analysis project entitled as "Theory and Reality of New Western International Intervention".

This topical research focuses on the developments related to the theories and practices of the Western international interventions in the post-Cold War era. Under the project, academic papers and books were published to present the relevant research fruits, written by the participant experts from domestic research institutions and universities. And, in order to exchange views and further promote the researches, the Institute of International Studies, has organized a symposium for this very purpose.

Zhou Hong, the deputy director of the Institute of International Studies, has written the preface part of the book, which not only gives information and comment on the research papers included in the book, but also expounds her unique research results on the topic.

I would like to extend gratitude to Tan Xiuying—chief editor of Journal of the World Economy and Politics, who greatly contributed to the selection of the papers included in the book, and to Ms. Li Mo from our Institute, for her meticulous work in the realization of this book.

We hope the publication of this book, will further promote the academic researches on the issue of international intervention, and provide the readers with valuable insight on the issue.

Zhang Yunling,
Director,
The Institute of International Studies of CASS,
March 20th, 2012, Beijing

Introduction
—Criticism on the Military Intervention against Libya

Zhou Hong[1]

I. The new development in international interference

The expression of "international interventionism" (interventionism) falls into two categories and is often taken in three forms. English writers often interchangeable use the terms of "intervention" and "interference" when referring to international interventionism. However, generally speaking, the former indicates that states involve themselves into the internal affairs of other countries by political and military means. Therefore, "intervention" in most cases, is translated as "干涉" or "武装干涉" in Chinese. Different from "intervention", "interference" is not limited to military interference; so "interference" in Chinese could also be referred as "干预", specifically "行政干预" or "经济干预". However, sometimes, "interference" is equal to "intervention". For example, "humanitarian interference" is almost the same as "humanitarian intervention" in that "humanitarian interference" is usually related to how to exploit armed forces to intervene into other countries' own business. International interventionism can be realized by military, economic and political means. And in the field of economy and technology, interference is comprehensively applied for foreign aid, foreign trade, military assistance and military trade to name but a few, and apart from economic sanction and the limiting conditions to the aid, the interference through media and new media platform is also categorized into technological interference. Considering the intimacy between political interference

---

1 Director of European Research Institute of Chinese Academy of Social Sciences, Committee member and Deputy Director Chairman of the Institute of International Studies attached to CASS.

and military interference, military interference has now been extended to the field of politics, which means the employment of armed forces against a sovereignty state in itself is a kind of interference, and other forms of non armed forces such as political and economic sanctions, arms embargo, and standing trials at international criminal court are also regarded as part of the content.

In the studies on international relations, the proposal of getting rid of international intervention or international interference which includes both the coercive interference and the non-coercive interference is almost always a failure. Even dated back to the Cold War, there already existed the international interferences. Military interference between the camps of socialism and capitalism has already left its footprint at that time. With the end of the Cold War, the world especially in the 21st century, has went through drastic changes in international configuration as a result of the frequent use of military interference which is now undermining the stability of the world in various ways. In such context, the international interference theories and practices have become a hot topic in the field of international relations and have drawn a wide attention around the world.

Different from the traditional international interventionism, the new modes of intervention have become more military-oriented with a tendency of undermining the sovereignty of the states. Though these have not yet been systematically theorized, the constant interference actions have already shaken the foundation of the UN Charter and adversely influenced the world pattern that is shaped on the basis of state sovereignty and equal status that every state should enjoy.

II. International interventionism in the post-cold war era

To learn and explain the non-defensive activities frequently undertaken against sovereign states since the end of the Cold War requires a basic judgment on the scope of state authority, especially in terms of the authority that states exert when involved in a foreign war or signing a peace agreement. In a discussion of the justice and the legitimacy of a war, Hugo Grotius (Hugo de Groot), an international jurist from the Netherlands, highlighted the rationality of self-defense within control, and he said, the law of nature allows self-defense against any dangers." He also mentioned that any kind of self-defense is permitted if our lives are under the threat of public violence or in the danger of assassination by thugs or enemies.[2]

---

[2] Hugo Grotius: the Rights of War and Peace. Trans. He Qinhui, Shanghai People's Publishing House, 2005, P. 54.

Similarly, the Christian "Just War" theory that is used for justifying wars in the Western world, is based on the premise of rational actions , and it argues that "wars are considered to be just if they are fought for a worthy cause, and are likely to achieve it, sponsored by a legitimate authority, undertaken as a last resort, and conducted in a way that uses no excess force than is necessary or proportionate use of force and which respects the welfare of non-combatants." The conclusion on the acts of war in the view of Christianity can be seen in Haass' book–Intervention: The Use of American Military Force in the Post-Cold War World.[3]

The Peace of Westphalia in 1648 initiated a new system of world order that features elements such as the national self-determination and the principle of equal sovereignty. In the treaties, not only do states have their own peoples and defined territory, but also the authorities to deal with both their domestic affairs and foreign affairs and to make right choice between war and peace. Performing acts of sovereignty on a territory of its own basically guarantees that every country goes in line with the world order. All emerging sovereign states in Europe need to take efforts to tighten their controls on their domestic issues and base their activities on the principle of "non-intervention" so as to handle multiple challenges from the inside out and to achieve a harmony between states. And the national capacity and state power will manifest themselves, if states are able to coherently strike a balance between the internal mobilization and the declaration of a war against any foreign states and between the endorsement with other countries and reaching domestic consensus.

In Europe, defining state boundaries has played a vital role during the process of "nation-building", not only in that the size of territory is closely related to a country's economic well-being, but also it is a backbone of contention between states. And states are have used, every diplomatic means, even resorting to war in order to gain supremacy over other states. As a spotlight in diplomatic activities and warfare, territorial boundary is also regarded as a means by which a country can be independent of others through its authority limits, which means state can merely handle the issues under its jurisdiction within its boundary, while issues outside this scope would fall into the relation category. Grotius believes that intervention by war must be performed on justified grounds.[4]

---

3 Haass, Richard N. Trans. Yin Xiong, Xu Jing, Beijing, Xinhua Publishing House, 2000, p. 9-10.
4 Hugo Grotius: the Rights of War and Peace. Trans. He Qinhui, Shanghai People's Publishing House, 2005, p. 73.

And the excuses should be able to be explainable with reasons. And if a state's involvement in a war is out of self-defense, only when the danger is imminent, can this war be justified.[5]

That is to say only when oppressed with humiliation, can state have a reason to involve itself in war. In the 18th century, as the undertaking of "nation-building" in West European soil was approaching completion, European countries, embarked into an era of overseas expansion, which has aroused theorists' reflections on the principle of non-intervention proposed in the Peace of Westphalia. Nowadays, when opposing the principle of non-intervention, people often refer to the theories proposed by John Stuart Mill in 1859. Living in an era when European colonists were trying to theoretically justify overseas expansion, John Stuart Mill has mentioned that there was a need that the whole doctrines of non-intervention should be re-evaluated. Although it is little justifiable to force people from other countries to submit to our will in any other respect, "to suppose that the same international customs, and the same rules of international morality, can obtain between one civilized nation and another, and between civilized nations and barbarians, is a grave error..."[6]

According to the arguments Mill asserted, the wars waged by French and UK against Algeria and India can be justified because the civilized countries' invading "barbarous countries" was legitimate. "Civilized countries" stick to different principles compared to "barbarous countries", and because of that, states do not share equal stance in the world; therefore, nowadays some people try to classify countries into different statuses such as the democratic states, failed states and rogue states to justify wars.

As a liberalism proponent of the 19th century, Mill was inevitably affected by the prejudices that lay behind imperialism at that time, prone to support the freedom of power, which may give the powerful states the impetus to oppress the weak states. However, when quoting the views held by Mills, people often neglect one point. As far as Mills was concerned, country is recognized with the right for self-determination. The so-called institutions of freedom established by the forces from outside, cannot survive because liberty cannot be gained externally. It is impossible for the native citizens to naturally rely on the alien mechanism, even if the country in itself lacks the liberal mechanisms. The practices in modern international politics have proved that although the "civilized countries" export their understanding

---

5 Hugo Grotius: the Rights of War and Peace, translated by He Qinhui, Shanghai People's Publishing House, 2005, p. 110.
6 John Stuart Mill (1859), A Few Words on Non-Intervention at the Online Library of Liberty.

of civilization to the "barbarous countries" without negotiation on equal terms, the so-called "mechanism of freedom" implanted in the "barbarous countries" through armed forces has virtually redoubled the level of barbarism in these states. Hence, after the Second World War, the theory and practices have been battered by the tide of national liberation movement and anti-colonial movement.

The Second World War has marked the watershed in the history of international relations. New world order has been established based on the Charter of the United Nations that has drawn lessons from the crimes committed by Hitler and laid down the principles of territorial integrity, political independence and non-intervention to help enhance the social well-being and protect the developing weaker states. For example, it is stated in Article 2, the 4th Principle that "all members shall refrain in their international relations from the threat or use of force against the territorial integrity or political independence of any state, or in any other manner inconsistent with the Purposes of the United Nations."

And in Article 2, the 7th Principle, "Nothing contained in the present Charter shall authorize the United Nations to intervene in matters which are essentially within the domestic jurisdiction of any state…"[7]

As a matter of fact, neither in the context of European colonialism nor the two world wars, nothing has ever shaken the principle of state sovereignty as the foundation of international relations. As the kernel of the customary international law and the Charter of the United Nations, the principles of national independence and non-intervention have been confirmed and justified repeatedly through international agreements. And during the process, weak countries are protected from invasion and the activities for maintaining peace and security are promoted. In the past 45 years after the Second World War, the principle of equal sovereignty has come in the spotlight in the discussions over the world order. However, since 1990s, with the reverse developments in the international situation, the outmoded theories have been brought to life. In this context, the world order founded on states sovereignty is going through dramatic changes.

The end of tension between the East and the West in 1990 signifies lower cost of interference and has marked the year with significant importance in that era.[8]

---

7 http://www.un.org/zh/documents/charter/chapter1.shtml.
8 Thomas G. Weiss, Humanitarian Intervention: Ideas in Action, Cambridge: Polity, 2007, p. 18.

From the time on, with the frequent cross-border activities, we have seen an unprecedented decline in the notion of territorial integrity of countries. And since 1990s, especially with the 21th century, Manfred B. Steger has made an observation on the population movements across the borders and other cross-border phenomena which are categorized as commodity trade, nationalism, foreign diplomacy, immigration, troop movements, use of missiles, computer information network, monitoring by management institutions on the globe, satellite communications, E-currency allocation, pollution across border, and so forth. He pointed that for these cross-border activities, except the ones like commodity trade, nationalism, foreign diplomacy, immigration, troop movements all of which are under the jurisdiction of state sovereignty and which are restricted by borders, the remainder six movements could occur across the border, thus directly impacting other states.[9]

In such context, the newly emerging theories around the point that a sovereign country can intervene in the domestic affairs of another, has far exceeds the scope of explanations on "the forced defense" in the traditional meaning of international relations. In short, the new questions are centered on the following aspects, below.

First, the function of power balance: why do some countries take so much interest in intervening in other countries' business, that they employ every possible means in the field of economy, culture, politics, or even resort to military means at the cost of domestic support by their citizens?

Second, the impetus behind the interests–what is behind intervention acts: to gain resources, geological/geopolitical advantages or whatever?

Third, seeking the backbone of righteousness and justice, especially in order to gain support of people; therefore, it is necessary to explain in what context the international intervention, especially the military intervention is legitimate and moral.

One of the supportive evidences is that, if properly consider the crimes against humanity committed by the Nazi Germany, the international society allowed intervention acts in such cases as the holocaust of Jews in Nazi Germany. What's more, according to the principle of equal sovereignty and non-intervention, many cases of international interference after the Second World War failed to gain legitimacy on the grounds of laws. And there lacked solid evidences to support the military invasion towards Iraq that was criticized by some Western countries for its use of weapons of mass destruction. Further, the recent NATO invasion of Libya has gone

---

9 George Joseph Stiglitz, Globalization, A Very Short Introduction. Trans by. Ding Zhaoguo, Nanjing: Yilin Press, 2009, p. 54.

far beyond the powers permitted by the UN. And, the U.S. even repeatedly involves itself in wars and without any declaration, it even captures or assassinates targeted political leaders to manipulate "regime changes" and "nation-rebuilding".

The examples above has led to doubts on the principles of equal sovereignty, and the U. N. Secretary-General Boutros Boutros-Ghali admitted in 1992 that sovereignty theory is always inconsistent with the facts. Some scholars have pointed out that "international community deems the organized hypocrisy as the normal rule."[10]

According to Thomas G. Weiss, state sovereignty is regularly infringed by power use. It is widely acknowledged that in tide of the recent globalization, the cultural, environmental and economic impacts are exerted beyond borders without permissions given by any country.[11]

All these above make it necessary to establish a world order which makes sense in the current tide of globalization. On the one hand, people cast doubt on the validity of the basic principles of Charter of the United Nations and on the significance of Peace of Westphalia in today's world. On the other hand, some scholars and international organizations attempt to testify whether the statement of equal sovereignty and non-intervention in chapter II is contradictory to the one in chapter VII. It is defined carefully and exactly in the chapter VII-Action with Respect to Threats to the Peace, Breaches of the Peace, and Acts of Aggression, that only when the acts of a state would breach or threaten the international peace and security, can the Security Council of the United Nations employ unarmed or armed forces in order to "maintain and restore the international peace and security."

Realizing that any military intervention performed by sovereign states is required to be authorized by the UN, most countries are prone to seek support from the United Nations in that circumstance, leading to an over interpretation of the necessity and rationality of intervention, which as a matter of fact, far exceeds the scope of self-defense. Many issues, previously regarded as domestic affairs, are now put on the table of the Security Council, such as the large-scale migration of the population of a country, as a pretext, of humanitarian intervention.[12]

---

10 Stephen D. Krasner, Sovereignty: Organized Hypocrisy, Princeton: Princeton University Press, 1999, p. 9 and Thomas G. Weiss, Humanitarian Intervention: Ideas in Action, Cambridge: Polity, 2007, p. 12.
11 Anthony Giddens, Runaway World, New York: Routledge, 2000, and others, from: Thomas G. Weiss, Humanitarian Intervention: Ideas in Action, Cambridge: Polity, 2007, p.13.
12 Lori Fisler Damrosch, Enforcing Restraint: Collective Intervention in Internal Conflicts, New York: Council on Foreign Relations, 1993.

III. From humanitarian intervention to responsibility to protect

The last decade of the 20th century has witnessed an increasing tendency towards humanitarian intervention in the international relations. From the end of the Second World War to the year of 1989, the claim that armed intervention legally breaches the principle of state sovereignty has been the mainstream of international law. However, since 1990s, intrusive manners have been widely recognized and supported. In the year of 1999, The Kosovo crisis and the massive bombing campaign NATO launched against Yugoslavia were not authorized by the UN, and the war waged against Serbia also ran contrary to the principle of non-intervention. However, "humanitarian intervention" sets up a new ethical system which considers the use of armed forces by sovereign states against another to be legitimate and reasonable, and the system is even simplified to the extent that heads of states only need to announce, the will of military intervention against another state is to protect people from human rights abuses. So far, the major problem is that there is neither any legal definition to standardize humanitarian intervention, nor a convincing description of the extent to which the human right abuses cannot be tolerated. This is because from different legal, moral or political perspectives, people may draw different conclusions or define "human rights abuses" in different ways. Humanitarian intervention obviously promotes the threat of using armed forces or resort to them directly. States are able to send troops on the excuse of humanitarianism even without justifying whether the military mobilization is on the ground of self-defense. Neither do states need to verify, if they have exhausted other options before resorting to military intervention to settle disputes. Therefore, the principle of state sovereignty is undermined.

The topic of "humanitarian intervention" has frequently come to the fore as a topic of discussion after NATO intervention against Kosovo in 1999. And the discussion on the concept of humanitarian intervention has brought about doubts on the legitimacy of the employment of armed forces and also some related empirical theories and normative theories. And the questions involved here are: when can be the armed forces employed, who can be authorized for military intervention and whether armed interference is effective or not. Western scholars, especially the US scholars have made a further step to classify humanitarian intervention according to its goals and have enumerated a series of means such as blockade (embargo), humanitarian aid and rescue so as to achieve the goals like threatening, prevention, enforcement, punishment, peacekeeping, military operation, arbitration and nation-building (regime change), among which nation-building is both the core content and the goal. Richard Haass, the special assistant to George Bush in his presidency, has unreservedly unearthed the fact that "nation-building is an extremely intrusive form of intervention, one basis that seeks to bring about political leadership and, more important, procedures and institutions different from those that already exist. In the case of the United States, nation building seeks to promote and sustain democracy and free-market practices."[13]

And Haass has also cited from an analyst that "this mission is of imperial proportions and possible of endless duration." Even so, he has mentioned for many times that the opportunity of intervention should be grasped promptly. In terms of humanitarian intervention theories, it is the interests not morality and integrity that gives rise to intervention, and this is because "interests are the only motive."[14]

Power is the ultimate driving force, and it is just as what Haass has admitted "Humanitarian intervention" has given the US "the right or even obligation to intervene to help people s vis-à-vis their own government or another."[15]

It is equal to say that the interventions assumed by the United States is to create tension, conflicts or even military intervention against other states.

In many circumstances, military intervention performed by a state or group of states against another state, is not authorized by the Security Council of the United Nations, and it is admitted that military actions infringe the basic human rights.

But, some states insist that only when military intervention is for self-defense or is authorized through the UN Security Council, should a military intervention be considered as legitimate. And considering this, it is obvious that the intervention against Kosovo by NATO betrays the principles in the Chapter II of Charter of the UN. Some countries claim there are still cases where the violation of the Charter of the UN can be tolerated and free from legal punishment, since it is in line with the spirit of the UN Charter evaluated from the moral perspective, though technically speaking, goes against it.[16]

---

13 Haass, Richard N., Intervention: The Use of American Military Force in the Post-Cold War World. Trans. Yin Xiong, Xu Jing, Beijing, Xinhua Publishing House, 2000, p. 60.
14 Ibid., p. 67.
15 Ibid., p. 13.
16 Simon Chesterman, Just War or Just Peace? Humanitarian Intervention and International Law, Oxford: Oxford University Press, 2001, http://en.wikipedia.org/wiki/Humanitarian_intervention.

Some states believe that the unauthorized humanitarian intervention may be still legitimate in some rare cases from the aspect of common law. Of course, echoing on this theme, some scholars and international organizations call for legalizing humanitarian intervention, and even request to revise the UN Charter to accommodate it.[17]

However, the concept of "the power of humanitarian intervention" is stoutly resisted by the developing countries, most of which have experienced the evils of colonization, since humanitarian intervention is nothing but revisiting the Western colonialism of 19th century. Though Western countries criticize the developing countries for undermining human rights when dealing with their social issues, , in fact these social issues pointed out by Western countries are virtually a left-over from the history of colonization, and all the efforts to legalize humanitarian intervention is to maintain an unreasonable exploitation.[18]

Humanitarian intervention is a means employed by "civilized countries" to achieve the long-term domination around the world. And they think that by claiming humanitarianism acts, the powerful states can successfully carry out their geo-strategies that are impossible to be implemented, if the victim states follow other paths. More specifically, it means that the US would make use of the humanitarian intervention to achieve its own global or regional goals.[19]

Therefore, the so-called humanitarian intervention is unanimously condemned in the G77 Summit where 133 heads of states have participated in 2000.[20]

Some contemporary scholars regard Hugo Grotius as the founder of humanitarian intervention, and cite his statements on the relation between states and peoples, which means if peoples are under the oppression of the ruler to the extent that they cannot be guaranteed and provided with basic human rights, then whoever the victims are, the whole human society is naturally empowered to rise against that oppression.[21]

---

17 Fernando Teson, "The liberal case for humanitarian intervention," Humanitarian Intervention: Ethical, Legal and Political Dilemmas, Cambridge: Cambridge University Press, 2003, http://en.wikipedia.org/wiki/Humanitarian_intervention.
18 Anne Orford, Reading Humanitarian Intervention: Human Rights and the Use of Force in International Law, Cambridge: Cambridge University Press, 2003, http://en.wikipedia.org/wiki/Humanitarian_intervention.
19 Noam Chomsky, A New Generation Draws the Line: Kosovo, East Timor, and the Standards of the West, New York: Verso, 2001. See also: Tariq Ali, Masters of the Universe? NATO's Balkan Crusade, New York: Verso, 2000.
20 Declaration of the South Summit, 10-14 April 2000, http://en.wikipedia.org/wiki/Humanitarian_intervention.
21 H. Lauterpacht, "The Grotian Tradition in the International Law," in Richard Falk, et al., eds., International Law: A Contemporary Perspective, Boulder, Colo.: Westview Press,

Meanwhile, Grotius also mentioned the point that "as the imperfect obligations of charity, and other virtues of the same kind are not cognizable in a court of justice, then neither of them can be compelled by the armed forces. Because it is not the moral nature of a duty that can enforce its fulfillment, some legal righteous basis should be possessed by one of the parties in order to execute the obligation. Because, the moral obligation receives an additional weight from such a righteousness. This obligation therefore must be properly combined to the former so as to give a war, the nature of a just war. Thus a person who has conferred a favor, has not, strictly speaking, a right to demand a return, for that would be converting an act of kindness into a contract."[22]

Grotius has made a clear distinction between the just nature of a war and the abuse of it and has separated the moral reasons from interests of a state. According to his statements, any humanitarian intervention for the sake of personal interests sails under false colors, ignorant of fallacy.

The biased concept of "humanitarian intervention by force" may dialectically give rise to the emergence of the norm -"responsibility to protect". In 2001, International Conference on Information Systems Security (ICISS) sponsored by the Canadian government proposed to establish a set of guidelines and standards with more clarity on international intervention and proposed to specify how and when interventions can be performed and in what circumstances and by which kinds of means intervention can be considered as legitimate and appropriate. What's more, ICISS symposium has also included both military intervention and non-military intervention in its discussions. Many speakers in the symposium have also mentioned that considering the fact that "intervention power" is contentious, there is a need to emphasize "responsibility to protect" which will avoid talking about some sensitive topics like the intervention in the domestic affairs of other states and will emphasize the international responsibilities to protect citizens of a state, the speakers have also argued that the concept of "responsibility to protect" should approach the issue from a positive side rather than stressing the importance of power.

We think, if Western theories of the "new international interventionism" and the discussion in the preface of the book demonstrated an agreement with the norm of "responsibility to protect", then it would be impossible to coherently develop the theory of "humanitarian intervention".

1985, p. 28. Quoted from: Shi Yinhong, HuoYaqing."State Sovereignty, Universal Morality and International Law–The Grotian Tradition in the International Law", "Europe". 2000.6.
22 Hugo Grotius, "The Law of War and Peace". Trans. He Qinhua Et al..Shanghai People's Publishing House. 2005, p. 334.

It is not only because the powerful states would fail to provide a reasonable explanation for their inconsistent standards and goals and also not only due to their incoherent intervention actions, but also they cannot prove the impartiality they claim to maintain when performing intervention or when fulfilling "the responsibility to protect". Kissinger has noted that the humanitarian intervention policies of President Clinton has been highly inconsistent. The US has made two interventions against Serbia but has ignored the genocide in Rwanda.[23]

IV. The content and characteristics of the book

With deep social changes and the development of the times, the publication of the collection of papers specifically coincides with the period when the West have been continuing military interventions against those states such as Kosovo, Iraq and Libya. The authors of the articles, have given an important space to the efforts of renown researchers across the world, who have meticulously explored those topics such as the "international interventionism", "the international intervention policy adopted by the West" "history and cases" and "the Middle East Situation and Western intervention". The articles also present the latest research results and theories in the Chinese academy, the views and thinking of Chinese scholars on the issues of world peace and security.

Professor Shi Yinhong in his discussion of "the theories of international intervention", has discussed the issue from the legal and moral perspectives, and expounds on the humanitarian intervention after the end of the Cold War, and he proposes strict limits on humanitarian intervention to prevent countries from abusing military intervention under the pretext of humanitarianism.

In her article Prof. Qi Haixia has selected the offense and defense as the key variables and established a dynamic game model of incomplete information to discover the rules of the US military intervention targeting Libya. What's more, Professor Qi Haixia compared the case of Libya war with the case of Korea and validated his game model, through which, she concluded that for the U.S., the nuclear dismantlement of Libya has been a sign of weakness, which has encouraged the U.S. to speed up the process of military intervention.

---

23 Henry Kissinger, Does the US Need a New Foreign Policy?, New York: Simon and Schuster, 2001.

Xiang Li has analyzed the trends in international interventionism listed in the Rome Statute of the International Criminal Court, and thought the international criminal courts actually act beyond the states authority over individuals and social organizations. And besides this, including non-state actors to the common parties also breaks the traditional principles of states sovereignty. But, the Rome Statute of the International Criminal Court and the system of international judicial cooperation are restricted by power politics for a long term. They underscore the obligation of cooperation between countries by persuasion, hence having no restrictive effects on the non-participating countries and posting no threats to states sovereignty.

Zhang Jiadong, in his discussion of "the Western policies of international interventionism", made a comparison between the strategies adopted by the U.S. in its foreign interventions, and he has asserted that the design of the strategy was shaped by considering a series of issues, such as the general international configuration, national power and geographical location of the targeted country, its ideology, and its relation with the U.S., international public opinion, the preferences of the U.S. authorities and the barometer of the domestic public opinion. The US foreign intervention usually takes the forms of "coercive diplomacy", "new interventionism" and "preemptive strikes", among which coercive diplomacy was mainly adopted in the Cold War. And in the post- Cold War era, as the sole superpower of the world, the U.S. continues seeking to enforce its hegemonic status. When the issue of security comes to the fore in the concerns of US public and the authorities, the strategy of preemptive strikes has been a usual option. But currently, , the decline of US national strength leads to public concerns over several domestic issues in America, which causes a different strategy that would probably be oriented towards US internal affairs. And president Obama has chosen to selectively implement the intervention acts.

By analyzing the theories of humanitarian intervention, relevant policies and practices, Zhao Huaipu has argued that engaged in an active collaboration with the U.S., EU has become the spokesman of humanitarian intervention and has enriched it with more sophisticated theoretical contents. As a result, new norms of international security and human rights, including the concept of "responsibility to protect" are proposed as the core of humanitarian intervention. There exist differences in the understanding of humanitarian intervention between EU and the U.S.. Europe mainly concentrates its intervention activities in its surrounding regions and Africa.

Professor Liu Guozhu has paid close attention to the elements of intervention contained in U.S. foreign aids after its launch of human rights diplomacy and democracy aid which was first proposed by the Carter administration. And Professor Liu holds that the U.S. is trying to advance its own interests and meanwhile, impacts on the political reform and the democratization of the beneficiary countries by exporting capital funds, material and human resources, which actually is an intervention through soft power.

Researcher Kong Tianping in his article has analyzed the case and detailed history of international intervention against Bosnia and Herzegovina. He has argued that after the war of Bosnia and Herzegovina ended, international society attempted to intervene into the internal affairs of Bosnia and Herzegovina, making them subject to international society. He has concluded that, it is rather the domestic political situation in Bosnia and Herzegovina, and not any senior representatives of international society that plays a detrimental role in settling such domestic issues as national reconciliation, restriction of nationalism, constitutional reformation.

Professor Li Kaisheng has discussed the intervention of the human rights in the developing countries performed by international non-governmental organizations. And in his eyes, the kind of "mobilization under the shame" has adversely influenced the international image of developing countries.

And Professor Li Kaisheng has discussed the religious intervention through the example of Kosovo war, and he believes that region has become an increasingly important political element in international relations after the end of Cold War. And religion has publicly been used to justify the foreign intervention, and religion in itself is a political tool used for states' own interests.

Researcher Wang Jinglie, in the article discussing "the Situation of Middle East and Western Intervention", has pointed out that to maximize their self-interests, the world's major Western powers try to intervene in the domestic affairs of small and weak countries, exerting political pressure, economic sanctions, military strikes, changing their regimes and also intervening through new social media. The impact of international intervention into the Middle East affairs is rather negative than positive. International interventions have violated the basic principles of international relations and changed the political configuration of the Middle East.

Researcher Xian Wu, in the article "Military Intervention by the EU targeting the Libyan Arab Jamahiriya" has argued that EU's such militarily intervening embodies an adjustment of the EU policies towards West Asia and North Africa and manifests the extension of the intervention through soft power such as the promotion of democracy in the neighboring countries. But due to limitations of its own military power, the EU still needs to rely on the US and the NATO.

Through an analysis of the Iran nuclear issue, Zhou Shixin, a research assistant, has made an interpretation of the coercive diplomacy tactics adopted in the international interventions. Zhou Shixin has also discussed the role and mechanisms of coercive diplomacy tactics in dealing with international conflicts and expounded ideas on the prospects of the Iran nuclear issue

V. Conclusion

Undoubtedly, the development of international interventionism during the past 20 years has increased the demand for academic studies with higher standards on this issue and calls for a deeper exploration. We can pleasantly say that the Chinese academy has achieved some initial good results in this exploration. However, if compared internationally, we have not effectively made use of various theoretical tools to explain the phenomenon comprehensively and profoundly and not yet meet the needs of current social practice. And we cannot adequately explain a series of new issues, such as the new development of international interventionism, the changes in the attitudes of major world powers in regard to international interventionism, which restricts our ability to propose predictions on the changes of international norms, and predictions on the development of world configuration in the future. A set of questions are still under extensive debates: whether the justice and morality can be achieved in a world that has already lost its balance, how to effectively maintain the peace and development causes? And how the later generations will describe and define our era and our efforts... I believe, just as me, many readers would question and then start their own journey on the exploration of them. By research, comprehension and analysis, they are on the way to reshape our era and will be contributing to the peace and development aspirations of all mankind. And if so, the collection of papers would be worth the efforts.

Zhou Hong
May 2012, Beijing

Humanitarian Intervention and Its Constraints — Criticism on the Military Intervention against Libya

Shi Yinhong[1]

Since the 1990s, especially recently, there has been an increase in humanitarian intervention acts. Under the banner of humanitarianism and in the name of UN Security Council Resolution 1973, NATO has intervened into the civil war in Libya for up to seven months. Such an international intervention, characterized by strong emotions with complex political intentions, as well as important social implications, has come again to the forefront of international attention and aroused divergent opinions in the media and public. And meanwhile, entailing issues related to ethics, law and politics, international interventionism has also been a hot topic for political commentators and scholars focusing on international relations and international law.[2]

---

1 Professor of School of International Studies, Renmin University of China, Director of Academic Committee.
2   Theoretically speaking, the essay is based on "the Analysis of the Constraints on Humanitarian Intervention on Legal and Moral Grounds", jointly published by Shi Yinhong and Shen Zhixiong. (Contemporary International Relations. 2001/8). Later on, I was invited to publish it in English with a few alteration in its contents. Shi Yinhong and Shen Zhixiong, "After Kosovo: Moral and Legal Constraints on Humanitarian Intervention," in the book Moral Constraints on War: Principles and Cases, Lanham, Maryland: Lexington Books, 2002, pp. 247-264, written by Bruno Coppieters (Editor), and Nick Fotion et.al, The motivation behind this paper arises from the large-scale intervention war against Kosovo by NATO in the name of humanitarianism in 1999. Ten years later, NATO is still waving the banner of humanitarianism in the name of UN Security Council Resolution 1973. Invited by International Research Department of the Chinese Academy of Social Sciences, I would prompt a rethink about the issues related to humanitarian intervention.

In China, great attention has been attached on the military intervention against Yugoslavia and Kosovo (part of former Yugoslavia) in 1999 and the one against Libya in 2011 that occurred 12 years later, both of which were performed by NATO forces under the pretext of humanitarianism. However, humanitarian intervention is mainly discussed from the political aspect, but due to the lack of adequate explanation from the aspectof international ethics and international law, there is a need to discuss the issue in its totality. What's more, frankly speaking, it is also necessary because, in China during the Libyan intervention we had many debates and confusion and doubts on the issue, besides the issue has given rise to broad public concerns related to international politics.

I. The concept of humanitarian intervention

Grotius, the father of modern international law, is also regarded as the founder of humanitarian intervention. He stated, in his work "Law of War and Peace" (1625): "in the relation between the states and peoples, if civilians are oppressed by the ruler to the extent that their basic human rights are not guaranteed, then whoever the victims are, the whole human society is naturally empowered to rise against this oppression".

According to H. Lauterpacht, one of the most famous international jurists in the 1900s, Grotius's work is the first authoritative statement on humanitarian intervention.[3]

During the past ten years, the author did not change his stance in terms of the morality and legality of humanitarian intervention after Kosovo, in that the basic principles of international law and international ethics are almost the same. The only changes may be the unprecedented proposal of UN Security Council Resolution Nr. 1793 and NATO's coarse implementation of it. And probably these changes have been the starting points for other countries to take subversive behaviors. Compared with the paper issued in 2001, this time, I have made some modifications in my arguments. But my current paper still reinforces similar points as follows: 1. In today's world, the humanitarian intervention in essence can only be justified on legal and moral grounds. 2. There must also be certain moral and legal restraints on the intervention. Meanwhile, the paper repudiates the righteousness of the humanitarian intervention against Libya since it cannot be supported by legal and moral arguments. Different from Kosovo war ten years ago, the intervention against Libya has been indeterminately authorized by the UN, and what were the reasons behind? Since my main arguments come from the previous cooperation with Shen Zhixiong, I would like to extend my gratitude to him.
3   H. Lauterpacht, "The Grotius Tradition in International Law," in: Richard Falk et al., eds., International Law: A Contemporary Perspective, Boulder, Colo.: Westview Press, 1985, p. 28. More detailed elaboration can be seen in "States Sovereignty, Universal Morality and International Law–The Grotius Tradition in International Law" authored by Yin Hong and HuoYaqing. "Europe". 2000.6., p.16.

Since the end of the Cold War, especially during the 1990s, there has come an unprecedented enthusiasm in the discussion of humanitarian intervention.[4]

More intervention activities were carried out during 1990s than ever. This activities has a dramatic impact on the international situation. Since the end of the intervention war against Kosovo that was waged by NATO in 1999, there has been a considerable decline in the number of international interventions compared with that in 1990s. However, due to the ambiguous authorization from the Security Council of the UN in the name of humanitarianism, the use of armed forces against Libya has come to the spotlight in the international community. This probably encouraged more cases of liberal interventionism that, in itself, is a kind of legal action on the basis of Western liberalism.

For different periods, there are some discrepancies in the comprehension of humanitarian intervention and its principles.[5] What's more, the differences in political structure, social culture, traditions and international position, may give rise to divergent understandings related to ideology, value and order. International community have had significant disputes about the concept of humanitarian intervention, and that's why it is necessary to define the concept before any discussion of humanitarian intervention from the moral and legal perspectives.

Definition on humanitarian intervention contained in Oppenheim's *International Law* (9th Edition, 1992), an authoritative international law book, has received broad acceptance.[6]

By using this definition as a reference and through observation on the pertinent preliminary international "common law", any just humanitarian intervention in its essence should be such an activity: international community can take intervention actions without getting the permission of the

---

[4] From the beginning of 19th century to 1980s, there occurred some international intervention activities in the name of humanitarianism, such as the intervention against Greece by French and Russia (1821-1827), the intervention against Lebanon by French (1860-1861), the American-Spanish War waged by America at the end of 19 century. And similar cases during the Cold War include the India invasion of Pakistan in 1970, Vietnam invasion of Cambodia in 1979 and intervention against Uganda by Tanzania. Robert Jennings and Arthur.

[5] Martha Finnemore, "Constructing Norms of Humanitarian Intervention," in: Peter J.Katzenstein, ed., The Culture of National Security: Norms and Identity in World Politics, New York: Columbia University Press, 1996, pp. 153-185.

[6] Robert Jennings and Arthur Watts, eds., Oppenheim's International law, 9th edition, Vol 1, Introduction and Part 1, London: Harlow Essex, 1992, pp. 430, 432.

authority of the targeted states only when the authority of the targeted state is incapable of prohibiting any large-scale and organized abuse of human rights from occurring within its border, or when the said authority in itself is the one who undertakes, commands or indulges such an abuse, or when the authority is unable or unwilling to shoulder the responsibilities to provide its citizens with the basic needs for living so that their livelihood is adversely affected. In such circumstances, the humanitarian intervention can be performed by neglecting the authority of that state (even the government or other political organizations). Also, in this case, intervention aims to put down the abuse of human rights and help the local people to survive. Within this defined conditions, a justified humanitarian intervention not only entails military intervention as we usually refer to, but also includes non-military intervention.

II. The political reasons behind frequent interventions

In the 20th century, starting from the early 1990s, the UN (or the UN as the representative of the international community) has waged, organized, authorized or carried on several international intervention operations on the humanitarian grounds in regions such as the south and the north of Iraq, Somalia, Bosnia and Haiti, which has brought about repeated heated debates on the issues pertinent to humanitarian intervention.

In the end of the 1990s, interventions by NATO (headed by the U.S.), without the authorization and approval of UN countries, airborne invasion and the large-scale bombing against Yugoslavia on Kosovo issues have once again placed the issue of humanitarian intervention into the spotlight in international community. Since then until 2011, the aforementioned cases of international intervention have dramatically decreased in frequency. However, NATO forces have made around 26,000 sorties and bombed Libya at the beginning of February 2011 which has once again put the issue to a prominent status in the world politics.

This cast doubt on to political legitimacy and even go so far as to increase suspicion and confusion among the people about the Kosova interference launched by NATO.[7]

---

[7] Although there is a lack of supporting evidence at present in our hand today, since the interventionists have used all kinds of manipulations with the aim of hiding their hidden aims about NATO's military intervention in Libya. According to the author's personal experience during international seminars and related diplomatic discussions in China, no person from a NATO member country could refute the author or call him into question in these meetings. Thus the author thinks that, according to the fundamental legal rules related to intervention

Furthermore, it should be noted that the NATO and UN authorized military forces have performed the interventions so casually and they did not act on the basis of the UN Charter, or according to international law and they have even infringed the international (customary) common law regarding humanitarian intervention.

Let us look into the UN Security Council Resolution Nr. 1975, adopted unanimously on March 30, 2011, on theworsening situation in the Ivory Coast.[8] After the UN intervention there occurred divisions of ideas with the African Union(AU) on the issue of civilian protection and regime change- of this country, therefore both ECOWAS and African Union held a common position with China and other BRICS countries to defend the spirit of this above Resolution. It was clear that the UN has taken sides in the domestic conflict of this country.By aligning themselves with the forces loyal to Ouattara regime, UN troops, have not abided by the principle of impartiality as set out by the UN resolution. In fact UN had merely made this resolution for the sake of resolution, and even more serious we can say that the resolution was distorted and abused. Aren't these cases the starting points to obscure the meaning of humanitarianism and developing liberal internationalism?

The international intervention on the humanitarian grounds occurs due to multiple factors, most prominent among which are the political, moral and legal reasons. On the political level, the Security Council has eased the embarrassing situation where it had been trapped for a long time. During the Cold War, the permanent members of the UN Security Council were often unable to reach agreements especially when it came to the issue of coercive intervention of the UN. But now, the UN Security Council is able to make decisions and carry out actions to eliminate similar problems.

During the past decade, the world has been divided into two political camps—-China and Russia on one side and the U.S, the UK and France on the other. It has become a common practice that above mentioned sides reach a compromise solution or they indefinitely defer decisions. And this method is to prevent any major state from exercising veto right when major

---

stipulated in the United Nations charter, the Libya war cannot be justified according to Chapter VII of this Charter – i.e acoording to Action with Respect to Threats to the Peace, Breaches of the Peace, and Acts of Aggression.

8   UN organs have estimated that after the presidential election held in Ivory Coast, a series of violent incidents, directly orindirectly have led to the casualty of up to 462. Quoted from "The UN Security Council Passed a Resolution to sanction former Ivorian President Laurent Gbagbo". Xinhua News Agency. 31.03.2011. http://news.qq.com/a/20110331/000170.htm. I should ask, was this a holocaust, was this a large-scale and organized abuse of human rights or a military intervention that threatens international peace and security?

disputes arise. As for the Iran issue, four resolutions passed by the UN Security Council to impose sanctions against Iran are typical examples.[9]

However, two points need to be added: 1. Roughly speaking, when a decision is required to be made on a controversial issue, in most cases, it is China and Russia who step back from their positions, which reflects the changes in the foreign policies followed by China and Russia. 2. China and Russia occasionally put a veto on the Resolutions of the UN Security Council that allow for coercive intervention. For instance, in October 2011 when Syria was charged by the West with large-scale humanitarian disaster, China and Russia firmly opposed military intervention and this stance has awakened the memories of their strong opposition to US-NATO military intervention over Kosovo in 1999.[10]

Secondly, America and its Western allies tend to make use of or distort the international norms related to human rights to intervene in other countries and even undermine their sovereignty to realize their strategic goals and achieve their ideological purposes. What's more, in the tide of globalization, the notion of liberal internationalism which aims to restrict and devalue the principle of state sovereignty prevails in the Western world.

Under such strong influence, there are increasing public concerns in the West over international human rights and humanitarian disasters in the other states of the world (especially against "the failed states" or "hostile nations"). Under such a a background the desire to intervene and the moralist sentiments of the ordinary Western people has grown dramatically.And with efforts of the dominant Western mass media and the internet which enables rapid spread of information, such emotions have increased and shaped the domestic public opinion and also the international public opinion and generates enormous public opinion pressure.

Sometimes such affects by media leads to overwhelming public supportfor the interventions of the West. For example, in February 2011 when the domestic conflicts in Libya started to escalate, Christian Science Monitor in the U.S. asserted: "if the international community continues to wait

---

9 Louis Charbonneau, "New Iran Sanctions: A Question of When, Not If; ICG: China Values Ties with U.S. Higher than Iran," Reuters, March 27, 2010; David E. Sanger and Mark Landler, "U.S. Says Major Powers Have Reached A Deal on Sanctions for Iran. The New York Times, May 18, 2010.
10 "Russia Defends Its Veto of UN Resolution on Syria," The Associate Press, the New York Times, October 7th, 2011. Medvedev in his presidency announced in Moscow that the U.S., UK and France's repudiation of Russia's proposal – no foreign military intervention against Syria, indicates other partners (the U.S., UK and France) would allow for such situation recurring.

passively and not react against the war in Libya, the former genocidal tragedies that occurred in Cambodia (1975) and Rwanda (1994) will repeat again.

What's more, many government authorities and renown scholars support the radical ideas of liberal internationalism. For instance, president Obama's reluctant attitude related to the military intervention against Libya has caused strong critiques by three female renowned figures. Therefore some partially rational proposals made by the realistic strategists who enjoy high status, was rejected. What's more, there do exist a small number of elites in developing countries, who affirm the humanitarian intervention; therefore, humanitarian intervention is widely favored by the public.

At last, the racial tyranny, and authoritarian acts related to political and religious issues do exist in some less developed countries, which, in some cases, sharpen and escalate into a large-scale, organized abuse of human rights. And although they are ostensibly tagged as countries which are in the political modernization process, these countries easily face political crises, hence fall into a status of "failed states" due to their immature political mechanisms and the lack of national cohesive power. And what comes along with these crises are serious ethnical, racial and tribal conflicts, which are regarded as communal conflicts, which constitute the most salient events of humanitarian disasters after the end of the Cold War. Western media describes these events as alarming, unusual and unstable situations. Thus the intervention by Western powers are affirmed and justified.

III. Legal and moral background of frequent intervention

In the early 20th century and especially in the period after the Second World War has witnessed a tendency to justify intervention on moral and legal grounds. This trend basing itself on moral and legal grounds.has become something deeper behind current humanitarian intervention. This trend seeks "justification" and gives an increasing attention to the righteousness of acts and conducts from the legal and moral perspectives. The above trend can be evaluated as a "historical revival" which emphasizes the adaptation of international law and international ethics to the problems of the current world, and bases itself on the classic ideas of Hugo Grotius, which is considered the starting point for modern international law. Another source it strives to revive is the international law of the 18th and 19th centuries which has shifted towards favoring of "positivism".

Besides, the idea of natural law—from the 17th and 18th centuries—as a basis for international law still remains to be influential, consequently contemporary international law and ethics starts from the natural law as one source of basic international norms, which endows an absolute freedom to states and to their acts regards the practice of the states, even regards this as the only basis.[11]

Since 1990s, especially after the World War II, international community has gone through dramatic changes in its common values, as H. Bull states: "the theory of international society has moved away from the emphasis of 18th and 19th century legal and historical positivism on existing practice as the source of. norms about international conduct, in favour of a return to natural law principles or to some contemporary equivalent of them; in political analysis as in. legal analysis of international relations the idea of international society has been rested less on the evidence of co-operation. In the actual behaviour of states than on principles purporting how they should behave."[12]

Besides state's practices, this is the most prominent and the most enduring character. In international society, the essence of such basic ethics includes those basic principles of mutual non-agreesion, non-infringement, equality, code of dignity and mutual understanding in state to state relationships, especially highlights respect to weaker and smaller states and puts individuals' basic needs for security,decency and human dignity in a prominent position.

As the extension of the above trend, today's international community, besides upholding the values of state sovereignty and equity among states advocates the common values of sovereignty and autonomy of a state in its internal issues, inter-ethnic equality and upholds that the basic human rights should be enjoyed by all groups including ethnical, racial, religious, social, gender, age, etc.. Recently new international norms have been formed which manifests the two above mentioned trends. The tendency expresses itself in the international law. With the U.N. Charter at its core, the contemporary international law not only retains the content of the previous positivist legal aspect but also takes in some contents from the natural law. The international legal documents such as international law and the U.N.

---

11 Hedley Bull, The Anarchical Society: A Study of Order in World Politics, New York: Columbia University Press, 1977, pp. 38-39.
12 The discussion on the justification of international law and morality can be seen in "New Trend, New Pattern, New Order". Beijing, Law Press, 2000, Chapter 9 "The New International Norms Formed By New Powers".

Charter have exhibited the balanced but sometimes antagonistic relations between the natural law and positive law.[13] The international law of human rights in the issue of humanitarian intervention does not wholly go in line with the traditional fundamental principles of state sovereignty and non-intervention.

International law and ethics are affected by the characteristic of the times historical period and dominant political forces. These influences have caused the rapid development of international law based on human rights conception. As a famous contemporary international jurist said: "at least, the concept of human rights has found broad acceptance in the international community in terms of its principles and discourse, and is reflected in the constitutions of contemporary states. It is widely acknowledged that issues of human rights should gain universal recognition in the international arena and be given more prominence in the discussion of international law, international institutions and international diplomacy.[14]

Since the end of the Second World War, the international law based on the concept of human rights has been enriched with more and more contents and became more sophisticated, followed with the appearance of widely accepted international treaties and declarations such as the Universal Declaration of Human Rights, International Covenant on Economic, Social and Cultural Rights, International Covenant on Civiland Political Rights. In addition, regional laws of human rights declarations also came into being in Europe, Africa and America. Moreover, the implementation of the norms of human rights has been guaranteed through some institutions that are responsible for investigating, supervising and making judgments. Consequently, these norms no longer stay on paper. The most important point in the development of international law of human rights is that the prohibition of genocide and large-scale massacre has become undoubted, unchallenged and non-violable norms, and any actions or treaties against them are evaluated as legally unacceptable. The international law of human rights is an international norm that every state should acoord and persist with. Recognizing the importance of self-determination is also becoming a similar norm, though some disputes may still exist.[15]

---

13 Louis Henkin, The Age of Rights, Tran. Xin Chunying. Beijing. World Affairs Press. 1997, pp. 22.
14 Simon Duke, "The State and Human Rights: Sovereignty versus Humanitarian Intervention," International Relations, Vol.7, No.2, 1994, p.30.
15 Jack Donnelly, International Human Rights, 2nd edition, Boulder, Colo.: Westview Press, 1998, pp. 19-20; Ian Brownlie, Principles of Public International Law, 4th edition, Oxford: Clarendon, 1990, p. 601.

Regarding to the stipulation in the UN Charter, the right of international intervention entailed in the current international law, an authoritative scholar in international law said: "The Security Council of the UN has the right to judge whether an event posits threats on the international peace and security... which means it is capable of internationalizing an issue to a higher level".[16]

Also according to an international jurist, in the current situation, the vertical allocation of authority has come into being, which highlights the international concerns and degrades the domestic jurisdiction of countries.[17] The UN has moved from a state-centered system to a world-people-centered one, elevating the issues which were previously regarded as domestic issues to international level, so that they can becaome pretexts for intervention. Interventions by the UN in most cases are considered legitimate since the domestic issues are regarded as object of international concerns. That's why the contemporary international law has become ambiguous and contradictory. In any case, it is really hard for a state to justify its resistance to an international intervention under the pretext of its state sovereignty. All in all, the development of international law based on human rights has caused the strengthening of the concept of humanitarian intervention.

IV. The restrictive law and the realities of the Libya intervention

The international humanitarian intervention can be justified with legal and moral evidences and can be partially recognized or allowed for some solid political reasons. Consequently, just for the above reason international humanitarian intervention should be restricted in theory and practically.[18]

First of all, any intervention on humanitarian grounds is just an exception of the principle of non-intervention. As the foundation of contemporary international law, "non-intervention" or the state sovereignty is recognized in the UN Charter as the first and also the most important principle. This principleis solidified through the establishment of the "Declaration on the Inadmissibility of Intervention and Interference in the Internal Affairs of States" in 1965, which recognizes the "full observance of the principles of non-intervention

---

16 Richard Falk, "The Grotius Quest," in: Falk et al., eds., International Law: A Contemporary Perspective, p. 130.
17 Lung-chu Chen, An Introduction to Contemporary International Law, New Haven: Yale University Press, 1989, p. 224.
18 The ICJ's finding in Corfu Channels rejects this narrow interpretation of article 2(4), which was included in the Charter to give more specific guarantees to small states, rather than to have a restrictive effect.

and non-interference in the internal and external affairs of sovereign States and peoples, either directly or indirectly, overtly or covertly."[19]

Legally evaluated, some of today's popular international humanitarian intervention ideas favoring them are making an ad hoc detour around the principles of non-intervention. This principle is carefully and exactly defined in the chapter VII of the UN Charter, "Action with Respect to Threats to the Peace, Breaches of the Peace, and Acts of Aggression", that only when the acts of a state would breach or threaten the international peace and security, the UN Security Council can employ unarmed or armed forces in order to "maintain and restore the international peace and security."[20]

After the establishment of the UN Charter, the international law and morality have progressed and a preliminary common law has come into being as a consequence. According to the law, a state can be targeted as the object of international intervention only when a large-scale abuse of human rights occurs in that state, even if this abuse does not posit any threat to international peace and security. However, this law has to be applied within certain restrictions since it is subordinated to the spirit of the chapter VII of the UN Charter that enjoys a superior position and wider recognition. Therefore, any international intervention based on such abuses needs to be grounded on a wider international consensus and scrutinized with more caution in terms of its application.

Without such tight cautious restrictions on the international humanitarian intervention, the authority and universality of the principle of non-intervention will be undermined which will put the international law system into disorder. It needs to be reiterated that the international law of human rights fails to adequately explain the international consensus and is only applicable in few cases (the hinderance of large-scale massacre and violence, the prohibition of racial segregation and race-baiting), although to some extent, it is universally coercible. Global or regional organizations make most of the current regulations on human rights through investigation, reports and supervision of the domestic situation of human rights in a particular state. As Henkin Louis wrote: "international law of human rights penetrates the shell of a country, but it is in fact still part of the international system which consists of states as the main actors and should still respect the doctrines and traditions of the international system".[21]

---

19 Ian Brownlie, ed., Basic Documents of International Law, 3rd edition, Oxford: Clarendon Press, 1989, p. 40.
20 The Chinese version of the UN Charter, http://wenku.baidu.com/view/5e9c8f11cc7931b765ce15e0.html.
21 Louis Henkin, International Law: Politics and Values, Dordrecht, the Netherlands: MartinusNifhoff Publishers, 1995, p. 184.

Similarly, just as one of the most famous Western scholar specialized in the international law of human rights wrote: "current norms of state sovereignty still prohibits states from acting coercively abroad in order to remedy torture and many other violations of human rights."[22]

However, contrarily y, the military intervention targeting Libya and relevant resolutions made by the UN Security Council do not accord with the international treaties such as the basic regulations of UN Charter and the preliminary common law on the issues of humanitarian intervention.

Shortly after February 21, 2011, military forces of the opposition made their first foray into capital Tripoli after gaining control of Benghazi. According to the major human rights organization, the HRW—that was responsible for observing the Libya situation, it was declared that 233 people has died in the suppression of the anti-Gaddafi security forces. After two days, president Obama publicly criticized the bloodshed, suppression and the torture incurred in Libya, which in his view, went against every international norm, and he bombastically announced his intervention intentions.[23] Three days later, in the circumstances where the estimated casualty did not increase, the UN Security Council passed the "United Nations Security Council Resolution Nr 1970" proposed by the US, UK, France and Germany. In the resolution, apart from the approval of intervention against Libya, the international Criminal Court in the Hague that is not recognized by the US, Russia and China, was authorized to make an investigation into the Gaddafi's "comprehensive and systematical attacks against Libyan citizens."[24]

Aif we evaluate the "UN Security Council Resolution Nr 1973" which authorized the no-fly zone in Libya and was misused by NATO for the intervention wars. İt is quite hard to justify and prove that the large-scale and systematical attacks towards citizens in Libya was a crime against humanity. In addition, there were no adequate evidences to frame and label Libya as a threat to international peace and security.Thus, the application of UN Charter VII to Libya situation has been an arbitrary interpretation.[25]

---

22 Jack Donnelly, "The Social Construction of International Human Rights," in Tim Dunne and Nicholas J. Wheeler eds., Human Rights in Global Politics, Cambridge: Cambridge University Press, 1999, p. 85.
23 David D.Kirkpatrick and Mona El-Naggar, "Qaddafi's Son Warns of Civil War as Libyan Protests Widen," The New York Times, February 21, 2011; Helene Cooper and Mark Landler, "Obama Condemns Libya Amid Stalled Evacuation, "The New York Times, February 23, 2011.
24 Edward Wyatt, "Security Council Calls for War Criminal Inquiry in Libya," The New York Times, February 26, 2011.
25 The whole text of United Nations Security Council Resolution 1973: http://baike.baidu.com/view/5430483.htm.

The requirement of the strict and cautious restrictions on international humanitarian intervention is essential also because of the fact that humanitarian intervention can be politically utilized by some states to implant and spread their own ideology in other states and pursue self-interests. In such circumstances, intervention motives do not stem from whether or not there is a humanitarian disaster or a threat to international security that arise from the internal situation of a particular state or such pretexts are not on the top of "reasons" list.. There is another circumstance which in some cases can regarded similar to the above case, as follows the humanitarian intervention is employed to please or bufferthe domestic internal disputes, i.e to deal with the internal politics of the intervening states. It is not strange that such a situation was described in the paragraph 4, "the political reasons" section, because the governments of intervening states sometimes will blow the foreign event out of proportion, dramatically fabricating and manipulating a humanitarian disaster, or irresponsibly and covertly coach the mass media in this direction, in order to serve certain interest groups and please some social groups.

The Libya war waged by NATO can be compared to one of the above cases. Although the intentions behind the NATO's intervention should not be only gauged through subjective suppositions or assertions, as mentioned by Bandow: "it is obvious that Libya gave the lie to the dubious doctrine of Responsibility to Protect. This was no humanitarian operation. Yes, the Qaddafi regime was brutal, but its forces had massacred no civilians before the campaign to "save" the Libyan people. Like other civil wars in Third World countries, this one generated most of its killing through the fighting itself."[26] (Gaddafi commented after the death of Gaddafi by Doug Bandow in the journal of National İnterest.)

The casualties of the Libya war is not yet certain but probably reached 15 thousand, most of whom died in the extended battles due to the careless intervention by Western states with minimal tolerance. And the humanitarianism disappeared into the air when NATO continued its strikes and bombing against the remnants of ex-leader Colonel Muammar Gaddafi's forces.[27]

---

26 Doug Bandow is a senior fellow at the Cato Institute. A former Special Assistant to President Ronald Reagan, he is the author and editor of several books, including "Foreign Follies: America's New Global Empire" (Xulon).
27 Doug Bandow, "Libya: Costs Outweigh Benefits," National Interest (Online), October 21, 2001, http://www.cato.org/pub_display.php?pub_id=13787.According to the article of Patrick, one factor pointed to the hypocrisy of humanitarian intervention performed by NATO is that the official of the provisional government admitted to extract information

V. The ethical significance of tight and cautious restrictions on international humanitarian intervention

The humanitarian intervention is expected to promote the protection of human rights and focuses on the realization and defending of particular rights and rights of indivudals rights (or the rights of racial or ethnic groups, religious groups, gender and age groups). However, this aim has gained an unproportional weight in the international relations, far exceeding the scope of humanitarian intervention.[28]

In the international relations, rights exist at four levels – the individual level, the level of inter-state relations, thirdly the level of which non-state groups or actors and at last the world level.[29] Generally these four levels coordinate with each other, but do not always enjoy harmony. Generally speaking, the individual rights cannot be detached from the remaining three since the individual rights cannot exist without the support given or without the premises laid by the other three. In most cases, individuals and all other groups in a country have to rely on states so as to provide the likelihood of the realization of their rights and security.[30]

Playing the most important part in the global system, states are still the only political entities that possess the most comprehensive and the richest material and organizational resources. Thus, generally speaking, effective implementation of the norms of human rights in any region has to seek recourse to states in the first place, although in some cases the states are the infringers or even destroyers of human rights. What's more, the tyranny of powerful states or discrimination by wealthy countries against the weak states, are still part of the common scene which is criticized by the public. There is no considerable improvement in the current situation compared to the one Hedley Bull described 20 years ago: "The hot topic of justice in international relations still centers on what states deserve".[31] Injustice could

---

by torturing detainees that were estimated over 2500. A lot of black Africans were arrested based the assumption that they were the supporters of Gaddafi. More details in: David D. Kirkpatrick, "Libyans Turn Wrath on Darkskinned Migrants," The New York Times, September 4, 2011.

28　Jack Donnelly, "The Social Construction of International Human Rights," p. 100.

29　More detailed and systematical elaboration in "the Discussion on the Justice in World Politics". Shanghai People's Publishing House.1998.

30　R. J. Vincent, "The Idea of Rights in International Ethics," in: Terry Nard in and David R. Mapel, eds.,Traditions of International Ethics, Cambridge: Cambridge University Press, 1992, p. 261.

31　Hedley Bull, Justice in International Relations, Waterloo, Ontario: University of Waterloo Press, 1984, p. 13.

arise around the world when international interventions including humanitarian intervention are performed on the pretext of protection of individual rights.

Gaddafi, the once notorious dictator in Libya, enforced his ideology through the long-term ethnic or tribal oppression, discrimination and divisions. "The development gap between Colonel Gaddafi's stronghold in Tripoli and the insurrection in the east region of Libya recalled Libya's pre-1931 years as three different countries—Tripolitania, Fezzan and Cyrenaica." It is undeniable that "Colonel Gaddafi seemed to fear from an emergence of any national institutions or networks that might check his power." The anti-Gaddafi groups in the army were gradually and quietly formed due to his lack of trust on his own military officers.

And it was the special brigade headed by his son and other battalions and African mercenaries loyal to Gaddafi, who carried out killing of Libyans which got orders from Gaddafi.[32]

It is certain that when evaluated from political, economic and social aspects, tGaddafi's tyranny over Libyan people has legally and morally justified the revolt of tribes and clans in eastern Libya with Tripoli as stronghold. But this is totally a different issue which should be separately dealt, and cannot justify NATO intervention and air strikes targeting Libya.

However, generally speaking, currently in the countries of the third world, which usually refer to those less developed and poor ones, are just like poor individuals who pursue a rich moral existence. And this is especially true because the state in these countries play a vital role in providing security, social welfare, identity and sense of justice to its citizens. Realistically evaluating, in the present and foreseeable future, only states are able to provide citizens those services that are needed by them, this is a necessity for the survival of these states. And any other organization will

---

32 Kareem Fahim and David D. Kirkpatrick, "Gaddafi's Grip on the Capital Diminishes as Revolt Grows," The New York Times, February 22, 2011; Kareem Fahim and David D. Kirkpatrick, "Qaddafi Strikes Back as Rebels Are Approaching the Libyan Capital, "The New York Times, February 24, 2011. Colonel Qaddafi has defined his authoritarian government as "rule by the masses" and, despite his pervasive security forces, cultivated a noisy disdain for centralized government. With little shared national and nation-state experience, except that of brutal Italian colonialism, Libyan people tend to identify themselves as members of tribes or clans rather than citizens of a country, and Colonel Gaddafi has governed Libya partly through the mediation of a "social leadership committee" composed of about 15 representatives of various tribes, said a Dartmouth professor who was an expert in Libyan studies. David D. Kirkpatrick and Mona El-Naggar, "Gaddafi's Son Warns of Civil War as Libyan Protests Widen," The New York Times, February 21, 2011.

not be able to properly fulfill this function. According to Bull Hedley, for an entity to be called a state it must claim sovereignty over (i) a group of people (ii) a defined territory, and it must have a government. And without these capabilities or arms, states will easily be ruled by others... Peoples of the third world have set up nation states to achieve their goals. After they have established their states, they have promoted nation building and develop domestic ethnic identity, through which, they have gained control of their national economy and became able to fight against the agents of hostile countries.

What's more, in the international arena, they foster relations with other countries, cooperate with their friends to break the citadel of the hostile countries and make their voice heard in the world arena. Western liberal internationalists frequently criticize the third world countries for their "statism" which means "no state if no government."[33]

At last, why humanitarian intervention should be strictly restricted also involves the issue of relations between justice and order which is a perennial topic in social philosophy and international ethics. There is always a tension between the justice and order.[34]

On the one hand, we see large scale of repression and abuse of human rights occurring in some countries. In some failed states, due to the atrocity and the loss of ethics and rule of law, the life of man is "solitary, poor, nasty, brutish, and short."[35]

In these two circumstances, the hands-off approach pursued by the international community is morally intolerable and pathetic. On the other hand, humanitarian intervention is inconsistent with the principles of state sovereignty and non-interference, and even has the possibility of undermining these principles. If without proper restrictions, the international order will face severe troubles. When the two sides are wisely weighed, the second one should be given more concerns especially after NATO's intervention targeting Libya. Philosophically speaking, justice and order should be given equal emphasis. Any form of justice can only be realized at the premise of order which also paves the way for right to equality.[36]

---

33 Hedley Bull, Justice in International Relations, pp. 6, 27.
34 Thomas G. Weiss and Jarat Chopra,"Sovereignity under Siege: From Intervention to Humanitarian Space," in Gene M. Lyons and Michael Mastanduno, eds., Beyond Westphalia? State and International Intervention, Baltimore: The John Hopkins University Press, 1995, p. 102.
35 Hobbes. Leviathan. Trans. Li Sifu, Li Tingbi, Beijing, The Commercial Press. 1986. pp. 95.
36 Hedley Bull, The Anarchical Society, p. 86.

Order is also based on justice, which is also true in terms of humanitarian intervention.[37]

VI. Why and how did NATO made use of and even abused the authorization given by the UN

The aforesaid indicates that NATO's role in the Libya war is essentially not the humanitarian intervention, and Libya war cannot be justified to accord with the international law and ethics. What's more, different from the intervention in Kosovo in 1999, NATO has abused the Resolution Nr.1973 in order to wage the Libya war, and this presents a dangerous precedent in the international legal system, this Resolution has jeopardized the fundamental principle of international law and undermined political order and moral justice.

Compared with the Kosovo war 12 years ago, a question is raised this time: how could the UN Security Council Resolution Nr. 1973 come into being, although it was predicable that NATO might abuse it? It is obvious that, the abstention votes by Russia and China have enabled the pass of the Resolution, but why did Russia and China abstented instead of firmly opposing the Western proposal as they had done in the Kosovo war 12 years ago, when NATO had made their decisions and the Kosovo war had been on the verge of breaking out?

It is well known that Russia has been taking sides in the US and Europe differences. Therefore, what we will discuss here is why China has forfeited its veto right.

Recently, there has been an assumption that Gaddafi has not been friendly to China. A famous expert of Africa has once mentioned that different from most state leaders of Africa who maintain friendly diplomatic relations with China, Gaddafi's Libya has only sent its foreign minister to participate in the China-Africa Cooperation Forum held by China. To estrange the relations between China and other African countries, Gaddafi wrote to many heads of African states, trying to persuade them not to participate in the 2006 China-Africa Summit Forum in Beijing. Furthermore, he has

---

37 But, this does not mean that order should be attached with more importance than justice in all cases. A just order in its essence features stability. Once the justice is distorted to the extent that most people cannot tolerate, the existence of order is jeopardized. Therefore, the humanitarian intervention should be considered with all related elements taking into consideration, and it can never be the case that sticking to convention can clear the path for future. It is strongly suggested that justice be considered at first when humanitarian intervention is on the plan.

retained an ambiguous relation with Taiwan. In his visit to Taiwan in 2006, Gaddafi not only invited Chen Shui-bian (the president of the Republic of China-Taiwan region from 2000 to 2008) to Libya, but also gave a warm reception to Chen Shui-bian when he dropped by Libya. Gaddafi has maligned China for imposing new imperialism in Africa and excluded China from investing in the oil and gas industries.[38]

However, just as the African research expert said, this was not the real reason behind Chinese attitude in the Libya case.

When big event happens or after it happens, the ideas derived from reflection, self-questioning and self-answering are possibly the most authentic thinking process although they may be adjusted, modified or even changed after the event. This is because this process of time involves the most intensive brain activities. And since the ideas that have been effective at that time has not been eliminated till today, I would like to share my reflection on the UN Security Council Resolution Nr. 1973 and NATO's intervention targeting Libya. The most important point is that, the reservation and regrets declared by China and Russia towards the Libya war are in fact much profounder than what they did in the voting process at that time. Actually, China and Russia's determination to fight against any unjust intervention and to safeguard international law is much stronger than what has been shown in the Resolution Nr. 1973.

Chinese government had considerable reservations towards some contents of the Resolution. But it is also understandable that China could do nothing but accept the pass of Resolution 1973 that allowed for the establishment of no-fly zone in Libya, since Western countries including France, UK and the US had made up their minds to carry out joint air strikes targeting Libya and already assisted the rebel forces to defeat Gaddafi. Moreover, since some Arab and African countries that are in good relationship with China, has been in favor of the intervention and even have attempted to play a part in it, China's opposition against the intervention could have heighten the tension between states. Obviously, even if the Libya resolution was rejected by China or unauthorized by the UN, the Western countries would carry out their unilateral air strikes, no matter how unpredictable the war process would develop.

For China, allowing the resolution to pass has been a tough decision, especially considering the fact that the Resolution Nr 1973 has set a dangerous precedent which will serve as a tool for Western countries to perform

---

38 PKU African Tele-Information (issue 66), November 1, 2011, http://www.zhong-fei.org/node/1426.

their foreign military intervention into the domestic conflicts or into the civil wars of some developing countries.

This dangerous precedent may well lead to repetition of situations we saw in the Kosovo crisis of 1999, although Libya situation has posited no threat to international peace and security. Though they did not say "no" and not rejected the Western resolution, the abstention vote of China and Russia has resulted in the misuse of the authority of the UN Security Council. In the future, the US and its allies may take advantage of it, to infringe the territorial integrity of other states, by the way of by-passing and getting aroundlegal rules.

There were probably two main reasons for China's response. Firstly, China's eagerness to foster peaceful and stable relations with the US has become stronger especially after Hu Jintao's visit to USA in January 2011. Besides, the long-term cordial relations with Saudi Arabia that as a matter of fact, supported the military intervention targeting Libya, has probably partially contributed to China's decision on abstention instead of vetoing the resolution. Later, Chinese government expressed deep concerns and regrets on the military strikes staged by NATO against Libya, highlighted the importance of UN Charter and relevant international law and norms and advocated respect for the state sovereignty, independence, reunification and territorial integrity of Libya.[39]

And then, President Hu Jintao pointed out to the French president Nicolas Sarkozy: "NATO's large-scale, intensive bombing of Libya ran against the intention and stipulations of the Resolution Nr 1973, and resorting to armed forces cannot settle issues but rather complicates the situation. Therefore, only by peaceful means such as dialogue and negotiation, can the disputes be resolved.[40]

However, compared with their stance during the Kosovo crisis in 1999, China and Russia appeared a bit timorous and hesitant when deciding on their votes concerning Libya war. Because of this, people may ask what if a similar situation occurs in a foreseeable future.

It is hard to guess the answer, but, they seem unlikely to use their veto right in order to defend the principle of non-intervention from any violation. In another words, in the foreseeable future, it seems likely that the US

39　The Question and Answer Session by Minister of Foreign Affairs on the Pass of Resolution on Libya Issues. Chinanews.com. March 18, 2011, http://www.chinanews.com/gn/2011/03-18/2915777.shtml
40　Hu Jintao, China Supports any Political Efforts on Easing the Tension in Libya, Xinhua Net. March 30, 2011, http://news.xinhuanet.com/politics/2011-03/30/c_121249967.htm.

and its allies may pass a similar resolution in the UN Security Council, if they insist on military intervention against a country that is not close to China and Russia, but I must add that such a resolution has to undergo a certain revision—a substantive but not essential revision.

Recently China and Russia have firmly rejected the Western originated UN SC resolution which proposed to adopt a strong military intervention targeting Syria, their attitude has encouraged and inspired the people around the world, who favor the proper implementation of the non-intervention principle, even though we cannot say or guarantee that their such attitude will continue in the long run.

Obviously, it looks somewhat astonishing to observe that, the rising China finds it hard or becomes reluctant when trying to check an abuse of power by a superpower, although it has left behind the times—not long ago—when its national power had been far behind.

We should say that a significant increase in the national strength does not automatically, or necesarrily mean the maintenance or realization of willpower of that country.

Analysis of the Motives behind US Military Interventions in the Post-Cold War Era

Qi Haixia[1]

At the beginning of 2011, the Arabic World has experienced a series of civil wars, and extensive political changes have occurred in Egypt, Tunisia, Libya and other countries. To maintain the stability of the existing regime, the Gaddafi administration in Libya responded by resorting to armed forces for suppression. On 26 February 2011, the United Nations Security Council (UNSC) unanimously passed the Security Council Resolution 1970 against Libya deciding to impose an open-ended embargo on the supply of arms and military equipment to and from Libya. On March 17, the establishment of a no-fly zone in Libya was authorized by the UN, and two days later (March 19) France started its air strikes against Libya followed by the military support of the US and NATO. The military invention of Europe and US was a major event in the existing international system. Why did the US specificly chose to intervene in Libya from among the countries which all suffered civil war, and why did the US insist on waging another war before completely putting an end to those in Afghanistan and Iraq? This article attempts to address these questions by focusing on the theories related to international intervention.

---

1 Doctor, Lecturer of China Institute of Contemporary International Relations of Tsinghua University.

I. Review of the literature on the causes of military intervention

International intervention has become a common phenomenon, ranging from China's dispatch of volunteer troops to North Korea to US led NATO intervention in the domestic affairs of Libya. But, there is still a dispute over the specific contents and the definitions of international intervention in academic circles. James N. Rosenau believes that intervention is an act adopted by external forces to intentionally change the status quo and influence other countries.[2] In Max Hilaire's opinion, intervention is any influence exerted by external forces on the domestic politics and foreign diplomacy of a state.[3] Ian Holliday has classified interventions into categories based on whether states serve as behavioral subjects, whether their actions are coercive, and whether the domestic politics or foreign diplomacy is targeted.[4] Shi Yinhong has asserted that the foreign intervention usually involves two aspects: (1) intentionally disturb the domestic policies of a state or constrain its political process (including its decision-making process on foreign policy) without obtaining permission of the targeted party; (2) initiatively intervening in the political affairs of other states that neither neighbor the intervening states nor are geographical parts of them, without reaching consensus among all concerned parties in the region.[5] To sum up, international intervention is divided in two parts: one usually refers to "interference" in internal affairs. According to Howard Wriggins, identifying the contents of internal affairs would assist scholars in classifying different types of international influences.[6] The other is called third party intervention with the goal to intervene in the foreign diplomacy of other states or to purely perform military actions. This paper attempts to explore the international intervention in a broad sense, and therefore, any military action practiced by a third party is under the discussion.

At present, there are mainly four explanations concerning why states wage third party interventions, which will be analyzed hereinafter in detail.

---

2 James N. Rosenau, "Intervention as a Scientific Concept," Journal of Conflict Resolution, Vol.13, No.2, 1969, p. 159.
3 Max Hilaire, International Law and the United States Military Intervention in the Western Hemisphere, The Hague: Kluwer Law International 1997, p. 4.
4 Ian Holliday, "Ethics of Intervention Just War: Theory and the Challenge of the 21st Century," International Relations, Vol.17, No.2, 2003, p. 120.
5 Shi Yinhong. Discussions on Foreign Intervention in the International Politics and the US Foreign Intervention after the Cold War. America Studies, No. 4, 1996.
6 Howard Wriggins, "Political Outcomes of Foreign Assistance: Influence, Involvement or Intervention", Journal of International Affairs, Vol.22, No.2, 1968, p. 218.

A. Power theories

With this focus, scholars are generally divided into two groups, one with the emphasis on "power balancing" as the major reason for military intervention, the other in favor of "bandwagoning".

1. Power balance theory

Most of the scholars with this view are theorists of power of balance in realism, such as Winston Churchill, who mentioned in his statement about the British foreign policies on the eve of the WWII, that "For four hundred years the foreign policy of England has been to oppose the strongest, most aggressive, most dominating Power on the Continent... Faced by Phillip II of Spain, against Louis XIV under William III and Marlborough against Napoleon, against William II of Germany, we joined with the less strong Powers, made a combination among them, and thus defeated and frustrated the continental military tyrant whoever he was, whatever nation he led... this is the British tradition of foreign policies. Today, our thoughts are based on this."[7] Realists believe that the balance of power theory and the policies to maintain it are not only unavoidable, but also indispensable elements to sustain the stability of sovereign states.[8] From the theory, one predicts that states will engage in balancing behavior, whether or not balanced power is the end of their acts. The expectation is not a balance, once achieved, will be maintained, but that a balance, once disrupted, will be restored in one way or another.[9] The response of other countries to one among them seeking or gaining preponderant power is to try to balance against it.[10]

Just as Joseph Grieco once said, "balancing of power is expected to be the uppermost prediction from the realist theory when a country is in an anarchic state."[11] According to Kenneth N. Waltz, balancing, not bandwagoning, is the behavior induced by the system.[12] Thereafter, Kenneth N. Waltz has further made a slight modification on his statement: states try various strategies for survival. Balancing is one of them and bandwagoning

---

7 Winston S. Churchill, The Second World War, Vol.1, The Gathering Storm, Boston: Houghton Mifflin, 1948, pp. 207-208. Quoted from Hans J. Morgenthau Politics among Nations: the Struggle for Power and Peace, trans. Lu Minghua et al., Shanghai Translation Publishing House, 1995, p. 257-258.
8 Hans J. Morgenthau, Politics among Nations: The Struggle for Power and Peace, p. 264.
9 Kenneth Waltz, Theory of International Politics, New York: McGraw Hill, 1979, p. 128.
10 Kenneth N. Waltz, "The Emerging Structure of International Politics," International Security, Vol.18, No.2, 1993, p. 77.
11 Joseph M. Grieco, "Realist International Theory and the Study of World Politics," in Michael W. Doyle and G. John Ikenberry, eds., New Thinking in International Relations Theory, Boulder, Colorado: Westview, 1997, p. 169.
12 Kenneth Waltz, Theory of International Politics, New York: McGraw Hill, 1979, p. 126.

is another…balancing theory does not predict uniformity of behaviors but rather the strong tendency of major states in the system or in the regional subsystem, to resort to balancing when they have to.[13] From the perspective of John Mearsheimer, multiple options are offered for states to act: blackmailing, buck-passing, being temporarily passive… and balancing is not the only or the uppermost option. The two most commonly used behaviors are balancing and buckpassing. In many circumstances, states have a strong tendency to pass the buck for self-defense and gaining of power. However, in bipolarity and unbalanced multipolarity, if there is a potential hegemon, balancing of power tends to be a more general behavior.[14] Considering the impact of asymmetric information, Ivan Savic and Zachary C. Shirkey have divided states into two types: a challenger, a revisionist state that wishes to change the status quo in a particular area and a respondent, potential balancer who prefers the status quo. If the cost of balancing is less than or equal to the relative value of the challenge, the respondent will balance.[15]

According to the power balance theory, military intervention is allowed by authorities to maintain hegemony. In explaining the British hegemony, Josef Joffe has pointed that "Britain utilized its regional advantages to stay offshore as an over-the-horizon presence in Europe, only performing military intervention when necessary to maintain the balance of the ground forces."[16] It's not only Britain, but also the US. Robert J. Art pointed out that the US adopted the offshore balancing strategy in Asia-Pacific region. To battle an emerging great-power hegemon, the US implemented military intervention as its last resort, which entails all necessary measures for waging a war and for containing and weakening the national power of the rising states to an acceptable level.[17] The major goal of the third party intervention performed by a hegemonic state is to maintain the balance. After the enemy state's alliance is formed, a major state usually performs military intervention targeting at the allies of its enemy states to expand its own power and maintain the

---

13 Kenneth Waltz, "Structural Realism after the Cold War," International Security, Vol. 25, No. 1, 2000, p. 38.
14 John Mearsheimer. The Tragedy of Great Power Politics. Trans. Wang Yiwei, Tang Xiaosong. Etc. Shanghai People's Publishing House. 2003, p. 387-392.
15 Ivan Savic and Zachary C. Shirkey, "Trust in the Balance: Asymmetric Information, Commitment Problems and Balancing Behavior", Journal of Theoretical Politics, Vol. 21, No. 4, 2009, pp. 483-507.
16 Josef Joffe. Defying History and Theory: the United States as the "Last Remaining Superpower", in: G. John Ikenberry. America Unrivaled: The Future of the Balance of Power. Trans. Hanzhaoyin. Peking University Publishing House, 2005, p. 155-162.
17 Robert J. Art. A Grand Strategy for America. Trans. Guo Shuyong. Peking University Publishing House, 2005, p. 162.

balance.[18] After the end of the Cold War, the US has waged many foreign wars, but there have not been any third party military intervention against the US. Some scholars have provided explanations for this from a geographical standpoint. Mearsheimer's explanation is that the hegemony exerted by the US is constrained to the Western hemisphere, but not a global hegemony because the geographical barrier of the territorial waters has brought problems for the US to carry out power projections. Hence, states outside Western hemisphere do not need to balance the power of the US.[19] According to Jack Levy and William Thompson, the concentrations of hegemony fall into two types: land-based military power and maritime power. Seeking to expand the territory, states with land-based military power pose a big threat to other states thus are more likely being balanced by other states. But hegemonic states with maritime power tend to pursue trade and markets, with a preference for economic hegemony. Because the navy is not good at continental occupation and is less a threat to other states, it is seldom balanced, and other major states even favor to establish co-operation or alliance with them.[20]

2. The bandwagon theory

According to the power balance theory, it is usually a hegemonic state or a major state that performs military interventions as a third party. However, according to statistics, the third parties are not necessarily major states and actually a plethora of third parties are relatively weak states. What's more, it is believed that the third parties usually help the weaker. But, in effect, there are many cases on the contrary, and sometimes the third parties even assist the stronger. Paul Schroeder has made an example. Although the UK always adopted the balancing strategy, it still aligned itself with France and Austria to defeat Russia, the weaker side.[21] The statistics have shown that among the 572 conflicts occurring from 1816 to 1992, there are 337 without the involvement of the third parties, 126 with the third parties supporting the stronger side and 109 supporting the weaker side. Therefore, the power balancing theory has been challenged, and many scholars have made attempts to explain such a bandwagon of states.

---

18 Herbert K. Tillema, "Cold War Alliance and Overt Military Intervention, 1945-1991," International Interactions, Vol.20, No.3, 1994, p. 263; Marita Kaw, "Predicting Soviet Military Intervention," Journal of Conflict Resolution, Vol. 33, No. 3, 1989, p. 425.
19 John Mearsheimer. The Tragedy of Great Power Politics, p. 526.
20 Jack S. Levy and William R. Thompson, "Hegemonic Threats and Great Power Balancing in Europe, 1495-1999," Security Studies, Vol. 14, No.1, 2005, pp. 1-33; Jack Levy and William Thompson, "Balancing on Land and at Sea: Does States Ally Against the Leading Global Powers?" International Security, Vol.35, No.1, 2010, pp. 7-43.
21 Paul Schroeder, "Historical Reality versus Neorealist Theory," International Security, Vol. 19, No.1, 1994, pp. 125-126. Paul Fritz and Kevin Sweeney, "The (de) Limitations of Balance of Power Theory," International Interactions, Vol. 30-No. 4, pp. 285-308.

When being threatened, many states opt for bandwagoning instead of balancing. Randall L. Schweller has divided states into two types according to benefit preferences: status quo states that seek to maximize security and revisionist states that seek to maximize power. Randall L. Schweller believes that balancing is to seek for security while bandwagoning is to gain benefits. Engaging in balancing or bandwagoning depends on the costs states are willing to pay to defend the status quo relative to the costs it is willing to pay to change the status quo. Revisionist states are usually willing to pay extremely high costs and even take greater risks to change the status quo. And the status quo states are usually willing to pay high price to defend the status quo. To pursue a greater benefit, states dissatisfied with the status quo will bandwagon the stronger revisionist states. Only those satisfied with the status quo adopt a balancing behavior. Schweller believes that bandwagoning with other states, the third parties perform military intervention to change the status quo and to share the spoils of war.[22]

B. The theory of norms

According to Alexander Wendt and Daniel Friedheim, five mechanisms are recognized to help create consenting identities in informal empire. The first mechanism is overt coercion, especially through military intervention.[23]

Effective and successful international intervention is favorable to enhance the legitimacy of hegemonic states. David Rapkin has listed several legitimate elements in US hegemony: common values, public procedures, self-restraint of hegemonic states; observation of international law, authorization of actions from the UN, the multilateral organization; universal consensus of the public, successful actions such as effective military intervention, generating economic growth globally and providing measures for fair distribution.[24] Therefore, hegemonic states usually implement third party military intervention.[25] By propagating and promoting its own ideology in the international system, a state can command the ideological loyalty of its bandwagoners, and eventually enhance its position and influence in the

---

22 Randall L. Schweller, "Bandwagoning for Profit: Bring the Revisionist State Back," in: International Security, Vol. 19, No.1, 1994, pp. 72-107.
23 Alexander Wendt and Daniel Friedheim, "Hierarchy under Anarchy: Informal Empire and the East German State," International Organization, Vol. 49, No.4, 1995, pp. 702-705.
24 David P. Rapkin, "Empire and Its Discontents," New Political Economy, Vol.10, No. 3, 2005, pp. 400-401; David P. Rapkin and Dan Braaten, "Conceptualising Hegemonic Legitimacy," Review of International Studies, Vol. 35, No. 1, 2009, pp. 113-149.
25 Nincic Microslav, Loss Aversion and the Domestic Context of Millitary Intervention." Political Research Quarterly, Vol. 50, No.1, 1997, p. 115.

international system.[26] Robert Gilpin has stated that the position of the dominant power may be supported by ideological, religious or other values common to a set of states.[27]

On the one hand, international intervention helps enhance the legitimacy of hegemony. And on the other hand, international norms sometimes impose restrictions on states' intervening behaviors. Christopher Cook has examined the different policies adopted by the US towards East Timor and Kosovo and refuted the ideas of realism. Two explanations on his argument are offered. 1. The US pays attention to regional stability. 2. The intervention is for preserving US credibility. According to his article the US aimed to intervene in Kosovo to strengthen NATO's legitimacy that has a direct connection with the European stability as a whole. As for the Timor crisis, it is regarded as a humanitarian crisis. Considering the facts that Indonesia is one of the US-allies and of significant importance to the stability of Southeast Asia, the US is unwilling to take the lead in denouncing and sanctioning Indonesian government, but only providing services of logistics and foreign diplomacy to fulfill its international obligation of peacekeeping in East Timor. However, if intervening in the conflicts of East Timor is not in the national interests of the US, why did the US still give a response to it though passively and restrictedly? This article believes that this was caused by international norms. Actually, the considerations from the perspective of international norms on human rights, national self-determination and the role as a member of the international organization (the UN), all have restricted the options for the US to adopt. Because of these international norms, the US could take intervening actions.[28] Martha Finnemore has studied the effect of the norm of use of force upon intervening behavior, and she believes that foreign military intervention has to be legally justified. For example, the recovery of contract debts by force has lost its legitimacy in terms of the arbitration agreement reached in the Second Hague Peace Conference in 1907. And as a result of it, similar interventions disappeared. European states have coordinately made clear that the legitimacy of interventions performed by major states is based on the premises that the security issues have crossed borders and all peaceful options have been exhausted. With the global popularization of the norms on human rights and state sove-

---

26 Nigel Gould-Davies, "Rethinking the Role of Ideology in International Politics During the Cold War," Journal of Cold War Studies, Vol. 1, No. 1, 1999, pp. 90-109.
27 Robert Gilpin, War and Change in World Politics, Cambridge: Cambridge University Press, 1981, p. 34.
28 Christopher Cook, "The Power of International Institutions: An Examination of US. Policy towards East Timor and Kosovo in 1999. "Journal of Politics and Law, Vol. 3, No. 2; 2010, pp.26-35.

reignty, more changes have been brought in the contents of humanitarian intervention.[29] Following the movements for the abolition of the slave trade, decolonization and national self-determination, the traditional norms on humanitarian intervention are no longer limited to the conventional identity with Christianity.[30] Richard Little has made an elaboration on the case that Britain did not intervene in the American Civil War, and this seems to run against Britain's insistence on the principle of balancing power and containment. He argues that the principles of state sovereignty and neutrality have been gradually recognized in the western international community since 1800s. Meanwhile, regarding the US as a legitimate member of the international community, the British policymakers thought that the US is also bound by international rules as themselves. Therefore, the legal rights of the US should not be infringed. With such considerations, the UK chose to stand by and did not interfere with the American Civil War.[31]

In ancient China, there are also the norms with influence on states' intervening behaviors. In B.C. 661, the emperor of the state of Lu passed away, and the state of Lu was struck in internal turmoil. The emperor of the state of Qi, wanted to send troops and occupy the state of Lu. But Zhong Sun, the official of the emperor of the state of Qi suggested that they should not take advantage of the precarious situation in another states. Zhong Sun said, "the rites of Zhou are the foundation for setting up a state. I've heard that a state was like a tree. When the tree is about to perish, its trunk will be the first to be brought down and then fall the leaves. The state of Lu does not discard the rites of Zhou, and we should not intervene in Lu state. Instead, you should be friend with the state of Lu and help it to overcome difficulties. Approaching countries of courtesy and propriety, relying on strong countries, estranging undisciplined countries and destroying troubled countries should always be the ways to cement your hegemony." Although Mencius did not emphasize the norms, he also stressed that winning the hearts of the public is the key to gain legitimacy. "Liang Hui Wang II: The people of Qi attacked Yan, and conquered it. The king Xuan asked, saying, 'some tell me not to take possession of it for myself, and some tell me to take possession of it. For a kingdom of ten thousand chariots, attacking another of ten thousand chariots, to complete the conquest of it in fifty days, is an achievement beyond mere human

---

29 Martha Finnemore, The Purpose of Intervention: Changing Beliefs about the Use of Force. Trans. Yuan Zhengqing, Lixin. Shanghai People's Publishing House. 2009.
30 Martha Finnemore, Constructing Norms of Humanitarian Intervention, in: Peter Katzenstein, The Culture of National Security: Norms and Identity in World Politics, p.153-85.
31 Richard Little, "British Neutrality versus Offshore Balancing in the American Civil War: The English School Strikes Back," Security Studies, Vol. 16, No.1, 2007, pp. 68-95.

strength. If I do not take possession of it, calamities from Heaven will surely come upon me. What do you say to my taking possession of it?' Mencius replied, 'If the people of Yan will be pleased with your taking possession of it, then do so. Among the ancients there was one who acted on this principle, namely king Wu. If the people of Yan will not be pleased with your taking possession of it, then do not do so. Among the ancients there was one who acted on this principle, namely king Wen. When, with all the strength of your country of ten thousand chariots, you attacked another country of ten thousand chariots, and the people brought baskets of rice and vessels of congee, to meet your Majesty's host, was there any other reason for this but that they hoped to escape out of fire and water? If you make the water more deep and the fire fiercer, they will in like manner make another revolution.'"

C. System theory

The system here is discussed at two levels: international system which generally refers to the treaty of alliance, and the domestic system which generally refers to politic systems such as democracy.

Arnold Wolfers thinks that alliance is the commitment made by two or more sovereign states to provide military assistances, and such commitment which has a strictly contractual spirit requires a state to join the fight when its allies are under attack.[32] Randolph M. Siverson and Joel King believe that if one or more allies join in a conflict, the state would choose the allies it trusts most at first.[33] On the occurrence of an international crisis, allies in the spirit of "defense treaty" will have a strong impetus to intervene so as to sustain the integrity of the alliance. And for the third party military intervention, if both sides of the conflicts have no relations with the third party, the chance of escalating the war into bigger war is small; if one side is allied with the third party, the escalation of war is of high probability.[34] However, allied states have a low chance of performing third party military intervention. From 1816 to 1965, the number of wars with the involvement of allied states accounts for 27% of the total.[35]

---

32 Arnold Wolfers, "Alliances," in: David L. Sills, ed., International Encyclopedia of Social Sciences, New York: Macmillan, 1968, pp.268-269.
33 Randolph M. Siverson and Joel King, "Attributes of National Alliance Membership and War Participation," American Journal of Political Science, Vol. 35, No.2, 1980, pp. 285-306.
34 Randolph M. Siverson and Joel King, "Alliances and the Expansion of War," in J. David Singer and Michael D. Wallace, eds., To Augur Well: Early Warning Indicators, in; World Politics, Beverly Hills, CA: Sage, 1979.
35 A.N. Sabrosky, "Interstate Alliances: Their Reliability and the Expansion of War," in: J. David Singer, ed., The Correlates of War II, New York: Free Press, 1980.

Looking from the perspective of the domestic system, it is less likely to intervene in states with similar domestic system. "The western system features a specific institutional structure, and the open form of government it entails has bond primary countries together, which as a result, minimized the impact of unbalanced power and reduced the likelihood of US's jettisoning or curbing other states. The systematic properties of the post-War international order is favorable to fully explain why balance of power does not exist after the Cold War."[36] According to Thomas Risse, the security community features three elements: collective identity and common value, interdependence in politics, economy and culture, international structures for adjusting social order. Ascribing the peaceful coexistence of liberal democratic states to the functions of security community and recognizing the three features of it have determined that these states will not balance the US.[37] Therefore, the US tends to promote liberal and democratic system or to rebuild such system in the targeted states.[38]

In terms of the international intervention performed by the US after the Cold War, there are still some deficiencies in the explanations above: since the US is the world hegemon in the Post-Cold War era, bandwagoning strategy was obviously not the option for the US. But from the angle of the power balancing theory, the US is supposed to intervene in the surrounding areas of China if the rise of China poses a threat to US's hegemonic position in the world. However, since the US interventions after the Cold War are primarily concentrated in Middle East, the power balancing theory fails to explain this fully. It can be seen that although the domestic politics of the targeted states for intervention do not always conform to the universally acknowledged humanitarian norms, there are also some other states such as North Korea, Iran with their domestic politics distinct from the US. But why did the US intervene in Iraq and Libya instead of the states above, and what considerations were taken by the US when making such decisions? Actually, US intervention against Libya was systematically influenced by France. But in 2003, the US ignored France's opposition to its intervention against Iraq, but why did France drag the US into war in 2011? Looking from the perspective of democracy, the states targeted by the US for military intervention were never democratic states. However, since there are

---

36 G. John Ikenberry, Democracy, Institutions, and American Restraint. America Unrivaled: The Future of the Balance of Power, pp. 214.
37 Thomas Risse. U.S. Power in a Liberal Security Community; G. John Ikenberry, Democracy, Institutions, and American Restraint. America Unrivaled: The Future of the Balance of Power, pp. 259-277.
38 Bueno de Mesquita and Downs. "Intervention and Democracy," International Organization, Vol.60, No.3, 2006, pp. 627-649.

many non-democratic states around the world, the argument of political system is inadequate to explain why Iraq and Libya but not other states were targeted by the US for its military intervention after the Cold War. The explanations above cannot cover all the reasons behind the US choices of military targets. And the next passages will discuss on this.

II. The US military intervention after the Cold War

The discussion above has analyzed the reasons of military intervention. However, after the Cold War, it is noticeable that the military interventions adopted by the US were entirely different from the ones before. What were the intentions for the interventions ranging from the intervention in Kosovo by Clinton Administration to the one in Libya by Obama Administration? In order to explore the reasons of US military intervention after the Cold War, the following passage will give the analysis of every military intervention adopted by the US in the Post-Cold War era.

A. Intervention in Kosovo

In 1999, without the UN approval the US and major European states launched a campaign of air strikes and started the Kosovo war. The war was led by the US and involved the active participation of European countries, practically by NATO forces. This was the first time, the US and European states have jointly resorted to unilateral use of forces against a sovereign state without obtaining explicit authorization of the UN after the Cold War. French president Chirac claimed, actions deviating from international norms could be adopted under humanitarian situation. France would perform interventions together with other states.[39] In April 22, 1999, during NATO's bombing against Yugoslavia, British Prime Minister Blair mentioned three points in his speech in Chicago. First, globalization was an international phenomenon. The world has become an international common entity with states depending on each other. Second, the internal affairs of any state will inevitably have an impact on other states. Therefore, other states have the right to intervene. The principles of states sovereignty and non-inferences have to be amended. Third, it is required to reform the existing international law and international organizations to establish the new international order based on humanitarianism thus justifying humanitarian intervention.[40] Blair has pointed out, "The US has once again shown that it

---
39 Catherine Guicherd, "International Law and the War in Kosovo," Survival, Vol.41, No.2, 1999, pp.19-34.
40 Tony Blair, "Doctrine of the International Community," speech to the Economic Club of Chicago on April 22, 1999.

has the vision to see that instability, chaos and racial genocide in the heart of Europe will never affect Europe alone."[41] This war has provoked the conflicts between states in the discussion of sovereignty and human rights.

In Kosovo war, NATO primarily adopted air strikes, imposed various coercive mechanisms through air forces supremacy, and compelled Milosevic to change his policies in a number of ways.[42] Although the US and Europe did not gain the explicit authorization of the UN when waging Kosovo war, they still strive for legalizing their actions through some resolutions concerned. After the end of Kosovo war, the Security Council has passed the 1244 Resolution that authorizes member states of the UN to rebuild Kosovo and maintain international peace and stability.[43]

B. Intervention in Afghanistan

After the Event of 9/11, according to the investigation by the US, the plotter of the event is Al-Qaeda, its leader, Bin Laden and the supporter behind the terrorists is the Taliban regime. Before 9/11, Afghanistan was in civil war where the north alliance and Taliban regime fought for the sovereignty. Burhanuddin Rabbani Administration of the northern alliance forces were on behalf of Afghanistan government in international community. But it was defeated by the Taliban regime that occupied more than 95% of the total territory of Afghanistan. Taliban regime was only recognized by Saudi Arabia, the UAE and Pakistan.

The US military intervention against Afghanistan has gained the support of the UN. From September 2001 to the end of that year when the US and its allies were attacking Afghanistan, the Security Council of the UN has issued six resolutions successively: (2001) 1368 Resolution (Passed in September 12, 2001 in the 4370th Conference)[44], (2001) 1373 Resolution (Passed in September 28, 2001 in the 4385th Conference)[45], (2001) 1377 Resolution (Passed in November 12, 2001 in the 4413rd Conference)[46], (2001) 1378 Resolution (Passed in November 14, 2001 in the 4415th

---

41 Warren Hoge, "Crisis in the Balkans: Britain; Blair under Domestic Pressure on Ground Forces," New York Times, May 18, 1999, p. A10.
42 Daniel R. Lake "The Limits of Coercive Airpower: NATO's 'Victory' in Kosovo Revisited," International Security, Vol.34, No.1, 2009, pp. 83-112.
43 Security Council Resolution 1244 (1999) on the situation relating Kosovo.http://daccess-dds-ny.un.org/doc/UNDOC/GEN/N99/172/89/PDF/N9917289.pdf/OpenElement.
44 http://daccess-ods.un.org/access.nsf/Get?Open&DS=S/RES/1368%20(2001)&Lang=E&Area=UNDOC
45 Ibid.
46 Ibid.

Conference)⁴⁷, (2001) 1383 Resolution (Passed in December 6 2001 in the 4434th Conference)⁴⁸, (2001) 1386 Resolution (Passed in December 20 2001 in the 4443rd Conference)⁴⁹. These resolutions have authorized the international community to adopt all necessary means to fight against terrorism and its supporters and asylum seekers, and support Afghan people for regime change.

From October 7, 2011 to mid-December, the US and the UK waged war against Afghanistan. During the fights, the US engaged about 180,000 troops. The UK engaged about 24 warships and 20,000 soldiers. NATO and EU supported the US militarily in different levels. Support also came from the Islamic world countries, African states and the neighboring countries of Afghanistan such as Russia (CIS), Ukraine and Central Asia. Thus, just within the span of two months, the US declared victory and succeeded in overthrowing Taliban regime.

C. Intervention in Iraq

Dated back to 1990s, the US has made a list of rogue states: Iraq, Iran, Libya, Sudan, Syria, and Afghanistan and so and so forth. After the 9/11 incident, the US singled out three countries, namely Iraq, Iran, and North Korea as the "axis of evil". The US highlighted the use of "preemptive strike" to fight against international terrorism and to prevent the proliferation of weapons of mass destruction.⁵⁰

At the beginning of 1991, when the Gulf War came to end, the Western states led by the US intervened in the domestic conflicts of Iraq in the name of protecting the Iraqi citizens. This was the first major western intervention activity after the Cold War. The UN Security Council has passed the 688 Resolution and announced that the oppression against the Kurds and Shiite Islamists by the Iraqi government had posed a "threat to international peace and security". In the words of former UN Secretary, General Javier Perez de Cuellar, "We are clearly witnessing what is probably an irresistible shift in public attitudes toward the belief that the defense of the oppressed in the name of morality should prevail over frontiers and legal documents."⁵¹ The coalition quickly defeated the Iraqi military.

---

47 Ibid.
48 Ibid.
49 Ibid.
50 Jiang Longfan, Wang Xiaobo, the New Development and the Future of the Nuclear Crisis in North Korea, Pacific Journal, No. 5, 2009, pp. 28.
51 Stephen Stedman, "The New Interventionist," Foreign Affairs, Vol.72, No.1, 1992.

In March 2003, in coalition with the UK, the US circumvented the regulations of the UN and waged the Iraq war after the intervention in Afghanistan. Although major countries such as Germany, Russia, France and China expressed a strong opposition against the US unilateralism, Bush Administration still insisted on its military intervention in Iraq. Though in power for 35 years, Saddam Hussein's Ba'ath regime was easily overturned by the coalition forces headed by the US. At the end of 2006, under the authorization and support of the US, Saddam Hussein was trialed and executed by the Iraqi government.

D. Intervention in Libya

Since Muammar Gaddafi came into power in 1969, he has taken the course of developing nuclear weapons. Because of this, Libya has been titled as a Rogue State since the middle of 1980s. In 1981, Washington cut its ties with Libya due to Libya's support of terrorism. In 1986, Reagan administration imposed an all-round economic sanction against Libya. Furthermore, the Bombing of Panam flight 103 in 1988 has left Libya isolated in the international community. The UN Security Council of started its comprehensive sanctions against Libya in 1992, which included the banning of all Libyan flights.

Libya's behaviors have come to a turning point in the 21st century. After the 9/11 incident, Libya extended its sympathy for the US and cracked down upon al-Qaeda at home. In August 2003, Libyan authorities announced their responsibility for the Lockerbie air disaster and made compensations for the relatives of the victims. On December 19, 2003, Libya renounced its nuclear plan. In March 2004, Libya agreed to permit the inspection of IAEA (International Atomic Energy Agency). In September 2004, less than one year since Gaddafi's announcement of the decision, the US State Department publically confirmed Libya's giving up its nuclear programs. Mr. Bush said that Libya has made an important step to prevent the weapons of mass destruction from falling into the hands of terrorists. If Libya fulfilled its commitments, the US would return in good faith. And the relations between the two states would be improved.[52] In such circumstances, the United States decided in June 2004 to restore the normal diplomatic relations with Libya. French president Chirac expressed his willingness to "establish a new partnership" with Libya when he visited Libya in November 2004. Moreover, the United States removed it from the list of sponsor states of terrorism in May 2006.

---

52 Ren Minjun, Gaddafi's Renouncement of Banned Weapons Makes the UK and US Happy, Global Times, August 8, 2006.

Libya stepped up its diplomatic efforts to woo the US and expected returns from the US. According to British "Daily Mirror", the former Libyan Foreign Secretary Mohammed Shalgam said to British Foreign Secretary Jack Straw that as a matter of fact, Libya had stopped the entire weapon.[53] Mohammed Shalgam said that Libya did not make any concession. Abandoning the program is for political needs…and this is not involuntary. We want to gain help from the US and the UK. This is much more favorable to us.[54]

Through the diagnosis of the Libya's behaviors, the US thought that in the context of the military coalition of the UK and US against Iraq, the nuclear program and the historical involvement in terrorism have made Libya become the target of the US. To avoid being trapped in the situation in Iraq, Gaddafi had to swiftly "change the course" of action considering the coercive diplomacy employed by the US.[55] When Libya sent a series of signals to show friendliness, the White House attributed this to "the security strategy of anti-proliferation of weapons of mass destruction by President George W. Bush"[56]. The US believed that Libya's behavior has reflected its weakness. Just like Kissinger's judgments on Gorbachev's disarmament initiative, "unilateral cuts of such magnitude signaled either extraordinary self-confidence or exceptional weakness".[57]

In February 16, 2011, there occurred an anti-government protest in Libya. With the escalation of the conflict, Gaddafi sent troops to crack down the protesters. "The suffering and bloodshed was outrageous, and it was unacceptable", and President Obama said at the White House: "These actions violate international norms and every standard of common decency."[58] On February 26, based on the Resolution 1970, "the UN Security Council called for an international war crimes investigation into the widespread and

---

53 Wei Jianfeng, Sinanet. Com British Report: with other Intentions, Libya Play Tricks with America and the UK. February 12 2004. http://news.sina.com.cn/w/2004-02-12/01531777116s.shtml.
54 Lin Shuo. Why Different Treatments are Taken for Libya and Iraq? December 22. 2003, China Daily, http://www.chinadaily.com.cn/gb/doc/2003-12/22/content_292403.htm.
55 Bruce W. Jentleson and Christopher A. Whytock, "Who 'Won' Libya? The Force Diplomacy Debate and Its Implications for Theory and Policy," International Security, Vol.30, No.13, 2005 /2006, pp.47-86.
56 Hussain Khan, "Gadhafi, Not a Victim of Bush Doctrine," http://www.yobserver.com/opinions/10095.html.
57 Kissinger, Diplomacy. Trans. Gushuxin. Haikou. Haikou Publishing House, 1998, pp. 733.
58 David D. Kirkpatrick and Mona El-Naggar, "Qaddafi's Son Warns of Civil War as Libyan Protests Widen," The New York Times, February 21, 2011; Helene Cooper and Mark Landler, "Obama Condemns Libya Amid Stalled Evacuation," The New York Times, February 23, 2011.

systemic attacks against Libyan citizens" [59]. And the investigation agency was the International Criminal Court in The Hague that has not been recognized by three permanent members of the UN Security Council. On March 10, Europe Congress issued a resolution and stressed that the EU and its Member States must honor their Responsibility to Protect, in order to save Libyan civilians from large-scale armed attacks.[60] On March 17, the Security Council 1973 Resolution authorized these setting of the no-fly area.[61] The no-fly zone was imposed as an excuse to launch a war in Libya. Under the encouragement of the UK and France, the US reluctantly joined the war. On March 19, in less than 48 hours before the 1973 Resolution was passed, air strikes against Libya were carried out by France, the UK and the US. France was involved in the direct air strikes against the Libyan government forces, and France and the US were responsible to attack the air defense of Libya. "No-fly zone" was imposed within a week.[62]

The US believed that Libya is not in the area of its core interests, and the issues on Libya should be handled in the hand of Europe.[63] At that time, trapped in Afghanistan war and Iraq war, the US was unable to lead the war. European states shouldered more responsibilities. At the early stage of "voluntary alliance", the US was responsible for commanding.[64] After that, NATO has taken over the command of the action and the right of control. As the High Representative of the Union for Foreign Affairs and Security Policy Catherine Ashton mentioned, there were some changes in the relations between EU and the US. EU's relationship with the US changes to being collaborative partners in solving problems rather than relying on it.[65]

---

59 Edward Wyatt, "Security Council Calls for War Criminal Inquiry in Libya," The New York Times, February 26, 2011.
60 European Parliament Resolution of 10 March 2011 on the Southern Neighborhood, and Libya in particular. http://www.responsibilitytoprotect.org/index.php/crises/190-crisis-in-libya/3248-european-parliament-resolution-of-10-march-2011-on-the-southern-neighbourhood-and-libya-in-particular.
61 Security Council 1973 Resolution. http://baike.baidu.com/view/5430483.htm.
62 James Blitz, "And now for the hard part: three reasons to fear a stalemate," Financial Times, March 27, 2011, p. 8.
63 Daniel Dombey and James Blitz, "Europe feels strain as US changes tack on Libya," Financial Times, April 6, 2011, p. 5.
64 Peter Spiegel and Daniel Dombey, "Allies at odds over command," Financial Times, March 22, 2011, p.3.
65 The Brookings Institution, "The European Union Response to the Arab Spring," A Statesman's Forum with Catherine Ashton, High Representative of the European Union for Foreign Affairs and Security Policy, Washington, D.C., July 12, 2011, https://www.brookings.edu/events/the-european-union-response-to-the-arab-spring/

III. Analysis of the motives behind the US military interventions

After the end of the Cold War, great changes have occurred in international configuration. The US detached itself from the proxy war and come to the frontline of military intervention. Hence, what are the motives behind the US military intervention, and whether we can identify its laws? The following paragraphs will make an analysis of it from the perspectives of power, norms and system.

A. The impact of power

In terms of power distribution, the military endeavors made by the US in the Post-Cold War era are for balancing instead of bandwagoning. As the bipolarity has disintegrated, America has been the only superpower left in the world. Therefore, consolidating its hegemonic position has become the strategic focus of the US.

The US intervention in Kosovo and in Iraq in 1990s was performed mainly for balancing Russia. Though the Soviet Union had collapsed, Russia still had strong military power. Since Kosovo was in Russia's traditional sphere of influence, the intervention in Kosovo can be regarded as a trial to test the national power of Russia. Although it voiced a strong opposition to this, Russia still made substantial concessions and let Milosevic accept the conditions imposed by the US. US's balancing strategy against Russia scored a success.

After the 9/11 incident, neither the power balancing theory nor the bandwagoning theory is adequate enough to explain the US interventions against Afghanistan, Iraq and Libya. Since the 21st century, the rise of China has become an important phenomenon. Clearly aware of it, the Bush Administration decided to practice containment against China and added Taiwan in the Nuclear Posture Review Reports to the regions that could probably possessing nuclear weapons.[66] In August 2001, "the war plan to defend Taiwan" made by US Pacific Command was upgraded from CONPLAN to OPLAN, one of only three completed and full-fledged war plans of the U.S. military.[67] But after the 9/11 incident, the US targeted terrorism in the Middle East as its primary strategic goal. And the diplomatic relations with China has been eased.

---

66 Nuclear Posture Review Report, Submitted to Congress on 31 December 2001, http://www.fas.org/blog/ssp/united_states/NPR2001re.pdf.
67 William M. Arkin, "America's New China War Plan," Early Warning (Washington Post), May 24, 2006.

After the interventions against After the interventions in Afghanistan and Iraq, President Obama has fully realized the deficiencies of Bush's policies: The US was overextended in all the wrong places ... in the Middle East neglecting other parts of the globe.[68] Under the impact of the financial crisis and the rise of China, the US is likely to experience a decline or a period of strategic shrinkage.[69] Therefore a series of new measures will be adopted, such as the reduction of military power, shifting of more responsibility to its allies and reducing its international responsibility, all of which can be evaluated as common responses to the decline of national power by any major country. And by such a shrinkage, a major country can maintain its great power status in the international community.

Therefore, President Obama has changed his diplomatic strategies towards the Middle East and adopted retrenchment and counterpunching[70]: reducing the total expenses on diplomatic policies, reallocating resources, abandoning marginal regions and making strategic focus.[71] As for the specific strategies adopted by the US in Middle East, Hillary Clinton proposed the "smart power" strategy to use the full range of tools at disposal – diplomatic, economic, military, political, legal, and cultural – picking the right tool, or combination of several tools, for each situation.[72] Although plunged into Iraq and Afghanistan wars, the US still intervened in Libya, which is really hard to explain this intervention from the perspective of power balancing theory.

Above all, after the 21st century, with its global hegemony strategy, the US takes military intervention less from the perspective of power balancing. And because of this, power balancing can only explain the US military interventions in the 1990s, but not the US military operations in the last decade.

---

68 Daniel W. Drezner, "Does Obama Have a Grand Strategy? Why We Need Doctrines in Uncertain Times," Foreign Affairs, Vol.90, No.4, 2011, p. 64.
69 Paul K. MacDonald and Joseph M. Parent, "Graceful Decline?—The Surprising Success of Great Power Retrenchment", International Security, Vol. 35, No. 4, 2011, pp. 7-44.
70 Daniel W. Drezner, "Does Obama Have a Grand Strategy? Why We Need Doctrines in Uncertain Times," Foreign Affairs, Vol.90, No.4, 2011, p. 58.
71 Paul K. MacDonald and Joseph M. Parent, "Graceful Decline? —The Surprising Success of Great Power Retrenchment," p. 11.
72 Hillary Rodham Clinton, "Nomination Hearing to Be Secretary of State Testimony," Statement before the Senate Foreign Relations Committee, Washington, DC, January 13, 2009, http://www.state.gov/secretary/rm/2009a/01/115196.htm.

B. The impact of international norms

Power balancing can only partially account for the US military intervention against Kosovo. The US could realize its strategic interests and reach its goals by unilateral military actions without the aid of NATO, through which, the US could be free from the restrictions of its European allies and increase its involvement in military interventions. However, in effect, instead of adopting unilateral strategies, the US coordinated its military intervention with its allies. From the above, we can see that, through intervention in Kosovo, the US endeavored to enhance the legitimacy of NATO, which on the other hand, was favorable to sustain the regional stability of Europe. Therefore, US's intervention against Kosovo was not only considered for power balancing but also for maintaining the prestige of NATO and the legitimate norms.[73]

Although power balancing was not the driving force for the US to take military interventions in Afghanistan, the intervention has still gained a legal support. From September 2001 to the end of that year, with the support of other states, six resolutions were issued to legally support America's anti-terrorism activities. National Security Strategy of the USA (2006) has made a summary of the democratic reforms practiced in Afghanistan and other states. According to the statement, the democratic reforms in these states have virtually provided a long-term guarantee for the national security of the US.. It has pointed out, "It is the policy of the United States to seek and support democratic movements and institutions in every nation and culture, with the ultimate goal of ending tyranny in our world…the goal of our statecraft is to help create a world of democratic, well-governed states that can meet the needs of their citizens and conduct themselves responsibly in the international system. This is the best way to provide enduring security for the American people."[74] Obviously, the US not only strived to legitimize its military intervention, but also hoped to establish its own democratic system in Afghanistan. The counterpunch of norms on anti-terrorism served to guarantee the US security interests.

The US intervention in Iraq in 2003 cannot be explained from the perspective of power balancing theory, and with the absence of approval by the UN, it has clearly violated the international norms. Mr. Bush believed and argued that the international norms had been outdated. The violation of

---

73 Cook, Christopher, "The Power of International Institutions: An Examination of the US. Policy towards East Timor and Kosovo in 1999." Journal of Politics and Law, Vol. 3, No.2, 2010.
74 http://georgewbush-whitehouse.archives.gov/nsc/nss/2006/.

the international norms could be permissible, when defending against the national security threats, even the the authorization of the UN was absent.[75] Eventually, the US adopted the unilateral strategy and its intervention did not gain international support. Except the UK which sent troops, other major countries such as France, Russia and China all expressed their opposition against it. Since the Bush Administration overly emphasized military superiority and military means, ignoring of the importance and function of diplomacy, various policy measures were self-contradictory, the advantage of national power failed to be effectively transformed to equivalent influence, and actually through its military interventions in the Middle East, the US did not realize its goals of anti-terrorism, promoting democracy, stopping the proliferation of the weapons of mass destruction.[76]

Nor can the US intervention against Libya in 2011 be explained by power balancing theory and interventional norms. Since Libya was beyond core concerns of the US, the military intervention against Libya was unexpected.[77] President Obama admitted that, the US should not and could not intervene in all crises around the world.[78] US Defense Secretary Robert Gates expressed firm opposition to the US intervention in Libya, and he believed it is impossible for the US to win three wars at the same time, since the US is still involved in Afghanistan war and Iraq war.[79] The US has waged Afghanistan war and Iraq war in 2001 and 2003 respectively, with more than 100,000 armed forces allocated to each war. Under such circumstances, the US was supposed to end the wars urgently. But, why did the US still decide to intervene in Libya? President Obama asserted that the military intervention was in line with the US's national interests, and no one has a bigger stake in making sure that there is some semblance of order and justice particularly in volatile regions.[80] Mr. Obama stressed that the cruel oppression of Qaddafi regime had lead to the chaos within Libya, and because of this, America's imposing

---

75　Shannon, Vaughn, "Leadership Style and International Norm Violation: The Case of the Iraq War."Foreign Policy Analysis, Vol. 3, No.1, 2007, pp. 79-104.
76　Jeremy Pressman, "Power without Influence: The Bush Administration's Foreign Policy Failure in the Middle East," International Security, Vol.33, No.4, 2009, pp. 149-150.
77　Richard N. Haass, "The United States Should Keep out of Libya," Wall Street Journal, March 8, 2011.
78　The White House, "Remarks by the President in Address to the Nation on Libya," March 28, 2011, http://www.whitehouse.gov/the-press-office/2011/03/28/remarks-president-address-nation-libya.
79　Mark Landler and Thom Shanker, "Gates and Clinton Unite to Defend Libya Intervention, and Say It May Last A while, "The New York Times, March 27, 2011.
80　Associated Press, "Obama says control of Libya operation can be turned over soon," The News Virginian, March 23,2011, http://www2.newsvirginian.com/news/wnv-news/2011/mar/23/obama-says-control-libya-operation-can-be-tur ned-o-ar-922114/.

military sanctions on Libya was on a just ground.[81] However, during the Arab spring in 2011, there were also other states encountered with those similar problems present in Libya. So, why America targeted Libya and not any other state in the region is worth exploring.

Obviously, norms are just one reason among the multiple causes for the US intervention. Justified on a normative basis, the US would more easily gain support from other states when performing military intervention, and this would also enhance the likelihood for success. Therefore, though norms did affect the means by which intervention is performed, they have not been the real motives behind US military intervention.

III. The impact of the system

From above, we can see that systematic factors entail both the international level factors primarily reflected in the form of alliance and the domestic level in the form of political systems such as democratic system. And the discussion below will focus on this two factors respectively.

A. Alliance factors

Except the intervention in Libya, the major military interventions after the Cold War were all led and initiated by the US, and after the US decision of wars, the European allies such as the UK and the France have decided whether they would join or not. And that is why the factor of alliance did not have a great impact on these two military interventions.

But, for allies, there were differences in terms of their partnership and ways of cooperation with the US. The US and NATO cooperated with each other when intervening in Afghanistan, while holding divergences on the issue of Iraq. The weakening of NATO's role is a result of the changes in international configuration, in the Post-Cold War era. After the break of the bipolarity, the US no longer had a complete trust in NATO. But to seek cooperation and support from NATO, the US still allowed it to play a role in the anti-terrorism activities.[82]

In Libya war, the US was significantly affected by its European allies when making decisions. From the perspectives of geopolitics and history, France regarded North Africa as its traditional sphere of influence, and France is

---

81 Wang Fengfeng. Linyu. The Protest by American Anti-war Organizations Opposing Military Intervention against Libya. March 27 2011. Xinhuanet. http://news.xinhuanet.com/2011-03/27/c_121235960.htm.
82 Renee de Nevers, "NATO's International Security Role in the Terrorist Era, "International Security, Vol. 31, No. 4, 2007, pp. 34-66.

one of the most active advocates of the intervention against Libya.[83] The UK stressed that "the region is vital to UK and EU interests.[84] France and the UK moved forward with their intervention against Libya, playing a leading role during the process.[85] The Joint Letter from Prime Minister David Cameron MP and President Nicolas Sarkozy on March 10 to the President of the European Council called upon the UN to evaluate and closely monitor the "humanitarian situation" in Libya.[86] What's more, under the concerted efforts by France and the UK, the UN has authorized the establishment of a no-fly zone by passing 1973 Resolution.[87] Finally, the lobbying by UK and US determined the US to intervene in Libya. On April 14 2011, Mr. Obama stressed in the joint declaration made by President Obama, British Prime Minister David Cameron and French President Sarkozy, that to remove Qaddafi by force was not the goal of their actions. And it was impossible to imagine a future for Libya with Qaddafi in power.[88] Sarkozy said that it was the first time that Europe has demonstrated its ability to deal with the conflicts through decisive intervention in its neighborhood. Since Libya borders the Mediterranean sea, the Libya crisis is firstly an European affair then an American one.[89] Since the intervention in Libya was primarily under the encouragement of France, UK and other European allies, the US did not take a leading role in this intervention. The US was mainly responsible to destroy the air defense in Tripoli. And claiming to protect the innocent people in Libya, Obama has made clear that the US would dispatch no ground forces.[90] Therefore, in the early stage of the voluntary alliance, the US only committed to take responsibility for commanding.[91] And then American experts were rushed in to boost NATO's

---

83 "France's foreign-policy's woes: Nicolas Sarkozy's diplomatic troubles," The Economist, March 5, 2011, p.53.
84 Nick Clegg: Transforming Europe's partnership with North Africa, March 2, 2011. http://www.libdems.org.uk/nick_clegg_transforming_europe_s_partnership_with_north_africa.
85 "France and Britain are leading the intervention in Libya. Rightly so," The Economist, March 26, 2011, p.48.
86 David Cameron and Nicolas Sarkozy, "Joint Letter from Prime Minister David Cameron MP and President Nicolas Sarkozy," March 10, 2011.
87 UN Security Council, (Paragraphs 6 and 8), Resolution 1973 (2011), Adopted by the Security Council at its 6498th meeting, on 17 March 2011.
88 Barack Obama, David Cameron and Nicolas Sarkozy, "Libya s Pathway to Peace," International Herald Tribune, April 14, 2011.
89 The Discussion on Rebuilding Libya by 60 States in Paris. Can Kao Xiao XI. http://world.cankaoxiaoxi.com/2011/0902/1763.shtml.
90 Wang Fengfeng. Lin Yu. The Protest by American Anti-war Organizations Opposing Military Intervention against Libya. http://news.xinhuanet.com/2011-03/27/c_121235960.htm.
91 Peter Spiegel and Daniel Dombey, "Allies at odds over command," Financial Times, March 22, 2011, p.3.

command centre.⁹² What's more, the US also provided a plenty of munitions. After 11 weeks of air strikes, the American National Defense Robert Gates pointed, "Yet many allies are beginning to run short of munitions, requiring the US, once more, to make up the difference."⁹³ From this it can be seen that the US is dragged in the intervention by its allies and does not shoulder primary responsibility of leading.

B. Domestic politics

From the observations about the US military interventions, we can notice that the major targets for the US are middle and small countries which are primarily in the Middle East and Yugoslavia (Balkan Region). Hence, what are the thoughts behind this?

The democratic system in the US is a crucial factor in analyzing US interventions. The domestic politics determine whether a state wages a third party intervention or not. As to the international intervention behaviors, Randall L. Schweller identifies four factors at the domestic-political level for analysis: elite consensus, elite cohesion, social cohesion, and the degree of regime stability or government's vulnerability. Elite consensus and elite cohesion are combined to reflect a state's willingness to act, and social cohesion, and the degree of regime or government vulnerability determine the state activity capacity. All four factors contribute to state's unity. Therefore, different from totalitarian states, democratic states will not perform international intervention easily.⁹⁴ The data from 1816 to 1990 have shown that democratic states have won 93% wars they waged. And the proportions for autocratic states and states with mixed regime are 60% and 58% respectively. According to Dan Reiter and Allan Stam, democratic states have more spaces in choosing wars than non-democratic states and tend to wage the wars with high probability to win.⁹⁵ Since the leaders in democratic states gain their authority from public support. Therefore only when confident in winning, will they join the war.⁹⁶ The logic of decision-making is based on two aspects. With strong incentives, the leaders of democratic

---

92 "Robert Gates parting shot exposes Europe's military failings," The Economist, June 16, 2011, p. 50.
93 Ibid.
94 Randall L.Schweller, Unanswered Threats: Political Constraints on the Balance of Power, Princeton, NJ: Princeton University Press, 2006, p.47. Dan Reiter and Allan, Stam, Democracies at War, Princeton, NJ: Princeton University Press, 2002. Chapters. 2, 6.
95 Dan Reiter and Allan, Stam Democracies at War, Princeton, NJ: Princeton University Press, 2002, p. 29.
96 Bruce Bueno de Mesquita, "Game Theory, Political Economy and the Evolving Study of War and Peace," American Political Science Review, Vol. 100, No. 4, 2006, pp. 637-642.

states are confident in winning wars or they are probably dismissed from their posts. But, for leaders of non-democratic states, the incentives are not strongly exhibited.[97] On the other hand, in democratic states, waging a war is based on the public consensus, which does not exist in non-democratic states. Considering from this, the democratic states can make better assessments on the possibility to win. Moreover, David Lake thinks that by means of a superior power, democratic states defeat their enemy more easily.98 According to the detailed analysis of John M. Schuessler, the democratic system made it difficult for President Roosevelt to perform military intervention at the early stage of the WWII.[99] Because of the democratic system, the US usually performs its military intervention against the states that are relatively easy to be defeated. With considerable odds of defeating Libya that has attempted to develop nuclear program, the US joined the intervention against Libya together with France and the UK, though Libya had little to do with terrorism. As the Secretary of State Hillary Rodham Clinton mentioned, if the US and its allies sat by and did nothing towards Libya; it was like sending a signal that the US dared not send military forces to protect Muslims and Arabic people.[100] The White House believed the US was very likely to win the Libya war without paying much costs, through which, the US could deter Iraq without dispatching ground forces to Libya. From the above, it is noticeable that the US military strikes against Libya were influenced by its domestic democratic system.

Elizabeth N. Saunders believes that the subjective cognizance of decision makers will have an impact on the ways by which interventions are performed. If the diplomatic behaviors of a targeted state are significantly influenced by its domestic political system, the decision makers will set their goal as rebuilding the democracy in the target states, and if not, a pure military intervention will bring no changes in the domestic politics of the targeted states.[101] After the "9/11" Event, the mentalities of American people and of their government have went through significant changes breeding

---

97 Bruce Bueno de Mesquita and Randolph M. Siverson, "War and the Survival of Political Leaders: A Comparative Study of Regime Types and Political Accountability," American Political Science Review, Vol. 89, No.4, 1995, pp. 841-885.
98 David A. Lake, "Powerful Pacifists: Democratic States and War," American Political Science Review, Vol.86, No.1, 1992, pp.24-37.
99 John M. Schuessler, "The Deception Dividend-FDRs Undeclared War," International Security, Vol.34, No. 4, 2010, pp.133-165.
100 Mark Landler and Thom Shanker, "Gates and Clinton Unite to Defend Libya Intervention, and Say It May Last A while," New York Times, March 27, 2011. http://www.nytimes.com/2011/03/28/world/africa/28policy.html.
101 Elizabeth N. Saunders, "Transformative Choices Leaders and the Origins of Intervention Strategy",International Security, Vol.34, No. 2, 2009, pp. 119-161.

a strong animosity towards the Arab World. Under such circumstances, The US thinks it is necessary to carry out democratic reforms in Islamic World. For example, in 2002, Richard N. Haass, the Director of Policy Planning for the United States Department of State, put forward a document named Towards Greater Democracy in the Muslim World.[102] With such an mentality, the US has successively waged the Afghanistan war and the Iraq war. Vaughn Shannon admitted that the Iraq war waged by the US in 2003 went against the international norms, but the extent to which actions were constrained was also related to leaders' comprehension of the international system. The Bush Administration with Hobbesian views lacked trust on other states, thus tending to take coercive policies. Therefore, Bush Administration insisted on waging Iraq war though opposed internally and externally.[103] From the above, we can get a hint of the motives behind the US's insistence on waging the Iraq war without bowing to international pressure.

IV. The Analysis of the Movies behind the US Military Intervention in the
Post-Cold War Era

In the Post-Cold War era, the US has implemented several military interventions ranging from the First Gulf war in 1990s to the intervention against Libya in 2011. But there are different movies behind each US president's engagement to these.

As for the Gulf war, US military intervention was practiced to balance Russia. With the same goal, NATO member states, the traditional allies of the US, with full support stayed behind the US. What's more, in the Kosovo war, US's enlisting the support of its European allies was also not the issue of humanitarian aid but rather power balancing. In the 21st century, the things have changed, US began to practice hegemonism and employed power balancing strategies lesser than before. Instead, US at this stage put more emphasis on a range of domestic affairs. With tension and contradictions between the US and the Islamic world becoming more acute, the US began military operations targeting Afghanistan, and was supported by nearly all countries on the just basis of fighting against terrorism which conformed to international norms. Also with the pressure of domestic concerns,

---

102 Richard N. Haass, "Towards Greater Democracy in the Muslim World," US. Department of State, Remarks to the Council on Foreign Relations, Washington, D.C., December 4, 2002.
103 Vaughn Shannon, "Leadership Style and International Norm Violation: The Case of the Iraq War," Foreign Policy Analysis, Vol.3, No.1, 2007, pp. 79-104.

the US has started its military intervention in Iraq, which on the contrary, failed to gain legal support and was opposed by France, China and Russia. The US intervention in Libya during 2011 was an act under the influence of its European allies, and the US did not dispatch ground forces to Libya.

From the above analysis, we can see that, with the change of its international status, in different eras, the US undertakes different positions as to military intervention. When the US, has targeted the states that were vulnerable to intervention, domestic politics has been the key cause, and the legitimacy of international norms was easily ignored. The US has also carried out the interventions when it deemed necessary, even if it cannot provide any legal support, , such as the intervention against Iraq performed by Bush Administration. But, undeniably, if legally justified by international norms, the US will have more room to maneuvervre, will more easily practice interventions. And with the decline of the US, it will require that its allies should undertake more important responsibilities. In conclusion, we can comfortably say that numerous factors intertwiningly determine the US military interventions, and it is impossible to explain them from a single perspective. To correctly understand and grasp the phenomenon requires the proper analysis of the US's current international positions in combination with all other factors we have mentioned above.

European Humanitarian Interventions after the Cold War —Theories, Policies and Practices

Zhao Huaipu[1]

Since the end of the Cold War, the foreign policies adopted by the US and Europe have introduced the "humanitarian intervention" and absorbed more contents into related theories, policies and practices of the past. Compared with the Cold War time, the post-Cold War "humanitarian intervention" has actually caused a more profound impact on the future. The author targets Europe as the subject for research, focusing on the theories, policies and practices concerning the humanitarian interventions performed by Europe after the end of the Cold War. Since in most cases European humanitarian intervention is closely related to the Western international intervention or in some cases is part of it, the interaction between Europe and the US on this aspect is inevitably included in the discussion. In another words, the paper attempts to put the discussion on the European foreign intervention in the context of Western international intervention and to explore the features of the theories, policies and practices followed by NATO and EU in their humanitarian intervention after the end of Cold War. The author believes that as a matter of fact, Europe assumes different roles and functions in NATO and EU: EU follows the steps of the US leadership in NATO, while seeking to develop its independent intervention mode . As one of the features of European humanitarian intervention, such a complexity has actually made the research on European humanitarian intervention more intricate. The paper serves for soliciting for valued opinions and hopes to be improved.

---

1 Professor of International Relations Institute, China Foreign Affairs University.

I. A new development of Western humanitarian intervention after the Cold War

The thought behind the humanitarian intervention has originated in Europe and it has a close association with the concept of "Just War" that is initially systematically elaborated by Saint Augustine, a medieval clerical canonist. The Augustinian theory of Just War is based on a series of conditions, among which, the most important are "just cause" and "right intention". Furthermore, St. Thomas Aquinas developed the Augustinian doctrine of "just war" with an additional condition: only the "legitimate authority" can wage a war. What's more, he introduced the "just cause" as "self-defense, restoration of peace, assistance of neighbors against armed attack and defense of the poor and oppressed. Therefore, a sign of humanitarian intervention can be seen here.[2] Spanish jurists Vitoria and Suárez made a further step to elaborate the principles of "just war" by adding three points: 1) the sin brought by war, especially in terms of the human casualties which should be counterbalanced with the injustice that the war attempts to prevent or redress; 2) all non-violent options must be exhausted before the use of force; 3) a war can only be just if it is fought with a reasonable chance of success.[3]

According to Suárez, the declaration of "just war" can be justified on the basis of protecting innocent civilians. Their viewpoints contained the thought of humanitarian intervention as it was called afterwards.[4] Later on, the Dutch jurist Grotius further developed a more systematical and comprehensive elaboration on the theory of "just war", and he mentioned in his work "On the Law of War and Peace" that the "just war" in a state would be legally justified if the treatment to the civilians of its own or of another state went against the international law and when other states waged the war to protect its own citizens or those from other states.[5] Grotius and his contemporary naturalist jurists' "just war" theory may be regarded as the earliest theoretical origin of humanitarian intervention, with its influence extended over time. Generally speaking, the "just war theory" entails six principles: 1) just cause; 2) last resort 3) legitimate authority; 4) chance of success; 5) principal of proportionality; 6) principle of difference, which means a

---

2 Peng Qiong. Discussion on the Legitimacy of International Humanitarian Intervention. http://cdzy.chinacourt.org/public/detail.php?id=4005.
3 Wei Zonglei, Qui Guirong, Sun Ru. Theories and Practices of Western Humanitarian Intervention. Beijing. Current Affairs Press. 2003, pp.5.
4 Peng Qiong. Discussion on the Legitimacy of International Humanitarian Intervention http://cdzy.chinacourt.org/public/detail.php?id=4005.
5 J. A. Hammerton, Outline of Great Books, He Ningtran, Beijing, Commercial Press. 1963, p. 114.

differentiation must be made between combatants and non-combatants. The "just war" principle has been absorbed into the International Humanitarian Law that was passed in Geneva in 1949. But it should be pointed out that in the Middle Ages when the state sovereignty was not yet established, the so-called "just war" was a purely moral principle. But for now, the Medieval principle as justification for a state intervention has become clearly incompatible with the current situation in which, the respect of state sovereignty has become the consensus in the international community. However, it is noticeable that the current international relations are full of suppression by exercise of power. Especially when the Cold War between East and West broke out after the World War II, the Western power states have been frequently attempting to distort the world order on the basis of western values (including the value of human rights) abusing the above-mentioned "just war" principle and frequently carrying out foreign interventions under the pretext of "humanitarianism". As a policy, the Western "humanitarian intervention" takes rejecting and challenging the principle of non-interference as its starting point and the communist countries as well as the third world countries as its main target. Taking shape in the Cold War period, the Western humanitarian intervention has gone through a sudden and vicious development after the end of the Cold War, its interventions becoming from rather unitary and limited increasingly diversified and intensified. The period of the World War II and after the Cold War is marked as a critical period in the development of western humanitarian intervention theories and policies.[6] It is followed by the outbreak of all sorts of contradictions that were previously concealed or suppressed under the bipolar US-Soviet pattern, leading to a variety of domestic and complex regional conflicts. Unrestricted by the Soviet Union, the US and some European countries resorted to foreign intervention attempting to expand aggressively their power and influence on the strategic regions of the globe. Due to the invalidation of such pretexts as "containing the communist expansion" or "defend freedom around the world," the US and Europe urgently sought new functional alternatives for their foreign interventions. During the process, the issue of "internationally displaced persons" has come to the frontline, which has become the breakthrough for western countries to achieve their goals. The frequent outbreak of civil conflicts after the end of the Cold War has caused a massive deplacement and immigration of people. Therefore, this new "humanitarian disaster" has aroused an enormous interest of the international community,

---

6 The formation of Western humanitarian intervention policies and their practices after WWII and during the Cold War: Zhao Huaipu. Analysis on the Western Humanitarian Intervention Policies, Europe, 2001/4.

and meanwhile, the international system set after World War II has also met challenges. On the one hand, considering the objective situation, the international community was required to provide aid to those people. On the other hand, the international system confined by the conventional concept of state sovereignty did not include the group of those displaced people as primary concern (the issue of international refugees was the primary concern in the Cold War.) As the population of displaced civilians has rapidly exceeded that of the refugees, a new call for seeking to restrict state sovereignty has emerged internationally. Adding fuel to the fire, US and Europe has attempted to take preemptive interfering actions in order to provide the factual ground for the formation of new theories on humanitarian intervention in the future.

After the end of the Cold War, the first humanitarian military intervention was carried out by the US and EU in 1991, when the end of First Gulf War was nearing. Under the guise of protecting Iraqi citizens, the US, UK and other countries made efforts to promote the issuance of the United Nations Security Council Resolution 688 and made a declaration that the persecution by the Iraqi government of its domestic Kurds and Shiite Muslims, already posed a threat to international peace and security. This was the first time that the UN had elevated the internal affairs of a state to the level of international threat, which was followed by a wide range of recognition for the argument that the domestic disputes including the violation of human rights within the sovereign territory, could also lead to large-scale internal conflicts, or even to the destruction of regional and international peace and security. This point was stated by Javier Pérez de Cuéllar, the UN Secretary General: "We are clearly witnessing what is probably an irresistible shift in public attitudes toward the belief that the defense of the oppressed in the name of morality should prevail over frontiers and legal documents"[7]. The above resolution of the Security Council has virtually given the green light to the US, UK and other European countries to send troops to Northern Iraq. Furthermore, in order to legitimatize their military intervention from the theoretical perspective, the US and EU have been striving for the formation of new norms on international security and human rights. At this point, the UK has performed a crucial role. Though UK for a long time insisted on the illegitimacy of humanitarian intervention without the authorization of the UN Security Council, later UK has changed its stance and attitudes dramatically since the end of the Cold War. In 1986, the Foreign and

---

7   Stephen Stedman, "The New Interventionist," Foreign Affairs, Vol.72, No.1,1992. Roberta Cohen and Francis M.Deng,eds., Masses in Flight:The Global Crisis of Internal Displacement, Brookings Institution, 1998, p.1.

Commonwealth Office of UK pointed in a policy document that the overwhelming majority of contemporary legal opinions oppose the existence of a right of humanitarian intervention for three main reasons: "first, the UN Charter and the corpus of modern international law do not seem specifically to incorporate such a right; secondly, state practice in the past two centuries, and especially since 1945, at best provides only a handful of genuine cases of humanitarian intervention, and, on more assessments, none at all, and, finally, on prudential grounds, that the scope of abusing such a right argues strongly against its creation... In essence, therefore, the case against making humanitarian intervention an exception to the principle of non-intervention is that its doubtful benefits would be heavily outweighed by its costs in terms of respect for international law."[8] But, sarcastically, as the Western world hyped up the international intervention after the Cold War, the UK assumed the role as the vanguard of breaking the non-intervention principle. Following the steps of the US in its intervention activities against Iraq, the UK has become the first that has made attempts to justify its intervention activities on the humanitarian grounds and meanwhile made the guidelines accordingly to determine under what circumstances and how to carry out humanitarian intervention.[9] Douglas Hurd, the British Foreign Secretary stated in 1992 "not every action that a British government takes has to be underwritten by a specific provision in a UN resolution provided we comply with international law... International law recognizes extreme humanitarian need."[10] Later on, the Foreign and Commonwealth Office argued, "we believe that international intervention without the invitation of the country concerned can be justified in cases of extreme humanitarian need."[11] As the first to propose this argument among the five permanent members of the Security Council, UK has exhibited its ambition to depart from the line of non-intervention and doing this has laid foundation for a more thorough and more systematic elaboration on the theories of humanitarian intervention in UK's following steps.

---

8 UK Foreign Office Policy Document No. 148, reprinted in Ian Brownlie and D. W.Bowett, eds., British Yearbook of International Law (1986), Oxford: Oxford University Press, 1988, p. 614.
9 Christine Gray, International Law and the Use of Force, Oxford: Oxford University Press, 2000, p. 27.
10 Ian Brownlie and D. W.Bowett, eds., British Yearbook of International Law (1992), Oxford: Oxford University Press, 1994, pp. 824-825.
11 Ibid.

The US and Europe have sought to impose the arguments held by the UK on the UN and the international community. The United Nations Secretary-General Annan admitted that internal displacement is an "unprecedented challenge for the international community: to find ways to respond to what is essentially an internal crisis."[12] Put it in another way, an effective balance needs to be found between accepting humanitarian assistance and respecting states' sovereignty. In 1992, Annan appointed Francis M. Deng to Special Representative on Internally Displaced Persons who was responsible to explore and investigate to form some kind of conceptual framework in order to reconcile the tension between the jurisdiction of a sovereign state and the internal displacement situations in the states targeted by the intervention of the international community.[13] Later on, Deng came up with the concept of "Sovereignty as Responsibility" and introduced the major principles of it to the UN. These principles identify the fundamental responsibilities of states to provide life-supporting protection and assistance for their citizens, and if they refuse or are unable to do so, the internally displaced people have the right to request and accept foreign offers of aid. States should accept international assistance, and this will not be regarded as an intervention in the domestic affairs of other states.[14] The concept of "Sovereignty as Responsibility" emphasizes that sovereignty has a limitation. Although these principles above are not legally binding, under the impetus of Western states, they have been recognized by the UN as "important tools" and "standards" when referring to the issue of internal displaced persons.

The outbreak of Kosovo war in 1999 has met with the climax of a new round of propaganda on humanitarian intervention by the US and EU. Western states continued their attempts to justify their military intervention by the means of "humanitarian exception". During the process, UK once again played the role of vanguard especially when it came to Tony Blair's vigorous preaches of military intervention. In April 22, 1999 when NATO's wanton bombing against Yugoslavia occurred, Blair raised in his speech in Chicago the "Doctrine of International Community" which was later called Blairism, and it signified the official announcement of the western "humanitarian intervention" theory.[15] Its main content is as follows:

---

12 Kofi Annan, Preface, in Roberta Cohen and Francis M. Deng, eds., Masses in Flight: The Global Crisis of Internal Displacement, Brookings Institution, 1998, p. 19.
13 Roberta Cohen and Francis M. Deng, eds., Masses in Flight: The Global Crisis of Internal Displacement, Brookings Institution, 1998, p. 3.
14 Roberta Cohen and Francis M. Deng, eds., Masses in Flight: The Global Crisis of Internal Displacement,Brookings Institution, 1998, pp. 275-280; Roberta Cohen, "Human Rights Protection for Internally Displaced Persons," Refugee Policy Group, June 1991; Francis M. Deng, Protecting the Dispossessed, Brookings Institution, 1993.
15 Tony Blair, "Doctrine of International Community," speech to the Economic Club of Chicago on April 22,1999.

First, globalization does not only concern world economy. It is also a phenomenon of international politics and security. We live in an "international community" where various nations are mutually dependent and have a common destiny. Secondly, any country's domestic affairs inevitably affect other countries and peoples so that they have certainly the right to intervene. Therefore, the principle of non-intervention in the traditional concept and international law of about sovereignty and national borders has to be revised. Humanitarian disasters, especially when ethnic genocide is concerned, do not belong to the scope of internal affairs any more. When oppression produces massive flows of refugees to neighboring countries then they can properly be described as "threats to international peace and security", which should be restricted and punished by the UN, or by the intervention of Western countries, if the UN is unable to act. Thirdly, the existing international law and international organizations (primarily the UN and the Security Council) have lagged behind the needs of the time. A "new humanitarian international order" must be established to make international intervention legally compatible with the UN Charter and the international order. It is easy to notice that the "Doctrine of International Community" highlights, in essence, the supremacy of human rights over state sovereignty. In order to make a theoretical footnote, the Foreign and Commonwealth Office of UK published the principles of "humanitarian intervention" in 2000. Later, in his defense of "the supremacy of human rights over state sovereignty" in his memoirs, Blair claimed "ethnic cleansing" and "killings" made him "abruptly awaken over foreign policy" and have completely changed his stance on it. Kosovo crisis made up the first test for Blair's liberal interventionism, and he said, "I saw it essentially as a moral issue. And that, in a sense, came to define my view on foreign and military intervention."[16] Ironically, Blair, who has a lawyer background, did not mention anything about the UN resolutions or international law when talking about his adventurous diplomatic actions in the past.

It needs to be pointed out that there is something mysterious that it's not the US but her minor friend UK to be the spokesman of the "human rights supreme to sovereignty" which is used for the purposes of Western powers as an important theory. The reason why the US herself does not make any general statements on the principles of humanitarian intervention is that, on the one hand, it is afraid it will be constrained and thrown into a passive position due to its too apparent hypocrisy, and on the other hand, calling upon revision or even cancellation of the state sovereignty principle will

---

16 Tony Blair, "Military intervention in rogue regimes 'more necessary than ever'", guardian.co.uk, September 1, 2010.

undermine the current international order, which in turn, may instead harm US' and the West's own interests. Given this, the US is glad to see UK to speak for their "special partnership". Being good at developing diplomatic theories and practices, UK is also glad to reach out her hands, hoping to exhibit its power and function. Apart from the UK as vanguard, other European countries such as France also joined in the chorus in support of "humanitarian intervention". France, preaching itself as "the motherland of human rights" and "defender of the ideal of liberty and solidarity", believes compromising on principles is a matter of shame.[17] French president Chirac said that "the humanitarian situation constitutes a ground that can justify an exception to the rule. If needed, then France would not hesitate to join those who would like to intervene in order to assist those that are in danger.[18] As a matter of fact, Blair's argument for the "supremacy of human rights over sovereignty" is just another variation of the views held by French Socialist Party. Michel Rocard, the French Prime Minister at that time and Bernard Kouchner, the Health Minister, attempted to associate the values of Socialist Party with the foreign policy of the party and claimed the right to intervene in other states' internal affairs so as to protect basic rights. And France's involvement in Kosovo war is primarily based on the "right for humanitarian intervention" created by Kouchner. Similar to the military intervention against Iraq, the US and Europe tried to impose their proposals on the international community and sought for the legitimacy of the intervention in Kosovo through the related resolutions in UN. After the end of the war, the Security Council Resolution 1244 (1999) on the issue of Kosovo war was passed to authorize member states to establish and sustain peace and stability in Kosovo, which also included the involvement of NATO in the issue.[19] The US and Europe claimed the resolution has legitimatized NATO's actions, though it did not indeed.[20] Although the Secretary General Annan admitted that to "gain peace, the use of force might be legitimate in some circumstances"[21], he meanwhile reinforced that the Security Council has the primary responsibility for maintaining international peace and security so that only the Security Council has to be authorized to take non-defensive military actions. [22] But, it is undeniable that the US and

---

17 Edouard Balladur, "Une attitude exemplaire dans l'avenir," Le Monde, April 7, 1995.
18 Catherine Guicherd, "International Law and the War in Kosovo," Survival, Vol.41, No.2, 1999, pp.19-34.
19 Security Council Resolution 1244 (1999) on the situation relating to Kosovo.
20 Christine Gray, Christine, International Law and the Use of Force, Oxford: Oxford University Press, 2000.
21 Ivo Daalder and Michael O. Hanlon, Winning Ugly: NATO's War to Save Kosovo, Brookings, 2000, p.127.
22 Press Release SG/SM/6938, March 24, 1999.

Europe's unilateral actions in Kosovo have been a catalyst for the formation of new international norms on humanitarian intervention. The Kosovo Crisis has aroused wide attention on the discussion of the legitimacy of humanitarian intervention. Some organizations have published reports or announced their assertions hoping to both theoretically and practically explore the path that the humanitarian intervention would follow.

In December 2001, Gareth Evans, the president of International Crisis Group and Mohamed Sahnoun, United Nations' Special Representative for Africa in the International Commission on Intervention and State Sovereignty (ICISS) issued a report named "The Responsibility to Protect".[23] On the basis of "Sovereignty as Responsibility", the responsibility has three essential and integral components: the responsibility to prevent violence against citizens, which emphasizes the use of peaceful means (development and foreign diplomacy) to address the root cause of the conflicts; the responsibility to react to large-scale violation, which attempts to prevent violation by diplomacy, sanction or military intervention in extreme situations; the responsibility to rebuild, which means the commitment to rebuilding states after the end of conflicts, especially after the end of international intervention. Concerning the question whether unauthorized military intervention is legitimate, the report points out that the authorization from the Security Council is the golden standard for the assessment, and in any circumstances, attempts should be made to gain the authorization. If failing to be authorized, states can take into consideration the alternative solution that is seeking to gain the sanction of the UN urgent meeting, and if it still does not work, actions can be taken under the jurisdiction of related international organizations listed in UN Charter before gaining the approval of the Security Council. In 2002, Gareth Evans and Mohamed Sahnoun further put forward an idea that the any military intervention in the name of "Responsibility to Protect" has to conform to six principles: just causes, precisely defined intervention objective, use of forces as the last resort, authorization from the Security Council of UN, appropriate intervention means and reasonable chance of success. Secondly, "Responsibility to Protect" allows for the violation of state sovereignty, though also stressing the importance of state sovereignty. International community is able to impose coercive measures, when local authorities fail to fulfill the responsibilities to protect their citizens from large-scale violation of human rights and from the harms resulting from crime against humanity, ethnic cleansing and genocide, or when the authority in itself is the perpetrator. Therefore, it is

---

23 International Commission on Intervention and State Sovereignty, The Responsibility to Protect, September 2001, http://responsibilitytoprotect.org/ICISS%20Report.pdf.

permitted to resort to minimum level of armed forces when peaceful means do not work effectively.

The concept of "Responsibility to Protect" has won acclaim in western countries, and shortly after it was put on the agenda of the UN. What's more, in December of 2004, "Responsibility to Protect" (R2P) was also adopted by High-level Panel on Threats, Challenges and Change that states that it is "exercisable by the Security Council authorizing military intervention as a last resort, in the event of genocide and other large-scale killing, ethnic cleansing or serious violations of international humanitarian law.[24] Later on, the panel has further come up with the principles that the Security Council should stick to.[25] However, the "Responsibility to Protect" is not applicable when the Security Council is unable to take actions. In May 2005, Annan called for a new security consensus in his report "Larger Freedom".[26] He suggests that the Security Council should adopt a resolution and provide primary principles as the guideline to decide in what circumstance and by what means the use of force is allowed to protect citizens.[27] But, Annan still fails to address the issue what if Security Council is unable to take actions. On September 2005, United Nations World Summit incorporated the "Responsibility to Protect" into the World Summit Outcome Document 2005 and admitted that the principles concerned have provided "an international framework of vital importance to protect the internally displaced people".[28] It is reinforced that every state is responsible to protect its people from ethnic cleansing, war crimes, genocide and from the crimes against humanity. If a state is unwilling or unable to shoulder this responsibility, the responsibility will be shifted to the international community and the international community will be prepared to take collective actions.[29] The UN's acknowledgment on the declaration in April 2006 has manifested the consensus international community has reached on the "Responsibility to

---

24 High-Level Panel on Threats, Challenges and Change, A More Secure World: Our Shared Responsibility, NewYork: United Nations, 2004, p. 66.
25 High-Level Panel on Threats, Challenges and Change, A More Secure World: Our Shared Responsibility, para. 207, (a) Seriousness of threat, (b) Proper purpose, (c) Last Resort, (d) Proportional means, (e) Balance of Consequences.
26 In: Larger Freedom: Towards Development, Security and Human Rights For All. General Assembly A/59/2005.
27 In: Larger Freedom: Towards Development, Security and Human Rights For All, para. 126.
28 United Nations, 2005 World Summit Outcome, para. 132, Resolution A/RES/60/1, September 15, 2005; Walter Kalin, "The future of the Guiding Principles on Internal Displacement," Forced Migration Review, special issue, December 2006.
29 United Nations, 2005 World Summit Outcome, para.139; Report of the International Commission on Intervention and State Sovereignty, The Responsibility to Protect, International Development Research Centre, Ottawa, December 2001.

Protect", which tends to be absorbed as part of international norms. For the US and Europe, the "Responsibility to Protect" has offered new theoretical grounds for their implementation of humanitarian interventions.

It should be noticed that with the increase of internal conflicts after the Cold War and with the appearance of new humanitarian crises such as internally displaced people standing out, the stronger awareness of the protection of human rights and the change of attitudes towards the concept of human rights has a certain historical rationality. And because of these, how to deal with the relations between human rights protection and state sovereignty has become a big challenge the international community has to face. However, the issue is complex since the US and Europe made use of the objective situations mentioned above, took preemptive actions on the humanitarian grounds, and then sought to force their actions upon the UN and the international community. By doing this, they hoped to establish new norms on international security and human rights, and the newly established norms will justify their following foreign interventions from the legal perspective. Although the proposal of the "Responsibility to Protect" had also a certain historical basis, it was practically utilized by western countries as a theoretical excuse for their interventions. The humanitarian intervention on the ground of "supremacy of human rights over sovereignty" and the "responsibility to protect" is merely a myth created by the US and Europe to safeguard the current western-led international order in the context of the new international political configuration formed after the end of the Cold War. Taking advantage of these concepts as the preparation for the thoughts in theory and law, the US has opened up and widened the path to western intervention. And acting as the spokesman of related theories, Europe also played an important role in shaping the new humanitarian intervention theories.

II. Policies and practices of European humanitarian intervention

In current international system, European countries are not only a component part of the western coalition but also an independent political power. As for humanitarian intervention, European interventions constitute a part of the western intervention and meanwhile retain its own features. Therefore, their functions and characteristics have duality: Atlantic-oriented, on the one hand as an ally of the US within the framework of NATO; on the other hand, Euro-oriented, seeking to realize its independent intervention within the framework of EU.

A. The European humanitarian intervention within the framework of NATO

The European humanitarian intervention within NATO framework entails two phases: first in the 1990s when EU's involvement in major intervention activities have focused on the Balkan region. At the end of August 1995, under the promotion of the US, NATO performed the intervention against Bosnia-Herzegovina, which also involved the participation of European countries such as the UK and France, among which France exhibited an aggressive ambition to maintain its major power status. Under the proposal of France, the Security Council of the UN has passed a resolution which authorized the establishment of safe areas in Bosnia-Herzegovina. What's more, in 1994, France prompted NATO to issue an ultimatum for air strikes in Bosnia-Herzegovina. According to French officials, France was the biggest contributor to the international intervention and peacekeeping operations in the former Yugoslavia.[30] After the end of the Cold War, the relations between France and the US reached its peak due to their cooperation in the intervention against Bosnia-Herzegovina. It is also noticeable that Germany's involvement in the NATO's military actions in Bosnia-Herzegovina is virtually its first attempt to send military troops abroad after the WWII, and this can be explained from two aspects: First, by doing this, Germany endeavored to change its public attitude towards the use of force and hoped and aimed to set it as a legal precedent, thus making legal basis for its future military intervention. Second, Germany aimed to prevent the refugees in Bosnia-Herzegovina and Balkan from flowing massively into Germany (Germany was the preferred destination of refugees at that time). 1999 Kosovo War was the first situation after the Cold War where US and Europe have employed unilateral use of force against a sovereign country without obtaining an explicit authorization of the United Nations, not only directly violating the principle of national sovereignty, sovereign rights but also setting "precedents" limiting the rights of sovereignty of non-democratic regimes "including the inherent right to seek whatever weapons a regime may choose." [31] Many European countries in the name of "humanitarianism" have actively involved themselves in the wars that were mainly plotted and led by the US. France and Italy declared in the

---

30 Ministry of Foreign Affairs Press Service, Speeches and Statements, No. 57 (April 29, 1993), No. 1 (January 12, 1994), No. 25 (February 10, 1994), No. 72 (April 12, 1994), No. 85 (May 4, 1995).
31 Walden Bello, Foreign Policy, "The Crisis of Humanitarian Intervention," Foreign Policy in Focus, August 9, 2011, http://www.fpif.org/articles/the_crisis_of_humanitarian_intervention.

joint declaration issued in October 6, 1998: "our shared position of principle... is that, before any military intervention... the Security Council of the United Nations must issue a resolution authorizing that intervention... But we must keep a close eye on the humanitarian aspect of the situation... which can demand very rapid... implementation of measures to deal with an emergency."[32] The Prime Minister Tony Blair insisted on the moral legitimacy of Kosovo war and the leadership of the US which, in his words, "has once again shown that it has the vision to see that instability, chaos and racial genocide in the heart of Europe will never affect Europe."[33]

Generally speaking, the European humanitarian intervention policies and practices during this period has featured an active engagement of European countries in NATO intervention in the Balkan region, although most of the interventions mainly served the interests of the US. The expansion of NATO is another long term consequence, which would lead to a new established situation in which the "security vacuum after the Cold War" in Eastern Europe and the Balkans will be filled by the leading position of US in Europe. But, since Europe alone was incapable of implementing effective intervention, it had to rely on the US to safeguard peace and stability in Europe. Undeniably, other states such as France, German and the UK also attempt to pursue their own interests by the means of intervention, and for whatever reasons, it is certain that the foreign intervention of European governments was interest-driven. Actually, some European left-wing (social democrat or green-green) parties have upheld the use of force for so-called humanitarian interests instead of emphasizing strategic aims. In Europe, the most fervent supporters of military intervention mostly came from these above left-wing parties who advocate the protection of human rights. Even in Germany, where pacifism was quite strong, the public support for humanitarian intervention became gradually prevalent, but this had something to do with left-wing's change of attitude. The majority of members from Social Democrat Party and Green Party tended to support the use of force for humanitarian aims. In 2003 the German government led by the German Social Democrat Party opposed the US led Iraq War, because it thought that the war was not grounded on humanitarian aims. During the Kosovo war, Joseph Martin Fischer, the leader of the Green Party and also the Foreign Minister of Germany was an active supporter of the NATO bombings of

---

32 Quoted in Richard McAllister, "French Perceptions," in: Mary Buckley and Sally Cummings, eds., Kosovo: Perceptions of War and Its Aftermath, New York: Continuum, 2001, p.94.
33 Warren Hoge, "Crisis in the Balkans: Britain; Blair under Domestic Pressure on Ground Forces," New York Times, May 18, 1999, p. A10.

Yugoslavia and he believed that air strikes must be carried out even without the authorization of the UN since the situation in Kosovo was quite unusual.

The first decade of 2000s is the second phase where NATO led the two significant interventions – the Afghanistan War and Iraq War, both of them being included in the US war on terror. After the 9/11 incident in 2001, the Bush administration has put the fight against terrorism on its agenda and has performed larger scale of foreign interventions together with NATO. In October the same year, The US initiated the Afghanistan War and toppled the Taliban regime, shortly after which, the US persuaded NATO to assume the military operation in Afghanistan. NATO's military operations in Afghanistan have substantially contributed to changes in NATO strategies after the Cold War, breaking the limits of territorial defense imposed by the member states and undertaking the "out of area" missions outside the territories of member states. NATO, to a great extent, acted in the interests of the US that aimed to strengthen its control on regions of strategic importance and thereby justify the existence of NATO after the Cold War. Although recognizing the fight against terrorism, European countries still retained a reserved attitude towards US strategies like "global NATO" and "preemptive strike". What's more, though based on the humanitarianism pretext, in the first phase France, UK, Germany and other countries did not send troops to Afghanistan. As a matter of fact, NATO's actions have plunged Afghanistan into continuous turmoil instead of bringing peace and security. After taking office, Obama announced his new strategy for Afghanistan, and asked European countries to increase their troops in order to alleviate NATO's increasing troubles in Afghanistan. Under the domestic public pressure, European countries tended to act with more cautiousness and reservation. Netherlands withdrew its troops in August 2011; France only provided troop reinforcement; and even the UK, the closest partner of the US, was encountered the same domestic public pressure. It was heatedly argued in the British public that the UK should not follow the US blindly in their cooperation but instead keep the independence of its policies. Although it was the domestic public opposition and other domestic reasons behind the cautious stance maintained by European countries, as a whole, it is caused by their reserved attitudes towards the implementation of the "out of area" (especially military interventions to be performed far away from European territory) missions. The unilateralism in Bush's diplomatic policies combined with his preemptive strategy has further intensified Europe's dissatisfaction and antipathy over the US policies. In 2003, the divergence between the US and Europe came to the surface and became acute related to the Iraq issue. Initially, US bypassed the UN and waged the Iraq war by pointing the finger at Iraq's possession of weapons of mass destruction. And after discovering the weapons, the US justified its actions on the humanitarian grounds. US's unilateralist intervention has triggered a strong dissatisfaction among some "old" Western European countries such as France and Germany which publicly announced their critical opinions – there occurred a pro-Iraq camp and the against-Iraq one. All in all, due to the apparent divergences on diplomatic strategies and "out of area" missions after the 9/11 Event, NATO's "out of area" intervention had to be gradually implemented through "voluntary alliance".

To summarize, the European humanitarian intervention within the framework of NATO has become an important component of Western international intervention. Its policies and practices have also gone through changes since the end of the Cold War. In 1990s, when dealing with the frequently-occurred regional conflicts in Balkan region, Europe had to rely on the US and NATO to sustain the peace and security in Europe since it lacked effective military intervention capacity, and because of this, Europe lost its independence in its foreign intervention during this period. After the 9/11 Event, US's unilateralism and unipolar hegemony have influenced its cooperation with other countries on foreign interventions. US has incorporated foreign intervention in its global strategies to fight terrorism and pushed further "out of area" intervention policy of NATO as witnessed in Afghanistan and Iraq. Owing to the doubts, most European countries display opposition against the "out of area" missions and their dissatisfaction towards the US's unilateralism, most European countries have remained reserved towards US military intervention and even boycotted it. Recently under the impact of global financial crisis and European debt crisis, the European community has become less enthusiastic to take part in global security issues. What's more, participating in Iraq War and Afghanistan War has also undermined Europe's desire for liberal interventionism.[34] However, this does not mean that Europe will also adopt neutral policies towards the crises in its own territory and periphery when its vital interests are endangered. The intervention practices Europe has adopted since the end of Cold War were mainly exercised in Europe and its surrounding regions, especially the African regions which previously were part of the European colonies. And in terms of the intensity and frequency of intervention, southeastern Europe (Balkan region) comes first followed by African regions, Middle East and other regions as targets.

---

34 "A Score card for European Foreign Policy," http://www.brookings.edu/reports/2011/0330_european_scorecard_vaisse.aspx.

B. Intervention policies adopted by EU and its characteristics

During the Cold War, European Economic Community acted as an economic entity and was regarded as a civilian force in the international system. During the period, European Economic Community very rarely engaged in any "high-level political issues" related to diplomacy and security. Since the end of Cold War, EU has committed itself to the establishment of the EU defense integration, and strives for a transformation from a "civilian actor" to a heavy-weight all-round international actor. What's more, through certain policies and actions, EU has also vigorously promoted its common security and common defense, building up an independent military force through reforming its policy mechanisms. In the field of foreign intervention, EU seeks to develop humanitarian intervention within the framework of ESDP (European Security and Defense Policy), in order to deal with conflicts and aims to establish a crisis management mode in an "European way".

EU seeks to develop intervention policies and practices as the component part of its Common Diplomacy and Security Policy. (CSDP)

- The Common Security and Defense Policy (CSDP) is the security and defense policy for the EU. It forms an integral part of the EU's foreign policy, the Common Foreign and Security Policy (CFSP). Created when the Treaty of Lisbon was signed in 2009, the CSDP replaces and enlarges the former European Security and Defense Policy (ESDP).

Moreover, the policies and practices are also employed by EU to implement its international strategies. EU has expressed its basic stance on humanitarian intervention, and has stated that a plan basket to deal with the political, civilian and economic reconstruction issues in the targeted states has to be considered when any military intervention is implemented to end violence. Both the US and NATO underscore the use of military forces for intervention, while EU puts more emphasis on comprehensive intervention measures and especially highlights the function of civilian intervention. In December 2003, Javier Solana the European Union's high Representative for the Common Foreign and Security Policy, has issued a report named A Secure Europe in a Better World: European Security Strategy.[35] The report was officially passed in the EU summit in Brussels in December 12, 2003, highlighting the importance of the establishment of a more powerful and more effective European security and defense policy that will enable EU to

---

35 Javier Solana, A secure Europe in a better world: European security strategy, Institute for Security Studies, Paris, France, 2003.

manage humanitarian crises, prevent internal conflicts, strengthen the regional security and build up sustainable partnership among member states. As what has been pointed by some scholars, Europe should be able to act in the following areas. 1. Humanitarian operations, including humanitarian aid, disaster relief and rescue tasks; 2. Crisis prevention operations that include preventive diplomacy, economic initiatives or military support; 3. Peacekeeping or peacemaking operations. 4. Peace enforcement.[36] After the end of Cold War, in order to accommodate the requirements for handling the complex conflicts and crises, EU was required to take into consideration the importance of the closeness between civilian issues and military issues and meanwhile to integrate military intervention with civilian intervention.

Independent military forces act as the carrier for international intervention. EU's has exhibited a strong overall military power, its military spending constituting up to 20% of the total in the world. Back to 1987, German and France jointly set up a mixed troop of 5,000. After the establishment of EU, five states including France and German replenished the "Eurocorps" that ended up with 60,000. In November 2004, the member states of EU jointly issued the Declaration on European Military Capabilities. In March 2005, EU announced its decision on the establishment of 13 quick response battle troops before 2007, and in January 2007, the troops were successfully set up, signifying another significant breakthrough EU has made in its military actions. And this will guarantee EU's ability to sustain its common security and defense policies. At the beginning of 21st century, although EU had carried out some independent interventions in Europe, Middle East, Africa and other regions, its power of intervention was decentralized and constrained by factors such as the divergences among member states. For example, all EU members kept silent in the face of the Darfur issue, and France, which had always played an active role in the intervention activities in Africa, even excluded the possibility of sending troops. In terms of EU diplomacy and security policy, a significant reform has been pushed through by establishing the Treaty of Lisbon that has came into effect since 2009, and the adjustments on the common security and defense policy were also made accordingly. However, these reforms failed to bring substantial changes to the policies on common security and common defense that were still parts of the intergovernmental mechanism. Undoubtedly, European External Action Service was of significant importance, but the measures still needed to be adjusted to further improve and impose the mechanism.

---

36 Katia Vlachos-Dengler, "Getting there: building strategic mobility into ESDP, " ISS Occasional Paper, No.38, 2002.

What's more, in recent years, the ongoing and spreading euro-zone crisis had a detrimental effect on EU's capability of defense, and because of this, except the UK and France that still have strong intention for intervention activities, EU, as an international security actor, is meeting challenges in general.

Having underscored the construction of civilian capability for a long time, EU put more emphasis on developing its intervention ability to deal with civilian crisis after the end Cold War.[37] The management of civilian crisis covered a wide range of areas such as police management, humanitarian assistance, and reconstruction of civilian and judicial systems, supervision of elections, human rights activities and so and so forth. The major tasks of civilian crisis management were to handle the issues of public order, legal system and civilian protection. EU sought to develop its civilian intervention ability within the framework of security and defense policies, hoping more tasks and missions can be fed into these policies. In July 2004, EU issued a report named "The military Headline Goal with a 2010 horizon and an Action Plan for Civilian Aspect of ESDP".[38] The first goal is to develop the ability consistent with what has been mentioned in the European security strategic report in 2003. At the end of 2004, EU issued the Civilian Headline Goal with a 2008 horizon.[39] Although it is still hard to give proper assessment in its implementation of these goals and plans, it is noticeable that EU will put more emphasis on the ability of civilian intervention, and EU has made relentless efforts for it.

What's more, EU also attached great importance to the employment of managerial resources for managing all sorts of civilian crisis, especially under the help of humanitarian NGOs. In the field of security, EU has provided foreign aids by funding NGOs since 1970s. From 1980s to 1990s, EU increased its foreign aids up to 1 billion dollars in 1995 through NGOs which account for 15%-20% of EU's total foreign aids.[40]

According to some studies, EU crisis prevention policy went through drastic changes in 1995, which was the result of the sustained dialogues between EU committee and NGOs to cope with issues in some critical

---

37 Text of the Action Plan in: EU security and defence-Core documents 2004, Chaillot Paper, No.75, Paris, EUISS 2005, pp. 121-128.
38 Council of the European Union, 2004b.Civilian headline goal 2008 (15863/04), December 7. Available from: http://register.consilium.eu.int/pdf/en/04/st15/st15863.en04.pdf.
39 Daniela Irrera, "Civil society and NGOs roles in ESDP operations," http://www.uaces.org/events/conferences/bruges/researchpapers/abstract.php?recordID=258.
40 Ian Manners, "Normative Power Europe Reconsidered," Paper presented to the CIDEL Workshop, Oslo, 22-23 October 2004.

regions, especially in Africa where the reconstruction after the end of the conflicts between southeastern Europe and Bosnia-Herzegovina and where the policies for development were urgent.[41] Playing an active role in the conflicted areas, humanitarian NGOs have worked in all phases from the burst of conflicts to the process of reconstruction. Due to their valuable experience, professional expertise and early warning capability to meet the requirements of the diversified missions of ESDP, EU embraced NGOs to the framework of its common diplomacy, CFSP and ESDP, and hoped to enhance the credibility of ESDP, thus more effectively performing humanitarian intervention. After the mid of 1990s, EU has made new attempts in its cooperation with NGOs. NGOs have been invited to take part in meetings or forums on a regular basis and were granted the right to negotiate on some humanitarian issues for which, NGOs are capable of providing related functional resources. At present, the dialogue and cooperation on a strategic level between both sides have come in shape and have achieved accomplishments to some extent. With NGOs more frequently engaging in the EU foreign intervention activities, their cooperation has become a characteristic of EU humanitarian intervention policies and practices. However, some problems still exist in their cooperation such as the lack of formal structural coordination and the dissatisfaction of NGOs for their lack of presence in ESDP. All of these have demonstrated EU's unwillingness to provide civil actors with more room to work with and most of their co-operations are based on tentative needs. In all, in the fields of security and humanitarian intervention, the cooperation between EU and NGOs is constrained due to the lack of institutionalization, though there is still great potential for both to cooperate.

It is undeniable that EU humanitarian intervention policies are still immature and imperfect. Compared with the model of western intervention within the framework of NATO, EU humanitarian intervention still exhibits some European features, among which, the most conspicuous are EU's emphasis on multilateral intervention and on the justification of its interventions from legal perspective. From 2003 to 2007, EU carried out nearly 20 interventions in Europe, Middle East, Africa, Asia and other regions, and most of its interventions were justified on the legal ground, for example, the resolutions of UN Security Council and the invitation from conflict parties.

---

41 The importance attached to this not only lies in the fact that EU has conventionally positioned itself as the civilian actor, but also in some kind of connection between EU and NATO, both seeming to cooperatively engage in the labor division in the field of international intervention with NATO performing military interventions of high intensity and EU undertaking the less intensified civilian interventions.

In another words, EU intervention activities are generally implemented within the framework of international law, conform to the principles of the UN, and are based on the consent of countries concerned. However, it needs to be pointed out that the quotation of resolutions from the UN Security Council on a legal basis does not mean that EU thinks that interventions should be operated within the limits of the UN system nor indicates EU's willingness to act under the UN's leadership. It comes to the conclusion that the pursuit of multiple interests is the primary impetus for EU to perform foreign intervention.

Since the security interest is the most important, EU hopes to stabilize Europe and its surrounding areas through interventions and meanwhile, to legitimatize its development of discretionary security and defense system. By promoting and strengthening its own military capability, EU strives for a leadership for the security in Europe and even around the world. Economic interests and political interests are also important, the former serving for the substantial interests. The interventions within Europe play an important role during the process of promoting the integration of Europe. In Africa, Middle East and other regions, interventions are used to disseminate the value systems of EU and are used to expand EU's impact on world politics, which has been demonstrated fully in EU's intervention against Libya.

III. Intervention by EU in Libya and its impact

After the end of Cold War, Libya war was a new attempt in the western humanitarian intervention practices. Although it was waged in the name of NATO, EU played an important role during the process. In March 2011, through British's efforts, the 1973 Resolution, which was allowed for imposing no-fly zones in Libya, was passed by the Security Council in a claim to protect Libyan citizens. Afterwards, in the name of the Resolution, France and UK initiated air strikes against Libya. After taking over the leadership for military intervention, NATO even continued the bombing against Libya until the opposition in Libya overturned the Gaddafi regime. The Western intervention against Libya has embarked a brand-new model of intervention, during which, western countries grasped opportunities when a sovereign state stuck in domestic turmoil. Using UN resolution and their support for the opposition as moral pretext, Western countries claimed to protect the citizens, pressed ahead with air strikes and eventually realized their goal to overthrow a government.

Compared with the previous western interventions, the intervention in Libya waged by Europe contains new contents. First, it is ostensibly regarded as a foreign intervention on the ground of "responsibility to protect", though European states take different means and perform intervention to different extents. In this aspect, France and UK demonstrated high-profile stances. British Foreign Secretary William Hague reiterated that "responsibility to protect" should be fulfilled to stop the humanitarian disasters from occurring. However, claiming this is not equal to a noble act in that the real intention of UK is to exhibit its capability for leadership to the outside world. When other European states hesitated to take actions due to domestic constraints, UK took coercive diplomatic and military activities. Similarly, with impure motives, France attempted to reshape its image as friend of Arabic people through interventions and to safeguard its reputation as the tough defender for human rights. Just as the intervention performed in Balkan region, European intervention against Libya is out of its own interests. As Europe's backyard, Northern Africa is not only geographically related to Europe, but also colonially tied with Europe. North Africa has brought Europe with huge energy interests in that the oil exploration in Libya is at relatively low cost and also of good quality. Most of the oil export goes to Europe and the statistics has shown that about 7% of EU energy import comes from Libya: of Italy 22%, of France 16% and of Spanish 13%. Therefore, energy security has been prioritized on the European states' diplomatic agenda. And the issue of immigration is another topic concerning European interests. Regarding the illegitimate immigration as a threat to European security, Europeanity and European welfare, EU has made attempts to establish the system to control the immigrants from North Africa. In all, Europe seems to fulfill its "responsibility to protect", but it virtually does this in order to promote its major interests in North Africa.

Secondly, Libya war has exerted a significant impact on the EU humanitarian intervention policies and practices, and it is the first crisis EU encountered in the after Lisbon. It is well known that The Lisbon Treaty has introduced some critical reform measures which should have better prepared EU for the challenges in diplomacy and security, while, in effect, have brought about divergent opinions among member states thus restraining EU's ability to act. But the divergences should not be exaggerated since, after all, the intervention against Libya was different from any interventions in the past. It is obvious to notice that the Libya crisis has become a driving force for member states of EU to change their manner of handling internal conflicts. Different from the Iraq issue in 2003, the leaders of UK and France went directly to Brussels and sought help from European Council instead of gaining support from the UN Security Council. The divergences between member states did not lead EU to a dilemma. UK and France's active engagement in the intervention has prevented EU to govern by non-interference in EU and has eventually assisted the opposition in overthrowing the Gaddafi regime. In dealing with the relations between Europe and US, the European leaders have got rid of the past timidity in their treatment on diplomatic and security issues. They have independently taken initiatives to carry out interventions instead of depending on the leadership of the US. In general, in the eyes of Europeans, EU has learned lessons from Iraq war and become experienced in dealing with the Libya crisis. Additionally, the intervention against Libya has further strengthened the European humanitarian intervention policies and practices which have been narrowed down to focus on the independent interventions in the surrounding areas instead of serving for the "out of area" missions within the framework of NATO. Just as Catherine Ashton, High Representative of the Union for Foreign Affairs and Security, noted, since Libya and North Africa are neighboring states of Europe, EU needs to fulfill certain functions and shoulder more responsibilities in its surrounding areas, and these functions are different from those of the US. She also mentioned that there are some changes in the relations between US and EU: currently, EU is rather in a partnership with the US than being tightly controlled by the US.[42] Compared with other major interventions Europe participated in after the Cold War, the intervention against Libya has demonstrated European features.

Furthermore, the intervention against Libya caused and contributed to adjustments in EU's security policies towards neighborhood states. Reflecting on the turmoil in North Africa, EU has become aware of the necessity of reframing its neighborhood policies, especially those towards its Mediterranean neighbors which include new diplomatic thoughts and more comprehensive strategies. EU has become aware that in its current policies towards North Africa, there lacked a well-defined policy of democracy and human rights criteria ,absence of which caused an inefficiency in coordinating economic and financial aids with the targets of EU policies, especially those related with democratization. EU aims to promote democratization reforms in North Africa and hopes to sustain the good momentum on the premise of its own interests. From this perspective, EU decided to reframe its neighborhood policies, which in the new sense, emphasized the ability to

---

42 The Brookings Institution, "The European Union Response to the Arab Spring," A Statesman's Forum with Catherine Ashton, High Representative of the European Union for Foreign Affairs and Security Policy, Washington, D.C., July 12, 2011, http://www.brookings.edu/events/2011/0712_ashton_arab_spring.aspx.

serve political functions as well as to handle economic issues, development of the livelihood of the people and immigration agreements. The EU good-neighborhood policy focuses on the political reform which stresses the political involvement of EU in the affairs of North Africa. What's more, with the policy of supporting democratization and progress of human rights, EU hopes to strengthen the political bonds with these states, their people and the whole region and states Catherine Ashton has claimed: The path to genuine democracy, reform and social justice is not easy, but the EU stands ready to help the Arab world, EU aims to promote "deep democracy" to take deep roots in North Africa. That is to better the current political system to one which includes, respect for the rule of law, freedom of speech and other civil rights, an independent judicial system, and which respects fundamental human rights.

As a future prospect, EU, as usual, aims to attach its economic aid and investments to gradual and progressive reform achievements whic are promised by the recipient countries of the region. What's more, to promote the political reforms in the region, EU also plans to encourage the local NGOs and other civilian social organizations, promotes the social groups like the youth and women to participate in political life.

EU believes that it has accumulated sufficient experiences of democratization reforms from its previous efforts in the Middle and East Europe, and it advocates applying this experience to the democratization reforms in North Africa. Apart from the promotion of "deeper democracy", EU has also worked out a plan to enhance its economic support targeting this region. Ashton in her strategy paper used "3Ms – market access, money and mobility" to describe the policies she suggested for EU in order to support the momentous changes in its Southern Neighbourhood (North Africa) contributions EU has made for the economic development in North Africa[43].

Market access means that EU will open its market to its neighboring states in the South through coherent efforts and in the mode that goes in line with the national needs and the market preparation. And it is also expected in the region that trade will promote the national economic growth. Financial aid refers to resources required in the short and middle term and are used when more challenges and more unstable risks are presented during the process of reform. EU will also introduce additional resources by various means such as attracting other investors to invest in the construction of North Africa. Mobility means that EU will open its door to welcome more young people and businessmen from North Africa and Middle East to

---

43 The Brookings Institution. "The European Union Response to the Arab Spring".

enjoy the education opportunities and also business opportunities provided by EU. Ashton realized that to fully fulfill the political and economic goals above was painstaking, but she firmly believed only by this, Europe's interests could be guaranteed.[44] She also mentioned that the assessment of EU should be based on the judgments on its ability to act in its surrounding areas.

All In all, the political changes in North Africa have delivered challenges to EU's interests and policies. To deal with this, EU attempted to exert influence through active intervention in the political reforms in this region and through the adjusted policies to enhance its political involvement in the process so as to transform its strategic passivity into initiative and promote the construction of genuine "deep democracy" in this region. At the beginning of Libya crisis, it was claimed that failing to serve certain functions at critical time might lead to the loss of the political capital EU has in North Africa. However, opportunities also came along with crisis. EU endeavors to reshape its policies on North Africa and strengthens its involvement in the region in order to restore the reputation that has been partially tarnished due to

EU's long-term friendship with totalitarian regimes in the region. By further promoting the deep democracy and the European style of democratization, EU hopes to defend and advance its interests in the fields of regional security, economics and politics. Ashton argued that EU would commit itself to functioning in North Africa for long term. If the neighboring states could sustain security, democracy and economic growth, it would be favorable to Europe. It can be seen from this, focusing on the comprehensive management and the export of system is another feature of EU's humanitarian intervention, and this is different from the interventions taken by US and NATO both of which have the preferences on power expansion through intervention.

The last point needs to be pointed out is that Libyan war has also demonstrated some changes in the relations between Europe and US besides some differences in respect to the mode of the Western military intervention.

After the Cold War, the western international intervention has been led by the US with Europe at a subordinate position, but vise verse in terms of the intervention against Libya. Although the intervention is carried out in the name of NATO, EU is allowed by US to play a major role in the process. The reasons can be analyzed from three aspects. First, the strength of the US has begun to decline. Foreign Affairs has published an article named "The Wisdom of Retrenchment—America Must Cut Back to Move

---

44　Ibid.

Forward" co-authored by Joseph M. Parent and Paul K. MacDonald.[45] In the post- Cold War era, US foreign policies have undergone a profound transformation. Unrestrained by superpower competition, the US' ambitions spilled over their former limits. The US has increased its military spending far faster than any of its rivals, expanded NATO, and started carrying out humanitarian aid missions around the world. These trends have even accelerated after 9/11. The United States went to war in Afghanistan and Iraq, ramped up its counter-terrorism operations around the world, sped up its missile defense program, and set up new bases in distant lands. From the historical perspective, a policy of retrenchment could help provide breathing room for reforms and recovery, and renew the legitimacy of US leadership. Washington appears to have rediscovered the advantages of multilateralism and a restrained foreign policy. Before the Libya war broke out, the US has compressed its responsibilities and objectives in Afghanistan and Iraq and temporarily removed expansion from NATO's agenda. Another reason is related with the security relationship between Europe and US. After the Cold War, EU has been committed to developing its defense policy so that it would able to take military actions even if the US is unwilling or less willing to be involved. The mode of intervention against Libya appears to be another variation of "Berlin Plus Agreements".[46] Bowing to give the leadership to France and the UK in performing military actions in Libya, the US hoped to encourage European countries to independently undertake more responsibilities and lessen its burden for defense. However, the puzzlement of the US lies in its hope for Europe to take more responsibilities for defense while meanwhile fearing the enhancement of EU's defense ability will impair the function of NATO and also its impact on Europe. Furthermore, Libya was conventionally Europe's backyard without significant strategic importance for the US or at least, was less important than Iraq and Afghanistan, which was why the US allows Europe to lead the intervention against Libya. Concerning whether the new mode of intervention can continue or not, more observation needs to be made.

IV. Humanitarian intervention by the EU facing challenges and dilemma

After the end of Libya war, once again Europe and the US targeted Syria, announced the illegitimacy of Assad regime and compelled Assad to step down. In an attempt to pass the anti-Syria resolution of the UN, UK, France

---

45 Joseph M. Parent and Paul K. MacDonald, "The Wisdom of Retrenchment—America Must Cut Back to Move Forward", Foreign Affairs, November/December 2011.
46 Berlin Plus agreement, http://en.wikipedia.org/Berlin_Plus_agreement.

and German called for the Security Council to make an investigation on the oppression of protestors and the infringement of human rights in Syria. In the current situation, the continuous violence in Syria is likely to be further escalated; therefore there exists the possibility of intervention performed by Europe and US against Syria. However, it is unavoidable for Europe and the US to encounter challenges and difficulties in their humanitarian interventions.

First of all, there lacks adequate legal support for the humanitarian intervention led by Europe and US, and the concept of humanitarian intervention often brings about confusions and misinterpretation.[47] Without a universally accepted definition of humanitarian intervention in the international community, the current elaborations on humanitarian intervention by western institutions and scholars have aroused doubts on its justice and rationality. The major reason for people's doubt on the legitimacy of humanitarian intervention lies in the suspicion on the motives of intervention performers, and for now, such suspicion is growing. When humanitarian consideration is the only motive for intervention, states are less likely to perform intervention. As some scholars mentioned, many examples have demonstrated the distinctiveness of humanitarianism. When the political interest and economic benefits of the outsiders are not under threats, states are obviously less enthusiastic in carrying out foreign interventions.[48] Countries are extremely unwilling to perform interventions for humanitarian purpose and there are usually other motives behind the interventions.[49] There are nearly no cases of legitimate humanitarian interventions, since the humanitarian intervention with legal spirits will not involve any interest-linked participants in intervention. The pure intervention is beyond the humanitarian concerns, and it does not involve political, economic and other factors related to the intervention performers. Even L. Fonteyne who advocates embracing the humanitarian intervention to international common law, admitted that there were no so many cases of humanitarian interventions. As a matter of fact, the western humanitarian intervention after the Cold War is interweaved with complex political and economic concerns, or in some cases, it is performed even out of some leaders' likes or dislikes. It is suggested from the experience of Iraq war and Libya war, that the humanitarian interventions by Europe and US in most cases are related to their

---

47 Sheng Hongsheng, Yang Zewei, Qin Xiaoxuan, Boundary of Forces. Beijing. Current Affairs Press. 2003, p.133.
48 Daniele Archibugi, Cosmopolitan guidelines for humanitarian intervention, http://findarticles. com/p/articles/mi_hb3225/is_i_29/ai_N29085497/.
49 Xiao Fengcheng, Humanitarian intervention: Veto and Rethinking from the Perspective of International Law. Journal of Xi'an Politics Institute. 2002. 1.

intention for overthrowing the regime (and the rule of a particular leader), thus making preparation for the future overthrow of the regime. And this is in fact an intervention by force. Blair admitted that the western humanitarian interventions were doubly guided by self-interest and ideology: Peace, stability and order brought from the interventions help to sustain the status quo in favor of Western countries and to promote the spread of "values of liberty, rule of law, human rights and open society" that are not only in their national interests, but also meet their ideological needs. Blair commented: "the spread of our values makes us safer."[50]

Regardless of these interests, the western humanitarian intervention still cannot be justified by the international law. Although some western scholars such as L. Fonteyne attempted to legalize the humanitarian intervention as part of the international law, the humanitarian intervention has not only encountered strong oppositions from many targeted states, but also has been criticized by the international community. Therefore, it seems hard to hold the view that humanitarian intervention conforms to the modern international law.[51] Even a British scholar of legal studies in favor of humanitarian intervention argued that the humanitarian intervention has never been part of international law truly.[52] Though accepted by most states and regions, the "responsibility to protect" still needs to be clearly identified in terms of when and how to fulfill it (including the issue whether intervention should be authorized by the Security Council of the UN in the first place). American scholars and think-tank analysts do not believe that the international law and the lack of legal support for intervention will block the way for the US and other states to take actions though they admit the authorization from the Security Council is required for any international humanitarian intervention. And because of this, they attempt to figure out a replacement to legalize potential intervention. For example, intervention can be permitted through some regional organizations or some tentative alliances before being authorized by the Security Council. Also in favor of the idea of "responsibility to protect", European think-tank analysts adds that any intervention without political intention and coercive measures will turn out to be ineffective. However, although accepting the argument of "responsibility to protect", most developing countries still emphasize the importance of the authorization of Security Council on any humanitarian interventions by

---

50 Tony Blair, "Doctrine of International Community," speech to the Economic Club of Chicago on April 22, 1999.
51 Peng Qiong, Discussion on the Legitimacy of International Humanitarian Intervention http://cdzy.chinacourt.org/public/detail.php?id=4005.
52 Mu Yaping, Studies on International Law in a Global Context, Peking University Press, 2008, p. 22.

force, some even arguing to set a threshold for international intervention. Intervention performers have to provide evidences for ethnic genocide and holocaust in the targeted states and these evidences have to be scrutinized by "objective analysts" judgment on justice.[53] In terms of the "responsibility to protect", there have existed divergences in the international community. Having not yet fully embraced the concept, many North Africa states fear that their national security and states sovereignty will be subject to the maneuver of western states in the name of the "responsibility to protect". This has exhibited to some extent the unsuccessful endeavors Europe and US have made to legalize their military interventions through international law, and actually more doubts will be cast on the foreign interventions in the future.

Secondly, the humanitarian interventions by Europe and the US usually lead to inhumane results and are questioned. Instead of eradicating "humanitarian disasters", the military interventions have caused heavy civilian casualties and put the targeted nations or states in turmoil and aggravated the already awry situation. Henry Kissinger, a former statesman, has realistically commented that the problems derived from the intervention in the name of humanitarianism and democracy seem more than the problems intervention aims to solve. Any use of force will trigger potential disorder no matter how noble it intends to be.[54] Take Kosovo crisis as an example[55]:

Due to the humanitarian disasters, allegedly ethnic cleansing, in Kosovo, NATO has waged a military intervention. However, it was just after NATO's air strikes that there appeared the massive flow of refugees. General Klaus Naumann who served as NATO's Military Committee chairman in Kosovo war, admitted that although interventions were based on humanitarian needs, it was still difficult to defend the NATO interventions logically and politically since the initial bombing could not provide Kosovars protection, but led to the massive flow of refugees which was embarrassing.[56] He commented: I would say first of all, never start to threaten the use of military force if you are not ready to execute it the next day. And secondly, if you do crisis management, never again change horses mid-stream. Similarly, the Afghanistan war and Iraq war have also caused heavy civilian casualties

---

53   Susan E. Rice and Andrew J. Loomis, "The Evolution of Humanitarian Intervention and the Responsibility to Protect", in Ivo H.Daalder, ed., Beyond Preemption: Force and Legitimacy in a Changing World, Washington, D.C.: Brookings Institution Press, 2007. pp. 59-95.
54   Mu Yaping, Studies on International Law in a Global Context. Peking University Press.2008.pg.26.
55   Tony Blair, "Doctrine of International Community," speech to the Economic Club of Chicago on April 22, 1999.
56   Klaus Naumann, "Nato, Kosovo, and Military Intervention," Global Governance, No.8, 2002.

and put the two states in turmoil for a long term. Compared with the situation before, the intervention strategy against Libya has changed, but the result was the same. Western states believed that one should even be willing to choose sides, namely when one party of a conflict is clearly the better choice for its own country and when choosing sides is likely to end a conflict.[57] However, this argument does not hold water. It is extremely perilous to intervene in the domestic conflicts of a state and to take sides with one party since more serious turmoil and disasters will be triggered. Libya crisis, which began as some domestic social unrest, has evolved into a civil war, when people raised their protests to an armed uprising. Shortly afterwards, France, the UK and other states involved themselves in the civil war to stop Gaddafi from massacring civilians and to stand with the opposition on their attempt to overthrow the Gaddafi regime. However, the investigations by some institutions like "Amnesty International" and "Human Rights Watch" do not reveal any evidences to show the signs of genocide and the large-scale planned infringement on human rights. The casualty resulting from the military interventions by Europe and US far exceeds what has been expected, and this obviously went against the declaration of "the responsibility to protect" on citizens made by Europe and US. Some European analysts have expressed concerns over the current policies on Syria, fearing the European interventions would result in a variety of religious and ethnic conflicts, and this would start another round of bloody mayhem and expose religious groups and ethnic minorities to disasters. According to the analysts, the actions taken by US in the Arabic world are based on two unshakeable principles – controlling the oil in Arabic countries and protecting Israel. And Europe, by blindly following the US, will undermine its own interests.[58]

Additionally, western foreign interventions have also reflected the unfair and undemocratic status quo in the international relations. During the post-Cold War period, holding the flag of humanitarianism, western states attempted to deprive other countries of state sovereignty but without giving up their own authority. Primarily targeted at the developing countries with weak political, economical and military power, the military interventions performed by Europe and the US after the end of Cold War are "acts of authority" (the hegemony of military forces, economy, politics and culture)

---

57 "Doing It Right: The Future of Humanitarian Intervention," http://www.brookings.edu/articles/2000/fall_humanitarianintervention.aspx.
58 Sylvia Kotoni Following America Lead to the Damage of Europe's Interests. Website of Spanish Elcano Royal Institute of International and Strategic Studies. May, 21 2011. http://news.xinhuanet.com/world/2011-05/27/c_121464167.htm.

exerted by so-called western democratic states to non-democratic states.[59] It is noteworthy that during the interventions adopted by Europe and US against Kosovo, Afghanistan, Iraq and Libya, they have attached some humanist values to their declarations to persuade their soldiers and victims that they are defending "humanity". On the one hand, Europe and US were motivated by the "responsibility to protect". On the other hand, the methods adopted for foreign interventions do not resemble the domestic police interventions on their own territories. It is hard to imagine air strikes carried out by Spanish and the UK in an attempt to solve the violent issues in Basque region and Northern Ireland. But as a matter of fact, air strikes have become an important tool for western states to perform their foreign interventions. The casualty caused in the air strikes in Kosovo and Libya amounts to almost the same as the total of population western states claimed to protect. These interventions are akin to a medicine that is worse than the disease and they are, at best, only "half-humanitarian" interventions.[60] At last, it needs to be mentioned that although there have been full of propaganda about European humanitarian intervention, as a matter of fact, the intervening states' capabilities and also the methods they adopted do not correspond to their policy goals. Within the short term, it is difficult to overcome the limits in EU's diplomacy and in its mechanism of making security policy. Taking into consideration the constraints of the European debt crisis, EU has committed a lot to deal with the continued crisis that has reversely affected EU's ability to implement external operations. In order to overcome the debt crisis, the member states of EU have to take a further step to cut down military spending, which goes against EU's intention for building up EU military strength. The lack of financial support due to debt and economic crisis, has also posed threats to EU's strategy of "deep democracy" in North Africa. If the investment of financial aid is insufficient, it will be hard to help North Africa to realize its economic transformation. Moreover, a negative impact is exerted on the stability of regional politics in this area. Furthermore, to cope with the debt crisis requires the support from some emerging countries. But most of members in G20 oppose to intervene in the domestic affairs of other states. In all, under the impact of such complex and destabilizing factors, EU has encountered multiple constraints in its foreign intervention operations.

---

59 "Humanitarianism and Humanitarian Intervention," chap. 8 in: Sovereignty, Rights, and Justice, Cambridge: Polity Press,2002.
60　Daniele Archibugi, "Cosmopolitan Guidelines for Humanitarian İntervention", http://findarticles.com/p/articles/mi_hb3225/is_1_29/ai_n29085497/.

V. Conclusive comments

Over hundreds of years, state sovereignty and the principle of non-interference have always been regarded as unshakeable notions which have contributed to stability in the international relations. However, the end of the Cold War seems to have opened the Pandora's box. To defend the existing Western-led international order in the context of newly emerging international political configuration, US and Europe started to practice foreign interventions on humanitarian grounds claiming to avoid "humanitarian" disasters occurring in regional or national conflicts and with the pretext of strengthening the human rights around the world. And by exerting the concept of humanitarian intervention on the UN and the international community, they expect to promote the formation of new international security and the formation of the norms on human rights, thus justifying their interventions from the legal perspective. Based on the analysis of the theories, policies and practices concerning European humanitarian intervention, the author suggests the following conclusions and thoughts.

Firstly, generally speaking, EU lacks the power to independently to carry out interventions alone, within the framework of NATO, and its intervention activities are significantly affected by US' policies. Although there are not many cases of interventions in this aspect, European interventions have exerted detrimental and lasting effects. For example, Kosovo war has initiated the practice of intervening in the domestic affairs of other states and has provided pretext for Europe's violation of the principle of state sovereignty in the later interventions in Afghanistan, Iraq and Libya. Secondly, EU has taken diametrically opposed attitudes towards the issues and missions within its region of influence and towards those "outside", being deeply involved in the former while less enthusiastic or even resistant to the latter. Such differences have something to do with Europe's different geographical preferences, its doubts on the "out of area" missions of NATO and its resentment of US' unilateralism. EU has criticized Bush Administration for its destructive adventurism in dealing with the Iraq issue, which as a matter of fact has sabotaged the purity of humanitarian intervention. Third, the European intervention within the framework of EU has exhibited some "European characteristics". There is a strong tendency to make further progress in the process of integration, and independent intervention is also a practice in EU's common diplomacy and security policy. The European humanitarian intervention entails three parts. First, focus on comprehensive intervention. The combination of military intervention and civilian intervention with the aid of NGOs' works well in the aspect of humanitarianism.

Second, focus on multilateral intervention. Importance is attached to provide interventions with legal explanation, although this does not indicate that the practical intervention adopted by EU conform to the principles concerned (the intervention against Libya has gone against related UN-resolutions and interventional norms). Third, there are geographical preferences for interventions. During intervention, expressing the most concern over the security and stability of Europe and its surrounding area, EU hopes to sustain and promote the peaceful stability in Europe and meanwhile to legitimize its actions for self-defense and self-security. With a special feeling towards Africa, EU plays an active role in its interventions in Africa, hoping to realize its own political and economic interests by sustaining the security and stability in Africa and to propagate European values and ideas to promote the democratic reform in Africa. Additionally, one of the impetuses for the independent intervention is to reduce EU's reliance on US and to strengthen its autonomy. What's more, revolutions in military affairs have had a significant impact on the western humanitarian intervention after the end of the Cold War. Generally speaking, the biggest constraint for intervention comes from intervention performers' reluctance to bear the enormous casualties. But, with the appearance of a new generation of military weapons, the use of drones, smart vehicles, smart bombs and so and so forth will reduce the consumption of resources and lower related labor costs, and all of these will reduce the risk to at least politically acceptable levels for intervention intenders. Kosovo war has foreshadowed the advent of a new era of warfare, which means that countries with strong military power could arbitrarily perform foreign intervention without any sacrifices on its own soldiers. The Libya war has further verified this.

Some thoughts are offered at last. It is an unavoidable fact that the increasing foreign military interventions performed by Europe and US after the Cold War has considerably challenged some important principles in the current international order. The domestic conflicts have been embraced in the concept of "international peace and security", and the "responsibility to protect" has also been added to the new norms on international peace and human rights. All of these have shaken the basis of the concept of state sovereignty, though state sovereignty still remains as the foundation of international system. There are some disputes over the concepts of "responsibility of sovereignty" and the "responsibility to protect". International intervention seems to be accepted to deal with civilian displacement and abuse of human rights resulting from internal conflicts. In recent years, the UN Security Council has defined the internal conflicts in Haiti, Liberia, Cambodia and Bosnia and Herzegovina as threats to international security and peace and has provided some regional organizations with more freedom to handle the regional humanitarian crisis and political crisis in their respective areas. Since the inviolability of national borders has been "jeopardized", it is impossible for western states to withdraw from the front line of humanitarian intervention. Considering the fact that the increasing military intervention by western states has undermined the effectiveness and the authority of the UN, how to cope with the humanitarian crisis after the Cold War and how to deal with the protection of human rights and the relations between humanitarian interventions and state sovereignty will be put on the agenda of the UN. What is also needs to be mentioned is that any autocratic use of armed forces outside the UN is dangerous no matter what kind of principles it goes in line with. In reality, more and more cases of foreign intervention outside the UN have strengthened this development. To make a breakthrough in the field of humanitarian intervention, the UN is not only required to push through structural reforms, but also to establish new values and thoughts so as to implement effective intervention when needed, or group interventions directly performed by Western states bypassing the authorization of the UN will repeatedly occur, thereby further undermine the reputation and function of the UN. As former Italian Prime Minister D'Alema stated, if UN is unable to take action, "an international organization made up of democratic nations" will be needed to replace the function of the UN to defend peace and stop humanitarian disasters massacres.[61] China as a non-western, developing country and also as one of the permanent members of the Security Council needs to take more efforts on the studies on humanitarian intervention in theoretical and policy level, streamlining the criteria to legalize humanitarian intervention, promoting the process of standardization as to protect human rights and meanwhile to impose limits on the abuse of humanitarian intervention from the legal perspective. Based on the conclusions of international humanitarian theories and practices, some Chinese scholars have come up with some conditions that humanitarian intervention should meet. 1. Humanitarian intervention can be legitime when it aims to prevent large-scale conscience-shocking violations of human rights which are already occuring or predictable. 2. Humanitarian motive and consideration regarding the event should be overriding and political, economical and ideological considerations should be avoided, or should only be subordinate to humanitarian evaluation. 3. Humanitarian intervention should be employed as the last resort after all peaceful options are exhausted. 4. The impact of intervention on the political authority structure of the targeted states should be kept at the minimum level. 5. The humanitarian intervention actions

---

61 Neo-interventionism, http://baike.baidu.com/view/362365.ht.

should be performed according to proportionality principle in appropriate with the degree of severity of the situation. 6. Humanitarian intervention should not pose any threat to international peace and security and should not cause greater disasters and sufferings. 7. Intervening forces should be withdrawn within the shortest time once the mission of humanitarian intervention is achieved. 8. The final decision on whether to perform a particular humanitarian intervention or not should be exclusively decided by the UN Security Council. If the international community hopes to keep the humanitarian intervention in the framework of morally, politically and legally acceptable means, simultaneously, a state, when taking part in a humanitarian intervention, has to conform with the basic principles mentioned above."[62] I hope these constructive views and positions can be a basis for further in-depth reflections.

---

62 See, Sheng Hongsheng, Yangze Wei, Qin Xiaoxuan, "Boundary of Force", Beijing, Shishi Press, 2003, pp.156-157.

A Discussion on the Means, Results and Influences of International Intervention Performed by Western Major Countries
—Taking the Middle East as an example

Wang Jinglie[1]

Aesop's Fable tells a well-known story called "Wolf and Goat":

Once upon a time a Wolf saw a lamb drinking water. "There's my supper," thought he, "if only I can find some excuse to seize it." Then he called out to the Lamb, "How dare you muddle the water from which I am drinking?" "Nay, master, nay," said Lamb "if the water be muddy up there, I cannot be the cause of it, for it runs down from you to me." "Well, then," said the Wolf, "why did you call me bad names this time last year?" "That cannot be," said the Lamb; "I had not yet been born last year." Snarled the Wolf; "if it was not you it was your father;" and with that he rushed upon the poor little Lamb…"

In the story, the seemingly moral wolf made up some lame excuses and finally bared its ferocious teeth at the little goat. Narrated widely for more than 2,000 years, this old tale has reflected the wisdom of human beings and implied the thoughts behind it.

The real-life "wolf and lamb" has staged on the international arena. In the existing international relations, "the civilized major countries or powerful states" in the West occupy strong positions and barbarously trample on the basic norms of international law. The relations between the Western powers and the smaller or weaker states just resemble that between the wolf and lamb. The rise of Western powers records a history full of bloodsheds

---

[1] Director of Middle East Department under the Institute of West Asian and African Studies, attached to CASS.

and interventions. For major countries, the realization of their interests is based on the devastation and intervention of the weaker.

I. The primary means used by Western powers for intervention

Western powers have never stopped their intervention in small and weak states, resorting to whatever means to maximize their own profits, for instance, political squeeze, economic sanctions, military strikes, overthrowing hostile regimes, new-media intervention...some of which are frequently employed by Western states while some are brand-new and characteristic of the times.

A. Political squeezing

Talking of the "political squeezing" by hegemonists against the hostile states in the Middle East, we observe that Western powers have adopted multiple policy measures primarily as: demonizing hostile states, blockading them, intervening in the Middle Eastern countries for the sake of democracy promotion. And making scathing comments on hostile states or demonizing them are the common practices that aim to expose the hostile states to public criticism at first. Specifically speaking, the hostile states in the Middle East are often denounced for their supports for terrorism. Under the Pahlavi dynasty rule, Iran was an important ally of the US in the Middle East, and Western countries like The US even assisted Iran in its nuclear reactor building. Since the success of Islamic revolution in 1979, the relations between The US and Iran have deteriorated. In November 1979, The US froze Iran's whole assets in U.S. In 1980, the US government severed ties with Iran, which was followed with a series of sanctions. In 1984, the US criticized Iran as the strongest supporter of terrorist activities and for the murderous activities around the world, and meanwhile put it on the list of states sponsoring terrorism. To curb the spread of Islamic revolution, The US sided with Iraq during the Iran-Iraq war, but also secretly sold arms to Iran. And this was revealed as the so-called Iran-Contra story, another notorious disgrace after the famous Watergate scandal. In short, all of these are just the manifestations of US's endeavors to impair its enemy states.

Since 1990s, a number of states are labeled by the US as Rogue States—Iran, Iraq, Libya, Sudan, Syria, Afghanistan and so forth.[2]

2　http://www.answers.com/topic/rogue-state.

In 2002, once again, the US defined Iraq, Iran and North Korea as Axis of Evil. In 2005, the US claimed Iran as the "outposts of tyranny". West powers are never bored with the opinion spreading, condemning the so-called rogue states as the headquarters of terrorism. These states are asserted by the US to support terrorism in a number of ways, for example, researching and producing the large-scale weapons of mass destruction. By doing this, Western powers amass the public animosity against these states, paving the way for their military strikes in the near future. After the 9/11 Event, Western media tends to associate terrorism with some religion (usually Islamism) in their news coverage.

What's more, the US also accused Iran of advocating some terrorists and anti-US armed groups and believed the extremists from Syria had disturbed the regional security in Iraq, preventing the normal progress towards constitutionality. In September 2005, U.S. ambassador to Iraq issued warnings against Syria, and in his words, the US is losing its patience with Syria.[3]

Allied with Western powers, the US tries to blockade its hostile states and impose sanctions on them with the aid of some international organizations like the UN. At the beginning of March 2009, the International Criminal Court at Hague issued a warrant arrest for Sudanese President Omer Hassan Ahmed Elbashir. However, the United Nations Secretary General, Mr. Ban Ki-moon proposed the same day in his statement that all parties to Sudan should endeavor to reach a political consensus and sort out a way to address the conflicts in Darfur. And he also stated that the UN will continue its humanitarian aids and peacekeeping activities in Sudan. On 4 March of that year, Montas, the spokesman for the UN Secretary General stated when responding to reporters' questions, that the UN would keep in contact with Sudanese President Bashir when necessary.

In June 2011, International Criminal Court at Hague issued a warrant arrest for Libya leader Gaddafi, and his son Saif al-Islam Muammar al-Gaddafi and the former intelligence chief Abdullah Senoussi due to their crimes against humanity. But in effect, this is merely political squeeze against Gaddafi before the military strikes against Libya regime was performed.

As for the Israeli-Palestinian conflict, though recognizing Pakistanian's endeavors for independence, the US still takes sides with Israel and has even imposed a series of bans on Palestinian. In July 2011, due to the efforts by Western powers, South Sudan became the 193rd member state in the United Nations after gaining independence. But, the US ruled out Palestinian's application for its accession to the UN, considering Israel's tough stance.

---

3   Associated Press, 12 September 2005, Tishreen (Arabic), 13 September 2005.

In October of that year when UNESCO came to the decision to include Palestinian to the UN member states, US refused to pay its membership fees to UNESCO to oppose the proposal. Under the obstruction of the US, to be officially introduced as a member state of the UN would be painstaking for Palestinian in the near future.

The US regards the Middle East as a region lacking democracy, where tyranny, terrorism and all evil antagonism towards the US have come from. "Supporting and extending democracy has long been a centerpiece of the US foreign policy."[4]

Spreading the Western values and Western democracy in the Middle East has always been a policy measure encouraged by the US and other Western countries. Shortly after the end of the Cold War, the US-led Western countries hastily launched a series of programs to reform the Middle East. In November 1995, EU came up with the Barcelona Process.[5]

This is a platform where the EU and the countries in North Africa and West Asia at the Mediterranean coast could engage in political dialogues, economic cooperation and culture exchanges thus promoting the construction and development of the democratic system in the Middle East. In July 2008, "the Mediterranean summit" was held in Paris and the "Union for the Mediterranean" was officially launched.[6]

After the "9/11" event, the attitude and mentality of the US government and citizens have gone through significant changes, with more emphasis on their increasingly serious security problems. In their eyes, "the anti-American hostility in Arab world has been rather alarming" and implementing the Western-style democratic education, is undoubtedly an effective way to detach the people in the Middle East from terrorism. The "US National Security Strategy" published in September 2002 particularly laid great stress on maintaining US dominant position in the world, promoting democracy on the globe, taking preemptive unilateral military actions against terrorists and tyrants. By the end of 2002, Richard N. Haass, the Director of Policy Planning for the United States Department of State put out with the proposal "Towards Greater Democracy in the Muslim World".[7]

---

4 Richard N. Haass, "Towards Greater Democracy in the Muslim World," U.S. Department of State, Remarks to the Council on Foreign Relations, Washington, D.C., December 4, 2002.
5 Countries at the coast of the Mediterranean: Morocco, Tunisia, Egypt, Israel, Jordan, Lebanon, Malta, Syria, Turkey, Cyprus and the Palestinian National Authority.
6 French President Nicolas Sarkozy and Egyptian President Hosni Mubarak co-chaired the summit. The so-called "Union for the Mediterranean" is considered as the replication of "Barcelona Process".
7 Richard N. Haass, "Towards Greater Democracy in the Muslim World," U.S. Department of State, Remarks to the Council on Foreign Relations, Washington, D.C., December 4, 2002.

In early 2004, US Vice President Dick Cheney advanced the idea of "Great Middle East Democracy Program" at the World Economic Forum for the first time, and in February the same year, US Secretary of State Colin Powell explained the proposal again. In June 2004, the G8 Summit officially launched the "Partnership for Progress and a Common Future", which was an improved version of the US' "Greater Middle East Plan". This program would serve to push through the political, economic, cultural and social reforms in the Middle East and North Africa. Judging from this, the United States actually employed the carrot and stick policy, requiring the Middle East countries to promote political, economic reforms and social democracy in exchange for acquiring Western financial aids.

Some US scholars have argued that "Greater Middle East Plan" and the "Helsinki Accords" (Helsinki Final Act) in 1975 are two tools or methods to achieve the same result. "Helsinki Final Act" is regarded as one of the most influential international treaties signed after World War II, and even conservatives have argued that this treaty helped to accelerate the evolution of the "Warsaw Pact" led by Soviet Union.

Despite the widespread opposition by the Middle Eastern countries against Western values and "democratic model", Western countries have continued its relentless efforts to advance their values and influence deeply and widely in the Middle East.

B. Economic sanctions

Financial aid is also an important way for major world powers to intervene. Major world powers economically support their allies and followers, draw them over and put them under control, through which, Western countries pursue to achieve their strategic goals. However, different from financial aids, major world powers impose economic sanctions aiming to restrict those "hostile forces" and economically weaken their opponents so as to serve their own strategic goals.

US have imposed long-term economic blockade and sanctions targeting Iran, Libya and other hostile labeled countries, and as a result, these targeted countries have suffered substantial losses. For the US, the sanctions against the hostile countries in the Middle East are mainly supported by US domestic laws, of which the most important is the "D'Amato Act". "D'Amato Act" is named after US Senator Alfonse D-Amato who believed that Libya and Iran advocated terrorism thus proposing a bill in September 1995. The "D'Amato Act" sanctions the foreign companies that export oil or energy extraction technologies to Libya and Iran. After several revisions, the 'D Amato bill was passed by US Senate in July 1996. And in August 1996, it was signed by President Clinton and has taken into effect since then. In 2001 and 2006, the law went through two supplementary extensions and has remained effective until December 31, 2011.[8]

This law prohibits the foreign companies from investing in the energy industry on a large scale in Libya and Iran. According to the law, United States would impose economic, trade and financial sanctions targeting those countries and companies which are in energy cooperation with Libya and Iran. Countries or companies that have investment of more than 400 million Dollar (later changed to 200 million Dollars) within a year would be subject to sanctions. The sanctioned countries, companies or individuals would be included in the blacklist of the federal government. However, the US president, in accordance with the national security interests, would have the power to exempt the violators from the backlist. Additionally, the bill also authorizes the US president to provide support to the democratic associations and human rights groups in Iran.

US sanctions have not only plunged Iran in extreme shortage of material goods, but also caused the unbalanced industrial structure in Iran. In order to resist sanctions and foreign interventions, Iran had to concentrate on strengthening its national defense with priority. Over time, the result is that although Iran has a developed its own military programs in the Middle East, the civilian and other industrial products are still extremely scarce. What's more, for Iran, there also existed the problem of structural imbalance, regarding the oil industry that serves as the pillar industry of the national economy. Iran has nearly 100 oil fields, but only few refineries. The relatively low production capacity of refineries cannot meet the needs.

The United States and Western powers have taken a series of measures against their hostile countries including Libya during the reign of Gaddafi, Iraq under Saddam Hussein as well as Sudan and Iran. These measures include economic sanctions and freezing their financial assets. In the spring of 2011, after the political unrest erupted in Libya, the United States and Western countries had frozen Gaddafi's assets in Europe even long before launching the military strikes against Libya. These grabbed assets of Gaddafi were even allocated to the Iran anti-government organizations, and used to buy weapons for them.[9]

---

8 http://news.sina.com.cn/w/2006-04-28/08228809909s.shtml.andhttp://gzdaily.dayoo.com/html/2006-10/02/content 15418884.htm.
9 And it was reported that Libyan assets abroad (Including overseas investment) exceeded 100 billion dollars, with approximately 30 billion dollars in the United States.http://cn.wsj.com/gb/20110301/bus103704.asp?source=article.

In early June 2011, the International Conference on Libya which was dominated by the Western countries has once committed to provide 1.3 billion Dollar funds to the Libyan opposition forces. And undeniably, these funds would be eventually transferred from those Libyan's frozen government funds.

In November 2011, the report issued by the IAEA on the Iran nuclear program arose uproar. The nearly 10-year nuclear crisis leads to another round of tension, and as a result, the Western countries intensified their sanctions on Iran. US, UK, Canada and other countries enforced more stringent measures in Iran. In addition to the general economic measures, an attempt to financially bring down Iran was also made. US not only announced the sanctions against the oil and petrochemical industries, banks and financial institutions in Iran, but also threatened to punish the governments and agencies in ties with Iranian banks and financial institutions.[10]

Britain announced cutting financial ties with Iranian banks, and Canada publicly stated that it would "stop any transaction with Iran", including the cooperation with the Iranian Central Bank.

This is a common practice employed by major countries to expand the scope of sanctions, deter any countries from normally contacting the hostile countries, ensure the success of sanction programs to further isolate the targeted countries and make them succumb to major countries. With the rapid development of the world economy and the deepening economic globalization, the economic exchanges between countries have heavily relied on each other, and no longer only in the form of simple commodity trade. The inter-penetration of mutual investments and joint research sites, have become common phenomena. Some "multinational" companies have become true "international companies" having shareholders from different countries. Looking from the social and historical perspectives, economic sanctions won't succeed without the sanctions targeting other related parties. But, those companies having normal trade relations might be negatively impacted only by joint sanctions, which can truly damage the trading parties.

According to "D'Amato Act", the sanctions imposed by the United States against the third party are typically "joint sanctions". For example, in 2004 and 2005, Union Bank of Switzerland and ABN-AMRO were successively sanctioned by the US. As a response to it, the international community, including US's European allies condemned and boycotted this Act which is claimed to clearly constitute a serious and unwarranted intervention in trade

---

10 http://world.people.com.cn/GB/16350740.html.

policies of sovereign states. What's more, the EU even threatened to start official counter measures through the WTO.

C. Military strikes

To maintain the world hegemony, United States has broadly practiced military interventions or directly launched wars against its hostile countries. In 1981, 2 trillion Dollars were allocated by US government to enhance US ability to project military power, especially the US Navy, aircraft carriers, amphibious ships, long-range Air Forces, special warring forces and so on. The then US Secretary of Defense, Caspar Weinberger has argued that they and their allies increasingly depended on the unstable regions of the world and the urgent need for West was, to better react to crises erupting away from their shores and retain the intervention capability when necessary.[11] And because of this, The US made some adjustments in its global military strategies. In 1983, the Central Command was established.[12]

This strengthened the US hegemony over the Middle East and also enhanced its military presence in the region establishing its headquarters in Bahrain, the US Fifth Fleet is responsible for the navy forces in the Persian Gulf, Red Sea, Arabian Sea and in some parts of the Indian Ocean, through which the United States increased the rapid response capability and the capacity to intervene.

As for the US military interventions, the US waged Iraq war and Libya war, directly resorting to armed interventions to overthrow the regimes of hostile countries and supporting the pro-American regimes to consolidate its sphere of influence. In March 2003, the United States, together with other allies, by-passed the United Nations and launched the Iraq war devoting fighting forces up to nearly 170.000 (120.000 US troops, 45,000 British troops) and mobilized ample US air forces and navy air forces which were stationed in the Gulf region. Through concerted efforts, the US-led joint Western forces easily overthrew the Iraq's Ba'ath Party regime that had been in power for 35 years. Besides, Saddam Hussein who ruled Iraq for 24 years was also captured after more than 9 months of hunting. After the invasion of Iraq, US adopted a series of measures such as the banning of Ba'ath Party, de-Baa'thification, disbanding the Iraqi army, hunting down Saddam Hussein and his senior officials, issuing warrants of arrest for them ... these measures were carried out until the Iraqi court authorized the execution

---

11 Peter J. Schraeder, Intervention into the 1990s, The U.S. Foreign Policy in the Third World, Boukler and London: Lynne Rienner Publishers, 1995, pp. 153-174.
12 http://en.wikipedia.org/wiki/CENTCOM.

Saddam Hussein by the end of 2006, and this execution has eradicated the last "symbol" of the Baath party rule. Bush described Saddam Hussein's execution as a milestone in Iraq's road to democracy.[13]

Kofi Annan said: "the U.S.-led invasion of Iraq was illegal because it violated the UN Charter." Indeed, the US military intervention hasn't alleviated the suffering of the Iraqi people, but increased the sufferings and the hatred bore by people in Iraq. At present, Iraq is still bogged down in the war and turmoil. The Former UN Secretary General Kofi Annan has sharply pointed out that the U.S.-led invasion of Iraq was illegal because it violated the UN Charter.[14]

Libya war is another example of the employment of military means by Western countries to subvert the regime of a sovereign state, and it was also a "non contact war" without the involvement of the Western ground forces.

After the Gulf War, claiming to protect the Iraqi Kurds and Shiite Muslims, the United Kingdom and France jointly imposed the no-fly zones over the northern parts and southern parts of Iraq in March 1991 and August 1992 and prohibited military flights in Iraq in the airspace between the north of the 36 degrees North latitude to the South of the 32 degrees North latitude.

In September 1996, the United States announced the extension of "no-fly zone" over the southern part of Iraq to Baghdad suburban districts, the south of the 33 degrees North latitude, and the employment of forces to limit Iraq's airspace controlled by the Iraq government in the range centered around Baghdad.

If the no-fly zone imposed by the US to Iraq can be evaluated as a limited no-fly zone measure, then the one in Libya is an "unlimited no-fly zone". Utilizing UN's allowance of a no-fly zone as a pretext, the US launched a war targeting Libya. By providing Libyan rebels with abundant funds, weaponry and military advisers, the US has introduced a modern version of "proxy war." Compared with the wars in Iraq and Afghanistan, though less costly, the Libya war achieved the goal of overthrowing the Gaddafi regime, almost without any losses of troops on the side of United States and its NATO allies. The Western media and think tanks have called it the "Libyan model" thus the West has ushered in new intervention by major countries in the Middle East.

---

13 http://news.bbc.co.uk/2/hi/middle_east/6126404.stm.
14 http://www.gulfnews.com,2004/09/16.

In addition to economic sanctions US also performs low-intensity war against its hostile countries in the Middle East, consuming the opponent's strength, forcing them to surrender. In general, the US "limited military strikes" against Libya, Iraq, Sudan and other countries are all within the scope of low-intensity war.

In 1970s, after the relations between Libya and the United States had deteriorated, Iran has repeatedly faced military strikes by the US in 1980s. In August 1981, the two countries fought an air war in the Gulf of Sidra and Libyan fighter planes were destroyed. In March 1986, the United States attacked Libya's missile speedboats and missile bases near Surt. In April the same year, once again US raided the capital city of Libya-Tripoli and Benghazi on the pretext of fighting terrorism. In January 1989, the US Navy was stationed outside the Libyan sea, shooting down two MiG-23 airplanes. Similarly in August 1998, the United States launched military strikes against Sudan and Afghanistan and fired about 100 cruise missiles targeting the two countries.

After the Gulf War, the United States not only imposed economic sanctions but also continued its air strikes targeting Iraq. In December 1998, the United States launched the military operation named "Desert Fox" against Iraq, which was achieved by the aircraft carrier group stationed in the Gulf region. First, hundreds of satellite-guided cruise missiles gave a devastating blow against Iraqi military targets and its security facilities. In order to hinder any threat to United States, the US Navy's EA-6B aircraft fired anti-radar missiles to destroy the air defense facilities of Iraq. Subsequently, taking off from aircraft carriers and air bases, the US bombers and British fighters launched a large-scale bombing and attacks targeting Iraq. After the Gulf War, the United States has continued to implement its policies against Iraq. In 2001, more than 400 air strikes were launched against Iraq who suffered seriously as a consequence.

D. Subverting hostile regimes

Assassinating hostile political leaders, instigating coups to overthrow hostile governments are all common practices used by US, and they are also an important part of CIA's regular covert activities. Two of the three coups staged in Syria in 1949 were plotted by the U.S, and in 1953, the coup in Iran was also schemed by the US. In the Reagan administration era, the United States tried to assassinate the Hezbollah leader Sheikh Mohammed and assisted the anti-government forces in Yemen in their sabotage activities.

As for Libya, the US first supported the opposition in the neighboring countries of Libya to overthrow or undermine the Gaddafi regime. In 1986, Reagan signed the "National Security Presidential Directive" which authorized operations to overthrow Gaddafi rule.[15]

In 1990, the CIA and its allies in the Gulf countries reached an agreement to provide arms, funds and intelligence to Kurdish rebels in the north part of Iraq, particularly providing media equipment and training to Kurds and the exiled Iraqis, smuggling forged banknotes into Libya to disrupt its economy, and spreading disinformation through international media so as to weaken the military support for Saddam, and Iraq.[16]

Osama bin Laden, the leader of the notorious terrorist organization, was once trained by CIA. His initial task was to lead military resistance against the Soviet occupation in Afghanistan. After the withdrawal of Soviet Union, Bin Laden gradually began to resist the intervention of the US in the Islamic world and plotted the "9/11" Event.

The "New Yorker" magazine and the Cable News Network (CNN) revealed that by the end of 2007, Bush presented a highly confidential bill to Congress which indicated that the government would allocate 400 million Dollars, mainly for the covert activities of the US Special forces in Iran, as well as for supporting dissidents in Iran, and for gradually expanding the secret operations against Iran. The aim of this bill was to split the leadership in Tehran, and trigger a "revolutionary coup" in Iran, and secretly subvert the Tehran government.[17]

Supporting anti-government organizations or related opposition forces aim to apply political pressure on the hostile countries.

Regarding Iran as a "thorn in the eye", the United States offers long-term support and financial aid to anti-government organizations in Iran. The most important one of them "MKO" (Mojahedin-e Khalq Organization)—the exiled Iranian fighters and militants who mostly live in Europe. In July 2004, the United States announced to entitle the exiled "MKO" members with the prisoners-of-war status, stipulated in the "the Geneva Convention". But formerly this organization had been listed as a "terrorist organization" by the United States and the European Union.[18]

---

15 Christopher Simpson, National Security Directives of the Reagan and Bush Administrations The Declassified History of U. S. Political and Military Policy, 1981-1991, Boulder: Westview Press, 1995, pp. 646-647.
16 Ibid., p. 930.
17 http://www.norislam.com/?viewnews-8125, http://www.alarabiya.netand http://news.cnhubei.com/ctjb/ctjbsgk/ctjb30/200807/t359616.shtml.
18 www.xinhuanet.com, September 7, 2004.

The United States and Western countries have supported Sudanese rebel organizations for a long term, providing them with overseas advantages: legal space for their activities, funds and even weapons, so that the Sudanese rebel groups has grown, and eventually led to the split of South Sudan.

In the spring of 2011 (the Arab Spring) when the political crisis sweep through the Middle East, the US and other Western politicians repeatedly stated that the Libyan leader Gaddafi, Syrian President Bashar al-Assad and Yemeni President Ali Abdullah Saleh must step down, and that they would support anti-government forces in these countries. Leaders of France, Britain, the United States and other countries have met with the leaders of the National Transitional Council of Libya and expressed their support for the armed struggles against the Gaddafi regime. In the early December of 2011, US Secretary of State, Hillary Clinton met with the seven leaders of the Syrian opposition in Geneva, expressing support for the Syrian opposition and encouraging Syrian opposition to engage in the anti-government demonstrations.

Since 1979, "regime change" has been an important policy option against Iran. Since then the United States has believed that only by achieving a regime change in Iran, can the threats against its interests cease once and for all. United States has not only criticized the Iranian government for its "human rights record", but also officially provided funds to the so-called "pro-democratic forces" in Iran and increased intelligence activities in Iran. After the "9/11" Event, the Bush administration laid more emphasis on strengthening the "regime change" campaigns.

In January 2002, Bush himself included Iran in the "axis of evil". In his second inauguration speech and subsequent State of the Union speech, Bush exhibited more intense determination to promote regime change in Iraq. On March 8, 2006, Deputy US Secretary of State Nicholas Burns, indicated in the House International Relations Committee that US would strengthen its diplomatic missions in the neighboring countries of Iran by increasing the number of diplomats who are fluent in Persian, and launched a project called as "observers of Iran" in the US diplomatic mission in Baku-Azerbaijan. In addition, the State Department in Washington has expanded its "Iran office", and one of its tasks is to keep in contact with the Iranian opposition forces exiled in the United States. The US government has set up a virtual "US embassy in Iran" on the Internet in order to export American culture and values and strengthen the contact with the anti-government activists and organizations in Iran.

In early December 2011, the two Republican presidential candidates in the US consistently expressed their political intentions. The former Governor of Massachusetts Mitt Romney declared that in the end, it is necessary to change the government of Iran. Another presidential candidate, the former House Speaker Newt Gingrich directly appealed to "regime change" in Iran, and he also extended his will to subsidize every dissident group in Iran.[19]

E. Interventions by the "new media"

In the history of mankind, every major scientific and technological revolution has played an important role in promoting social development. New media refers to those digital media that are interactive, incorporate two-way communication and involve some form of computing including smart phones, Internet and other tools, which feature a rapid and convenient transmission of information, its function in promoting social development are obvious. As the main tools of the new media, Mobile phones especially smart phones and the Internet complement with each other. Mobile phones perform very fast in disseminating information, and they are easy to operate even when people are walking, with a fingertip, people can spread a message instantly. While, the Internet which slightly requires more equipment, is also very convenient having more and multiple advantages. For example, it has a data saving space and transmit huge amounts of data with the cloud technology, including large charts thus being more informative. Internet is the fruit of contemporary scientific and technological progress.

But currently we are living in the era of asymmetric information, once a severe scandal is disclosed in the web, people tend to blindly believe it due to the lack of transparency. As a result, the disclosure of government corruptions, mismanagement of the web would stir up disappointment and rage among the masses thus causing a serious impact on social stability. Tunisian upheaval has been instigated by the "Wikileaks" which disclosed unchecked information about the corruption by the Ben Ali government. An unemployed Tunisian young man had performed self-immolation in order to protest against the brutal enforcement of the law by city inspectors, and this has triggered huge demonstrations on the streets and caused the president to fled the country. Global media also call the Tunisian upheaval as the "Wikileaks Revolution" or "Internet revolution".[20]

---
19   http://www.chinanews.com/gj/2011/12-09/3519709.shtml.
20   "The List: How Much Did the WikiLeaks Cables Change the Arab World?", http://www.foreignpolicy.com/articles/2011/03/09/best_of_arableaks.

The political crisis in Egypt also involved the multi-intervention by foreign media outlets including the "new social media". "Facebook", "Twitter" and other US government-supported sites are among the most active social media outlets.

For The US, apart from the warfare fields of air forces, army, and the navy, the Internet has become the fifth field of warfare. According to some reports, the US military has developed more than 2,000 kinds of network weapons. Generally speaking, the US cyber warfare entails three modes.

First, the physical blow, dropping the "graphite bomb" so as to cut off the enemy's computer networks, or partially make them paralyzed, blocking the networks temporarily or permanently. Second, launching virtual strikes or mobilizing "hackers", sending a deadly virus attack to the enemy's networks, interference and sabotage the enemy's network operating system so that it cannot run any more. The third is to identify strikes or "deception tactic". Create virtual images or signals through network to deceive or mislead the operators in wrongdoing so that their command will fail.[21]

Generally, the virtual strikes by the US do not target the international Internet in the common sense but the internal security network of the enemy. Via keyboards and screens, a thrilling battle on the network gets started. In Virginia, there is an inconspicuous building in a common industrial park, where is the headquarter of the CIA monitors the network of overseas public opinions – "open source center".

According to the reports, the US military is working secretly with a local company to develop new software, using forged identity of users to publish propaganda in favor of the United States on the website. The world popular social networking site "Facebook" and micro-blogging website "Twitter" will be the major tools used by U.S.for "manipulation". U.S. Central Command spokesman Bill said that the U.S. military would apply this software to a "psychological war" in Iraq.[22]

For the United States, the "cyber war" cannot only effectively weaken the unfavorable ideological propaganda, but also won favorable responses and supports. Therefore, it can be said as "two birds with one stone". The United States is the first to launch the "cyber warfare", using its "absolute monopoly" on the Internet to pursue its own interests. The Internet has overcome the slow dissemination of layered information in the past and spreads information quite fast and much broader.

---

21 http://www.chinanews.com/it/2011/11-19/3472432.shtml.
22 British Guardian, 19 March 2011. Reference: http://www.chinanews.com/gj/2011/03-29/2936979.shtml.

The Middle East, region which features a much younger demographics, with the population below 25 years accounting for around the half of the total, 42.1% in Tunisia, 47.4% in Libya, 52.3% in Egypt, 60.6% in Iraq and 65.4% in Yemen.[23]

Young people can easily accept new things and they have a natural affinity for the new media. There have been a lot of people joined in the "Internet E family". As for the recent political crisis in the Middle East, new media has served to mobilize and organize people, acting as yeast or a catalyst in the process. Disseminating information and announcing the demonstration or meeting time and place through smart phones and the Internet has become a common practice used by the demonstrators in the Middle East.

When resorting to the new media, demonstrators and anti-government forces strengthened themselves and accumulated energy, the course of which not only makes their voice heard aloud but also enhances their expectations for their actions, holding a strong power to challenge the government.

In fact, the United States already had a trial of the "new media war" in the Middle East. The Spanish newspaper "Uprising" reported that, during the Iran's presidential election in 2009, the CIA took advantages of the new media to "incite internal chaos in Iran." It is said that the CIA has instructed Iranian opposition forces who are exile in the United States, UK and other Western countries, to spread various misleading information concerning the political crisis in Iran via mobile phones and blog websites, so as to create chaos and incite public opinions against the government for the purpose of overthrowing the government.[24①]

In the recent political crisis in the Middle East, the United States just employed the new media much more extensively.

From the Iranian presidential election in 2009 to the ongoing political turmoil in the Middle East currently, the United States has intervened in other states and attempted to alter their political direction by the means of "cyber war".

---

23 http://media.economist.com/sites/default/files/media/2011InfoG/Interactive/ArabLeague_Jan16/Arab5.
24 http://www.norislam.com/?viewnews-8125.

II. The results and impacts of the interventions by major powers

Overall, the impact brought about from the Western intervention policies and activities, has been far more negative than positive. The so-called positive influence can only manifest itself in typical cases. In the Middle East, such cases are particularly rare. Generally speaking, the results and impact of the interventions performed by Western powers focus on the following aspects.

A. Trampling upon the basic norms of international relations

In essence, the intervention policies adopted by the Western powers are not based on the basic norms of international relations, but performed out of their own interests. It is noticed that in fact, the Americans themselves acknowledge the injustice of Iraq war, and the US government and media have once described the war as "the invasion of Iraq" as in the case of the war in Libya performed by the United States and the Western powers.

In early 2002, Iraq, Iran and North Korea were defined as the "axis of evil" countries by Bush Administration, and they were considered as a threat to the world security and interests. Then the statement was followed with a "preemptive" strategy. Though the US government justified its preemptive strategy as a "preventive war", but the war in essence is a "challenging war" and has set a very bad example in the field of international relations. Bruce Blair the Director of the US Center for Defense Information, believed that as the world's most powerful nation, the United States, would not allow any presumably hostile country or dictators to arm themselves with weapons of mass destruction, and would not allow the existence of any threat to the United States.

Bruce Blair also admitted this strategy has set a bad example for the world. It did not comply with international law, and was inappropriate to the international community.[25①]

Many Americans have said bluntly that in fact the United States has already enjoyed a hegemonic' status. For US interventions around the world, a quite number of Americans believe that it is not that the United States wants to intervene in the affairs of other countries, but that the world needs the United States to do so. The United States has declared its determination to check and reform those "failed states' which were labeled as posing severe

---

25 Washington Observer, No.3, September 25, 2002.

threats to its security. Although indirectly expressed, the failed states are expected to transfer their sovereignty to the international community.[26]

Based on this logic, the United States can put any country it targets or resents in the list of "hostile countries" or "failed states". Taking the pretext of defending the US security interests, the US relying on its preemptive strategy, has become ready to commit itself to the military strikes and political transformations in the targeted states.

B. Important components of the "unstable structure" of Middle East

"Interventions by great powers" have become an important factor in the Middle East for long, which have caused the lasting turmoil in the Middle East and intertwining with the "transformation period in the Middle East" and which trigger "manifold contradictions in the Middle East region". The weaved "unstable structure" has not only impacted the Middle East in the past but also will control the situation in the Middle East for a quite long time in the future.

Judging from the situation in the Middle East since the World War II, we can clearly see this "unstable structure" consisting of the three elements mentioned above, which have exerted profound impacts in the region's politics, economy and social development.

We have proposed the three points in the early 1990s, and the long-term studies on the Middle East have offered us with new understandings and upgraded theories about the Middle East problems at the turn of the century.

The 10-year experience has shown that these views have stood the time (see Figure-1 below).

Through comprehensive analysis of a variety of factors, we believe that, this unstable structure will not only continue to exist, but also will have far-reaching effects on the Middle East situation. In other words, analyzing the unstable structure becomes an important theoretical tool to recognize, analyze and grasp the situation in the Middle East.

C. The political configuration in the Middle East has changed

The Great Power interventions have had a significant and far-reaching impact on the situation and the political structure of the Middle East. During the multi-polarization, the United States is facing fierce competition in the overall national strength. In future competition, energy is a constraint of

---
26 Ibid.

great importance. Therefore, for the United States, to control the oil-rich Middle East is equal to have true weapons to constrain its Western allies and its rivals. By controlling the oil supply and oil prices, the US tries to draw over allies and at the same time squeeze its rivals. By beating off the challenges and competitions in the political and economic fields, the US will try to maintain its strong position.

The unstable structure influencing the Middle East

External forces	Transition period	Regional conflicts
Colonialism	Basic social ideology	National and religious conflicts
Major countries' intervention	Inheritance of the crisis creation and institutional construction	Competition for national interests
Globalization	National state building	Arab-Israeli conflicts and wars

Figure 1. The unstable structure influencing the Middle East

After the World War II, the Middle East has become the most volatile region which has been frequently inflicted by wars. More than 10 wars have occurred in the region with significant impacts. These wars include Palestine War, the Suez war, the Six Day war, the October War, the war of Lebanon, eight-year Iran-Iraq war, the 10-year Soviet war in Afghanistan before the end of the Cold War, the Gulf War, the war in Afghanistan, Iraq War and Libya War and so on. In the 20th century, there also occurred also about 70 military coups in the region.

Some of these wars or coups are directly waged or participated by major countries, while some were manipulated behind the scenes. But in general, all of these have some to do with the major powers. The turbulent environment and warfare prompt countries in the region to arms races and buying arms, increasing military expenditures, which has caught them in a vicious circle.

Arab-Israeli conflict seems to be a regional conflict, but the founding of the Israel state and the generation and escalation of the conflict without any solutions for 6 decades can all attributed to major countries' constantly meddling and intervening. Arab-Israeli conflict reflects the most fundamental contradiction in the Middle East, exerting a long-term impact on this region.

In the post-Cold War era, the United States regarded itself as the "undoubted power center" and as the only state capable of leading the world. After the outbreak of the Gulf crisis, Bush believed that USA should seize this opportunity to achieve the goal of establishing a new world order.[27]

In the post-Cold War period, the United States had consolidated its leadership in the world order. Waging the Gulf War, Afghanistan war and Iraq war, the US has seen the Middle East as a platform where it could show off its strength and a test field for its new weapons and demonstrate its leadership in "the new world order" in the post-Cold War period.

D. The countries at stake have fallen prey to major powers

Long-term war situation and unrest in the Middle East have severely affected its normal economic development. Some countries have suffered enormous economic losses from direct sanctions or blockades. United States has created the concept of "failed state" which in fact, is a direct product of interventionism. Afghanistan, Iraq, Somalia are all typical examples of this aspect.

After the World War II, major powers have never ceased their interventions in the states in the Middle East. During its 50-years of development period, Afghanistan has suffered from foreign invasions and wars exceeding more than 20 years: firstly, the Soviet Union invasion over 10 years which ended up in failure; secondly, the Afghanistan war launched by the U.S.for more than 10 years, at a cost of 444 billion Dollars, with the soldier casualty up to 1,738.[28] And the US seems determined to increase its military engagement. During the nearly eight-year invasion of Iraq, about 4,500 soldiers were dead and 34,000 wounded and became disabled.[29] Military expenditures have exceeded circa 800 billion Dollars.[30]

---

27 President Bush's State of the Union issued on 29 January1991.
28 "Casualties in Afghanistan", http://icasualties.org.
29 American Military casualties in Iraq, http://antiwar.com/casualties/.
30 "The War in Iraq Cost," http://www.nationalpriorities.org/Cost-of-War/Cost-of-War-3.html, the statistics was made through a dynamic calculation on the website. The war consumption increased by tens of thousands of dollars the moment when the author was checking the figures.

The death toll of the Iraq population has reached nearly a million. However, with so much "sacrifice", the US hasn't been to deliver happiness to the people of Afghanistan and Iraq, but caused them suffer from the bombings, bloodshed, terror and turmoil in these two "failed states" (see Table 1).

Table 1. Global ranking of the 4 failed states

States/Years	2008	2009	2010	2011
Somalia	1	1	1	1
Sudan	2	3	3	3
Iraq	5	6	7	9
Afghanistan	7	7	6	7

Data Sources: Failed States and Detailed Indexes, http://www.foreignpolicy.com/files/fs2011/FSIgrid 2011.swf.

The world's major powers have never ceased their intervention in the Middle East. The US does not bring happiness to the people of Afghanistan and Iraq, but making them suffer from the explosion, bloodshed, terror turmoil, in the two "failed state". Afghanistan and Iran have become "failed states". US attempts to implant the Western values and democracy are not only logically absurd, but also unfeasible in practice. The United States is the only superpower in the world, but it cannot be strong enough to transform a civilization.

E. The rampant violence and social unrest as a consequence

International fight against terrorism have only deteriorated the situation. The root of it lies at its narrow utilitarianism, and also driven by it, the anti-terrorism has become a tool for major powers to achieve their own interests. Major countries adopt quite divergent "anti-terrorism" criteria in their fight against terrorism: oppose terrorist activities threatening their national interests, have no objection to those terrorists to their own advantage or even support them as freedom fighters. What is more, under the guise of "combating terrorism", states even perform an act of terrorism to fight back the hostile states or organizations in order to achieve their own political goals. In the Middle East, this is known as the "state terrorism".

The most difficult task for a state after accomplishing its state building is to establish and consolidate the supremacy of states sovereignty, grant people the citizenship and national identity, construct and popularize the core values of national states. All of these require a relatively long time in history of the development. After smashing the old mechanism, the external intervention, usually causes the lack of structure and institution, the corruption and impotence of government and even the rampant violence and social unrest. Still struggling with the pain from the unrest, Iraq and Afghanistan are just the proofs. Foreign invasion triggers various forms of resistance including the continuing armed struggle and is an important cause of the long-term turmoil and endless violence in the occupied countries. But it must be emphasized that the armed struggle against foreign invasion is just, not terroristic. Although the United States and other Western countries have strong media, tending to confuse the armed struggle against foreign invasion with terrorism, we must strictly distinguish the two behaviors. Actually, the armed struggles against foreign invasion in Palestine, Iraq, Afghanistan can be justified from the legal perspectives.

War and poverty breed further violence. Poverty is not necessarily connected with violence and terrorism. But being trapped and troubled with warfare in poor areas for a long term will inevitably lead to violence and terrorism. So the hope for life can only be brought through the elimination of poverty and wars and by the efforts to sustain the social stability, developing economy and enhance people's living standards. Only by achieving such goals, will it be possible to gradually hinder and eliminate violence and terrorism.

F. Double standards get widespread critique and opposition

The Western powers have often held self-contradictory double standards in their intervention policies and actions, which have become the scales to determine the interests of major powers. Under the intervention and manipulation by the major powers, democracy becomes optional and the human rights can also be freely identified. And the standard is whether the action is in compliance with the interests of the United States and other Western powers.

Iran's nuclear program began in the late 1950s, during the reign of the Shah Pahlavi. At that time, Iran was one of US allies, one of the pivots of the Middle East policy-Twin Pillars Policy. Therefore, Iran's nuclear development program has once gained technological support from the United States, Germany, France and even Israel, and this has made Iran nuclear facilities take shape. After the Islamic revolution in 1979, the nuclear program was interrupted and resumed in 1990s with the support of Russia. After the break of Iranian nuclear crisis in 2003, the IAEA after repeated supervisions and verifications has declared that there was no evidence to show Iran is developing nuclear weapons.

In early December 2007, several US intelligence agencies released a report that also made clear that the nuclear program has not been restarted so far since Iran stopped its nuclear weapons program in 2003. However, for now the United States and other Western countries once claiming the supports for Iran's nuclear program, repeatedly stress that Iran's nuclear program has posed a serious threat to regional security and world peace and constantly launch sanctions against Iran, even resorting to the threat of force.

The US and other Western countries have made a shift in their attitude from the initial assistance and policy support to oppose, prohibit and even threatened Iran with military strikes, which demonstrates a 180-degree change in their political stand.

The inherent logic is that, allies can freely develop nuclear programs, but opponents are never allowed. In fact, the discrepancies between Iran and Western countries are not merely reflected on the nuclear issues. The core of the contradictions lies in the differences in their ideologies and the distinct security concepts. The US and its Western allies imposed tough sanctions against Iran, while conceding on the nuclear program of Israel, which has made Israel, the only state possessing nuclear power in the Middle East.

And this has are stimulated the Middle East states to think about developing the nuclear weapons since the Middle East cannot become a "nuclear-free zone".

In the Middle East, the human rights situation in Israel could not be worser. capturing at random, shooting Palestinians (in the name of combating terrorism). News reporters who have lost their lives in the muzzle of Israeli soldiers are more than any in the other regions of the world. But the United States has never really condemned Israel (perfunctory when has to).

G. Aggravation of the conflict between the Western powers and the Middle East

After the "9/11" Event, the American public and the media wondered, "Why do they hate us?" But, the general public in the US have never imagined another question which is frequently raised by the people of the Middle East, "Why do they hate us, as is always the case". In fact, these two observations are the true reflection of the general relationship between the US and Middle East and not of the differences in their understanding on some specific issues.

For a long time, the US government is pushing its hegemony in the world, and claiming itself as the world leader. And with such a "big nation mentality", many Americans have bred a sense of superiority (this is not the big nation mentality in the general sense, but one as superpower). Driven by this mentality, many American citizens subconsciously feel proud, assume a sense of mission and superiority over those people living in any other country of the world. However, security problems in this most powerful country of the world are also the most intractable ones. US embassies in the Middle East and Africa are the embassies which are protected with the most strict security measures in the world, heavily guarded and equipped with the side of the road made of cement and the fence for isolation. Americans working or travelling in the Middle East do not have a sense of security and many American scholars also admit those insecure feelings for themselves, they dare not to go to the Middle East alone.

The U.S.Middle East policy in itself has some deficiencies. The US bases its foreign policy starting always from its own narrow national interests, does everything to weaken and control other countries so as to strengthen its hegemonic status and policies. Different from this, China's foreign policy, generally attaches importance to mutual respect, mutual benefit and win-win policies, which is why the Chinese are often welcomed in the Middle East and African countries.

III. Conclusion

Many scholars, thinkers and officials in the United States believe that, the United States is in pursuit of democracy, happiness and freedom, rather than hegemonic power. But the US leaders and government officers are more clear on the issue, who claim that, without a power based authority, it will be impossible to protect democracy, happiness and freedom. Therefore, the United States always seeks hegemony and try its best to maintain its hegemonic position. Clyde Prestowitz also admitted in his book: the US is the biggest rogue state.[31]

The United States recruits and chooses its allies, according to its own strategic needs, at the same time coaches and treats its allies in a skillful manner with blatant defiance. And regarding surrendering hostile countries, it launches various kinds of interventions.

---

31 The Director of US Economic Strategy Institute Clyde Prestowitz published a series works to reflect on the US diplomacy, a major book of him is "A Rogue Nation: American Unilateralism and the Failure of Good Intentions". He has argued that the US is the biggest rogue state.

In 2009, US President Barack Obama said in a speech at the UN General Assembly "Democracy cannot be imposed on any nation from the outside. Each society must search for its own path, and no path is perfect. Each country will pursue a path rooted in the culture of its people and in its past traditions. And I admit that America has too often been selective in its promotion of democracy. But that does not weaken our commitment; it only reinforces it. There are basic principles that are universal; there are certain truths which are self-evident and the United States of America will never waver in our efforts to stand up for the right of people everywhere to determine their own destiny."[32]

The author believes that Obama has hit the nail on the head and his remark is fabulous. But regrettably, the United States has never acted as Obama advertised or spoke, instead it always conducts the opposite approaches. The United States and Western powers have never ceased their interventions and meddling in the Middle East region. In the post-Cold War era, the United States and Western powers have hastily launched a number of changes and adjustments in the Middle East, or even launched several direct wars. On the other side, the application of Internet technology and the new media has broken the national boundaries in the traditional sense, made the world a "global village" more closely connecting all countries, we think that all these challenge the conventional diplomacy and conventional international politics.

Simultaneously, the Internet especially IT technology has become a new warfare in the hand major powers states to develop neo-interventionism.

The United States still plays a "leading" role in the Middle East. After the recent political crisis—Arab Spring—in the Middle East, the US and other Western countries have adopted some selective interventions, i.e. sheltering allies, subverting the regime of its foes such as the Libya, continuing to exert pressures on Syria… all of which demonstrated the capacity of US to control and influence the Middle East. It must be noted that the United States cannot "dominate" the Middle East. The new governments being formed in Tunisia, Egypt (Morsi government), Libya and other countries may not challenge or disturb the US interests, but they will never blindly follow the orders of the United States. In order to achieve its global strategy, United States has taken various measures to safeguard its strategic interests in the Middle East. But no matter they are strategic objectives of the US

---

32 Obama's speech in UN General Assembly 2009, http://www.whitehouse.gov/the-press-office/remarks-president-united-nations-general-assembly.

or the specific acts or operations to achieve partial goals, both go against the interests of most countries in Middle East. Therefore, we can say that in the region the struggles of control and counter-control, between the US and Middle East countries will be a long-term phenomenon, which implies a "repeated gaming relation" between the two sides.

Major powers of the world exert global influences, this is much true especially for the United States, possessing huge powers. Any progress or introduction of a benevolent manner by the U.S.regarding global affairs will contribute much to the well-being of humanity, while conversely erred acts or discourteous behaviors of the US will cause mankind suffer a lot.

Coercive Diplomacy and the Issue of International Conflict Management — Case Analysis of Iran Nuclear Crisis

Zhou Shixin[1]

Since 2003, the abundant complicated issues surrounding Iran's nuclear program have become a hot topic in the Middle East and posed important challenges to certain interests of the world's major powers and international community. The dynamic power game and dealings between Iran and the international community have repeatedly gone through ups and downs, without reaching any ultimate solution until now. Even more severely, such conflicts have a tendency to deteriorate the circumstances around the globe.

With its nuclear program, Iran is regarded as a challenger to the existing global nuclear non-proliferation regime, thus the international community aims to hinder Iran's nuclear ambitions. However, Iran believes and argues that its nuclear program is essential for its energy needs and for the development of its national economy. Iran also believes that their nuclear program does not oppose the rules of the global nuclear non-proliferation regime, thus argues that the demand for the abandonment of its uranium enrichment efforts is just a coarse interference infringing its sovereignty. In the current situation, the settlement of the issues surrounding Iran's nuclear program still proceeds through diplomatic channels, and each involved .party tries to compel the adversary to accept its policy proposals through diplomacy. The prospect of the coercive diplomacy lies in whether both sides are able to enhance the effectiveness of coercive diplomacy.

---

1 Assistant Researcher in Foreign Policy Research Institute at the Shanghai Institute for International Studies.

Coercive diplomacy as a conception is essentially a diplomatic strategy, one that relies on the threat of force rather than the use of force. If force must be used to strengthen diplomatic efforts at persuasion, it is employed in an exemplary manner, in the form of quite limited military action, to demonstrate resolution and willingness to escalate to high levels of military action if necessary.

Coercive diplomacy can be more clearly described as "a political-diplomatic strategy that aims to influence an adversary's will or incentive structure. It is a strategy that combines threats of force, and, if necessary, the limited and selective use of force in discrete and controlled increments, in a bargaining strategy that includes positive inducements.

The aim is to induce an adversary to comply with one's demands, or to negotiate the most favorable compromise possible, while simultaneously managing the crisis to prevent unwanted military escalation.[2]

I. Theoretical aspects of coercive diplomacy

The concept of coercive diplomacy has emerged from the reflections on the facts where threat of force (deterrence) was employed to keep adversaries from acting. The term compellence initially coined by American scholar Thomas C. Schelling. According to Schelling's definition: "it (compellence) usually involves initiating action that can cease, or become harmless, only if the opponent responds." Schelling distinguishes compellence from deterrence and argues that "Since physical force is often employed to harm another state until the later abides by the coercers demands. It is important to recognize the difference between two types of threats, compellent threats and deterrent threats. [and]since deterrence is merely passive and static while compellence (coercion) is too active and dynamic, a new term completely distinct from the above two is necessary". Schelling also argues that "the threat that compels rather than deters often requires that the punishment be administered until the other acts, rather than if he acts". Deterrence, the better known of the two, is the threat to use force in retaliation if the opponent takes a certain action. In the words of Robert Art, "its purpose is to prevent something undesirable from happening". Schelling elaborates that the difference between the two types of threats is the "difference between inducing inaction [deterrence] and making someone perform [compellence]". Many Western scholars including Art, R. Pape, and L. Freedman, assume that compellence should be more difficult to achieve

---

2 Alexander L. George and William E. Simons, eds., The Limits of Coercive Diplomacy, 2nd ed., London & Boulder: Westview Press, 1994, p. 7.

than deterrence, Schelling affirms this idea by saying that "[in a] world without uncertainty... [i]t is easier to deter than to compel." Coercion is the power to hurt, not the one directly exerted to hurt. The potential violence involved may influence others' choices and make adversaries obey or compromise.[3]

R. Pape evaluates the Gulf War as a failure for a coercive military strategy of decapitation, but it was a success for a coercive military strategy of denial. Therefore, successful coercion is not achieved by wars. The coercer does not resort to violence though it is capable of doing so.[4]

Clearly, deterrence and compellence are two types of coercion, or two sides of the same coin. Both concepts depend on risks, threats, and choices. The coercer, whether seeking to deter or compel, is exploiting the potential risks the opponent faces in resisting the coercer's threats. Lawrence Freedman, argues that the coercer bases coercion "on the exploitation of threats and latent violence," what is yet to come unless the target complies.

Lawrence Freedman also suggests that the strategic employment of coercive measures, which are performed thoughtfully, purposely and publically to influence others' strategic decisions. General demands from Iraq, such as "Don't invade Kuwait," appear to fall clearly in the deterrence camp, whereas those calls to withdraw seem like compellence. The in-between areas are more ambiguous. "Don't go further" involves both stopping an existing action and avoiding a future one—both immediate deterrence and coercion. Moreover, a call to withdraw carries with it an implicit demand not to engage in the offense again and affects the credibility of the deterrence call to not invade Kuwait in the future."[5]

Another scholar argues that coercive diplomacy is a tool used by a state to undo the actions of its adversary that go against its own interests and a tool to persuade adversaries to cease their destructive actions.[6]

Moreover, coercive diplomacy also imposes the will of a state on others, which, if put in another words, embodies the inherent meanings of deterrence and compellence and highlights the use of threat to compel opponents into some actions. Deterrence is to stop the actions that has yet to take

---
3 Thomas C. Schelling, Arms and Influence, New Haven: Yale University Press, 1966, p. 3.
4 Robert Pape, Bombing to Win: Air Power and Coercion in War, Ithaca, NY: Cornell University Press, 1996, pp. 12-15.
5 Lawrence Freedman, Strategic Coercion: Concepts and Cases, New York: Oxford University Press, 1998, p. 3.
6 Alexander L. George, Forceful Persuasion: Coercive Diplomacy as an Alternative to War, Washington, D.C.: United States Institute of Peace Press, 1991, p. 5.

place, and compellence includes attempts and acts to prompt opponents to take some actions to change the status quo. Deterrence is achieved through stopping opponents from taking actions, but compellence is to compel opponents into actions by threats.[7]

Deterrence is passive while compellence is active.[8]

Deterrence is practiced when a state clearly issues a specific threat of using military force against an opponent. Compellence is to deter an opponent to change the status quo with respect to a specific issue in dispute by using military force.[9]

Deterrence is to stop the actions that have already been taken by opponents, and even to restore the situation to the former.[10]

Coercive diplomacy attempts to overcome the logical deficiencies in deterrence and compellence and to fulfill its potential strategic advantages. In terms of deterrence, the sense of time is blurred and static. The party on deterrence tries to create an environment where the opponents don't dare to take any deterring actions, and then wait quietly and timelessly. When we discuss compellence, some punitive measures will be put into force within a period of time. Deterrence indicates that the signals of threat are enough,

but compellence means once the conditions offered cannot be met, threats will probably become reality. In general, the goal of compellence is to change the opponents' behaviors, and it requires active actions of the opponents. Under such circumstances, compellence is not only more complex than deterrence, but also makes easier for opponents to regard it as a shame.[11] [12]

Therefore, the coercive diplomacy performer may constantly signal threats to its opponents, and make them realize the enhanced likelihood of threatening by increasing pressure on them so that the opponent will make the required responses. Therefore, coercive diplomacy can be regarded as the tool employed in the early stage when states deal with their conflicts. A

---

7 Thomas C. Schelling, Arms and Influence, New Haven: Yale University Press, 1966, pp. 3-4, 76.
8 Thomas C. Schelling, The Strategy of Conflict, p. 196; Arms and Influence, pp. 69-72.
9 Walter Peterson, "Deterrence and Compellence: A Critical Assessment of Conventional Wisdom," International Studies Quarterly, Summer 1986, p. 270.
10 Bruce W. Jentleson, "The Reagan Administration and Coercive Diplomacy: Restraining More than Remaking Government," Political Science Quarterly, Vol.106, No.1, 1991, p. 57.
11 Lawrence Freedman, Strategic Coercion: Concepts and Cases, Oxford: Oxford University Press, 1998, p. 54.
12 Robert J. Art, "To What Ends Military Power," International Security, Vol.4, No.4, Spring 1980, p. 10.

state's intervening in the international conflicts can be shown at three levels: coercive diplomacy, suppression by force and war. Poyueh Wang Hsu says that "Coercive diplomacy has several defensive objectives. Firstly, the aim may be limited to merely stopping the action of the adversary. Secondly, aim is the reversal of what the adversary has already accomplished. Then the aim is the cessation of the adversary's hostile behavior by demanding for a change in the composition of the adversary's government or in the nature of the regime."[13]

Coercive diplomacy is a policy with a combination of diplomatic negotiation and threat of force, and coercer regards threat of force as a tool to restore peace.[14] Threat of force is not only a tool to deter but also an instrument to tentatively compel the opponents to stop their aggression.[15] Any coercer hopes to seek out a peaceful solution to some severe international conflicts. For example, coercer demonstrates its resolution, provides credibility for threat of force and tries to dissuade opponent from aggression not merely to demand by exerting pressures on the opponents to some extent.[16]

Features of coercive diplomacy

Coercive diplomacy has several features: in terms of its goal and intention, it implies compellence and means more than deterrence. As for its contents, it mainly focuses on some traditional political, military, economic and cultural security aspects-. For the means of the implementation, coercive diplomacy is achieved through threat of force, sanctions, diplomatic pressures, ultimatum and so forth. Themajor coercers include state actors and non-state actors such as international organizations. Additionally, the components of coercive diplomacy entail demanding a request, setting a scenario, tempting or punishing. The factors affecting the decision of coercive diplomacy are the contrast of the overall strengths between the coercer and its adversary, the effectiveness and efficiency of foreign decision-making regimes, the attitude of international community and the recognition of security threats.[17]

---

13 Poyueh Wang Hsu, "US Coercive Diplomacy in the North Korean Crisis: From the Crime-and-Punishment Approach to Diplomatic Give-and-Take, 1993-1994," Tamkang Journal of International Affairs, Vol.9, No.4, 2006, pp. 56-57.
14 Alexander L. George, Forceful Persuasion: Coercive Diplomacy as an Alternative to War, Washington, D.C.: United States Institute of Peace Press, 1991, IX.
15 Ibid., p.5.
16 Alexander L. George and William E. Simons, The Limits of Coercive Diplomacy, Boulder: Westview, 1994, p.10.
17 Thomas C. Schelling, Arms and Influence, New Haven, CT: Yale University Press, 1966; Robert Jervis, The Meaning of the Nuclear Revolution: Statecraft and the Prospect of

However, the transmission and the reception of the information can only be achieved through diplomatic channels. The core of coercive diplomacy is diplomacy not coercion. Diplomacy serves for coercion and embodies the functions of coercion in the process of coercive diplomacy.

Coercive diplomacy highlights diplomatic negotiation as the primary coercive mean. Without abandoning the threat of force, coercer obliges its opponent to reach the conditions it offers. Coercive diplomacy is a combination between coercive goals and diplomatic means. With the employment of forces as its back-up plan, coercer tends to influence, demand, persuade or even tempt its opponent through diplomatic channels to satisfy its needs. Coercive diplomacy weighs the communication between states through diplomatic channels. Coercive diplomacy also prevents coercer from overly paying attention to the costs and benefits of their behaviors may lead to without considering whether their opponents will respond and how the response will be made. Coercive diplomacy helps to promote the interaction between the two sides in the conflicts and averts the disadvantageous situation where the coercer takes unilateral risks in carrying out its strategies. Hence, coercive diplomacy contributes to the settlement of disputes. Although attaching importance to threat of force, coercive diplomacy lays more emphasis on the smooth transmission of message. It also emphasizes on the assurance that the coercer is able to demand its adversary to make some commitments and take some actions to ease the tension between them and reduce the intensity of the conflict.

The judgment of the effectiveness of coercive diplomacy depends on whether the opponent is willing to make concession eventually and whether the coercer reaches its goals as it is expected. To be more specific, coercive diplomacy primarily produces the following results. Firstly, when adversaries initiatively agree the conditions offered by the coercers, the coercive diplomacy ends and succeeds. Secondly, when adversaries are obliged to negotiate with coercers, there are several possibilities: adversaries are forced to completely act at the will of coercers and at this point, coercers score total success. Alternatively, by bargaining, both sides partially make concession. Thirdly, if adversaries refuse to respond to the demand of coercers and coercers fail to force adversaries to respond, the coercive diplomacy will fail. Lastly, when adversaries adopt strong confrontational policies and escalate the conflict, which probably leads to the outbreak of a war, in such context, coercive diplomacy also fails.

Armageddon, Ithaca, NY: Cornell University Press, 1989; Patrick M. Morgan, Deterrence: A Conceptual Analysis, Beverly Hills, CA: Sage Press, 1977; Keith Payne, Deterrence in the Second Nuclear Age, Lexington: University Press of Kentucky, 1996.

II. The coercive diplomacy in international conflict management

International system is the outcome of a series of intentional integrations between traditional major states, and it reflects the interests of major states and their hope to sustain such international system to their advantage in most cases. The anarchic feature of international system has determined not only the principle of sovereignty of equal states but also the structural contradictions due to the differences in national powers between states. Once the structure of the existing international system encounters dramatic changes with the rise of emerging states and the decline of traditional major sates, the state actors in the system will correspondingly adjust their strategic demands significantly. In the context, emerging states will be regarded as threats to the existing world order and challengers for the international system.[18] International conflicts arise when both sides surface the potential and static contradictions.[19] International conflicts and disputes become common phenomenon as international relations deteriorate.

In the international system, state actors that challenge and responding constitute important parts of coercive diplomacy. In coercive diplomacy, challenger and responder are the opposing sides. What is worth mentioning is that the identity of actors is not unilateral and absolute.[20] Challenging-responding model helps to make a description and an analysis of the process of coercive diplomacy. When a state or state group attempts to sacrifice another state or state group to establish authority, the threatened state or state group will passively take actions to respond. Such response will be reversely regarded as a threat to the state that utters threat first.[21] Pressed with the demand of challenger, responder may take overreaction and have a tilt-for-tat demand on challenger, prompting the challenger to abandon its previous demands. So here is the reciprocal challenge. Challengers will adopt certain strategic procedures and expect adversaries to respond. If I adopt plan A, what kind of response my adversary will make? By analyzing this, challenger proactively comes up with countermeasures against adversary's

---

18 A. F. K. Organsky, World Politics, New York: Alfred A. Knopf, 1958; A. F. K. Organsky and Jacek Kugler, The War Ledger, Chicago: University of Chicago Press, 1980; David Dapkin and William R. Thompson, "Power Transition, Challenge and the (Re)Emergence of China," International Interactions, Vol.29, No.4, 2003, pp. 317-321.
19 Quincy Wright, "The Escalation of International Conflict," Journal of Conflict Resolution, Vol.9, No.4, 1965, pp. 434-435.
20 Frank C. Zagare and D. Marc Kilgour, Perfect Deterrence, Cambridge: Cambridge University Press, 2000, p. 181.
21 Andrew M. Scott, "A Challenge Response Theory of International Relations," American Behavioural Scientist, Vol.1, 1958, pp. 24-26.

responses. In this context, challenger does not intentionally break the existing international system but only hopes to promote its national interests by reforming the system. Challenger may also be the revolutionary in the international system, and thinks that there are no needs to sustain the stability of the current international system and the maximization of its national interests can be achieved only by breaking the current system. Challengers may make strategic requirements that the current international system cannot meet, and arise strong responses from the potential beneficiaries, through which drastic changes in international configuration may occur. Under such circumstances, the coercive diplomacy has to be changed and addressing the disputes by forces may be taken into consideration.[22]

The security dilemma has demonstrated a crisis of confidence due to the uncertainty of both sides about the strength and intention of each other. Such crisis intensify arms races and results in the escalation of conflicts. Afraid of being aggressed by other states, every state gathers its strength and pursues authority in all endeavors to ensure its own security. At this point, the other side who is inevitably feeling unsafe, will also tries to improve itself in case of emergency. However, this situation would intensify the already existed worries about the security between the two sides.[23] The fear among states is real and natural. Even if challenger has no intention to harm, the other may misinterpret the intention. Under such circumstances, both sides regard the other's behaviors as hostile and irrational, and refuse to make promise of mutual security.[24]

Due to the chaotic environment of the international system, every actor is considered not only as a potential threat to others, but also an enemy in reality. No actor is aware that its behaviors are seen as a threat. But it believes that the only possible explanation for the hostility of the other side is its aggression.[25]

The main objective of the international conflict management is to ease or eliminate the security dilemma. Lack of authority in the international system and symmetry of national strength between states lead to a security dilemma that is difficult to eliminate due to the differences in security, benefits and recognition between states. An important function of international conflict

---

22 Richard Smoke, War: Controlling Escalation, London: Harvard University Press, 1977, p. 27.
23 John H. Herz, "Idealist Internationalism and Security Dilemma," World Politics, Vol.2, No.2, 1950, pp.157-158; John H.Herz, Political Realism and Political Idealism, Chicago: Chicago University Press, 1951, p.3.
24 Herbert Butterfield, History and Human Relations, London: Collins, 1951, p. 21.
25 Robert Jervis, Perception and Misperception in International Politics. Tran. Qin Yaqing. Beijing. World Affairs Press. 2003, pp. 68-69.

management is promoting mutual trust between countries, reducing false judgments and eliminating misunderstandings. Therefore, the main forms of international conflict management are diplomatic negotiations in which the parties to the conflicts clarify their positions, make demands and seek solutions to the problems by mutual agreements. Considering the international war as the ultimate mean of settling international conflicts, foreign policy makers tend to use it as the last resort to resolve international conflicts. International conflicts reflect two main trends: the escalation and the ease. Conflict escalation marks qualitative and quantitative changes in conflict relations. Such strategic steps not only intensify the degree of conflicts, but also change the nature of them.[26]

Conflict escalation signifies the changes in the conflict structure towards a vertical growth, rather than the linear and the horizontal direction. It likes the ladders with different height, rather than a "conflict life cycle".[27]

The potential function of conflict escalation is that the managers of the international conflicts try to exploit opponents' fear about the disasters resulting from the conflict escalation in order to force them to succumb.[28] And easing the conflict does not mean that the conflict is resolved but implies a prolonged conflict and reduced cost. It creates a benign environment where political parties can settle the conflicts. International conflict managers by threat of force or diplomatic negotiations, consciously control the process of escalation and mitigation of conflicts, put the opponents under the control and determine the opponents' policy choices in international conflicts, through which, conflict managers will exploit the most favorable situation for management.

Conflict management is a way to deal with conflicts rationally, through which, parties take further actions to change opponent's behaviors. State actors in international conflict management tend to make rational choices, because of two basic principles: to maximize the benefits and to minimize risks. In international conflicts, state actors prone to make strategic decisions on the ground of realism in order to achieve the maximization of the relative benefits. What's more, state actors attempt to maximize its own benefits and minimize the benefits of its components thus keeping the biggest

---

26 Dean Pruitt and Jeffrey Z. Rubin and Sung Hee Kim, Social conflict: Escalation, Stalemate and Settlement, New York: McGraw Hill, 1994, p.69.
27 Michael S. Lund, Preventing Violent Conflicts: A Strategy for Preventive Diplomacy, Washington D.C.: United States Institute for Peace, 1996.
28 Lisa J. Carlson, "A Theory of Escalation and International Conflict," Journal of Conflict Resolution, Vol.39, No.3, 1995, p. 53; Liu Junbo. Introductory Discussion on Conflicts Management. International Forum, NO.1 2007, pp. 38.

gap of strength between the two sides and maintaining its strategic advantages. Meanwhile, state actors also try to take whatever means to minimize the risks involved in the conflicts, in order to avoid the negative effects of international conflicts that may arise. Of course, the state actor may also adopt the new liberal institutionalism as their strategy, trying to harness the power of international mechanisms and international organizations for binding its opponent's behaviors, protecting and safeguarding its own strategic interests. Because the international mechanisms propose relative equality, state actors, could merely achieve absolute benefits by using international mechanisms to resolve international conflicts. In other words, state actors have to allow other states to obtain the corresponding benefits when maximizing their own interests,. From the evolution of the international system, the strong countries tend to adopt more realistic strategies, while weak countries are more willing to accept the concept of neo-liberalism. Coercive diplomacy is an important tool to deal with international conflicts. All parties involved in international conflicts, especially the conflict parties, often threaten each other and try to force the other side to yield to their political will. This situation helps to create a strategic environment for coercive diplomacy. Before the escalation of international conflicts, those countries who want to achieve maximum benefits will not resort to military force at first, in order to solve problems. However, they are in a demanding position based on their own requirements, they demand that the other side act or cancel the actions that might threaten their own interests, and all these are achieved through diplomatic channels. In other words, during the process, the diplomatic request usually implies coercion. Even more severely, if failing to meet the declared demands, the other party may be politically isolated, economically sanctioned and even encounter military strikes. International conflicts could escalate into international crisis, during which enormous diplomatic pressures will be exerted on the rival side. But that does not mean coercive diplomacy is a catalyst to the escalation of the international conflicts. On the contrary, an appropriate coercive diplomacy is likely to buffer the conflicts.

Coercive diplomacy is not a one-way strategic game but an important means to buffer or intensify the international conflicts. Coercion and diplomacy are both bidirectional. Instead of resulting in the shutdown of international conflicts, coercion and diplomacy coach that the international conflicts repeatedly encounter ups and downs. Coercion and diplomacyalso promote the emergence of new situations as results of the continuing development of various factors. Therefore, it is required that the parties involved in international conflicts to maintain a relative balance between coercion and diplomacy when resorting to coercive diplomacy for their own strategic goals. Pure coercion easily leads to conflict, and pure diplomacy cannot solve problems. Coercion through diplomatic channels open the possibility of mutual understanding and heighten the expectation about the potential threats, through which, policy space is kept as large as possible in order to resolve conflicts.

III. The coercive diplomacy in Iran nuclear issues

Since the outbreak of Iran nuclear issue in 2003, the U.S. has firmly asserted that the ultimate goal of Iran's nuclear program is to develop nuclear weapons and threaten the security in Middle East since Iran possesses abundant in oil resources, which rules out the necessity of developing nuclear program in Iran. To prevent Iran from further undermining the strategic interests of the U.S.in Middle East, the U.S. has significantly strengthened its efforts to constrain Iran and compel Iran to abandon its nuclear program in multiple ways.[29]

After rounds of negotiation and argument, Iran and international community endeavored to address the issue to enable the best interests of involved parties. The U.S.and Israel are in the camp that strongly oppose the development of nuclear program by Iran. Although, the UK, France and German also object Iran's nuclear program, they rather put strong emphasis on Iran's termination of its uranium enrichment program, and argue that this would hinder the likelihood of Iran's developing of nuclear program. Sharing similar ideas, China and Russia have both underlined Iran's rights to develop its nuclear program for peaceful aims. The actions performed both by the U.S. and Iran with respect to the nuclear program, embody some fundamental features of coercive diplomacy. Firstly, there is always a possibility of military confrontation. After the Cold War, due to the lack of balancing world powers against it, the U.S. has lost its patience in negotiation and compromise. Resorting to armed forces has become the shortcut way for the U.S.to realize its strategic goals. All of which, however, has on the contrary lead to the failure of the coercive diplomacy. For the U.S., properly dealing with Iran nuclear program would make a breakthrough in the status quo. Since international community will not tolerate the proliferation of nuclear weapons in general, once Iran is identified as proliferator of nuclear weapons, some measures will be taken into consideration as in the case of the air strikes against Gaddafi regime and the voluntary alliance

---

29 Kathleen J. McInnis, "Extended Deterrence: The U.S. Credibility Gap in the Middle East," The Washington Quarterly, Vol.28, No.3, Summer 2005, pp. 169-186.

being forged to forcefully change the regime in Iran. Since 2006, the U.S.in the name of the International Atomic Energy Agency has one-sidedly and unfavorably reported on Iranian nuclear program. Security Council of the UN has passed a series of resolutions for imposing economic sanctions against Iran and banned its enrichment of uranium. Furthermore, allied with other European states, the U.S. also imposed unilateral economic sanctions against Iran. On 1 December 2011, the U.S. repeated its economic sanctions and was followed by EU.

Secondly, the emphasis is laid on the coalition of powers to build up pressure on Iran. During the process of implementing coercive diplomacy, the U.S. once tentatively established an alliance so as to enhance the credibility and intensity of its military threats.[30]

It is clear for the U.S., its reliance on the military forces of its own may also lead to accomplishment of its strategic goals. However, some political risks are there due to unilateral actions by the U.S. For example, the lack of international legitimacy and justice, and the high war costs America may pay. Once the actions end up with failure, no state would like to offset the loss of the U.S. What's more, the tug of war will contain the U.S.'ambition to implement its global hegemony strategies. Additionally, anti-war emotion in the public is probably bred weakening America's hegemonic will. Therefore, even though a big part of the U.S. military activities bear the characteristic of unilateralism, the U.S.will not let itself isolated.[31] Meanwhile, many states that participate in the process, enhances the effectiveness of coercive diplomacy.[32] The U.S, not only aligns itself with the UK, France and Germany to create pressure on Iran, but also secures the legitimacy of any of its actions to stop Iran from developing nuclear program. To realize its strategic goals in the Iran issue and force Iran to give up its nuclear plan, the U.S. endeavors to draw all parties to its side: China, Russia, IAEA, Board of Governors, other member states, and also the non-permanent member states of the Security Council of the UN.

---

30 Robert O. Keohane, "Multilateral Coercive Diplomacy: Not 'Myths of Empire'," Duke University, November 2002, http://www.ciaonet.org/special_section/iraq/papers/ker02/ker02.html; Branislav L. Slantchev, "National Security Strategy: Credible Commitments in Deterrence and Compellence," February 7, 2008, http://polisci.ucsd.edu/~bslantch/courses/nss/lectures/09-credible-commitments.pdf.

31 David C. Hendrickson, "Preemption, Unilateralism, and Hegemony: The American Tradition?" Orbis, Vol. 50, No. 2, 2006, pp. 273-287.

32 Robert J. Art and Patrick M. Cronin, The United States and Coercive Diplomacy, Washington, D.C.: United States Institute of Peace Press, 2004, pp. 275-278.

Coercion takes on different forms: indirect coercion, extended coercion, counter-coercion and so forth. Indirect coercion indicates the situation where coercion is performed by the party behind the scene, concentrates to drive its allies to enforce coercive measures. As for extended coercion, though sharing a lot of similarities with indirect coercion, it puts more emphasis on increasing pressure by the primary coercer on the subordinate coercer and encouraging the subordinate coercer to take coercive actions. Concerning the counter-coercion, the target state facing coercion will consciously make response with measures that can likely subdue or even eliminate the effects of coercion on itself. Judging from the current development, the coercive measures adopted by UK, France and Germany against Iran are more likely originates from the U.S. impact on them rather than pursuing their own interests. Under the diplomatic efforts by UK, France and Germany, Paris Agreement was reached. On November 22, 2004, Iran abandoned all of its activities that is related to the enrichment of uranium. However, UK, France and Germany were still required by the U.S. to adopt coercive measures against Iran's nuclear program. Due to Iran's non-performance regarding the Paris Agreement and Mahmoud Ahmadinejad, the representative of neoconservatives coming to power in Iran, the tensions between the U.S. and Iran on the nuclear issues are on the verge of breaking out. As a result of it, on August 2005, Iran tore the IAEA seals that barred Natanz nuclear facility and announced the recovery of uranium enrichment plant. Thirdly, it has shown some obstacles and defects in diplomatic information transmission and flaws in the communication channels.[33]

Although coercive diplomacy requires the targeted state to respond according to the will of the coercer state, it in itself features strong defense nature and underlines the importance of negotiation and even compromise.[34]

If the goals are realized by armed forces, the coercive diplomacy is switched into a blackmailing strategy. Since the U.S. did not have normal diplomatic relations with Iran for a long term, the political messages with respect to Iran issues cannot be transmitted successfully from the U.S.to Iran, which is why the relations based on mutual trust was not be possible to be established between the two.

During the Six-party talks, always being in a passive position, Iran could not negotiate the issue with the U.S. on equal terms. Although China and Russia remained neutral and acted as a buffer between Iran and the U.S., the

---

33 Alexander L. George and Richard Smoke, Deterrence in American Foreign Policy: Theory and Practice, New York & London: Columbia University Press, 1974, p. 608.
34 Alexander George, Forceful Persuasion: Coercive Diplomacy as an Alternative to War, p. 5.

lack of diplomacy between the two sides (US-Iran) has inevitably resulted in disastrous effects.

Iran's nuclear issues have experienced twists and turns for a long time, which includes too much uncertainty. In 2003, Iran's nuclear problem raised extensive concerns, and Iran shifted its role from a challenger for global nuclear non-proliferation regime to a responder. Under the huge pressure from international community, Iran had to cooperatively admit that its nuclear program is just for peaceful use. To eradicate the skepticism that was prevalent in the international community in Iran's enrichment facility at Natanz, Iran signed the Nuclear Nonproliferation Treaty on December 18, 2003. With this treaty, Iran agreed to stop its enrichment of uranium temporarily and accepted supervisions by the IAEA inspectors. Although the international environment for developing its nuclear program looks negative, Iran, under the mounting pressure from the major powers such as the U.S. and EU states, has not surrendered and has a strong political will to act against the Western countries. Iran continued its enrichment of uranium and has made some progress with the enrichment level-it announced reaching 3.5 percent on 9 April 2006. This has made a solid foundation for its nuclear fuel production which is suitable for industrial scale.[35] On May 2 of that year, Iran has achieved even higher uranium enrichment level of -4.8 percent.[36] On 29 January 2008, Iran has started to install the advanced centrifuge (IR-2) technology that has speeded up the process of enrichment.[37] The total weight of the Uranium Hexafluoride processed has reached 348 tons.[38] In December 2010, according to IAEA, Iran has achieved self-sufficiency in precipitating the "yellow cake"[39], an important mixture of uranium oxides in nuclear industry.

Shortly after Iran's announcement of achieving advanced centrifuge technology innovated by Iran itself for enriching uranium on 15 February 2012, Iran started to apply this brand-new technology to the enrichment facility in Natanz. There are political disagreements and divergence of interests among the non-proliferation camp, i.e. between the U.S. and Israel, the UK, France and Germany, China and Russia. Iran attempts to take advantage of

---

35 Nazila Fathi, David E. Sanger and William J. Broad, "Iran Says It Is Making Nuclear Fuel, Defying U.N.", New York Times, April 12, 2006.
36 "Iran Achieves Higher Uranium Enrichment Level", Agence France Presse, May 2, 2006.
37 The Director General, "GOV/2008/4", IAEA, February 22, 2008, p. 8.
38 The Director General, "GOV/2008/59", IAEA, November 19, 2008, p. 3.
39 Yellowcake (also called urania) is a type of uranium concentrate powder obtained from leach.. Modern yellowcake typically contains 70% to 90% triuranium octoxide (U3O8) by weight.

these discrepancies in the non-proliferation camp and in this way reduce the negative impacts resulting from the outside pressures through balancing tactics. Obama administration has sought for direct negotiations with Iran since taking office.

After Obama administration ended up with failure, the U.S. changed its attitude drastically and become tough on the Iran issue. Driven by the U.S., the Security Council of the UN passed the Resolution Nr. 1929 on June 9, 2010, which imposed more strict sanctions against Iran. Iranian citizens' march to protest British Embassy in Iran on October 29, 2011, has led to the recalling of ambassadors of both sides, and the diplomatic relations between the two countries has sharply deteriorated. This situation has brought more perils in the international conflict which is another result of resolving nuclear issues through coercion.

In terms of the international conflict management, on the one hand, Iran is able to consciously swift its status and role from challenger to a responder country and control the escalation of conflicts at a critical time. The management of the tension has brought more opportunities and offered time for Iran to use its resources, and Iran enhanced its ability to independently engage in nuclear research. On the other hand, the U.S. and European countries have made relentless efforts to increase the tension, which would generate pressure on Iran materially and psychologically and weaken the will of Iran on this issue. Under the concerted efforts by the international community, Iranian nuclear issues tends to become more complex. With Iran's increasing power to resist external forces, the U.S's costs to strike and hinder Iran has increased greatly. What's more, the U.S.' withdrawal of its troops from Afghanistan has also boosted Iran's confidence in developing its nuclear program.

Iran has always emphasized the peaceful use of its nuclear program when struggling with the non-proliferation camp in the international community. In terms of the coercive diplomacy on the Iran issue, Iran is both a challenger and a responder state. Iran has challenged the bottom line of the global nuclear non-proliferation regime. All member states concerned have the desire to regulate Iran's behaviors in its nuclear program, restrict the risks of Iran's nuclear plan and ask Iran to adopt proper measures to eradicate the skepticism in international community, in due time. Due to the asymmetry of power between the struggling sides, Iran generally takes defensive tactics. With flexible policies and measures Iran strives to increase its diplomatic space and bids for time to develop its nuclear technology, in order to maximize its state interests that can be possible in the current framework of the global non-proliferation regime. Although having limited powers against the international community, Iran has clearly set its bottom line for its compromise: the right to develop the nuclear program for peaceful use.

IV. The prospects of conflicts management through coercive diplomacy

On the Iran issue, the International community needs to pay attention on the following aspects when resorting to coercive diplomacy. Firstly, the emphasis on the authority of international laws and mechanisms are important and should be required. The coercive diplomacy adopted by international community against Iran's nuclear program not only entails the Nuclear Non-Proliferation Treaty and relevant provisions which provide the legal basis, but also embodies the obligation of the international community to maintain the nuclear security and to maintain the authority of the nuclear non-proliferation regime so that the regional and international security can be promoted. As a member of Nuclear Non-Proliferation Treaty, Iran has the responsibility to report to IAEA its history of nuclear activities and also the status quo of its nuclear development efforts. IAEA is supposed to supervise the Iran nuclear issue neutrally and objectively. The UN Security Council should evaluate the characteristics of Iran's nuclear program on the basis of IAEA reports and then adopt corresponding measures to it. To avoid the sanctions by the UN, Iran has to reassure the international community especially the U.S. and Israel by providing adequate evidences to demonstrate the peaceful nature of its nuclear program. And because of this, Iran has repeatedly reiterated that its nuclear program was not used for producing nuclear weapons but developing its national economy out of real needs.

Secondly, intervening states or institutions need to avert the direct participation in the international conflicts which is one important component of coercive diplomacy. The participants in the international conflicts constitute the opposing parties. The roles of challenger and defender are not unidirectional and absolute but bilateral and relative.[40]

Intervenors may be directly related to one of the parties in the international conflicts or they, themselves are the third parties. Third parties may challenge or oppose the direct participants in the international conflicts. Therefore, the international intervention and conflict management through coercive diplomacy has become more complicated.

---

40 Frank C. Zagare and D. Marc Kilgour, Perfect Deterrence, Cambridge: Cambridge University Press, 2000, p. 181.

During the six-party talks on the Iranian issue, the U.S. as a major intervener, strongly disagrees with Iran on its nuclear program, and it has a dominating position in the global non-proliferation regime. At this point, the U.S. has been able to take the control of political discourse with respect to Iranian nuclear issue. As a matter of fact, the barriers built through the US coercive diplomacy have given rise to considerable uncertainties about the peaceful prospect of Iran nuclear program.

Thirdly, asymmetric structure of power causes gaming relations between the parties. The major powers in the international community do not always hold the same stand points.

And when it comes to the specific means to stop Iran from its nuclear activities and hinder nuclear proliferation, these major powers have divergent opinions. Iran has no leverage with Western countries due to its vulnerable state security, and due to some economic dependence on the outsiders, which means it needs to show good will to sustain its relations with international and regional institutions.

With an absolute supremacy over Iran in all aspects, the Western states headed by the U.S. attempt to force Iran to make concession by multiple means including military deterrence, economic sanctions and so forth. During the negotiations, Western countries attempted to deprive Iran of the right to enrich uranium and to push Iran on the verge of counterpunch. Since an unchecked situation would put Iran in a real dilemma, China and Russia on the one hand, acted in good faith, endeavoring to persuade Iran to cooperatively accept the inspection of IAEA and proposed some constructive solutions to the issue. On other hand, they also requested that the Western countries should benignly interact with Iran and negotiate with it without breaking their political insistences. The asymmetric powers we observe in the international conflicts help to retain the credibility of coercive diplomacy, and the benign interactions and communication between conflicting parties is favorable to avoid further development of unilateral coercive diplomacy.

Fourthly, a relative balance between coercion and diplomacy can be achieved. The policies adopted by the parties in the Iranian issue have shown that the coercive pressures of both sides have far exceeded the buffer of diplomacy. Under such circumstances, where the UN Security Council was less likely to impose hard policies against Iran. Western countries attempted to overthrow the Assad regime when Syria was struck in internal conflicts, through which an important ally of Iran in the Middle East would be eliminated from its side. The evidence for their intention of using military forces by Western countries against Iran is shown in their increasing deployment of military forces in the Middle East and their large-scale military exercises. On the Iranian issue, China and Russia acted as mediators to sustain the stability of the situation. But, what they can do is neutrally and objectively requests both sides of the conflict to act in accordance to international law and mechanisms, which however, cannot determine whether peaceful means or armed forces will be employed when addressing the issue. What's more, being tough on the issue, Iran has repeatedly signaled threats to Western countries. The imbalance between coercion and diplomacy requires China and Russia to contribute more to the settlement of the issue, and try to reduce the perniciousness of coercive threats, and enhancing the capacity and certainties of conflict management by diplomacy. Coercive diplomacy not only considers the asymmetric structure of power but also the irrational factors involved in its process.[41]

The effectiveness of coercive diplomacy is closely related to the subjective opinions of coercer and its adversary and also related to the cognition of their mutual identities.

If the coerced party believes that its adversary does not have a firm political will, the coercive diplomacy carried out will fail to create enough deterrence. Although it recognizes the importance of force employment, coercive diplomacy only underscores the use of force for threatening which means maximization of the potential role of military force instead of using it in reality.

The fulfillment of the strategic goals and certain policy purposes only by resorting to potential forces signifies the success of coercive diplomacy. When both sides fail to develop effective diplomacy, or the coercer has strong incentives to resort to war, or when the coercer has unlimited strategic goals, such as overthrowing the regime of the targeted state is its ultimate goal, or when the coercive diplomacy is rejected by the adversary, the coercive diplomacy will have a high probability of a failure. From this perspective, whether coercive diplomacy succeeds or not is not positively correlated with whether the international conflicts management and international intervention are effective or not. For example, the outbreak of a war after a conflict and the lack of diplomacy all indicate the failure of coercive diplomacy. But, this does not directly influence the settlement of international conflicts leading to a war, which is the most extreme tool for resolving international conflicts. Moreover, an international intervention without coercion may also lead to failure.

---

41 Robert Jervis, "Deterrence and Perception", International Security, Vol. 7, No. 3, Winter 1982-1983, pp. 3-30; K. J.Holsti, International Politics: A Framework for Analysis, New Jersey: Prentice Hall, 1995, p. 221.

Looking from the current situation, whether or not Iran gives up its enrichment of uranium, , has become a key point for Western countries to make a judgment on Iran's opposition against the nuclear non-proliferation regime and will also be an important model for a successful coercive diplomacy in the management of nuclear proliferation issues by international community.

The essence of the issue lies in the concerns of both sides over their security. The U.S.casts doubts on the Iran's nuclear activities while Iran is worried about the U.S. might and involvement in the regional affairs of the Middle East. The U.S. has announced that no tolerance would be made towards Iran's nuclear program, but Iran insisted on its rights to independently master nuclear technology and apply it for peaceful use. International community asserts that, Iran nuclear issue should be resolved—within the framework of the UN Charter—through diplomatic channels and the authority of global nuclear non-proliferation regime should not be violated. Although challenging the non-proliferation regime to some extent, Iran by cooperatively accepting the inspection of IAEA and clarifying unsettled issues. Iran is still hopeful to rely on the IAEA rules to properly deal with the issue in favor of its interest and still hopeful to convince others of the peaceful nature of its nuclear program by diplomacy and negotiation in the framework of IAEA and the UN Security Council.

Therefore, the settlement of Iranian issues partially lies in the Iran's wiliness to accept the oversight of the IAEA, through which Iran can prove that its nuclear program is for peaceful purposes and that its act conforms to the global nuclear non-proliferation regime. In addition, the settlement also depends on whether the international community, especially the U.S. and Europe would like to make conditional offer of peaceful talks with Iran instead of blindly exaggerating the threats related to Iran's nuclear program. In order to safeguard the interests of all states, and global security Western countries are suggested to restrict the process of Iranian nuclear development through strict verification procedures, but meanwhile admit and guarantee Iran's right to utilize nuclear power for peaceful purposes.

Nowdays we have reached a critical point whether Obama administration will show a strong political will and whether it will resort to any means so as to force Iran to sacrifice its national dignity and sacrifice its security considerations and make concession on this issue.[42]

---

42 William Galston, "What Israelis Hear When Obama Officials Talk About Iran", The New Republic, December 7, 2011, http://www.tnr.com/article/the-vital-center/98207/israel-america-nuclear-iran.

All in all, due to rapidly changing international system, international relations have become more and more complex during the post-Cold War era. Further transparency and justice are required in managing international conflicts. The employment of armed forces instead of diplomacy deviates from the normal international development. But, meanwhile there is an increasing pressure or demand for justifying international intervention in international conflicts, with the pretext of moral and legal anxiety and these proponents of international interventions exclude the likelihood that the interveners may well take side in the relevant conflicts. The peace and war are the important manifestations of the current international conflict management. The range between them provides coercive diplomacy to have more space to function. If we evaluate the development of the Iranian nuclear issue, the coercive diplomacy still remains an optimal option to promote and realize the common interests of all parties concerned. With the focus of the U.S. global strategy shifting to East Asia and Pacific region, drastic changes have occurred in the Middle East. With steady development of its nuclear program, Iran's position in the security pattern of Middle East has elevated. But the prospect of coercive diplomacy on Iranian nuclear issue is facing abundant uncertainties. None of the states, including United States, Israel, China, Russia, S Arabia or others want to see a nuclear-armed Iran. Therefore, these countries not only strengthen their supervision over Iran's continuing nuclear activities, but also introduce new initiatives to limit Iran's nuclear program, and thus maintain the pressure of coercive diplomacy at a very high level. These countries are forcing Iran to cooperate on the issue and also trying to avoid a possible isolation of Iran by the international community.

The Evolution and Development of Judicial Intervention — A Survey on the Practices of the International Court of Justice (ICJ)

Song Jie[1]

On 31,May 2010, considering Japan's ongoing Antarctic whaling the government of Australia filed an application at the International Court of Justice (ICJ) to commence proceedings against Japan in relation to Japan's "scientific whaling program"[2]. Australia has contended that Japan "had breached and is continuing to breach" its obligations under the "International Convention for the Regulation of Whaling" it has signed in 1946.[3]

Since Australia did not demand or gained any specific material benefits in this law case, but merely sought for a kind of abstract, general legal interest; .looking from the entire background of the jurisdication rules of the ICJ, this case against Japan has exerted significant influence on the protection of the universal legal interests and demonstrated the increasing importance of judicial intervention through the International Court of Justice. As known to all jurisdiction is often a crucial question for the ICJ in contentious cases. The key principle is that the ICJ has jurisdiction only on the basis of consent.

---

1 Doctor of Law, the Associate Professor of Zhejiang Gongshang University, Law School, and the Director of the Department of International Law.
2 Scientific whaling refers to intentionally killing a whale for the purpose of scientific research.
3 Relevant information on this case is available on the ICJ website: http://www.icj-cij.org/docket/index.php?p1=3&p2=3&k=64&case=148&code=aj&p3=0. Last visit on August 24, 2011.

In order to fully discuss and evaluate the importance of this case concerning the legality of "whaling in the Antarctic" and also its effects to the case law of the ICJ, this essay will focus on the following four aspects.[4]

In the first part of my essay, the concept of general legal interest will be defined, to lay the foundation for the latter discussions. In the second part, the essay will discuss the ICJ and those cases concerning the protection of the general legal interest and will provide a brief analysis and evaluations on the issues handled in these cases.

In the third part, our essay will discuss and analyze the judicial intervention by the international Court of Justice from the technical aspect. And the fourth part of the essay will give a brief summary of my discussion.

I should mention that in this essay, judicial intervention issue will be discussed in the framework of the International Court of Justice.

Although the current research on judicial intervention in the international community is mainly focused on the intervention of the international criminal judicial institutions, the results of this research are:

Since the national litigation by the states and litigations by the ICJ are "parallel" proceedings that are applied by two equal subjects, the judicial intervention by the ICJ is completely different from the one implemented by the international criminal bodies such as the International Criminal Court.

The International Criminal Court was designed to be a permanent venue to try individuals accused of the most serious international law violations. It was to replace the UN's system of creating ad hoc tribunals with more limited jurisdiction like the International Tribunal for the Former Yugoslavia and the International Tribunal for Rwanda. It is also supposed to be an independent judicial body which can investigate alleged crimes wherever it holds jurisdiction.

Although, currently, the relavant studies mainly focus on the intervention by the internationalized criminal bodies.[52] In particular, the judicial intervention by the International Criminal Court:

---

4 Ed. jus cogens, is the case law of the International Court of Justice which it helps to clarify and interpret.
5 Studies on this field Andrea Birdsall, The International Politics of Judicial Intervention, Routledge, 2009; Lorna McGregor, Military and Judicial Intervention: The Way forward in Human Rights Enforcement?, 12 Ind. Intl & Comp. L. Rev., 2001-2002; Rachel Kerr, International Judicial Intervention:The International Criminal Tribunal for the Former Yugoslavia, International Relations, 2000/8 .

For instance, the International Criminal Court has issued an international arrest warrant for the incumbent President of Sudan Omar al-Bashir,which indeed created dramatic impact on international relations. In the cases related to Libya and Sudan (Darfur), the International Criminal Court had to intervene in Sudan's Darfur situation and deal with the situation in Libya which were important successive interventions by the International Criminal Courtand have caused radical changes in these countries' regional statuses.

However, the above trend of study focus, does not mean that one should ignore the judicial intervention by the International Court of Justice, and also it does not mean that the judicial intervention by the International Court of Justice, is not a kind of judicial intervention, and is less important.

For the intervention implemented by the International Court of Justice has the essential features of judicial intervention, see my below article.[6]

On the one hand, the judicial intervention by the International Court of Justice is more disguised and complex compared to the one implemented by the international criminal bodies.

On the other hand, the judicial interventions performed by the states—on the basis of—with the assistance of the ICJ help to strengthen the legal basis for international humanitarian law and humanitarian intervention and encourage and promote the further development of other forms of intervention thus will cause more profound effects on the international relations. Therefore, I think this issue is worthy of more attention and more in-depth studies.

I. The concept of universal interest and the international law

The notion of universal legal interest has derived from the concept of "erga omnes obligations" (erga omnes means) towards all") recognized by the International Court of Justice in the "Case Concerning Barcelona Traction, Light, and Power Company, Ltd" There are certain very important principles of international law which emerged out of this case.

In the international law erga omnes has been used as a legal term describing obligations owed by states towards the community of states as a whole. An erga omnes obligation exists because of the universal and undeniable interest in the perpetuation of critical rights (and the prevention of

---

6 Judicial intervention features, see, Song Jie "Judicial Intervention in the International Relations: a New Era of Intervention", Journal of World Economics and Politics, 2011/7, pp. 112-114.

their breach). Consequently, any state has the right to complain of a breach.

As stated by the ICJ, on a circumstance when universal interest being infringed, every state under the protection of legal interest is entitled to the legal interest: "[A]n essential distinction should be drawn between the obligations of a State towards the international community as a whole, and those arising vis-à-vis another State (...). By their very nature the former are the concern of all States. In view of the importance of the rights involved, all States can be held to have a legal interest in their protection; they are obligations *erga omnes*." But such universal legal interest is different from the one in common sense.

In this case, the specific, realistic, perceivable and immediate material interests of the states are not jeopardized, but the potential, unperceivable and indirect legal interests of them do indeed suffer.

Article 53 of the 1969 Vienna Convention, "TREATIES CONFLICTING WITH A PEREMPTORY NORM OF GENERAL INTERNATIONAL LAW ("JUS COGENS")" It says: A treaty is void if, at the time of its conclusion, it conflicts with a peremptory norm of general international law. For the purposes of the present Convention, a peremptory norm of general international law is a norm accepted and recognized by the international community of States as a whole as a norm from which no deroga tion is permitted and which can be modified only by a subsequent norm of general in ternational law having the same character."

The main features of the universal legal interest are reflected in the following aspects. First, universal legal interest is abstract and indirect, which is different from the specific and concrete legal interest in common sense.

Such abstractness and indirectness will impose limits on the exercise of sovereign rights of for the states having universal legal interests. Obviously, the scope of the former is more extensive than that of the latter. Infact, the article 48 in the draft articles on

Responsibility of States for internationally wrongful acts adopted by the International Law Commission at its 53rd, session (2001) has explained this issue clearly. In this regard, I will present a more detailed discussion in the part three later.

Secondly, the universal legal interest is committed to protect the interest of the international community which is altruistic in nature. While being generally figurative or abstract, material legal interest is for protecting the particular interest of states or state groups, hence it is specific.

The rights enjoyed by the states based on the material interest embody "equality" and "reciprocity", which reflect the "bilateralist" and community character, we see in the system of international law.[7]

But the universal legal interest is something else. International law aims to protect the common interest or the interest of the international community. The rights enjoyed by the states based on the universal legal interest do not directly imply "equality" and "reciprocity"

The next section of our essay will specifically provide further elaboration on this issue.

Third, the universal legal interests mainly exist in the treaties related to human rights, the treaties related to protection of the environment and other treaties as such. Since either of the two types of treaty aim and concern concerning the protection of the basic human rights of all people, or the improvement of the environment for the whole human survival, here interests of a particular country is not the issue when they are deciding to join such a treaty, a state's pursuit of specific interests is not the aim, however their attitudes have an altruistic or solidarity nature, which also manifest that their these altruistic attitudes reflect the natures of indirectness and consciousness—a rising awareness of the common interests of the international community.

It is precisely due to the above characteristics of universal legal interests, that when the maintenance based on universal legal interests, in did not suffer any damage to its specific, material benefits, the International Court of Justice filed lawsuits against another country,

That means this kind of litigation, started by a country does not pursue to defend and maintain its own specific interests, but the interests of the whole world community. As a result, act of the country which starts a litigation in such a situation, obviously has the nature of altruism and the nature of international solidarity consciousness. In such a litigation, the action of state targeting another, certainly possesses the nature of intervention, thus constitutes a judicial intervention.

---

[7] For the issue of bilateralism: see Bruno Simma's brief quotation the from Professor Philip Allott, "international law has been the minimal law necessary to enable state-societies to act as closed systems internally and to act as territory owners in relation to each other." See. Bruno Simma, "From Bilateralism to Community Interest in International Law,"Recueildes Cours, Vol. 250, 1994, p.229.

The Relevant Practices of the International Court of Justice on the Protection of Legal interests of the International Community

Generally speaking, the protection of the legal interests of the international community by the ICJ has encountered four stages in which its judicial practices and stand has further developed. The first stage is marked by the "Advisory Opinion On The Genocide Convention"and the judgement on the "South-West Africa Case" of the ICJ. At this stage, evaluating the judgements of the International Court of Justice, we notice that the progressive and conservative stand seems to co-exist intertwined, therefore in this same stage we can observe totally different positions at different phases of the same case.

The secondstage is mainly marked by the judgement of the "Barcelona Traction Case"and"the judgement "Legal Consequences for States of the Continued Presence of South Africa in Namibia (South West Africa) notwithstanding Security Council Resolution" At this second stage, ICJ's practices demonstrated a more progressive nature, and ICJ had not only stressed the "obligations erga Omnes" as commitments towards the international community as a whole but also explicitly and officially affirmed and confirmed the concept of "legal interest of the international community".

The third stage is the intermediate stage, which can be evaluated as one step forward two steps back..

The main cases of this stage include the case concerning the "atmospheri cnucleartests"and"EastTimor case" which we will examine below.

At this stage, the position of the International Court of justice has been quite contradictory, wavering between progress and retreat. The fourth stage includes another important step forward, "the Genocide Convention" (Bosnia and Herzegovina versus Serbia), as the representative case of this stage.

At this stage, the relevant judicial practice of the International Court of justice seems more positive, and demonstrated a clear willingness to protect the new paradigm of the international law.

A. The first stage with controversial stands intertwined: Advisory Opinion On the Genocide Convention" and the "South-West Africa Case"

The Advisory Opinion On the Genocide Convention by the ICJ

The UN General Assembly adopted the "Genocide Convention"[8] in 1948 in response to the atrocities committed during World War II. When the Convention was opened to ratification gathering,some states held different opinions and declared reservations against certain rules of this Convention and brought forward different ideas on its probable effects and its utility, and others declared their opposition to reservations. Among the 19 already deposited instruments of ratification and accession, Philippine and Bulgaria have agreed with the reservations while Britain, France, Australia, Ecuador and Cambodia and other states declared their opposition to reservation.[9]

Therefore, the United Nations General Assembly decided to get advisory opinions from the ICJ.

Firstly, the advisory opinion of the International Court of Justice, in the introduction part clarified the nature, the objectives and purpose of the Convention and brought forward the issue of reservations to the Convention, and opened the way for further discussions.[10]

ICJ recognized that the principles underlying the Convention are principles which are recognized by civilized nations, and that these principles had binding on the States even without any conventional obligation.

ICJ emphasized that the features of the Genocide Convention were obviously different from the features of the general "contractual" treaties.[11]

---

8   Ed. See, ICJ's Advisory Opinion on Reservations to the Genocide Convention, Malaysia (its reservation was opposed by the Netherlands and the United Kingdom), Philippines (reservation opposed by Norway), Rwanda (its reservation opposed by the United Kingdom), Singapore (reservation opposed by the Netherlands and the United Kingdom), United States (its reservation opposed by Denmark, Estonia, Finland, Greece, Ireland, Italy, Mexico, the Netherlands, Norway, Spain, Sweden and the United Kingdom).
9   Among the 19 already deposited instruments of ratification and accession, Philippine and Bulgaria have agreed with the reservations while Britain, France, Australia, Ecuador and Cambodia and other states declared their opposition to reservation.
10 For background information see: Li Haopei. "Introduction to the Law of Treaties". Beijing, Law Press,2003, pp.135–144; Wan Exiang, Shi Lei, Yang Chengming, Deng Hongwu, "International Law of Treaties", Wuhan University Press, 1998, pp.141-142.
11 No extra discussion will be made in terms of the opinion that International Court of Justice has made on the issue of convention reservations.

Sixteen nations conditioned ratification, accession, or succession to the Convention on one or more declarations, reservations, or understandings which explicitly require that the nation-state should grant consent to trial of its citizenry before an international court for the crime of genocide

The Convention is initially used by the United Nations as a means to condemn and punish the genocide which is regarded as a "crime under international law."

The Convention provided a precise definition of the crime of genocide, "In ratifying the Genocide Convention, the parties "confirm that genocide, whether committed in time of peace or in time of war, is a crime under international law which they undertake to prevent and punish" (Article I). And gave a definition particularly in terms of the required intention and the prohibited acts (Article II).

The parties have also agreed to enact the domestic legislation necessary to provide effective penalties for those committing genocide. This provision anticipates and establishes a decentralized control scheme under which the crimes defined by treaty are subject to enforcement under the national criminal law of states. At the same time, the Genocide Convention also refers to the possibility that those charged with genocide might be tried by "such international penal tribunal as may have jurisdiction" (Article VI). This set the stage for efforts to create a permanent International Criminal Court.

The concept of the "crimes under international law" has two consequences. Firstly, civilized nations recognize the principles on the basis of the Genocide Convention as the ones that bind the states' acts and behaviors, even without fulfilling any obligation in the Convention. The second is that the condemnation of genocide and the cooperation to save humanity from this "odious catastrophe" which universally exists. As for the purpose, the Convention is merely a pursuit of a pure humanitarian is mand civilization. In this Convention, contracting parties have no interest of their own but merely a general interest. Achieving these noble purposes justifies the presence of the Convention. Therefore, in this Convention it is neither allowed to talk about the states' own interest, nor the balance between the rights and obligations.[12]

---

12 International Court of Justice believes that the "contractual" nature is the characteristic principle of many conventions. This point is obviously affected by the Israeli argument. See, ICJ Reports 1951, p.21. For related arguments about Israel see also Li Haopei's above book: "Introduction to the Law of Treaties," pp.143-144.

In this sense, the International Court of Justice draws from its traditional principle of reservation, and proposes a new rule of "coordination between object and purpose".

This case is ICJ's first attempt to classify treaties based on their attributes. Through the investigation of the origin of *Convention Genocide* and definition of its objective and purpose, the International Court of Justice distinguishes the Convention from the others states in pursuing their own interest. Since contractual treaties and public treaties have their own uniqueness, there should be special rule systems for their applications, and this should not be confined to the reservation area. But in which other areas it can be extended, depending on the further development of the international legal system. Therefore, in this case, this classification by the ICJ is of particular importance. On the one hand, it provides the basis for the formation of the concept of peremptory norms in the Vienna Convention on the Law of Treaties of 1969. On the other hand, it is the source of inspiration behind the ICJ's formulation of "erga omnes obligations" in its future judicial practice. This concept establishes the first theoretical foundation for the protection of general legal interest.

"South West Africa Case"

The South West Africa cases (Ethiopia *versus* South Africa Liberia *versus* South Africa), held in the International Court of Justice which relate to the continued existence of the Mandate for South West Africa and the duties and performance of South Africa as Mandatory there under, were instituted by Applications of the Governments of Ethiopia and Liberia filed in the Registry on 4 November 1960. The Government of South Africa raised preliminary objections to the jurisdiction of the Court to hear the cases

Ethiopia and Liberia have alleged that South Africa broke the obligation of accepting the supervision from the United Nations and of surrendering the petition of the local residents in the mandated territory of South West Africa. There questing state cited the Article 7 (2) of the Mandate Letter and the Article 37 of the "Statute of the Court" as the basis for proceeding. . As for the allegation, South Africa raised four preliminary objections and believed that there questing state had no just and I and the court had no jurisdiction. Since the third preliminary objection involves the discussion on the nature of the disputes on this case and the question of whether the party has legal rights or legal interests, this essay only introduces the third preliminary objection.[1310]

---

13 See, I C J Reports 1951, p.23.

The third preliminary objection proposed by South Africa is: according to the nature and content of the conflicts, especially considering that the material interest of the requesting state or of its citizens were not affected, the conflicts between the two sides did not constitute the kind of "dispute" listed in the article 7 (2) of Mandate Letter.[14]

In the oral arguments, the legal representative of South Africa stressed that although the Article 7 (2) mentioned the words of "regardless any dispute", if the state in the appeal did not enjoy legal rights or legal interest, then the proceeding did not fall into the scope of "dispute" in the meaning.[15]

Given that the supervision of the International Union Member States is of significant importance on the implementation of the Mandate system, Ethiopia and Liberia argued that the plain tiff was not required to enjoy the "material interest" in the matter of the appeal. And this is on the aspect of monitoring the behaviors of the Mandate state in Article 7 (2).[16]

In1962, on the verdict on the preliminary objections, the International Court of Justice argued that the basic principles of the mandate system recognized the rights of the people in the under-developed regions, and the purpose of the mandate system was to promote the wellbeing of the people and development of them and ated regions. According to the precises cope and purpose of the Article 7 (2) that refers to the "regardless of any dispute", the Member States of the League of Nations are considered to have legal rights or legal interest when the Mandate stateful fills its obligation with respect to the people in the mandated territory, the League of Nations and the member states of League of Nations.[17]

Thus, the third preliminary objection should be dismissed. After the rejection of the other three, the Court regarded that it was entitled to adjudicate.[18]

---

14 The dissenting opinion of judge . Tanaka made such definition in his judgment in 1966. See, Dissenting Opinion of Judge Tanaka, South West Africa, Second Phase, Judgment, ICJ Reports 1966, p.250.
15 See, ICJ Reports 1962, p. 327.
16 See, CR1962/35, p. 201, available at: http://www.icj-cij.org/docket/files/47/9291.pdflast visited on December 12, 2011.
17 See, CR1962/35, p. 324, available at: http://www.icj-cij.org/docket/files/47/9291.pdf last visited on December 12, 2011.
18 See, ICJ Reports 1962, pp. 342-345, available at: available at: http://www.icj-cij.org/docket/files/47/9291.pdf last visited on December 12, 2011.

As a result of multiple corrective factors after a periodical re-election in the International Court of justice, the final judgment made in1966 is diametrically different from the one in 1962.[19]

In its judgment, the Court first clarified that the issue concerning the jus standi of the plaintiff state had been addressed in the 1962. However, whether the plaintiff possessed the legal interest in the subject of this "standing" had not been resolved.[20]

Through the review, the International Court of Justice drew a negative conclusion, holding that the Plain tiff State had not enjoyed the legal rights or legal interest based on Article 7 of the Mandate Letter.

Therefore, ICJ rejected the appeal filed by the plaintiff state. In the judicial practice of ICJ, this case was the first lawsuit touching the protection of the general legal interest. The plaintiff state in the name of the former member state of the League of Nations, filed the lawsuit on the basis of protecting the interest of the mandated territory of West Africa. And actually the direct, specific and material interest of the plain tiff state was not infringed. The legal basis of the proceedings was also the only foundation for the "jus standi" which lied in the general legal interest performed by Mandate Letter and claimed by the former member state of the League of Nations on the basis of Mandate Letter. In the judgment of the preliminary objections, ICJ recognized the proceeding qualification that the plaintiff state enjoyed on the basis of the general legal interest, and determined the justifiability of the general legal interest. But in these condphase of the proceedings, mainly due to the changes in the composition of judges, the International Court with the technical excuses, "transformed" its own jurisprudence on this issue. And this change also showed that on one hand, ICJ did not follow the usual legal principles established by PCIJ in the "Wimbledon case" and "Interpretation of the Statute of the Memel Territory", but took completely different approaches. On the other hand, it did not conform to the legal principle selaborated by the International Court of Justice in the advisory opinion of the "Genocide Convention". Because the Mandate System pursued the interest and wellbeing of the people in the mandated territory which was based on the "sacred trust of civilization". The exercise of the mandate should rely on the purpose and the spirit of Mandate System.

19　The text of the judgment verdict states: The Court finds that it has jurisdiction to adjudicate upon the merits of the dispute.See. South WestAfrica Cases (Ethiopia versus South Africa; Liberia versus South Africa), Preliminary Objections Judgment of December 21, 1962: ICJ Reports 1962, p.347.

20　Related Background available at: Song Jie. "Responsibility to Protect: the Study on the Related Judicial Practice of the International Court of Justice" Science of Law, Vol. 2009, p. 59.

B. The breakthrough stage: from the "Barcelona Traction Case" to "the Legal Consequences for States of the Continued Presence of South Africa in Namibia"

1. "Barcelona Traction case"

"Barcelona Traction,Light and Power Company" was incorporated and registered in 1911, and its headquarter was in Toronto, Canada, and the company possessed a subsidiary in Spain.

The company issued a series of bonds which met the company's solvency from the subsidiary company in Spain. The payments were interrupted in 1936 due to the Spanish Civil War. After the war, the Spanish Exchange Control Authority refused to approve the subsidiary company to pay the necessary foreign exchange to the company for debtpaying.[21]

In 1948, the Spanish company was declared by the Spanish court to be bankrupted. After that, because Canada did not make a claim, Belgium filed a lawsuit in the International Court of Justice against Spain in order to protect the rights of their shareholders.[22]

In the lawsuit against Belgium, Spain made four preliminary objections. On July 24, 1964, the Court rejected the first and second objections and joined the third and fourth to the merits. After a hearing on the entity issue, the Court dismissed the claims of Belgium, holding that they lacked legal basis on Belgian's exercise of diplomatic protection for the actions taken by the shareholders of Belgian in Canada against the Spanish. Due to the limitation of research topic, here only the discussion on the "the obligation erga omnes" elaborated by the International Court of Justice will be presented. The concept of "the obligation erga omnes" appears in paragraph 33 to paragraph 34 of the Court judgement. For research purposes, the text is as follows.

In particular, an essential distinction should be drawn between the obligations of a State towards the international community as a whole, and those rising vis-à-vis another State in the field of diplomatic protection. By their very nature, the former are the concern of all States. In the view of the importance of the rights involved, all States can be

---

21 ICJ here made a distinction between the two concepts:jus standi of the genus humanity (jus standi rationae personae) and jus standi in the case of physical properties (jus standi rationae materiae). The Court held that that the plaintiff belongs to the "jus standirationae personae", which has been recognized in the judgment in 1962, but in the case of the "jus standi rationae materiae", it was not resolved in the 1962 judgment. See, ICJ Reports 1966, pp. 38-39, para.60.
22 See, ICJ Reports 1970, para.10-12.

held to have a legal interest in their protection, they are obligations erga omnes.

Such obligations derive, for example, in contemporary international law, from the outlawing of acts of aggression, and of genocide, as also from the principles and rules concerning the basic rights of the human person, including protection from slavery and racial discrimination.Some of the corresponding rights of protection have entered into the body of general international law, and others are conferred by international instruments of a universal of quasi-universal character.[23]

In order to make a distinction between these two types of obligations, the International Court of Justice extended its explanation further in paragraph 35. The fulfillment of those obligations for diplomatic protection does not fall into the category of "the obligation erga omnes". When on the occasion of disputes over specific cases, it cannot be said that all states possess legal interests in fulfilling their obligations of supervision.[24]

From the background of the ICJ case law and in the practices of the ICJ in the protection of the general legal interest, the case concerning "Barcelona Traction, Light and Power Company ltd." has served as a link between past and future.

It is mainly because on one hand, the inconsistency of the Court in the practice of "South West Africa case" has left international community a bad impression, adversely influencing the confidence of the emerging countries in resolving international disputes through the Court. And on the otherhand, there action from international community has made the court realize that it might make some mistakes on the protection of the general legal interest. In this context, the ICJ needs a case to redress its treatment on the similar issues which will undoubtedly provide a perfect opportunity.

The ICJ seized this opportunity advisedly. By distinguishing the two different types of obligations based on different treaties, the International Court of Justice on one hand has retained its logic in its advisory opinion of "Genocide Convention" and has responded to the development of international law since the World War II through practices. On the other hand, detaching itself from the judicial records in the past, the International Court of Justice has provided necessary theoretical basis for the protection of the general legal interest.

---

23   ICJ Reports 1970, para. 19-25.
24   ICJ Reports 1970, para. 33-34.

Although the International Court of Justice devoted two paragraphs to fully explain the positions and implications of "the obligation erga omnes" in the contemporary international legal system, it did not touch the potential practical legal consequences the concept might lead to, especially in terms of the scope of actions that the international community was capable of taking in the protection of such interest.

2. "The Legal Consequences for States of the Continued Presence of South Africa in Namibia" (South West Africa) notwithstanding Security Council Resolution 276 (1970)

The UN General Assembly was extremely disappointed about the judgment in the second phase of the "South West Africa case". Under such circumstances, the General Assembly adopted the Resolution Nr. 2145 in 1966, there solution "decides that the Mandate conferred upon His Britannic Majesty to be exercised on his behalf by the Government of the Union of South Africa is therefore terminated, that South Africa has no other right to administer the Territory and that hence forth South West Africa comes under the direct responsibility of the United Nations."[25]

Unfortunately, this resolution failed to make South Africa terminate its mandate for South West Africa. Contrary to the facts, it even intended to incorporate South West Africa into its own territory. In this context, the Security Council made the Resolution Nr. 276 in 1970, and there solution declared that "the continued presence of the South African authorities in Namibia was illegal and that consequently all acts taken by the Government of South Africa on behalf of or concerning Namibia after the termination of the Mandate were illegal and invalid." "Calls upon all States, particularly those which have economic and other interests in Namibia, to refrain from any dealings with the Government of South Africa which are inconsistent with paragraph 2 of the present resolution."[26]

On July 29 the same year, the Security Council adopted the Resolution 284, and decided to request the International Court of Justice to provide the advisory opinions on the following question, "what are the legal consequences for States of the continued presence of South Africa in Namibia not with standing the Security Council Resolution Nr. 276 (in 1970)?"[27]

On June 21,1971, the International Court of Justice made an Advisory Opinion of 21, saying "the continued presence of South Africa in Namibia

---

25 ICJ Reports 1970, para.35.
26 See, UN documents: A/RES/2145(XXI). Body Part: Paragraph 1.2. 3. 4.8.9.
27 See, UN documents: S/RES/276. Body Part: Paragraph 1.2.4.5.

being illegal, South Africa is under obligation to withdraw its administration from Namibia immediately and thus put an end to its occupation of the Territory" and "that States Members of the United Nations are under obligation...to recognize the illegality of South Africa's presence in Namibia and the invalidity of its acts on behalf of or concerning Namibia, and to refrain from any acts and in particular any dealings with the Government of South Africa implying recognition of the legality of, or lending support or assistance to, such presence and administration."

Thus, in the South West Africa Case, on one hand, the International Court of Justice gave "sacred trust of civilization" to the legal forces, which was consistent with its previous judgments in the preliminary stages of this case. On the other hand, the Court directly addressed the effect of the "erga omnes" in the Security Council resolutions. This was the first time that ICJ applied the concept of "erga omnes" ("towards all" or "towards everyone") in its judicial practices and clarified the legal effect of this concept.

In the 126 paragraph of the advisory opinion, it is stated that non-Member States of the UN also need to follow the Security Council Resolution 276 so that the legitimacy of the continued presence of South Africa in Namibia will not be recognized and the International Court noted that the non-Member States of the UN were not bound by Article 24 and Article 25 in the UN Charter. The paragraph 2[28] and paragraph 5 of Resolution Nr. 276 in the main text "call upon" all states particularly those which have economic and other interests in Namibia to assist the UN's actions against the Namibian situation and refrain from any dealings with the Government of South Africa.[29]

Therefore, in the opinion of the International Court, the termination of the Mandate Letter and the declaration of the illegitimacy of the continued presence of South Africain Namibia targets all countries, and the termination of the legitimacy of a situation contrasting international law has the nature of "erga omnes". Therefore, even if a country is not a member state of the United Nations, it is still required to act in accordance with UN Security Council resolutions.[30]

---

28   See, UN documents: S/RES/284.
29   Paragraph 2: "Declare that the continued presence of the South African authorities in Namibia is illegai and that consequently all acts taken by the Government of South Africa on behalf of concerning Namibia after the termination of the Mandate are illegal and invalid."
30   Paragraph 5: "Calls upon all States, particularly those which have economicand other-interests in Namibia,torefrain from any dealings withthe Government ofSouthAfrica which areinconsistent with paragraph2 ofthe present resolution."

ICJ also stressed that as for the general consequences of South Africa's continued illegal presence in Namibia, all countries should keep in mind that, the Namibian people as the victim entities expected that the international community could offer their help to realize the "sacred trust of civilization".[31] Clearly, here the International Court did not only emphasize the obligations to terminate South Africa's continued illegal presence in Namibia, but also ruled that that non-Member States of the UN had to fulfill the same obligations assumed by United Nations Member States. More importantly, the international Court of Justice also underlined them oral value goals of the fulfillment of this obligation for the "international community". Regarding the perspective of the inheritance of the cases, if the ICJ's final opinion (in1970) on the "the case concerning "Barcelona Traction, Light and Power Company ltd" had aimed to indirectly correct its impropriety in the "South West Africa Case", (Second Phase) then it could be said that the performance of the ICJ in the Barcelona case had directly aimed to address the "mistakes" in the aforementioned law suit.

All in all, in the "South West Africa Case" (Second Phase), the International Court of Justice partially elaborated the legal consequences of the breach of the obligations, and to some extent clarified the obligations and responsibilities, that states should undertake the protection of the general legal interest. All these decisions have demonstrated that all States have general interest in the legality of actions (exercise of power) that affect community values.

C. The stage of one step further and two steps back: from the case concerning "atmospheric nuclear tests" to "East Timor Case" (a) start and wandering stage: the punishment of the crime of Genocide Convention "advice and southwest Africa litigation case." the Genocide Convention "advisory opinion case" Although ICJ explicitly divided the international obligations into two parts in the "the case concerning" Barcelona Traction, Light and Power Company Ltd.", it affirmed the obligations that all States should undertake on the ground of Resolution 276 and the "civilized sacred trust" in the case concerning "the Legal Consequences for States of the Continued Presence of South Africa in Namibia" in order to terminate South Africa's continued illegal presence in Namibia. Although the interest on the basis of this obligation is abstract and universal, there are still a number of legal gaps in the paths of protecting the general legal interest since ICJ's discussion on the relevant obligation is not based on its practicality and operability. Therefore, filling the gaps with specific cases in practice may require theoretical, and practical and technical efforts.

---

31   See, ICJ Reports 1970, para.126.

Case concerning "the atmospheric nuclear tests"

In 1973, Australia and New Zealand brought applications to the I.C.J. demanding cessation of atmospheric nuclear tests being carried out by France in the South Pacific, and accused France by causing nuclear contamination in their territories due to radioactive fallout[32] as a result of the atmospheric nuclear tests in the South Pacific.

France issued a series of statements declaring that the purpose of its atmospheric nuclear tests had been achieved, and it would shift to an underground nuclear tests in the near future.

Considering France's attitude ICJ issued a judgment in1974, declaring the following: "It is clear from these statements that if the French Government had given what could have been construed by Australia and New Xealand as "a firm, explicit and binding undertaking to refrain from further atmospheric tests", in the South Pacific the applicant Governments would have regarded its objective as having been achieved." "For these reasons, The Court, by nine votes to six, finds that the claim of Australia no longer has any object and that the Court is therefore not called upon to give a decision thereon".[33]

Due to the declaration of refrain and binding commitment byFrance,the ICJ declared the following: Thus the Court faces a situation in which the objective of the Applicant has in effect been accomplished, inasmuch as the Court finds that France has undertaken the obligation to hold no further nuclear tests in the atmosphere in the South Pacific." and added "However, the Court having found that the Respondent has assumed an obligation as to conduct, concerning the effective cessation of nuclear tests, no further judicial action is required. The Applicant has repeatedly sought from the Respondent an assurance that the tests would cease, and the Respondent has, on its own initiative made a series of statements to the effect that they will cease. Thus the Court concludes that, the dispute having disappeared, the claim advanced by Australia no longer has any object. It follows that any further finding would have no raison d'être."[34]

In this case, although the Court did not address the "the obligation erga omnes" and the issue of the general legal interest, it is still worth studying the obligation because based on the "the obligation erga omnes" in their appeal, plaintiff states put forward the question concerning applicable rules of international law.

---

32 Radioactive fallout is the radioactive particles that fall to earth as a result of a nuclear explosion.
33 See, ICJ Reports 1970, para.127.
34 See, ICJ Reports 1974, para. 50.

In the law suit filed by Australia, it was referred that the atmospheric nuclear tests conducted by France in the South Pacific did not comply with the obligations that should have been assumed by French under the international law, and accordingly when Australia requested ICJ to sentence against France, Australia are marked, "these obligations include, first of all, the general one of abstaining from any kind of atmospheric nuclear test. In the opinion of the Australian Government this obligation is clearly imposed one very State by a rule of general international law and it is clearly one owned by each state towards every other states; Australia, like any other country, is entitled to claim respect of that legal prohibition."[35]

In terms of the legal interests enjoyed by Australia in the claim, Australia considered the duty to refrain from the atmospheric nuclear tests not being directed to the one particular states, but the absolute one. The duty is thus owed to the international community; it is a duty of every state towards every other state. For this reason and- "to use the very language of the Court in the Barcelona Traction case-because "of the importance of the rights involved, all states can be held to have a legal interest in their protection".[36]

In this sense, "Australia undoubtedly has a legal interest in the protection of its right to claim from the observance of the obligation to abstain from conducting atmospheric nuclear tests." Therefore, "it has just and it obtain a declaratory judgment to this effect; and its application is fully admissible."[37]

---

35 Nevertheless, the ICJ may also be aware of the impropriety of their arbitrary understanding to some degree: what, then,in paragraph 60 of the judgment (See, paragraph 60 of the ICJ judgment on Australia versus France and New Zealand versus France) The paragraph says: "Once the Court has found that a State has entered into a commitment concerning its future conduct it is not the Court's function to contemplate that it will not comply with it. However, the Court observes that if the basis of this Judgment were to be affected, the Applicant state could request an examination of the situation in accordance with the provisions of the ICJ Statute" " the denunciation by France, by letter dated 2 January 1974, of the General Act for the Pacific Settlement of International Disputes, which is relied on as a basis of jurisdiction in the present case, cannot by itself constitute an obstacle to the presentation of such a request.

In 1995, referring to this paragraph 60, New Zealand made an application to the International Court of Justice again demanding the review of the situation. From the perspective of New Zealand, the underground nuclear tests made by French since the judgment by ICJ in 1974, were still unable to deliver sufficient protection and concern over the dangers of its nuclear tests. With regard to the application of New Zealand and the study of the situation in 1995, please refer to the book by Shaping Shao "The Studies on the Recent ICJ cases", published by Commercial Press, Beijing 2006, see, pages between. 258–291.

36 See, Australian Memorial, para. 431, available at: http://www.icj-cij.org/docket/files/58/9443.pdf, last visited on February 10, 2011.

37 See, Australian Memorial, para. 448.

Australia also noted that in terms of supervising France to observe the obligation to abstain from conducting atmospheric nuclear tests, every state possesses a legal interest. However, Australia has a higher title than most states to claim such protection because of its geographic situation and the deposit of radioactive fall-out from French tests landing on its territory.

In the case concerning the nuclear tests (New Zealand versus France), New Zealand, classified its claims into five points in the proceeding as referred to the paragraph 191. The rights asserted under heads (a) and (b)[38] fall into a different category from those under heads (c), (d) and (e). The former reflects a community interest in the protection of the security, life and health of all peoples and in the preservation of the global environment. The rights are held in common and the corresponding obligation imposed on France is owed in equal measures to New Zealand and to every other member of the international community.[39]

On the issue of the legal interests and jus standi, New Zealand also express edits views. The content of the notion of legal interest varies from case to case. And it has also been extended with the development of substantive rules of the international law. The international law has never exclusively been concerned with the protection of the material interests, narrowly defined, of individual states.And in an increasingly interdependent world, there has been an accelerating shift in the emphasis of the judicial enforcement of the substantive rules of the international law towards the protection of legal interests.[40] New Zealand also believed that in the development of there cognition of the right of States to bring issues before international tribunals in the general interests and without the direct in jury to interests vested in the mal one, the separate and dissenting opinions of Judge Kess up in the South West Africa cases were a landmark.[41]

New Zealand thought it possessed legal interests in the five heads, especially for (a) and (b). And its ought the protection that could reflect the community interests. The obligation to hold no nuclear test similar to the obligations stemming from the outlawing of aggression and genocide- is owed to the international community as a whole. Importantly, the Court

---

38   See, Australian Memorial, para. 449.
39   The rights listed under (a) and (b) are: (a) the rights of all members of the international community, including New Zealand to prevent that nuclear tests that give rise to radioactive fallout and other dangers; (b) the right of all members of the international community including New Zealand, to get rid of the artificial radioactive contamination to the terrestrial, maritime and aerial environment.
40   See.New Zealand Memorial Volume II, para.191.
41   New Zealand Memorial, para.194-196.

clarified the distinction between obligations and erga omnes as follows, "Obligations the performance of which is the subject of diplomatic protection are not the same category. It cannot be held, when one such obligation in particular in question, in a specific case, that all States have a legal interest in its observance".[42]

New Zealand and Australia have made claims based on the "the obligation erga omnes" that France undertook and partially made their jus standi on the basis of rights. Especially for New Zealand, it took quite a time for this country to address the issue of jus standi on its own rights.[43]

However, unfortunately, the International Court of Justice did not touch this issue whether it was in Australia's or New Zealand's appeal. The Court merely "understated" the issue as something concerning the "legal interests". ICJ stated that "it cannot be assumed a priori that such claims fall completely outside the purview of the Court's jurisdiction, or that the Government of New Zealand may not be able to establish a legal interest in respect of these claims entitling the Court to admit the application".[44]

The main significance of this case lies in: either ICJ as a whole or a judge as individual, or Australia and New Zealand as the parties in this case, all cases provide many inspiring and constructive arguments on the issue of the jus standi and classification and protection of legal interests.

First, the request of New Zealand is different from that of Australia in there al sense, and actually they touch upon the types of rights with different natures: one lies in the individual of interest; while the other in the interest of the international community. As far as the former concerned, Australia safeguards its direct rights, self-serving; and as for the latter, New Zealand acts as the "spokesman" of the international community to some extent, maintaining the interest of the international community thus being altruistic. Without carefully studying the request of New Zealand and decidedly responding to it, the International Court of Justice based on French unilateral declaration of "binding", simply regarded that New Zealand's "concerns" had been met and believed that the appeal of New Zealand had lost its effectiveness which was quite regrettable.

Secondly, in terms of the legal interest, whether it was Australia or New Zealand, both exemplified the ICJ's arguments on the "related obligation" in the aforementioned "Barcelona Traction Case", emphasizing the nature

---

42 New Zealand Memorial, para. 198.
43 New Zealand Memorial, para. 207.
44 See, Nuclear Tests (New Zealand v. France), Interim Protection, Order of 22 June 1973, ICJ Reports 1973, p. 140, para. 24.

of France's obligations in its atmospheric nuclear tests and accordingly asserting that they possessed the legal interest. Especially for New Zealand, it made a "further" step on this aspect and expounded the expanding trend of legal interest from the perspective of the international law. What's more, it also stressed the importance of possessing the abstract legal interests based on the public welfare of the international community.

Thirdly, in terms of the jusstandi under the protection of general legal interest, the case also has raised several questions of great importance. Firstly, the question lies in the relationship between the jus standi and matters of substantive law. In fact, Judge Castro has mentioned this in his dissenting opinion. According to the Judge's opinion, the question of admissibility and the matters of substantive law are the questions of different natures. Therefore, the two different issues should not be discussed at the same level. The second question lies in the relations between the juridical provisions and the protection of the general legal interest. Whether a state can have a right of jus standi, is directly based on the regulations of the judicial provisions. Accordingly, whether a state can file the lawsuits related to the protection of the general legal interest also caused debate in the "South West Africa Case". In this case close ties between the substantive provisions and dispute settlement provisions that are actually the guarantee of the rights and obligations in the substantive provisions exist. If the independence of the dispute settlement provisions and the decisive significance of it in solving the jusstandi of a state are not recognized, then, when the other conditions of jus standi are met, the request of a state based on its non-self interest, especially when related to the protection of the general legal interest, will lead to the "powerlessness" of the state and the ICJ in protection of the corresponding rights, which is not conducive to the development of the relevant rules of international law.

II. "The East Timor Case"

Historically, the Netherlands and Portugal had both colonized certain parts of Timor Island. In 1960, the 15th UN General Assembly adopted Resolution Nr. 1542, stipulated that the East Timor and its subsidiaries were among its list of non-self-governing territories. At that time East Timor was a colony of Portuguese. Portugal therefore rejected the view that East Timor was a non-self-governing territory. According to Article 73 of the UN Charter, a non-self-governing territory is an area whose peoples have not yet attained a full measure of self-government. In 1974, Portugal finally succumbed to international pressure and accepted East Timor's status as a non-self-governing territory.

In 1975, the Indonesia annexed East Timor and imposed effective domination on the region. The UN General Assembly and the UN Security Council has issued a number of resolutions condemning Indonesia's annexation of the East Timor and demanded the immediate withdrawal of Indonesian military forces from the region.

However, since 1976, the United Nations Security Council has notanyresolutions relatedtothe issue of EastTimor. And since 1982, the UN General Assembly has not issued any resolutions on this issue, either.

On February 20, 1978, Australia de facto recognized East Timor as part of Indonesia. On December 15, in the sameyear,the Australian Foreign Ministry announced that it would start negotiations with Indonesia on the issue of the delimitation of the continental shelf between Australia and EastTimor region of Indonesia.

On December 11, 1989, the two sides Indonesia and Australia signed a treaty: "Treaty on the Zone of Cooperation in an Area between the Indonesian Province of East Timor and Northern Australia". The Zone of Cooperation was composed of three parts: part A, B and C. To implement the treaty, and Australia specifically issued its relevant laws in 1990.

According to the treaty between Australia and Indonesia, Portugal considered that the continental shelf in the A and C regions should be exclusively owned by East Timor. During the negotiation on the agreement, Portugal repeatedly put up strong oppositions. And when the protest failed to achieve the effect, Portugal filed a lawsuit against Australia on February 22, 1991.

On June 30, 1995, the International Court of Justice made a judgment on the case, claiming that since this case was involved in the legitimacy of Indonesia as the third party, the ICJ could not exercise jurisdiction on the case as Indonesia did not agree to the Court's jurisdiction.

The first major contention was whether Portugal had "jus standi" and enjoyed separate legal interest in the complaint or not.

Australia believed that the rights enjoyed by the Portugal could not be equated to the rights enjoyed by East Timor. Since the withdrawal of Portugal from East Timor in 1975, the East Timorese people no longer recognized Portugal as the regulatory authority, and the international community (especially through series of United Nations resolutions) did not recognize Portugal's right to represent the East Timorese people anymore.[45]

---

45 From this sense, although Australia and New Zealand filed a lawsuit against French nuclear tests, the NewZealand's appeal is fundamentally different from Australia's. Australia's

According to Australia, a state had to prove its legal interest when filing a lawsuit against another state through the ICJ. Generally speaking, there was no principle in the general international law that is in support of Portugal's proposal of the principle of "international public service". In this case, the right of self-determination gives rise to consequential obligations for the third States. Therefore, the right should be exercised by the international community. To allow States to proceed-assuming a jus standi in the absence of collective decisions would lead to decisions of high subjective character. And the result would be practically chaotic and self-serving.[46]

Portugal in its pleadings refuted these doubts of Australia, emphasizing its proceeding did not depend on the notion of "mass action". On the contrary, it was in the identity of the representative of the people of East Timor. Therefore, it should possess the legal rights and have the right to take actions.[47]

In its 1995 judgment, ICJ skillfully handled the disputes over the jus standi and the disputes over legal interests.

ICJ started from the main arguments made by Australia to address the problem of whether the "third party rule" advocated by Australia should be established or not.[48]

In this regard, after mentioning the proposition of Portugal- "the rights to possess as the regulatory authority" of Portugal, the International Court of Justice immediately delivered and announced its "solemn" position: According to "Third-party consent" principle which was established in the case called "Monetary Gold Removed from Rome in 1943." ICJ without getting the consent of any relevant state, cannot judge the case.[49]

"Portugal agrees that if its Application required the Court to decide any of these questions, the Court could not entertain it. The Parties disagree, however, as to whether the Court is required to decide any of these questions in order to resolve the dispute referred to it."

---

appeal focused on the nuclear tests in the atmosphere while the appeal of New Zealand is for the general nuclear tests not limited in the atmospheric nucleartests. Therefore,inthissense, the ICJ treated the cases equally without actively and positively responding to the wider demands of New Zealand in the judgment, which also led to the review of the case in 1995.
46 See, Counter Memorial of the government of Australia, para. 242-252, available at: http://www.icj-cij.org/docket/files/84/6837.pdf, last visited on February 12, 2011.
47 Counter Memorial of the government of Australia, paras.258-263.
48 See, Reply of Portugal, para. 8.15, availableat: http://www.icj-cij.org/docket/files/84/6838.pdf, last visited on February 12, 2011.
49 ICJ Reports 1995, para. 23-24.

The ICJ specially rejected Portugal's additional argument that the rights which Australia allegedly breached were rights erga omnes and that accordingly Portugal could require it, indi vidually, to respect them regardless of whether or not another State had conducted itself in a similarly unlawful manner.

ICJ noted that the national self-determination which Portugal advocated came from the "UN Charter" and previous the practices of the UN.

The UN Charter had the nature of erga omnes, and this argument in itself was blameless. However, having a certain norm for all (erga omnes) was entirely different from whether a state accepted the rules of the jurisdiction of the International Court of Justice.

In a lawsuit, regardless of what property of the responsibility that the parties have cited, when a decision involves the evaluation on the legitimacy of a certain state's behaviors, the court will not make any judgment on the legitimacy.[50]

This case is unique and essential in terms of the fulfilling "the obligation erga omnes", In this case, ICJ found irrelevant to rely its judgement on the principle of the required consent of the third party to the Court's jurisdiction mainly on the technical basis of the "third party rule". However, whether or not the technical reasons exist is a very big controversy.[51]

Admittedly, ICJ's evasive attitude towards the supervision of the "the obligation erga omnes" undoubtedly "weakened" its previous discussion on it to great extent. On the one hand, as what scholars have commented, although the Court did not make a summative comments on the "jusstandi" of Portugal and appropriately averted it through some techniques, the ICJ's performance in the cases till meant that compared to the previous situation, it greatly retreated in its stance on the "the obligation ergaomnes"[52] But on the other hand, from the perspective of legal interest, although the national self-determination had the property of "universality", Portugal was not purely and completely based on the "self-determination" to "build" its

---

50   ICJ Reports 1995, para. 25-26.
51   ICJ Reports 1995, para. 29.
52   For example, as Judge Weermantry stated in his dissenting opinion that it was not difficult to differentiate the case from the case concerning "Monetary Gold removed from Rome". Once the cases were distinguished, the "thirdparty"wouldnotconstituteamajorobsta cleforthiscase.See.Dissenting opinion of Judge Weermantry, ICJ Reports 1995, pp.156-168. The other judges pointed out that in terms of the so-called "third party rule", the International Court of Justice did not always strictly comply with it in its judicial practice. See, Separate opinion of Judge Ranjeva, ICJ Reports 1995, pp. 130-131.

own "jusstandi". On the contrary, it was primarily in the status of "management authority". In this regard, as pointed by Australia, the UN General Assembly and the Security Council did not authorize Portugal to exercise the rights of management arbitrarily. And as a result of it and also the lack of universal support regarding the "mass action" theory in the international law, the "jus standi" of Portugal lacks sounded to have theoretical basis.

D. The stage of another small step forward: Genocide Convention to "Antarctic

"Whaling Case"

The case concerning "Genocide Convention" (Bosnia and Herzegovina versus Serbia)

Whether the case is the "nuclear tests" or "East Timor Case", jus standi is the issue which all parties are concerned with and the focus of the discussion as well.

When evaluating this issue, ICJ unexpectedly only discussed the issue from a technical point of view instead of explaining the "jus standi" in details, especially in terms of the concept of jusstandi around the universality of legal rights. However, that did not mean the Court had "closed the door" on this issue. Because the primary function of the ICJ is tore solve the disputes, rather than develop the international law; however the International Court of Justice has the right to develop international law according to UN General Assembly Resolution No.171 in 1947.

Therefore, in the process of disputes settlement, the International Court of Justice has been extremely restrained in the exercise of the function of developing international law unless the "situation is urgent". The ICJ's cautiousness on the development of international law was very obvious in the case concerning the "Genocide Convention".

On March 20, 1993, Bosnia-Herzegovina submitted a request against the Federal Republic of Yugoslavia, alleging Yugoslavia's violation of its obligations based on the "Convention on the Prevention and Punishment of the Crime of Genocide".

On February 26, 2007, the Court made a final judgment on the request. In the judgment, the Court confirmed that, Serbia and Montenegro had not performed genocide acts via its government agencies or individuals, so that there was no breach of the Convention rules. And the court concluded that Serbia and Montenegro it neither had not committed an "intended genocide" nor was it responsible for "complicity in genocide" a which was defined in the Convention:

But on the other side as for the massacre that occurred in Srebrenica in July 1995, the Court concluded that the acts committed at Srebrenica falling within Article II (a) and (b) of the Convention were committed with the specific intent to destroy in part the group of the Muslims of Bosnia and Herzegovina as such; and accordingly that these were acts of genocide, committed by members of the VRS (the Army of the Republika Srpska) in and around Srebrenica. The court added: Serbia government had violated its obligation to "prevent genocide" stipulated in the Article 1 of the Convention.[53]

Confined to the subject, here we only describe and comment on the relevant parts of "the obligation ergaomnes" and general legal obligations in respect with the judgment of the preliminary objections and the final substantial judgment. With reference to the connotation "prevention" and "punishment" under the Article 1 of the Convention.[54]

Serbia argued that since the genocide did not happen within its own territory and it did not involve in the genocide, it should not bear any responsibility.[55]

Bosnia and Herzegovina argued that according to this provision, Serbia had the obligation to prevent genocide from happening. In the preliminary objection judgment in 1996, the Court declared that the rights and obligations under the Convention had the property of universality, and the Convention did not impose any geographic limitations in terms of prevention and punishment of genocide.[56]

In the substantial judgment, the Court started from the point above and expounded the contents of the preventative obligation.

The Court noted that, since the first article denoted the meaning of "undertake", it symbolized an acceptance of a binding obligation and a formal commitment to it. The obligation to prevent should be a direct, normative and mandatory obligation In the aspect of undertaking the obligation, the Convention does not require the State to succeed in preventing genocide from occurring, but only requires the State to take all means reasonably available to them. When States do not take all effective measures within

---

53　Christian J. Tams, Enforcing Obligations Erga Omnes in International Law, Publisher: Cambridge University Press, 2005, p.183.
54　See, the operative part of the ICJ Judgment of 26 February 2007.
55　See, the operative part of the ICJ Judgment of 26 February 2007, para. 153.
56　See, ICJ Report 1996, para.31, pp.615-616.

their power to prevent genocide from happening, they should bear the responsibility. Therefore, to undertake the preventative obligation requires the State to act with "due diligence". In determining the extent of the "due diligence" (such as the geographic distance), it is necessary to consider the effective influence of a state on another state that practices or is going to practice the genocide. When the genocide and the behaviors forbidden in the Article III of the Convention begin, the preventative obligations based on Article I also begin at the same time. The state should start to fulfill the preventative obligations when the states come to know or should be informed under normal circumstances that there is a serious risk of genocide.

The discussion above actually highlights the concept "interference as an obligation". According to the statements of the ICJ, as long as the States are the parties to the Convention, even if they do not perform genocide or the genocide does not occur within the geographical scope of their own jurisdiction, the parties still be art the preventive obligations to different levels. .This means that when the genocide has occurred or is about to occur, states cannot refuse to fulfill the obligations under the Convention on the excuses of "nothing to do with them" and "no participation". All States parties undertake the sacred obligations and responsibilities in the aspect of supervising and ensuring the fulfillment of obligations under the Convention. Such obligations and responsibilities are apparently non-self-serving and are based on the maintenance of the community interests. States possess abstract legal interests in supervising the fulfillment of obligations under the Convention.

"Antarctic Whaling Case" (Australia versus Japan)

As for the judicial protection of the general legal interest, since the International Court of Justice has shown signs of loosening stance in the case concerning the "Genocide Convention (Bosnia and Herzegovina v.Serbia)", The "Antarctic whaling Case" (Australia v Japan) has become the one of extremely importance cases, serving as a link between past and future. And if the case proceeds smoothly, it will not only help to display the relevant juris prudence of the Court, but also is conducive to the further deployment of judicial intervention in the future.

Article 48

Invocation of responsibility by a State other than an injured State

1. Any State other than an injured State is entitled to invoke the responsibility of another State in accordance with paragraph 2 if:

(a) The obligation breached is owed to a group of States including that State, and is established for the protection of a collective interest of the group; or

(b) The obligation breached is owed to the international community as a whole.

2. Any State entitled to invoke responsibility under paragraph 1 may claim from the responsible State:

(a) Cessation of the internationally wrongful act, and assurances and guarantees of non-repetition in accordance with article 30.

III. The intervention by the ICJ ruling: Its procedural and technical rules

As can be seen by the aforementioned studies, on one hand, the International Court of Justice has played an important role on the protection of the general legal interest and on the other hand, the judicial practice of the International Court of Justice is commendable for promoting the judicial protection of the interests.

The concept is proposed by the ICJ therefore it is of great importance. Because the ICJ comes up with the concept of "the obligation erga omnes" in the "Barcelona Traction case" and stresses that all States possess legal interests in supervising the realization of the interests, the legal interests States enjoy are kinds of general legal interest, obviously different from the ones with emphasis on "equal" and "reciprocal" legal interests based on the contractual treaties. The proposal of this concept has obviously enriched the content of legal interests and given states the ownership and responsibility of community interests. From the perspective of the commendable judicial practices, ICJ has been holding the issue partly concealed. As can be seen by the aforementioned studies, in different cases and at different stages, ICJ's practices and stances on the issue of judicial protection of the general legal interest show some changes tending to actively advocate it in some occasions while tending to remain relatively negative stance in others. The commendable practices of the ICJ can be explained and understood only from the perspective of the operational law. The importance of rights and interests are important is one thing, and on the other hand, the judicial protection of the rights or interests having to follow certain technical rules and procedural rules is another thing. We should separate the procedural right and substantive right in the aspect of the protection of the general legal interests. Firstly, if only the conditions for the procedural right and technical rules are met, can the corresponding appeals start through the International Court of Justice? Without the compliance with the procedural and technical rules, even if the right is important, the ICJ may not open the door of "judicial protection" to the relevant States. Therefore, this section will focus on the procedural and technical rules on the protection of the general legal interest. Generally speaking, in the matter of the protection of the general legal interest, the procedural and technical rules that states need to follow include the following aspects.

The Rule of Agreement For International Court of Justice, agreement is the most critical and important element in the pre-trial stage of the case. As for con the concerned proceeding, the all three different power sources of jurisdiction of the ICJ, whether it is the voluntary jurisdiction, agreement jurisdiction or optional compulsory jurisdiction, they all reflect the importance of agreement.

"Agreement", especially in the form of "request" in the proceedings of the International Court of Justice, means that the agreement of the respondent State is particularly important.

In the case that the respondent State explicitly refuses to accept the jurisdiction of the International Court of Justice, even if the plain tiffs tates agree to accept the jurisdiction, the ICJ still has no jurisdiction over the case and should not hear the case as a result During the Cold War, there are many cases like this. The refusal of the jurisdiction of the International Court of Justice by the defendant states leads to the disruption of the case.[57]

The Rule of the Consent Agreement of the Third-party

This rule mainly comes from the ICJ case concerning the "Monetary Gold Removed from Rome in 1943" and has so far been applied in two cases.[58] The main implication of this rule is as follows: On the condition that the case between the parties involves a third country, and the results of the case are concerned with the vital interests of the third country, and the third country does not explicitly express an agreement to the jurisdiction of the International Court of Justice or before the third country participates in the proceeding concerned, ICJ should rule that it has no jurisdiction on the case. The "East Timor case" is the direct result of the practice of this rule.

The rule of "the Right to Access to the Court"

The rule of "the right to access to the Court" is a new procedural element proposed by the ICJ in the 21st century. The meaning of the rule can be stated as: Does the state have the right to resort the ICJ to dispute settlement

---
57 See, ICJ Judgment of 26 February 2007, para. 428-438.
58 To start the proceedings in such situation implies the distinction between "the Plaintiff State"and the "Respondent State".

only when possessing the access to the court? Without the access to the court, even if the state agrees to accept the jurisdiction of the ICJ, the ICJ should not consider the disputes. Under such circumstance, the International Court of Justice should not open its door to specific states.

The Rules of the Actual Effect of Judicature

The Actual Effect of Judicature mainly means that if the decisions made by the ICJ cannot produce the practical consequences, the ICJ should avoid obliging them. The ICJ should avoid clarifying or even elaborating a question of law purely on the basis of the rational sense in any case

The effectiveness of judicature mainly comes from the "North Cameroon Case". As exhibited previously in the introduction of the case, it is in the context that the UN General Assembly dealt with the ownership of North Cameroon and that the disposal practices were implemented accordingly, that the issue concerned was submitted to the International Court of Justice by North Cameroon. In this context, the International Court of Justice has clarified that the court ruling should produce some practical consequences –effect the existing legal rights and obligations of the parties and eliminate the indeterminate relations between the parties.[59]

The strict effect of "United Nations system"

The UN system is a normative concept proposed by the International Court of Justice at the time when the World Health Organization raised an advisory opinion on the legality of suing nuclear weapons by a state in war or other armed conflict. The meaning of the notion is that the United Nations system is a large system, and the agencies that operate within the system even including the specialized agencies in the United Nations should pay attention to the roles and functions of other organs. The bodies of United Nations including the specialized agencies should play their functions respectively by coordinating with each other rather than contradicting.

Regarding the ICJ's implementation of the UN system, the normative concept in its practices, the most obvious example for the restraining effect is embodied in the "Lockerbie case". In that case, when faced with

---

59 For example,the Aerial Incident case (United States versus USSR) on September 4, 1954. In that case, the United States submitted a request and started the lawsuit, hoping to stimulate the Soviet Union by this means to accept the jurisdiction of the International Court of Justice. After the Soviet Union clearly expressed its rejection, the International Court of Justice issued orders on December 9, 1958, declaring that it has no jurisdiction over the case. Andthe caseis withdrawn as a result.

the pressures exerted by Britain and the U.S. through the Council, such as the pressure to resolve the challenges against its own the constitutional system, Libya based on the provisions of Montreal Convention, filed a lawsuit against Britain and the U.S. in the International Court of Justice. And on the same day, Libya also requested the ICJ to make the order indicating provisional measures. When the International Court of Justice reviewed the Libyan provisional measures, Britain and the U.S. prompted the Security Council resolution Nr. 748 on March 31, 1992 ahead. In the Resolution, the Security Council asserted that the Libyan behavior had constituted a threat to international peace and security, and thus as for the requests of Britain and the U.S, Libya had to comply with the paragraph 3 of Resolution 731 without further delay. What's more, the Council also required all other states to take appropriate sanctions against Libya.[60]

In this context, Resolution Nr. 748 obviously pushed the International Court of Justice to the "corner". It is impossible for the ICJ to make the order indicating any provisional measures to support Libya's request. Once ICJ indicated a similar command, the command worked directly against the Security Council resolution Nr. 748. Based on this, the ICJ directly quoted from the Security Council Resolution 748 and concluded that the resolution had constituted an obligation of Libya under the Article 25 of the "UN Charter". While according to the statement that "the obligations under the present Charter shall prevail" in the section 103 of UN Charter, it cannot be considered that the rights enjoyed by Libya on the basis of "Montreal Convention" can be protected by provisional measures because it might undermine the rights of the United Kingdom in lines with the Security Council Resolution Nr. 748. On this basis, the ICJ rejected Libya's request for the indication of provisional measures.[61]

IV. Summary

As can be seen, on the one hand, as we have presented above, the International Court of Justice has played an important role in the protection of the general legal interest. And on the other hand, the judicial practice of the International Court of Justice is commendable for promoting the judicial protection of the interests.

The concept is proposed by the ICJ, therefore it is of great importance because the ICJ came up with the concept of "the obligation erga omnes" in the "Barcelona Traction case" and stressed that all States possess legal

---

60 East Timor Case is another example apart fromthe case concerning "Monetary Gold removed from Rome".
61 ICJ Reports 1963, p. 34.

interests in supervising the realization of the interests, the legal interests which States enjoy are kinds of general legal interest, obviously different from the ones which emphasizes "equal" and "reciprocal" legal interests, we see in contractual treaties. The proposal of this concept by the ICJ has obviously enriched the content of legal interests and given states the ownership rights and responsibility based on the community interests.

From the perspective of the commendable judicial practices, ICJ has held the issue partly concealed. As can be seen in the previous parts of my essay, in different cases and at different stages, ICJ's practices and stances on the issue of judicial protection of the general legal interest has shown some changes it tends to actively advocate it in some occasions while it tends to hold a relatively negative stance in other occasions.

The commendable practices of the ICJ can be explained and understood only from the perspective of the operational (procedural) law. The importance of rights and interests are important is one thing, and on the other hand, the judicial protection of the rights or interests having to follow certain technical rules and procedural rules is another thing. According to the previous studies, the technical rules and procedural rules include (not limited to these) the principles of agreement, the third-party agreement and the access to courts.

"Barcelona Traction (Judgment)" indicates that the lawsuit to be brought to the International Court of Justice must be based on the consent agreement of countries, as well as the acceptance of jurisdiction by the International Court of Justice For the third-party consent agreement, the case of East Timor is a clear example. And "the access to courts" means that only the members of the United Nation have the qualification to file with the ICJ.[62] If technical and procedural requirements above are not fulfilled, no matter how important the violated rights are—including universal rights or even unilateral coercive measures—the ICJ cannot open the door of "judicial protection" to the applicant States.

In conclusion, when states sought judicial intervention through International Court of Justice, and hoped to protect "general legal interest", the International Court of Justice gradually began to demonstrate an open position which is especially obvious in the post-Cold War era. The relevant practices of the International Court of Justice in the fourth stage, especially the practice in the case concerning Genocide Convention (Bosnia versus

---

62 Because Britain and the United States requested to extradite the Libyan suspects but the Libyan constitution prohibits the extradition of its nationals. In Security Council Resolution Nr. 731 (1992), the Council gave substantial supports for the request of Britain and theUnited States, and urged all countries individually and collectively to encourage the Libyan Government to respond to these requirements fully and effectively.

Herzegovina), clearly reflect this openness. If such a practice can continue itself to Antarctic Whaling Case (Australia versus Japan), the jurisprudence of the International Court of Justice might be clearer on the issue of protection of the general legal interest, with more obvious indication for the national behavior patterns. Of course, the protection of the general legal interest, especially when it comes to the judicial protection of the interest does not only depend on the position and the practice of the ICJ, but also on the continued exploratory practices that the states realize through their political will. And this is beyond the inherent limitations of the exercise of judicial functions by the International Court of justice. For the latter, its role and value may be more important. Since the judicial protection of the general legal interest is closely related to the jus standi of a state in the International Tribunal, the ICJ is less likely to clearly explain the jusstandi. On the contrary, the ICJ tends to be more willing to develop the explanation through the determination of individual cases. In this context, the political will of states and the Provisional Measures by the states are of great importance. States do not to pursue their own interests when they face issues of general legal interest. Therefore, due to the absence of altruism and strong political will, states generally do not initiate international judicial procedures easily, so as to safeguard this kind of interests, and even they decide to do so, it implies an existence of political will.

According to Statute and Rules, of the ICJ, on the condition that the Motions for the appropriate cases are not taken timely so as to start the judgment proceedings at the International Tribunal, the country cannot get jurisprudence in the international tribunals, consequently judicial protection of such interests will not be defended through the court. However, the Court, upon a request by the Palties, may extend the deadlines as seen in the case USA versus Mexico[63].

---

63 See, Order on the timely filing of the New Amended Indictment as modified and as directed in the Decision of 20 November 2000. See also Article 48 of the ICJ Statute and Rules: The Court shall make orders for the conduct of the case, shall decide the form and time in which each party must conclude its arguments, and make all arrangements connected with taking of evidence.

Principal Forms of Interventions by the U.S. and the Factors Behind Its Interventions

Zhang Jiadong[1]

Since the end of the World War II, the core national interests and national security of the U.S. has never been directly threatened. Hence, most of the external interventions by the U.S. since the World War II has nothing to do with the defense of its core interests. Its interventions are mainly for the maintenance of its national prestige or nationhood, or sometimes even just for the demonstration of its power, when it feels obliged to do. Besides, sometimes the U.S. has no choice but forcibly intervene. In this case, due to the constraints of the bipolar world political structure in the Cold War Era, and since its rival's position has generally limited US's external interference goals and scale, the dominant factor impacting the U.S. external intervention decisions were the degree of domestic public support and favorable domestic political factors. Evaluating from the perspective of its motivations, U.S. external interventions are roughly divided into coercive policies in coordination with coercive diplomatic activities; neo-interventionism motivated by humanitarian aid, and pre-emptive strategy for national security. At present, these three external intervention strategies constitute an integrated whole.

---

1 Prof. Zhang Jiadong has studied at the School of International Relationship and Public Affairs at Fudan University and got a Ph.D. in international relations for his studies on terrorism affairs. Since July 2004, he works in the Center for American Studies at Fudan University.

I. Development and evolution of the U.S. National Security Strategy

The United States is one of the few countries in the world that periodically publishes its National Security Strategy (namely the grand strategy). Since 1989, American President George H. W. Bush has started the tradition of publishing the *National Security Strategy* reports. President Clinton published National Security Strategy reports seven times, annually from 1994 to 2000. President George W. Bush published the report twice respectively in 2002 and 2006. Till today, President Obama has only published the 2010 National Security Strategy report. The national security strategy reports do not include the complete national grand strategy of the US, but merely provide some key documents and reports for reference. National grand strategy is also called the national security strategy because it is mainly composed of the twin pillars of defense and diplomatics trategies.[2]

It is an overall strategy that aims to "realize the fundamental national goals by using various national resources including military forces and others such as political, economic, technological, diplomatic, ideological, cultural, spiritual and so forth"[3]. In this sense, a state's grand strategy is never a simple strategy, but a complex system which includes a series of specific strategic behaviors and goals.

During the Cold War, both the Republican Party and the Democratic Party of the U.S. conformed and accommodated to the containment strategy against the Soviet Union designed and advocated by George Frost Kennan *et al.*, which led the U.S. grand strategy for several decades. After the end of the Cold War, the U.S. entered an era of strategic ambiguity, when the containment strategy had—as a matter of course—ended after its victory against the rival. From President H. W. Bush's doctrine of the New World Order to President Clinton's new strategy of democratic enlargement, and then to the Global Counter-Terrorism Strategy during the Bush Jr. tenure and President Obama's "selective multilateralism" strategy, American grand strategy has been in a state of constant adjustments.

On the whole, after the Cold War, the Clinton Administration emphasized U.S. leadership in international affairs in its National Security Strategy, besides cooperation with other countries to enable this leadership, also

---

2 Wang Weinan, Zhou Jianming: From "National Defense Reforming" to "Reforming Diplomacy", "World economy And Politics" Journal, in: 2006/12, p. 16.
3 For the relations between US' foreign economic diplomacy and its grand strategy constituents see Shi Yinhong's article, "A Comment on US' Foreign Economic Diplomacy", Journal of "US Researches", in: 2003/3, p. 130.

deterrence and pressure strategies against certain hostile countries. In its 7th National Security Strategy report, the Clinton Administration advocated international cooperation in order to maximize its national strategic interests, and also highlighted its resolute attitude to promote democratization in the other regions of the world even through military interventions when it deemed necessary. The National Security Strategy, issued by the Bush Administration, emphasized the U.S's leading role in world affairs, and implied that the U.S. would use compulsive power to force other countries to serve American interests. On September 20th, 2002, the Bush Administration issued its first National Security Strategy, which can be summarized as follows: to defend the peace by "fighting terrorists and tyrants" counter-terrorism, pre-emptive strategy against the enemy, preserve the peace by "building good relations among the great powers, , comprehensive superiority over rivals, promoting U.S. democracy and market economy.[4] In fact, this was a new imperial strategy which centered on unilateralism. This involved maintaining unipolar domination, wiping out terrorism, forestalling the enemy, compelling other states to accept their sovereign responsibilities, thus judging their behaviors, despising international treaties, international organizations as well as the international norms.[5] In comparison, the Bush administration's 2006 National Security Strategy was more adventurous and aggressive.[6]

President Obama, who undersigned the 2010 National Security Strategy report was opposed the internal and external strategies of President Bush, and rejected the former "pre-emptive" strategy, namely "making the first move and gain strategic advantage". Instead, Obama administration introduced the multilateral foreign policy which would deploy "smart power", thereby established a strategy of comprehensive engagement, the report said "successful engagement will depend upon the effective use and integration of different elements of American power." Thus this new foreign strategy focused on multilateralism and a diplomatic strategy based on "skillful use of hard strength"[7].

---

4 Yang Jiemian, US National Security Strategy, Report and Big Power Relationships, "US Research" in 2002, 4th issue, p. 7.
5 John G. Ikenberry, "America's Imperial Ambition," Foreign Affairs, Vol.81,No.5, 2002, pp. 44-60.
6 Xu Jia: "An Evaluation of US' National Security Strategy of 2006." Journal of "Peace And Development", 2006/3, pp. 11-13 and 32.
7 According to experts, in the 2010 National Strategy Report, the word engagement and the term "multilateral engagement strategies" has appeared 42 times. See: Walter Shapiro, "Obama's New National Security Strategy: More Questions than answers", http://www.politicsdaily.com/2010/05/27/obama's.new.national. security.strategy.more.questions.than.answ/print/. Access on 2011-12-3.

The new strategy report emphasized that using military force would be the final strategic choice of the U.S. Further, it would be employed only when other options do not work: "credible and effective alternatives to military action—from sanctions to isolation—must be strong enough to change others' behavior, just as we must reinforce our alliances and our military capabilities. And if nations challenge or undermine an international order that is based upon rights and obligations, they must find themselves isolated in invalid situations. Meanwhile, pursuing extensive widespread support by international organizations is the premise for selective military force".[8] However, in a similar and even consistent manner with the 2002 and 2006 National Security Strategy reports, the 2010 National Security Strategy report also analyzed the degree of security threats coming from Asia, and explained the objectives of the grand strategy in this continent as well as values and alliance system to be pursued in Asia.[9]

In fact, Bush Senior, Clinton, Bush Junior and Obama administrations have shared the same strategic goal as the core of their national security strategies which is how to retain the global hegemonic status of the U.S. and how to seek strategic interests for the U.S. by relying on its power status. In the 2002 National Security Strategy report, undersigned by President Bush Jr. it was explicitly pointed out that the U.S. would never allow other countries to challenge its status as the world's sole superpower. President Obama also stressed in his first State of the Union Address that the US would never accept being the world's second power...[10] Despite the decline in the US's national strength, Hillary Clinton, former United States Secretary of State, kept emphasizing repeatedly: "the U.S.' leadership in the world shall be strengthened rather than the opposite"11. As a whole, the U.S. as the world's largest economy, the world's leading military force and the world's leading scientific and technological power is not overtaken. Moreover, it still owns and leads the world's widest alliance system, all of which are the basis why together there is no significant change in the goals and means of the U.S' grand strategy. Precisely for this reason, President Obama, although he won an election victory with a campaign slogan of (change), he has in fact continued the U.S. long-existing national security

---

8   2010 National Security Strategy of the United States", p. 22, http://www.whitehouse.gov/sites/default/ files/rss_viewer/national_security_strategy.pdf. access on 2011-12-3.
9   See, Gan Junxian in 2010, 'US National Security Strategy Report Evaluation', 'Modern International Relations" in 2010, the 6th Issue, pp. 52-53.
10   Barrack Obama, "The 2010 State of the Union Address", Jan. 27, 2010, http://www.whitehouse.gov/thepressoffice/remarkspresidentstateunionadress, access on 2011-2016.
11   Karen De Young, "Obama Redefines National Security Strategy, Looks Beyond Military Might", Washington Post, May 27, 2010, p. 2.

strategies and did not make dramatic changes. Sarah Kreps has also confirmed this view in his book.[12]

Although we see no substantial change in the U.S's international status, its strategic security environment has greatly transformed. In the background of globalization, informationization, multi-polarization and diversification, the U.S. is faced with s uncertain and complicated threats compared to the previous certain and simple ones, thus the demarcation line between friend and foe is also becoming vague.[13] As a result, the influence of leaders' subjective judgments, ideas prevalent in the major political parties, and the general public opinion has began to play a more important role in the formation of U.S' concrete national strategies. Besides we can say that the making of the U.S' concrete foreign strategy can be more easily influenced by these above domestic factors.

II. Two External Intervention Strategies by the U.S.

Since the late Cold War age, the U.S. has been mainly implementing three external intervention strategies, which are coercive diplomacy, neo-interventionism and pre-emptive strategy. These three strategies comprehensively reflect the then international pattern, the U.S. public opinion environment and U.S's. strategic decision-making logic of those days. Below I will discuss these strategies respectively and make a comparative analysis.

A. Coercive diplomacy–in coordination with diplomatic activities

Coercive diplomacy means the diplomacy in which a country threatens an opponent to stop or avoid an adversary's behavior in an explicit or an implicit manner, otherwise, it attempts to punish the rival by military force or other means such as sanctions. This diplomacy generally includes 4 basic variables: placing a demand on the opponent, threat of force, diplomatic negotiation and enticing rewards.[14] Coercive diplomacy which enables sophisticated use of both diplomatic means and threat of force is generally much more effective than employing diplomatic means or military force separately as it can achieve one or more rational objectives with a lower cost and with lower risk.[15] In comparison with the U.S.'s traditional deterrence

---
12 See, Sarah Kreps, "American Grand Strategy after Iraq", Orbis, vol. 53, No.4, 2009, pp. 629-645.
13 Article by Pan Zhenqiang, Lu Yousheng: "Pondering On the US National Security", "Journal of US Issues Research", 2008 (1), p. 1-20.
14 Alexander George, Forceful Persuasion: Coercive Diplomacy as an Alternative to War, Washington, D.C.: United States Institute of Peace Press, 1991, Summary.
15 Bruce Jentleson, "Coercive Diplomacy: Scope and Limits in the Contemporary World," The Stanley Foundation, Policy Analysis Brief, December 2006, p.1.http://www.stanleyfdn. org/publications/pab/pab06CoerDip.pdf,access on 2011-10.25.

strategies, coercive diplomacy endows US with more initiative and coercive diplomacy is more aggressive. The deterrence strategy seeks to persuade an opponent to stop taking a dangerous action which it has not yet realized, here power threat is used to achieve this goal. On the other side coercive diplomacy is essentially a diplomatic strategy, one that relies on the threat of force rather than the use of force. If force must be used to strengthen diplomatic efforts at persuasion, it is employed in an exemplary manner, in the form of quite limited military action, to demonstrate resolution and willingness to escalate to high levels of military action if necessary, additionally we can say coercive diplomacy takes compellent actions only: to force a target to stop or reverse action already taken, rather than an offensive goal of forcing them to do something.

Although the coercive diplomacy employs both diplomacy and threat as its main means, it always keeps the actual usage of military force option open. In order to make diplomatic threats more effective, the coercive party often implements demonstrative and limited military actions and may also gradually upgrade them as seen in specific cases.

Coercive diplomacy is not new, and it refers to "a treaty deal attempt under coercion", and was even alternately used by both warring parties during the World War II. During the Cold War, especially under the shadow of nuclear missiles build-up, this strategy was replaced by the deterrence strategy. However, since the 1970s, the U.S. containment strategy could no longer cope with new and complicated international security situations due to the expansion of the Soviet-Eastern Europe and the continuous upsurge of the national liberation movements. Hence, the coercive diplomacy strategy emerged at this historic moment. During the Cold War, coercive diplomacy was mainly divided into three parts.

Firstly, the U.S. supported allies and strengthened their power to strike opposing forces; secondly, the U.S. coordinated with the military actions or other nonconventional military actions taken by allies or quasi-allies relying to its strong political and economic power and used its global diplomatic networks; thirdly, the U.S. acted as a peacemaker between its allies and its rival forces in good time and forced its adversaries to satisfy the political needs of its allies and itself in a powerful nonconventional manner.[16]

---

16 Article by Zhang Jiadong, "From Coercive diplomacy to 'preemptive strategy", Journal of "International Observation", 2003/6, pp. 67-68.

The coercive diplomacy strategy was fully practiced when dealing with southern African region. During the Cold War, the racist South African apartheid regime was a quasi-ally of the U.S. Both countries strived to maintain the white race's dominance in the region as a whole They cooperated in avoiding large-scale violent revolutions, and fought against the national liberation movements supported by the Soviet Union and deplored the political movements fighting against racist discrimination. For this purpose, the U.S. undertook proxy wars in collaboration with the South African authorities and gave logistic and propaganda support to right wing anti-government forces in neighboring countries. Angola was targeted as a communist country in which the USA should secretly intervene.

The U.S. also employed economic and diplomatic measures to oppress black South African opposition forces. Militarily, the U.S. vigorously supported nonconventional warfare and direct military operations in South Africa and backed armed anti-government paramilitary organizations in Angola.[17]

U.S. strongly supported the opposition factions in Angola financially, and imposed carried on economic embargo and sanctions against the Angolan government and prevented it from participating and benefiting from international economic organizations such as the World Bank.[18] Diplomatically, the U.S. on one side directly supported the racial discrimination policies of South African authorities but also played diplomatic mediator role successfully between South Africa and other Southern African countries. As a result, the U.S. managed to consolidate its interests in the form of diplomatic politics.

The U.S. also employed the coercive diplomacy in the Middle East. In the Arab-Israeli conflict, on the one side, the U.S. strongly supported Israel so as to maintain US's absolute superiority over its potential rivals militarily and economically. On the other hand, the U.S. used formidable propaganda and strong political and diplomatic network in order to legitimize military action of Israel in the international community, and demonized and illegalized the Palestinian resistance. At last, the U.S. actively reconciled the disputes between Israel and Palestine when necessary and helped Israel to reach its goals, so as to strengthen U.S's ability to solve

---

17 Sean Garvasi and Sybil Wong, "The Reagan Doctrine and Destabilization of South Africa" in Alexander George, ed. Western State Terrorism, Cambridge, UK: Polity Press, 1991, p. 238.
18 John A. Marcum, "Africa: A Continent Adrift", Foreign Affairs, Vol. 68, No:1, Special 1988/1989, pp. 164-165.

international disputes and further consolidate its hegemonic status, at the same time. Since the end of the Cold War, especially with the 21st century, during the U.S. centered unipolar world period, US has implemented coercive diplomatic strategies more effectively. In December, 2003, the Libyan government suddenly announced that it would eliminate all weapons of mass destruction, including guided missiles with a range of 300-km and a load of over 500kg, and relevant stockpiles and stop related weapon research activities... Libya's this decision stunned the whole world. In fact, Tripoli's disarmament was a success story for the U.S's coercive diplomacy after the Cold War.

From the case of Libya, we can see find the combined effects of the 4 essential factors: demand, threat, negotiations and awarding. Firstly, for a long term, the U.S. had explicitly urged Libya to stop researching and producing weapons of mass destruction and to admit its responsibility for Pan Am Flight 103 air disaster that occurred in 1988. Although these US demands were limited and rational the aim was to change the foreign policies of Libya without changing its political system. Secondly, by overthrowing the Iraqi regime and finally arresting President Saddam, the U.S. in fact posed a powerful threat to Gaddafi. Thirdly, diplomatic negotiations also played an important role in the case of Libya. Early in President Clinton's tenure, the U.S. carried out secret negotiations with Libya, and then President Bush Junior has continued this policy.[19]

Finally, the awarding mechanism also played a crucial role in the above case. The U.S. made a promise to Libya that it would lift sanctions on Libya once Libya eliminated their weapons of mass destruction and relevant programs. In that way, Libya would return to the international community and would enjoy the status of "normal" state again.

B. Neo-interventionism–in the name of humanitarian aid

Interventionism refers to the armed intervention conducted to another state on the legal basis of humanitarianism. Hence, it is often called humanitarian intervention. In fact, the theory of "humanitarian intervention" has a long history in both the East and the West. In ancient China, frequently a tyrant ruler was attacked by an emerging dynasty and the people under its yoke and oppression were relieved; and we all know that in the Western international legal system, there is the theory of limited sovereignty. Both imply that the exclusive right of sovereignty can be restrained when people

---

19 James Verini, "The Good Bad Son", http://nymag.com/news/politics/saif qaddafi-2011-10-12.

confront violence and maltreatment by the state authorities. Since modern times, more and more conscious humanitarian intervention has taken place. Even during the Cold War, several countries and international organizations have carried out over 10 humanitarian intervention actions.[20]

Actually, traditional humanitarian intervention was only temporarily conducted by countries and international organizations in certain international situations. It is more about an international code of conduct rather than a foreign strategy of a nation.

Since the Cold War, the possibility of wars among the great powers had radically decreased, and all of a sudden the U.S. became aware that its huge army, abundant intelligence and other security departments had lost their importance and practical utility. Meanwhile, the wave of nationalism after the Cold War has not only created a lot of independent countries, but also led to nationalist secessionist movements in many countries. Domestic conflicts and contradictions took the place of international ones, and became a new source of threat. Under this situation, the U.S. has developed new principles for foreign humanitarian intervention, which was also supported underpinned by its allies such as Britain. Blair, former Prime Minister of Britain, publicly stated that "As for external policies, the most urgent task of us is to provide legitimate reasons for our positive interventions in the domestic conflicts of other countries... We will be safer if we uphold our values.[21]

Also President Clinton emphasized that the U.S, in order to defend its traditional national interests would try its best to "maintain the will and conscience of the international community", "defend freedom and promote democracy all around the world" and employ military forces when necessary in order to "encourage democracy-oriented countries and make the anti-democratic countries pay the price in the true sense".[22]

As the main essence of neo-interventionism argues that a democratic world is a safer world..That means, democratic countries should promote the process of democratization in non-democratic countries. One important means to realize this goal includes initiating armed interventions in some non-democratic and inhumane countries. Compared with the theoretical

---

20 See, Zhong Mingyou, "Neo-interventionism Theory", "Lingling Institute Journal" in 2005, the 1st issue, p. 1.
21 April 22, 1999, British Prime Minister Blair's speech in Chicago Economic Club. Quoted by Xu Xueyin, "New Interference Theory: A Challenge to the International Law", Journal of Politics and Law Review, 1999/5 , p. 14.
22 Journal of US Research in 1993/4, pp. 17-18.

bases of traditional interventionism such as the "theory of limited sovereignty" and "irrelevance between human rights and internal affairs", neo-interventionist theory bases its arguments on the outdated character of state sovereignty concept and advocates individual-centered concept of "human rights to be respected beyond sovereignty". Upholding the principles of humanitarianism" and "protection of human rights" as its main values neo-interventionism is mainly practiced as armed interventions, but it is inevitably influenced by "real-politics".

Firstly, neo-interventionism is based on integrating moral pursuits with hegemonic objectives, but these objectives are often contradictory and mutually conflicting. For example, in the Kosovo case, the U.S., for a long time, had labeled "the Kosovo Liberation Army" as a terrorist organization. However, in order to disintegrate the Federal Republic of Yugoslavia, the U.S. later praised "the Kosovo Liberation Army" as the "freedom fighters" but on the other side treated "counter-terrorism activities" of the Federal Republic of Yugoslavia as "massacre" acts against humanitarianism. Here, we see that moral pursuits were obviously placed after hegemonistic objectives of the US. Secondly, neo-interventionism features dual standards. In the current world many countries are faced with extreme separatist forces and over 40 countries have to deal with or trying to suppress domestic ethnic-national separatist movements. Despite flaunting humanity, freedom and democracy all around the world, the U.S. actually favors and carries out selective interventions and employs moral standards to guarantee its benefits quite "flexibly". Colin L. Powel, former chairman of the Joint Chiefs of Staff of the U.S. , said: "use of military forces should be limited to those cases that can bring some concrete benefits and should truly guarantee that these benefits go beyond casualties and other costs".[23]

Lastly, we can observe that mainstream media outlets support neo-interventionism by misleading the public opinion. In the cases of Kosovo and Chechnya, most media outlets in the Western countries gave priority to instigate their audiences, and their reporters have repetitively transmitted bloody events while neglecting the backgrounds and roots behind them.

C. Pre-emptive strategies–serving national security objectives

The "pre-emptive strategies" were first proposed in a Chinese classic book entitled The Art of War: Thirty-Six Stratagems, and it originally refers to a situation in a war where the party taking earlier actions can always

---

23 Quoted from Richard N. Haass, in: Yin Xiong and Xu Jingyi, "Neo-interventionism", Xinhua Publishing House, Beijing, 2000, p. 69.

subdue the other party. This is also known as "gaining mastery and advantage by striking first, and allow yourself being defeated if you take late actions".[24]

Contemporary Western international relations theories and international law theory in particular has also made abundant elucidations concerning "pre-emptive strategies" and approves the rationality and validity of pre-emptive actions in cases of self-defense.[25]

Famous jurist of international law and thinker Grotius said: "It is legal to execute a person who aims to kill you." He believed: Anyone who remains in the status of moral superiority can properly execute punishment. The natural right to punish was an important innovation in Grotius' early works.

Emmerich de Vattel also pointed out in the Law of Nations that: "The safest plan is to prevent evil, where that is possible. A nation has the right to resist the injury another seeks to inflict upon it, and to use force and every other just means of resistance against the aggressor. It may even anticipate the other's design, being careful, however, not to act upon vague and doubtful suspicions, lest it should run the risk of becoming itself the aggressor."[26]

The Caroline Affair in 1837 was a typical example of "pre-emptive" method. Back then in Canada which was under the British rule, a rebellion occurred demanding a more democratic government, a U.S. steamship, the Caroline, carried men, weapons and supplies to a site on the Niagara River—a short distance above the falls—in order to render assistance to the rebellion. They were then arrested by British and numerous U.S. citizens (crew of Caroline) were wounded or killed. Although the U.S. side acknowledged that the British behavior could be deemed legitimate, it still argued that such preventive anticipatory self-defense action by Britain should comply with the principles of necessity and proportionality.[27]

In an era when the mechanism and institutions of power configuration in an international system has been inappropriate and became obsolete, or fell into anarchy, states have often preferred using the pre-emptive strategies. Moreover, pre-emptive strategies are used by certain aggressive countries

---

24 Ban Gu, "Book of Han Ji Biography" (Eastern Han Dynasty), China Publishing House, Beijing, 2011, p. 8.
25 C. S. Owens, "Unlikely Partners: Preemption and American Way of War", Quantico, VA: Marine Corps University, 2003, p. 3.
26 Emmerich de Vattel, The Law of Nations, Vol. IV, p.3, see, David M. Ackerman, "International Law and Preemptive Use of Force Against Iraq", September 23, 2002, CRS Report for Congress, RS21314, p.2.
27 See, Ouyang Chao, "Preemtive Strategy and International Law", Journal of Modern International Relations , 2005/7, p. 14.

which try to fabricate some "legitimate reasons" for their aggressive military acts. For this reason, even after the Charter of the United Nations was promulgated and the UN system was established, pre-emptive actions did not vanish completely. After analyzing the 30 cases of pre-emptive wars which involved 12 countries, between 1956-2008, Sun Degang has elaborated the following: "the domestic national public pressure and uncertainties regarding acute national security threats seem to be the primary causes of preemptive strategies."[28]

However, the legitimacy and the appropriateness of preemptive strategies are extensively questioned and their legal backing and legitimacy conditions status seem obscure and inconsistent. Almost no country regards pre-emptive strategies as an adequate security strategy.[29]

In fact, the academic circles have refocused on the issue of pre-emptive strategies after President Bush Junior issued pre-emptive strike orders. And we know that the U.S. government had used this strategy many times prior to 9/11 attacks. For example as early as the Cold War period, the U.S. government repeatedly thought about taking pre-emptive actions as seen in the Cuban Missile Crisis and the U.S's attempt to bomb China's nuclear facilities.[30]

In the Post-Cold War era, some U.S. politicians began to quest for a new world order which sought absolute security, absolute advantage based on the exclusive leadership of the US. In 1990, Richard B. Cheney, the U.S. Secretary of Defense at that time, entrusted assistant Secretary of Defense Paul Wolfowitz to initiate a research project for the new U.S. international strategies and announced that U.S. would seek to establish a new international order under the US leadership and utilize the golden historic opportunity, and that the US would never allow any other country to rise sharply or challenge the U.S's. superior status, to prevent this the US might employ pre-emptive actions to eliminate potential threats at critical moments.

The 9/11 attacks has been the first direct threat to the core security interests of the U.S. and also the second serious attack targeting its own territories after its independence in 1776. American peoples' faith and trust in home security was seriously shaken. As a consequence people and public started to reflect on the effectiveness and competency of the US security

---

28 Sun Degang, "Agent Analysis İn the Implementation of Preemptive Strategies" Journal of Diplomatic Review, 2009/5, p. 95-105.
29 Ouyang Chao, "Pre-emptive Strategy and International Law," Journal of Contemporary International Relations,2005/7 , p. 15-16.
30 Shen Yi: "The US National Security Strategy and Sino-US Security Relationship", Journal of World Economy and Politics, 2003/6, p. 52.

strategies, especially on the containment and deterrence strategies which were persistently employed for decades. Having the most powerful military might in the world, the U.S. was not able to stop or thwart a group of terrorist attacks, and suffered the most serious casualties since the 1812 US-Britain War. In order to cope with the asymmetrical, uncertain, unexpected and sudden threats arising from terrorism, the U.S. began to readjust its security strategies. In 2001, the United States Department of Defense proposed in the Quadrennial Defense Review Report that the U.S. would transform its defense paradigm from the threat based "defense planning" to "capability enhancement" based one.

In March 2002, the U.S. Nuclear Posture Review stated that the U.S. could develop new nuclear weapons and lower the "threshold of nuclear use"

Since May 22, 2002, when the U.S. President Bush Junior publicly stated in Germany that "the U.S. government will employ 'pre-emptive' measures when necessary" for the first time, the U.S. has formally confirmed the preemptive external intervention strategies, which was symbolized by Bush Junior's submission of the U.S. National Security Strategy report to the US Congress on September 20th in the same year. Preventing attacks before they occur as a preemptive strategy was also reaffirmed in the 2006 U.S. National Security Strategy report.

The report argued the following: those unqualified states as "rogue states" and terrorist groups which are trying to inflict as many casualties as possible and seek to produce or buy weapons of mass destruction, have become the biggest threats to the U.S., so the U.S. must take the initiative to eliminate the threats at their source.

Actually this report claimed preemptive "self-defense privilege" for the U.S. After the U.S. affirmed the pre-emptive strategies, the countries like Britain, France, Japan, Israel, India, Russia, North Korea and Pakistan also showed their intentions to employ pre-emptive strategies in different occasions, which seriously challenged the existing international legal system especially right of self-defense codified in the 51st article of the Charter of the United Nations.

This article states that on the condition of an armed attack taking place against a Member of the United Nations, it shall not impair the inherent right of individual or collective self-defence until the Security Council has taken measures necessary to maintain international peace and security. Therefore, the preemptive use of force constitutes a clear violation and ill-treatment of the UN principles which stirred debates in the international community and caused a great confusion.

Firstly, the use of nuclear weapons according to this preemptive strategy breaks the base line which regards nuclear weapons as the final defense means, a principle which has been tacitly upheld by the international community for decades. In fact, these new interpretations preemptive strategy can trigger the spread of weapons of mass destruction.

Secondly, the pre-emptive strategies have greatly shaken the existing international legal system. On the other hand such strategies have directly challenged the principle of state sovereignty, overthrown the fundamental principle of sovereign equality of states, violated the principle of non-intervention in internal affairs and fundamentally shaken the legal foundation of the current international order. Again, the implementation of this strategy is based on uncertain, opaque and unreliable judgments of the U.S. towards sources and degree of threats and fully reflects the US unilateralism and hegemonic mentality which leads to dissatisfaction and fear in most countries including allies of the U.S. At last, the strategy emphasizes on resolving problems through military force. It is important to note that these actions may not be the actions of self-defense..But worse still, they may be serious aggressive actions which violate the desire for peace in the international community. However, the U.S. rapidly winning the Iraq War at very low casualties led the U.S. government embrace the pre-emptive strategies very determinedly, and also win the support of many U.S. scholars. Joseph S. Nye, Jr. said: "the U.S. has strongly fought back to the public doubt about absolute superiority of U.S. military power."[31]

With this background, the pre-emptive strategies became the major principle of external intervention strategy which was jointly approved by decision makers and public opinions in the U.S.

III. Major factors influencing U.S. decisions on international interventions

According to the above analysis, we can see that the U.S. is not the first implementer or unique founder of coercive diplomacy, neo-interventionism and pre-emptive strategies. Nevertheless, in the past 30 years, only the U.S. has attached importance to them, and even elevated it to a sophisticated superior level intervention strategy through which the U.S. showed its hegemonic status and strong national power but also reflected its security culture. For over a decade from the end of the First Gulf War in the 1990s to the fall of Saddam Regime in 2003, the U.S. employed both the coercive diplomacy and the pre-emptive strategies.

---

31 Joseph S. Nye, Jr., "U.S. Power and Strategy after Iraq", "Foreign Affairs, Vol. 82, No.4, 2003, p. 60.

During the Iraq War, the U.S. employed the pre-emptive strategy at the very beginning, but it once again used the neo-interventionist "democratization strategies" and viewed democracy as a means of promoting moderation and stability and a tool that would prevent terrorism. This was also advertised by the US to obtain legality and promote a sense of righteousness for its launch of the Iraq War. In the Libya war which started in February, 2011, the U.S. and other Western countries firstly used coercive diplomatic means, then turned to neo-intervention policy, after the former strategy had failed. Finally, military intervention obtained a decisive position and overturned Gaddafi's regime in the Libyan Civil War by launching 26,000 air strikes which targeted 6,000 points, besides ground military forces were delivered. Evidently, the three external intervention strategies are closely related in many aspects. In the following part of the article we will respectively analyze international and domestic factors influencing U.S. decisions of external intervention strategies (see Table 1).

(1) International factors influencing U.S. decisions

International factors influencing U.S. decisions of external intervention strategies mainly include the general international pattern, national power and geographic position of potential intervention target countries, ideology of the potential intervention target country and its relationship with the U.S., etc. In addition, international and domestic public opinions also greatly influence U.S. selection of intervention strategies.

1. General international pattern

International situation can influence the strength and scale of U.S.'s outside intervention strategies. Under the general peculiar bipolar pattern of mutual deterrence during the Cold War, the strength and scale of U.S. outside intervention were limited except for the Vietnam War and the Korean War which aimed at serving the Cold War. The coercive diplomacy strategy was rooted from the Cold War. Back then, while being greatly hampered and balanced by the Soviet Union, the U.S. formulated the containment strategy as the basic national security strategy. The U.S. tried hard to intervene in internal and external affairs of other countries by armed forces, but could not break the baseline of launching any full-scale wars against the Soviet Union. In this case, the U.S. Government preferred using the coercive diplomatic strategy that featured controlling a state through either the threat to use force or the actual use of limited force and concealment. Neo-interventionism and pre-emptive strategies were derived when the U.S. superpower monopolized the world in the post-Cold War. At that time, the U.S. possessed an absolute military superiority and greater freedom of international actions, so it employed the more positive and proactive intervention strategy.

Table 1: Background and Implementation of The Three External Intervention Strategies

	Cold War	Post Cold War Period	Counter-terrorism Period	Post Counter-terrorism Period
National security strategy	Containment strategy	Sole Leadership strategy	Control or domination strategy	Selective multilateral engagement
External intervention strategy	Coercive diplomacy	Neo-interventionism	Pre-emptive strategy	Selective interventionist strategy
International pattern	Bipolar pattern	Unipolar Configuration	Unipolar Configuration	One superpower and multiple major powers
Domestic political state in the US	Government by 2 parties ruling in-turn	Democratic Party Government	Republican Party Government	Democratic Party Government
Public opinion basis	Support containment strategy, but oppose to hot wars against the Soviet Union	Public fond of peace dividend, don't advocate excessive employment of military forces in foreign countries	Give priority to topics of security, and support the government's overseas military operations	Give priority to topics related to economy, and oppose to overseas military actions
Strategic goals	Internal and Foreign policies of middle and small size developing countries	Domestic contradictions and conflicts in the middle and small sized developing countries	To hinder the ability of middle and small developing countries and non-state actors regarding terror activities	Internal affairs and foreign policies of middle and small developing countries

2. The national strength and geographic positions of potential intervention target countries

During the past decades, target countries of U.S's external armed intervention operations mainly included medium and small developing coastal countries.

The U.S. had to calculate cost and benefits of its' intervention actions carefully. Intervening in very large-scale countries, the U.S. would pay excessive costs and would have to change the domestic and foreign public opinions in case of long-term interventions. Intervening in an inland country, the U.S. can pay high expenses for logistics and transportation and potential costs can outweigh the benefits of intervening or the U.S. can hardly obtain intervention benefits, which were the reasons typically reflected in the U.S.'s opposition to intervene in the Rwandan Civil War. Hence, until 2011, the U.S. made direct intervention actions mainly to countries like Nicaragua, Angola, Afghanistan, former Federal Republic of Yugoslavia and Libya. The First Gulf War was launched by the U.S. in 1991, which was not an overseas intervention action, indeed. Instead, it was a large-scale conventional war. The Iraq War, started in 2003 was a typical practice of the pre-emptive strategies. The U.S. launched the war not because of the destruction of Iraq's continuing production of weapons of mass destruction, known ties to terrorist organizations and Iraq's continued violations of UN Security Council resolutions as it was alleged before the war, but actually after years of sanctions and strikes, the Iraq military system had been broken and the domestic public of Iraq had become increasingly discontent.. The invasion targets was reached swiftly leading to the collapse of the Iraqi government and the military of Iraq in about three weeks since Iraq had become a weak and inferior country and could hardly fight against U.S.'s powerful army effectively.

3. Ideology of potential targets of intervention and their relationship with the U.S.

In fact, as per standards and definitions of the U.S., it shall intervene in dozens of countries all over the world at any time. However, the U.S. generally made interventions in a few of these countries. Apart from limited national power of the U.S., ideology of potential intervention targets and their relationships with the U.S. also plays an important role in the US's decision making. One reason why the Reagan Administration implemented the coercive diplomatic policy in South African region and Middle East was to stabilize the situation through supporting the legal governments. However, the U.S. also strongly supported the anti-government forces in

Nicaragua, as well as anti-government terrorist organizations in countries such as Mozambique.[32]

In the neo-interventionist practices, the decision of the U.S.'s intervention depends on the country's relationship with the U.S. or on its relationship with other Western countries. In 1999, the U.S. carried on powerful military interventions in the so-called atrocity and violence in the Kosovo region of the Federal Republic of Yugoslavia, but turned a deaf ear to decades of ongoing humanitarian disasters faced by Palestinian refugees.[33][34]

Based on the same logic, when Bush Jr. continuously accused countries such as Iraq for "nuclear threat issues", strange enough, other countries nearly had no "nuclear" involvement. Currently, once again the U.S. and other Western countries have particularly focused on the Iranian nuclear issue and signaled their intention of launching another war. Obviously, the U.S. intended to "intervene" in the nuclear issue of the existing Iran Islamic regime. In order to solve this problem, the U.S.'s solid choices were take reliable actions by terminating the existing Iran regime or terminating Iran's nuclear program or a combination of both including toppling the regime.

4. The international public opinion environment

These three external intervention strategies of the US aim to cope with unconventional security threats, all of which require legal bases and public opinion environments that are different from those in conventional wars. Hence, in particular, the U.S. entails its international public opinion tools to create an environment which is beneficial to its military intervention activities both at home and overseas. In fact, "international terrorism has become a factor influencing the global diplomatic policy of the Reagan administration and also an important part for the U.S. to deal with East and West conflict", due to East and West contention the Reagan administration supported the racist apartheid regime of South Africa, it recognized the ruling government in this country and secretly provided materials and intelligence assistance to anti-government armed forces in leftist countries such as Mozambique, Zimbabwe and Angola.

---

32 Ihekwoaba D. Onwudiwe, The Globalization of Terrorism, Aldershot and Burlington: Ashgate, 2001, p. 109.
33 Zhang Jiadong, Journal of "Strategic International Observation", 2003/6, p.70.
34 G. John Ikenberry, Democracy, Institutions, and American Restrain. America Unrivaled: The Future of the Balance of Power, pp. 214.

South Africa's military was then engaged in an occupation of Namibia and proxy wars in several neighboring countries. Reagan Administration officials saw South Africa's apartheid government as a key anti-communist ally.[35]

After the Cold War, the NATO armed forces led by the U.S. blindly launched air strikes to all the military and civil targets in the former Federal Republic of Yugoslavia, carried out air strikes, night raids and special force attacks in the Iraq War and the Afghanistan War, and frequently employed drone strikes and the like in countries such as Pakistan and Yemen. All these actions brought international legal problems to the U.S., and some of its operations were criticized as state terrorism. In order to avoid supervision and opposition by domestic and foreign public, the U.S. government effectively "controlled" the media. Firstly, it transformed the U.S.'s open operations into covert ones. An U.S. officer once said that the Reagan Administration was distinctly characterized by effectively replacing diplomatic policies with secret deals and covert operations.[36]

After President Obama's taking office, despite the fact that the U.S. strengthened its special military operations in Afghanistan and Pakistan, only a few of them were effectively reported. Secondly, the U.S. has paid special attention to guiding and directing the information sources and news reports as well as combating and oppressing the dissident news and media outlets.[37]

Such media framing tricks of the U.S. were typically reflected in the news reports about Iraq, Afghanistan, Pakistan and during the recent Libya war. In this way, media tried to legitimize and beautify the U.S.'s military operations. Hence, such media control has become an inseparable part in the national security strategy of the U.S.

(2) Impact of domestic factors in interventions

International situation and other international factors have been the major factors influencing the U.S's external intervention strategies during the Cold War. In the post-Cold war era, especially when the U.S. became the sole superpower of the world, domestic factors of the US has played an

---

35 Marc A. Celmer, Terrorism, US Strategy, Reagan Policies, New York and Westport: Greenwood Press, 1987, p. 113.
36 Cited in National Security Archive, "Covert Activities in the Reagan Administration: Areas of Inquiry Suggested by Iran, Contra Investigation and Press Accounts", Memorandum for the Senate Select Committee on Intelligence, Washington, D.C., June 24, 1987, p. 2.
37 John Western, "Sources of Humanitarian Intervention: Beliefs, Information and Advocacy in the U.S. Decisions on Somalia and Bosnia," "International Security, Vol. 26, No.4, 2002.

increasing important role in its choice of external intervention strategies. In evaluating public support, the question remains to know the weight given to the opinion of the elite. As a whole, the strategic preferences of the U.S.'s elites and the international public opinion environment are important and sometimes even the primary factors influencing the U.S's external intervention strategies.

1. Different strategic choices of the U.S.' ruling elite teams

During the Cold War, for decades the two parties in the U.S. had agreed on the containment strategy. However, after the end of the Cold War, this consensus was greatly distressed. In general, the Democratic Party emphasizes the construction of international mechanisms, international cooperation and supports the democratization process, and diplomatic measure which is underpinned by military forces.

The Republican Party, on the contrary, generally supports unilateralism on bring fore the issues of national security believing in the ability and right of the U.S. to act without external support of allies in matters of its national defense. In the view of the mentioned difference, President Clinton adopted neo-interventionism as the external intervention principle, while President Bush Junior, has implemented the military-first pre-emptive strategy, which reflected that President Bush Junior was aiming to upgrade the US "leadership" to have control over global affairs, while President Clinton policies aimed to lead the world, with negotiations among allies . In fact, implementation of external intervention strategies by the U.S. was rather influenced by domestic interest groups such as the interest of the military-industrial complex. In those years, the Clinton administration was extremely reluctant whether to intervene Kosovo. However, he was more determined when the U.S. military-industrial group told him that a batch of U.S. guided missiles was approaching to the expiry date.

2. Domestic public opinion environment

The domestic public opinion environment of the U.S. involves 2 aspects: 1. whether the U.S. public is willing to see the government intervening in foreign affairs; 2. their viewpoints and emotions towards potential intervention objects. During the Cold War, the U.S. public basically held similar views regarding the national grand strategy, which laid a solid foundation for the U.S. to implement the containment strategy for a long term. However, in the post-Cold War Era, the general public of the U.S. was no longer certain and no longer in agreement regarding security issues. Following the collapse of the Soviet Union and due the uncertainties of the new post-Cold war era Clinton administration mainly focused on the creation of a new approach for handling international affairs, a policy called "doctrine of democratic enlargement" was introduced. Doctrine of democratic enlargement was based on the idea of expanding market democracies around the world, promoting free trade, implementing multilateral peacekeeping policies and it included a commitment of limited interventions in international affairs except severe global crisis situations when deemed feasible and practical (i.e. interventions with little risk and low causalities of U.S. troops) and morally defensible.

Therefore, the U.S. public in the Clinton era was mainly concerned about how to develop economy, improve social welfare and carried out a relatively more peaceful policy in foreign affairs.. However, in the tenure of President Bush Junior, the outbreak of the 9/11 attacks have transformed the U.S.'s public opinion. The U.S.'s public attached more importance and became more sensitive to security topics, thereby expressed broad willingness to support the government in expanding overseas military activities to combat terrorism. In 2002, when the United States Senate voted on the resolution for use of military force against Iraq, only one senator voted against. This result has fully reflected the then characteristic of the U.S's public opinion, which quite favored pre-emptive military intervention strategy. However, since 2007, the U.S. was confronted with a setback in the Iraq battlefield, failed to make substantial progress in the counter-terrorism war and was faced with increasingly serious domestic economic problems. The U.S. public fundamentally changed their attitude towards overseas wars, which forced President Bush Junior to adjust Iraq policies and withdraw the US troops during his last two years of tenure. Till recently, such a public opinion hasn't changed and lays an important foundation for President Obama's overseas intervention decisions. In the Libya event starting from March, 2011, at last the U.S. acted as a backstage leader mainly due to public opinion and domestic public pressure.

IV. Conclusions

From coercive diplomacy and neo-interventionism and to pre-emptive strategies, the U.S. has continuously upgraded and enlarged its possibility and scale of employment of military forces. Multiple presidents from both the Republican Party and the Democratic Party administrations have engaged themselves in upgrading and expanding US military machine. The significance and information involved in the logic chain appears to be very important, because the implementation of the coercive diplomatic does not necessarily mean that the U.S. is committed to addressing and solving the problems. Instead, the US leadership may intend to tell the domestic public that it is trying hard to defend the interests and ideals of the U.S. while at the same time providing legitimacy for future military solutions. The US leadership's attitude regarding the Libya intervention case, may be the proof of such assumption, accordingly Robert Art wrote: "Do not resort to coercive diplomacy, unless, you've gotten ready to start a war, or unless you have found a proper and a safe political way out,when the coercive diplomacy will fail."[38]

Precisely because of this, after President Obama took office, the U.S. has publicly stated that it would give up a series of external operations that was conducted by the former US government including global counter-terrorism operations, use military means and employment of the principle of unilateralism. However, in fact it has only changed the interventions in foreign affairs, as well as the goals and specific behaviors which aim to rebuild the national pattern.

At present, the U.S. demonstrates a trend of making comprehensive use of multiple external intervention strategies and use of relevant means. Particularly since the "Arab Spring Transformations" which started in the end of 2011, the U.S. has successfully led the development direction of the Libya intervention by comprehensively employing coercive diplomacy and neo-interventionism. At present, it is seeking to prepare the legal basis of a possible armed interventions targeting Syria and Iran. In this situation, another kind of U.S. intervention strategy—the selective intervention strategy—is taking shape: the U.S. will seek to weaken the military, political and economic capacities of a target country by employing coercive diplomacy, in the meanwhile provoke and intensify domestic discontent and turmoil in the target country; and when the conditions will be ripe it will make a military intervention, cloaked in a kind of humanitarian intervention, i.e. neo-interventionism. And as another trend, the U.S. and its western allies may launch pre-emptive military attacks to some countries in the name of important international security topics such as nuclear non-proliferation issue and fight against terrorism. Nevertheless, as Niall Ferguson said, "the decline and fall of the U.S. Empire may not be caused by terrorists hanging around about the gate of U.S., but by debt crises inevitable for a welfare state."[39]

---

38 Robert Art & Patrick M. Cronin, The United States and Coercive Diplomacy, Washington DC: US Institute of Peace Press, 2003, p. 388.
39 Niall Ferguson and Laurence J. Kotlikoff, "Going Critical: American Power and the Consequences of Fiscal Overstretch", The National Interest, Fall 2003, pp. 22-32.

In the face of serious domestic social and economic dilemmas, the U.S. is more likely to take military adventures overseas. However, in view of its increasingly weakening military strength, the U.S. will launch military interventions overseas in a more selective and indirect manner.

Democratic Aid and International Interventions by the U.S.

Liu Guozhu[1]

As a political term which emerged after 1980s, "democratic aid" belongs to the category of political aid, but it is different from traditional political aid. The traditional political aid generally refers to the political support by the US or shared solidarity among US and its allies, with the aim of consolidating its world hegemony and securing the political stability of the US allies..

Democracy aid can also be defined as the promotion of democracy, democracy support or promoting democracy building, as a part strand of foreign policies adopted by governments, established international institutions (including treaties) and non-governmental international organizations that seek to support the spread of democracy as a political system around the world.

Since 1980s, the U.S. has provided democratic aid to US friendly countries with the aim to maintain the friendly state with the U.S. in terms of ideology and political system, besides it included those countries being hostile to the US or those countries with dissimilar ideologies.

---

[1] Doctor of History, Professor in Department of History of Zhejiang University, special council member and special researcher of China Foundation for Human Rights Development. The paper was based on the thesis published in American Studies Quarterly, No.3, 2010.

Apart from traditional sovereign countries, the beneficiaries of aid also include various political organizations, social organizations and even opposition organizations of the aided countries.

The U.S. provides democratic aid goods, funds—mainly in the form of grants, various kinds of equipment and materials as well as some advanced technologies. Democratic aid, is an important component of U.S' democracy export strategy, and an important means for the US to promote democratization world-wide.

I. Development history of U.S.' democratic aid

Democratic aid by the U.S. is concerned the development aid and development paths, development modes of the recipient countries. By the facade of providing democratic aid, the U.S. can influence the development paths and development modes of the recipient countries, and this played an important role in foreign aid strategies of the U.S. during the Cold War.

The U.S. foreign aid during the Cold War had basically gained a strong ideological colors, targeted at non-Western development views. Under the grand framework of Cold War whose main actors were the U.S. and the Soviet Union, the U.S. aid primarily aimed to prevent developing countries from embarking on a socialist development path and the spread of international communism.

Due to the impact of the grand framework of the Cold War and due to the prevalent political development theories at that time, the U.S. leaders and officials, when designing the aid, did not prioritize, or did not make strict considerations about the status of beneficiaries' domestic status: whether they were indeed democratic states politically, or whether they practiced free-market standards for development

Over 40 years ago, many scholars of the Western political academia, strongly believed—the mainstream economic and political development view—that: the more developed a country socio-economically, the more likely will it be able to build a lasting democratic system.[2]

The core content of this development concept has argued that economic development would automatically lead to democratization. Some scholars even argued that authoritarian regimes could make better use of limited and poor economic resources to create a rapid economic growth, accordingly

---

2 See, relevant detailed discussions from Seymour M. Lipset, "Some Social Requisites of Democracy: Economic Development and Political Legitimacy," The American Political Science Review, Vol.53, No.1, 1959, pp. 69-105.

many scholars often doubted democratic regimes as being influenced by special interest groups.

Compared to authoritarian regimes which were generally isolated from the majority, those democratic regimes in the developing countries would always succumb to public appeals, thus easily compromise with public demands, which hinder them to plan and conduct comprehensive economic development plans.

In view of this, these scholars concluded that the process of democratization should be properly postponed till the realization of certain development goals. Influenced by the above development theories, Agency for International Development in the U.S., since its establishment, and even until the middle and late1970s, generally did not adopt the promotion of democratization in the developing countries as its strategic objective, when designing its international development aid programs. We can even say that, during the Cold War era, in most cases, except a few of them, the countries which were provided economic aid from the U.S. were mainly pro-U.S. dictatorships, such as the Syngman Rhee regime of South Korea, Nguyen's regime in the southern Vietnam, and other numerous militarist and other type of dictatorships in Latin America. However, we cannot say that the U.S. government lacked the desire and need to promote democratic aid, but the desire did not become a direct and full-fledged national policy. As a matter of fact, the U.S. government took promotion of democratization in the recipient countries as one objective of its foreign aid policy, but this aim only remained an indirect component of this foreign aid policy.

Whether the U.S. Agency for International Development or the Peace Corps both organizations intended to "shape and mould" the recipient countries with their projects. In other words, they concentrated their efforts to shape the economic and political systems of the recipient countries according to the U.S. model and standards. Through staff exchanges, Peace Corps volunteers, when working in the recipient countries, spread their thoughts and attitudes, communicated their experiences, but also gave abundant feedback to the U.S. government so that latter could better introduce its social system and advertise the superiority of its cultural system to the people of host countries. In this way, the aim was to persuade more people in the developing countries so that they would admire the American culture and its values, and aspire that their countries would to acquire adapt such a cultural and social system.[3]

---

3 On the surface, Peace Corps Volunteers helped to build clinics in villages, put books in schools, and improved access to nutritious food, this organization is still active in 60 countries.

This was the overriding motive why American policymakers have established the Peace Corps volunteer program and sent them to the developing countries.

During the late 1970s to the early 1980s, the first stage of the U.S. foreign democratic aid had started. The first stage started with the human right diplomacy of President Carter administration, then with the establishment of The National Endowment for Democracy which aimed to act as a grant-making foundation, by the Reagan administration, international democratic aid was gradually institutionalized.

After Carter took Office, the U.S. administration, made human rights issues a priority in the U.S. foreign policy.

President Carter believed that throughout the whole world, the inspiration and demand for human rights has become a world trend, including the free nations and the totalitarian countries. In his inaugural address, he declared: "Ours was the first society openly to define itself in terms of both spirituality and human liberty. It is that unique self-definition which has given us an exceptional appeal, but it also imposes on us a special obligation to take on those moral duties which, when assumed, seem invariably to be in our own best interests."

"The world itself is now dominated by a new spirit. Peoples more numerous and more politically aware are craving, and now demanding, their place in the sun—not just for the benefit of their own physical condition, but for basic human rights. The passion for freedom is on the rise. Tapping this new spirit, there can be no nobler nor more ambitious task for America to undertake on this day of a new beginning than to help shape a just and peaceful world that is truly humane."

"We are a proudly idealistic nation, but let no one confuse our idealism with weakness. Because we are free, we can never be indifferent to the fate of freedom elsewhere. Our moral sense dictates a clear-cut preference for those societies which share with us an abiding respect for individual human rights. We do not seek to intimidate, but it is clear that a world which others can dominate with impunity would be inhospitable to decency and a threat to the well-being of all people."[4]

---

4   Jimmy Carter, Inaugural Address, published in Inaugural Addresses of the Presidents of the United States, Beijing, Central Compilation & Translation Press, 1995, pp. 409-410.

On May 22, 1977, at the Commencement Exercises at the University of Notre Dame, President Carter elaborated on the new US foreign policy: "we have reaffirmed America's commitment to human rights as a fundamental tenet of our foreign policy." ... "I want to speak to you today about the strands that connect our actions overseas with our essential character as a nation. I believe we can have a foreign policy that is democratic, that is based on fundamental values, and that uses power and influence, which we have, for humane purposes. We can also have a foreign policy that the American people both support and, for a change, know about and understand.

I have a quiet confidence in our own political system. Because we know that democracy works, we can reject the arguments of those rulers who deny human rights to their people.

We are confident that democracy's example will be compelling, and so we seek to bring that example closer to those from whom in the past few years we have been separated and who are not yet convinced about the advantages of our kind of life.

We are confident that the democratic methods are the most effective, and so we are not tempted to employ improper tactics here at home or abroad.

Carter administration even believed that in order to promote and implement the human rights policy, the United States could well interfere in the affairs of other countries.

The Secretary of State of the Carter Government, Cyrus Vance said in a statement: "It is not our purpose to intervene in the internal affairs of other countries, but , as the President (Carter) has emphasized, no member of the United Nations can claim the violation of internationally-protected human rights as its own domestic affair, solely. United States "will speak frankly about injustice, both at home and abroad," while avoiding strident and polemical language. Vance cautioned, although, that our administration would not "comment on each and every issue" but would comment "when we see a threat to human rights" and when it was "constructive to do so." The administration also linked human rights concerns directly to the conduct of foreign policy, including support for a bill halting importation of Rhodesian chrome and the reduction of foreign aid to other nations that did not display sufficient respect for human rights."[5]

---

5 Zhou Qi: American Diplomatic Policies about Human Rights, Shanghai People's Publishing House, 2001, p. 69.

As argued by the Carter administration, the U.S. behaviors and foreign policy complied with both its liberal tradition and the spirit of United Nations Universal Declaration of Human Rights, and it is also the US' mission and duty to the world.

During the tenure of President Carter, there was no large-scale democratic wave in the world, in general. The Carter administration cared about basic breaches of human rights in some countries at that time, such as cruel tortures, political assassinations and other forms of infringement of basic human rights. Carter administration rarely paid attention to higher level of human rights such as freedom of speech, freedom of association, right to information and regular political elections.

In addition, the Carter administration also recognized that human right defence and maintenance should be a long-term objective of the U.S. foreign policy, Carter administration thought that except for a few individual cases, the U.S. government could not rapidly reduce human rights violation all around the world.

In the meantime, the Carter administration argued that some other objectives in U.S. foreign policies "are equally important as human rights or are even more important compared to it under some cases", such as Middle East peace talks, stabilization of the NATO (North Atlantic Treaty Organization), normalization of relations with China, and limitation of strategic weapons. Confronting the above problems, the U.S. would "not hesitate to declare its(our) ultimate objectives and to take concrete actions to move forward them., namely postpone or reduce the objectives of human rights, that would become subordinate to other important foreign policy objectives.[6]

Virtually all observers agree that the Carter administration's foreign policies changed over time. Hence, when pro-Cuba Sandinista Front overturned pro-Western, Somoza regime in Nicaragua and the Soviet Union directly sent troops into Afghanistan, the Carter administration began re-employing the former foreign policies and did not focus on human rights policy any longer.

With Reagan taking office, promotion of democracy in foreign countries gradually became an important content of the U.S' foreign aid. On June 8, 1982, in his address to the members of the British Parliament, President

---

6 David F. Schmitz and Vanessa Walker, "Jimmy Carter and the Foreign Policy of Human Rights: The Development of a Post Fort War Foreign Policy," Diplomatic History, Vol. 28, No. 1, 2004, pp. 127-128.

Reagan declared that the U.S. had very simple diplomatic objectives – "The objective I propose is quite simple to state: to foster the infrastructure of democracy, the system of a free press, unions, political parties, universities, which allows people to choose their own way to develop their own culture, to reconcile their own differences through peaceful means. It is time that we committed ourselves as a nation- in both the public and private sectors to assisting democratic development"[7].

Since then, one major objective of the U.S. foreign policies is to assist democratic development overseas and promote global democratization.

The Reagan administration's policy of promoting democracy in foreign countries, primarily was the product of its opposition to communist ideology. In the speech of the British Parliament, Reagan had also stressed the need to launch a crusade against Soviet despotism and the need to fight for freedom.

As part of the foreign policy that became known as the Reagan Doctrine, the U.S. supported anti-communist guerillas and resistance movements around the World to diminish Soviet influence as a part of the administration's overall Cold War strategy. While rearming, opposing the Soviet Union power, aiding anti-Soviet resistance movements all over the world and gradually returning to the former policies, the U.S. also obviously strengthened its aggressive manner in the ideological field.

The Wall Street Journal published in USA called the policy of the Reagan administration as the "War of Ideas"[8].

One major initiative launched by Reagan administration was the establishment of the National Endowment for Democracy (NED).

The purpose of setting up the NED was to provide the continuity of the U.S.' "Covert Strategy" in other countries in the new period. In earlier time of Cold War, the U.S. and its allies secretly provided consultants, equipments and funds to socialist countries of Eastern Europe on the other side of Iron Curtain via public nongovernmental volunteer organization (POV) in order to support opposition persons in these countries to conduct political activities like publishing newspapers and forming associations. In the late1960s, the U.S.' non-governmental volunteer organizations were found only to conduct activities for overturning regime in socialist countries. The

---

7 Ronald Reagan, "Address to Members of the British Parliament, June 8, 1982," State Department Bulletin, July 1982, pp. 24-29.
8 Gerald F. Seib, "Fearing Soviet Gains U.S. Counterattacks in the Propaganda War," Wall Street Journal, May 17, 1983, p. 1.

covert operations of these NGO's were funded by CIA. As a result, socialist countries raised an outcry against the U.S. in some international organizations which made Johnson administration issue commands to stop the mentioned covert activities. Hence, some senators in the US Congress began setting up public nongovernmental organizations which aimed to continue its subsidization for overseas democracy movements.

The Reagan administration took the lead in establishing the National Endowment for Democracy (NED).The establishment of the NED continued the U.S. "Covert Strategy" in the new period. In the earlier Cold War, the U.S. and its allies secretly provided consultants, equipment and capital to socialist countries in Eastern Europe on the other side of Iron Curtain via a nongovernmental volunteer organization (PVO) in order to help oppositions there to open newspaper offices and form associations. In the late 1960s, PVOs of the U.S. were found to obtain activity funds from the CIA and engaged in subversive activities in some countries. After the information was revealed, socialist countries strongly opposed to the U.S. in some international organizations. Meanwhile, the Johnson administration had to issue commands to stop the above covert activities. Hence, some senators in the United States Congress began building PVOs in order to continue providing subsidies for overseas democratic movements.

Furthermore, the largest labor union organization of the U.S. – American Federation of Labor and Congress of Industrial Organizations (AFL-CIO)—expected to establish an U.S. fund of democracy to provide public resources for international activities which could take the place of activities conducted by the CIA in the 1960s.

In February 1983, the Reagan administration formally suggested the establishment of the National Endowment for Democracy to the congress and obtained approval of most senators in the two parties. Afterwards, the United States Congress approved to establish the National Endowment for Democracy. According to regulations of the National Endowment for Democracy which were formulated by the United States Congress, the Endowment aims to complete the following objectives:

- to encourage free and democratic institutions throughout the world through private-sector initiatives, including activities which promote the individual rights and freedoms (including internationally recognized human rights) which are essential to the functioning of democratic institutions;

- to facilitate exchanges between United States private-sector groups (especially the two major American political parties, labor, and business) and democratic groups abroad;

- to promote United States nongovernmental participation (especially through the two major American political parties, labor, business, and other private-sector groups) in democratic training programs and democratic institution-building abroad;

- to strengthen democratic electoral processes abroad through timely measures in cooperation with indigenous democratic forces;

- to support the participation of the two major American political parties, labor, business. and other United States private-sector groups in fostering cooperation with those abroad dedicated to the cultural values, institutions and organizations of democratic pluralism; and

- to encourage the establishment and growth of democratic development in a manner consistent both with the broad concerns of United States national interests and with the specific requirements of the democratic groups in other countries which are aided by programs funded by the Endowment.[9]

For the first year, the United States Congress set the upper limit of fund allocation as 18 million Dollars for the NED operations. Afterwards, the US Congress gradually increased the appropriation provided to the NED, which reached up to 30 million dollars in the late 1990s.[10]

The establishment of the NED symbolized the institutionalization of U.S. foreign democratic aid. Since the Reagan administration, the NED has gradually played an important role for the U.S. to promote democratic movements overseas.

Although, the Reagan administration built a systematic democratic aid platform, democratic aid during Reagan's tenure still remained at an initial stage. In the meantime, except for Latin America, there were no large-scale democratization waves in other countries. In the late 1980s, when the waves of democratization swept across countries in Eastern Europe, Asia and Africa, the democratic aid platform built elaborately by the Reagan administration could be rapidly mobilized and thus quickly expanded the U.S' democratic aid.

---

9   Thomas Carothers, Aiding Democracy Abroad: The Learning Curve, Washington D.C.: Carnegie Endowment for International Peace, 1999, pp. 31-32.
10   David P. Forsythe, Human Rights and American Foreign Policy: Congress Reconsidered, Gainesville: University Press of Florida, 1988, p.135.

The 1990s saw the second stage of U.S. foreign democratic aid

During this period, U.S. foreign democratic aid was characterized by: firstly, democratic aid was mainly provided to Eastern Europe and the former Soviet Union, which were former socialist countries in the Cold War. Undoubtedly, the U.S. executed the democratic aid in order to consolidate achievements in the Cold War and accelerate transformation of the political systems in these countries; secondly, the aid expanded rapidly. After drastic changes took place in Eastern Europe, the Bush Senior administration and the United States Congress made a swift response. In particular, they specially set up a Fund for Democracy in Eastern Europe and funded 0.3 billion dollars to Eastern European countries in order to support their democratized transformation. After the collapse of the Soviet Union, the U.S. rapidly established the Freedom Support Fund, together with the Department of Defense Cooperative Threat Reduction Program, aided the former Soviet Union 2 billion dollars in one year. From 1990 to 1998, the democratic aid fund provided by the U.S. to Eastern European countries reached up to 0.33 billion dollars; from 1992 to 1998, the democratic aid fund provided by the U.S. to the former Soviet Union reached up to 0.32 billion dollars. In the same period, the U.S. NED provided 3-5 million dollars and 4-5 million dollars each year on average respectively to Eastern Europe and the former Soviet Union. Established in 1993, the Asia-Europe Foundation was also used for democratic transformation of some countries in the former Soviet Union and 5-10 million dollars were funded every year. Throughout the 1990s, the U.S. provided democratic aid fund of about 1 billion dollars to Eastern Europe and the former Soviet Union.[11]

With the 21st century especially after "9/11" Event, the U.S. entered a new stage of foreign democratic aid. The U.S. foreign democratic aid at this stage was characterized as the following:

Firstly, U.S. foreign aid is combined with democratic aid more closely and U.S. foreign aid mainly aims to promote democratization in recipient countries. According to the Strategic Plan jointly formulated by the United States Department of State and the United States Agency for International Development, the U.S. foreign aid aims to promote and deepen democratization of the recipient countries. In other words, the U.S. will "further develop democracy and good governance in respect to civil society, laws and regulations, respect for human rights and freedom of religion". It is declared in the Strategic Plan that "the U.S. diplomacy and foreign assistance will be

---

11 See, Thomas Carothers, Aiding Democracy Abroad, p. 41.

stalwart in support of democracy and human rights, not only because they are worthy of our traditions, but also because a more just world can lead to a more stable and prosperous world. We will support movements for democracy and human rights abroad consistently, responsibly, and prudently."[12]

Secondly, democratic aid was combined with U.S. global strategies more closely. After the "9/11" Event, anti-terrorism has become the most important content in the U.S. foreign strategy.

Accordingly, the U.S. has also adjusted the corresponding strategies in foreign democratic aid. The U.S. provides foreign democratic aid mainly to Middle East and the Islam world which are deemed as the originating places of international terrorism. Decision makers of the U.S. believe that only by implementing democracy and reform in Middle East can terrorism be fundamentally eradicated and the U.S. become safer. Thus democratic aid became an important part of the U.S.' strategy for countering international terrorism.

II. Modes and levels of U.S. democratic aid

The U.S.'s democratic aid can be classified into 2 modes: One is the traditional mode – economic and financial aid, with certain conditions attached to them. U.S. economic and financial aid is linked up with democratization promise of the recipient country, while conducting political and economic reform is the premise of U.S. financial assistance.

The other mode is governmental organizations or state-backed nongovernmental organizations (NGOs) of U.S. provide the recipient country or various political and social organizations in the recipient country with capital, materials, human resources and so forth, which directly intervene in transformation of political, economic and social systems of the recipient country, in this way.

When providing foreign aid, the U.S. often requires the recipient countries to implement democratization and democratic politics and promotes political and economic transformation of developing countries by virtue of U.S. economic aid. However, during different periods, objectives and emphases of the American government differ to a certain degree. For instance, during Reagan's tenure, the U.S. government paid more attention to promoting the development of private economy and market economy in developing countries. When addressing U.S. policies towards Africa,

---

12 Department of State/USAID, "Security, Democracy, Prosperity: Strategic Plan, Fiscal Years 2004-2009," Washington D.C., 2003, pp. 19-20.

Chester Crocker, Assistant Secretary of State in the Reagan Administration, emphasized that the U.S. would endeavor to make foreign economic aid more effective and useful no longer merely provide aid to some friendly countries like Sudan and Kenya, and try to promote the development of private economy in African countries.

He pointed out: "Under the Reagan Administration, our bilateral aid will be targeted on those areas where our interests are most clearly manifest and focused more to produce policy changes of broad and lasting impact. These changes include giving a much greater opportunity to the private sector, both within these countries and abroad."[13]

During the same period, the foreign aid strategies formulated by the USAID also centered on execution of market economy and private economy. For example, the foreign aid strategy issued by the USAID aimed to realize the following targets:

Firstly, policy transformation and reforms: the USAID hoped that the establishment of policies towards aided countries could promote implementation of free market principles and reduce government intervention in the economy such as tariffs, price controls, and subsidies, which hinder the effective play of free market forces.

Secondly, promotion of development of private enterprises: the USAID would support and assist in development of micro-, small- and middle-sized local private enterprises in developing countries,

Thirdly, implementation scope of schemes: the USAID would use nongovernmental organizations and enterprises to promote the execution of development-aid promotion plans in respect to population, healthcare, among others, in developing countries.[14]

During the Junior Bush administration, the U.S. paid more attention to political reform in aided countries and tried to use U.S. economic aid as bait to promote them to conduct political system reforms according to Western values.

For example, the new Millennium Challenge Account (MCA) built in 2002 set extremely strict political and economic requirements for aided countries. As per the Millennium Challenge Act of 2003, each aided country must reach the following standards in respect to political and economic democratization.

---

13 E. Brown, "Foreign Aid to SADCC: An Analysis of the Reagan Administration's Foreign Policy," A Journal of Opinion, Vol.12, No.3/4, 1982, pp. 29-30.
14 Mark F. McGuire and Vernon W. Ruttan, "Lost Directions: U.S. Foreign Assistance Policy Since New Directions," The Journal of Developing Areas, Vol.24, No.2, 1990, p. 142.

In order to implement just and democratic political governance, a recipient country must promote political diversification, equality and rule of law; respect human rights and civil rights including those of the disabled; protect private property ownership; encourage governmental transparency and strengthen governmental responsibilities; and oppose to corruption.

In order to realize free market economy, a recipient country should execute the following economic policies: it should discourage citizens and companies to engage in global trade and international capital markets; promote the development of private enterprises and sustainable use of natural resources; strengthen the role of markets in the economy; and respect rights of workers, civil mass organizations and labor unions.[15]

In 2005, the U.S. formulated stricter stipulations for aid especially regarding the political aid. For instance, each aided country must execute just governance in the following six aspects: civil freedoms, which is to conform to standards of Freedom House (USA) which include the freedom of speech, rights of assembly and association formation, adherence to rule by law and protection of human rights as well as independent and economic rights of individuals; political rights, which is also to conform to standards of Freedom House, including free and just elections of officers, citizens' organizing as political parties, possessing real rights as well as fair completion in election; freedom which is not controlled by army, foreign power, totalitarian party, religions & monks, and economic oligarchy, as well as guarantee of rights of ethnic minorities; speech and responsibility, which is to conform to standards of the World Bank, including constitutional protection of citizens' freedom, citizens' ability to choose the government, and independent media; governmental effect, which conforms to standards of the World Bank, namely provision of equal public services, guarantee of permission of citizen services, avoidance of being influenced by political pressure, and governmental ability to scheme and implement major policies; rule by law, should also conform to the standards of the World Bank, including the public's trust and compliance with the laws, violence incidents and non-violence criminals, efficacy and foresight of a judicial system. And ability to freely perform contracts should be guaranteed, corruption should be fought against which conforms to standards of the World Bank, including fighting against the influence of corruption on the commercial environment, major corruption in politics and also fighting against the tendency elite groups attempting to grasp the state control.[16]

---

15 MCC, Millennium Challenge Act of 2003, Washington D.C., 2002, pp. 4-5.
16 MCC, Report on the Criteria and Methodology for Determining the Eligibility of Candidate Countries for Millennium Challenge Account Assistance in FY 2005, Washington D.C., 2004, pp. 7-8.

Under such a background, some developing countries had to carry out political reform expected by the U.S. in order to gain economic aid from the U.S.

Since the end of the Cold War, modes of the U.S. foreign democratic aid have highlighted direct interventions in political, economic and social transformations of aided countries. Democratic aid of this mode mainly contains the following aspects. (1) Construction of the political system

In regard to construction of the political system, the U.S. democratic aid contains the following aspects:

Further Construction and institutionalization of the Political System

Electoral aid

Periodical elections are an important part of democratic politics and includes the election of administrative officers and the election of legislators, etc. The U.S. democratic aid has firstly started from the field of elections and then gradually expanded to other fields. In the meantime, elections are always highlighted in U.S. democratic aid. U.S. aid mainly has the following types in respect to elections. Firstly, the U.S. funds election organizations in aided countries. For example, in 1992, driven by the United States Department of State, the USAID set up the Africa Regional Electoral Assistance Fund, which is an aid fund mainly employed in U.S. elections. It was specifically operated by the African-American Institute, the International Republican Association and the National Democrat International Affair Association. In Middle East, the National Endowment for Democracy funded the elections and parliament reform plans in Yemen, the election system reform of Yemen and the reform of Kuwait Parliament, etc.

Secondly, the U.S. provides aid to establish election administrative bodies and train Professional officers for the election organizations. Besides, while aiding the developing countries, organizations like USAID and NED also help them to build and perfect the election administrations. The key is to improve the organizational and administrative abilities of election committees and consolidate the independent position of election committees in politics in order to establish authority of these organizations in general elections. The U.S. trains relevant officers in election organizations, including officers in central election committees and staffs at all districts in general elections, observers for general elections and volunteers for general elections, etc.

Thirdly, the U.S. assigns observers for general elections to supervise general elections and make arbitration and conciliation when disputes take place during elections. In 1982, the constitutional assembly election was held in Salvador, and the USAID organized a large number of observers to supervise it. Afterwards, the U.S. also sent election observers to 12 countries, which made the national elections more impartial at earlier stage of democratization.

In addition, the U.S. also provides support and assistance to other aspects of elections in aided countries. For instance, it helps countries in transition design the election system, including settings of election districts and the election manners of legislative institutions, presidents and local governments, etc.; it also carries out education on elections and voting and so forth.

Aid to political parties

Aid to political parties is specifically implemented by International Republican Association and National Democratic Institute for International Affairs. Since the late1980s, National Democratic Institute for International Affairs began strengthening its relationship with foreign political parties with which it shared similar conceptions, through funds provided by the National Endowment for Democracy. The International Republican Association mainly strengthened contacts with centre-right political parties in Latin America and provided technical aid and personal training to right-wing political parties in Columbia, Guatemala, Bolivia and Costa Rica, etc. After 1990, the U.S. rapidly expanded its political party aid, while funds provided by the USAID to the above two organizations each year reached up to 10 million dollars. During this period, political party aid mainly targeted at political party organizations in Eastern Europe and the former Soviet Union.

Political party aids by the US is realized mainly by: directly through assistance (whether training, advice, moral support and funding) to the political actors themselves- political parties or associations, politicians, or politically oriented nongovernmental organizations (NGOs). It can also be done indirectly through support to key institutions–an independent electoral commission, an independent judiciary, or independent media, for example–that help to level the political playing field by securing and guaranteeing fair procedures for the democratic actors and by checking the power of non-democrats.

For instance, "International Visitor Program" initiated by United States Department of State and renamed as International Visitor Leadership Program in 2004, directly provided chances for current or potential leaders in the government, politics, the media, education and other fields from all over the World to pay visit, do some investigation in the U.S. and gain firsthand knowledge about the U.S. society, culture and politics.[17]

For instance, the project of "International Visitor" led by the United States Department of State enabled political party elites in some countries to make visits and investigations to the U.S. Ma Ying-jeou, president of China's Taiwan, Karzai, president of Afghanistan, Sarkozy, president of France, Brown, the Prime Minister of the UK, to name just a few, were invited and educated by this project.

However, U.S. aids regarding political parties still focus on general elections and aims to help political parties join and win general elections. Specifically, U.S. plays a part in establishing election themes, selecting candidates, collecting election funds, employing and using volunteers, and dealing with media, etc. Such aid is generally realized by various kinds of training of U.S. political organizations. However, U.S. political party organizations often make direct interventions in elections of political parties in some countries. In the early 1990s, the International Republican Association made direct interventions in president elections of Romania and Bulgaria. Especially during the Romanian presidential election in 1992, the International Republican Association sent experienced political consultants to organize the opposition faction in Romania and tried to topple Ion Iliescu regime in collusion.

Aid to legislative bodies

Aid to Legislative Bodies is important content of the U.S. democratic aid which is highly supported by the US Congress, in order to institutional constructions in aided countries. And also this aspect enjoys great support from the US Congress. Members of the U.S. Congress argue that a powerful legislative body lays an important foundation for the democratic system. The Asia Foundation, the International Republican Association,The National Democratic Institute for International Affairs and some non-governmental consulting companies play a principal part in implementing such aid. Aid to legislative bodies is carried out mainly by training and technical aid provided to members in legislative bodies (namely congress members or

---

17 Krishna Kumar, "Reflections on International Political Party Assistance," Democratization, Vol.12, No.4, 2005, p.512.

legislators of aided countries) and relevant working staffs. Such aid contains settings of working manners in legislative bodies and legislative processes, expansion of influences exerted by committees in legislative bodies, holding of hearings and deepening of transparency in legislative bodies. In addition, the U.S. also helps some countries to follow the modes of the United States Library of Congress and build their own libraries of congress.

Aid to local government bodies

Such aid has started since the implementation of the USAID's "Strengthening of Local Governments" program in Latin America during the 1980s. Local governments are generally elected by the local people and have certain autonomy from the central political government.

After the 1990s, this kind of aid was expanded to Eastern Europe, the former Soviet Union, sub-Saharan Africa, as well as Philippines, Nepal and Mongolia in Asia. Such aid is carried out by strengthening rights of local governments and amending the constitutions accordingly in aided countries when necessary; providing training and technical support to officers and organizations in local governments; assisting in local construction of nongovernmental organizations and guiding cooperation between these nongovernmental organizations and the local governments.

Aids related to economic field

The U.S' aids related to economic field mainly includes promoting the development of market and implementation of marketization reforms based on private economy. The U.S. argues that most undeveloped countries are quite hostile to market economy and are unwilling to conduct, market mechanisms, market power and market's role in resource allocation, exchange, circulation or consumption, and therefore they cannot effectively use and allocate their national resources. "Countries which overextend influences of public departments and limit operations of private departments have confronted slow economic growth, heavy financial deficit and rise of debt burden."[18]

The USAID will coordinate with private enterprises to promote following affairs in developing countries:

Firstly, it will execute policy transformation. The USAID hopes that the establishment of policies in aided countries can promote principles of free market and reduce governmental interventions in economy; secondly, it

---

18 Mark F. McGuire and Vernon W. Ruttan, "Lost Directions: U.S. Foreign Assistance Policy since New Directions," The Journal of Developing Areas, Vol.24, No.2, 1990, p. 142.

will promote development of private enterprises. The USAID supports and assists in the development of micro, small and middle private enterprises in developing countries.

Aid for the judicial field

The US provides aid to promote judicial reform and judicial regulations construction. Judicial reform targets at establishing a court system which can operate more effectively, has more capacious legal knowledge, can provide more accurate explanation of laws, and is more independent of administrative authorities and other social right groups which may intervene in justice. Judicial reform mainly aims to establish a more rational and stronger management of the whole judicial system; increase judiciary budget, make innovation in existing judicial system and reforms in judicial occupational regulations, carry out trainings of judges and other judicial staff strengthen case management, etc. The judicial aid of the U.S. generally involves the above aspects, but the emphases vary in different areas; for legal reform aid, it mainly helps aided countries to revise the existing laws or reformulate new laws. The U.S. has provided aid to formulate commercial laws, criminal laws and civil laws in some Latin American and African countries.

Aid to civil society construction in aided countries

Political schools in different countries have different understandings of the concept of civil society. The USAID and the NED argue that a civil society is "an organization defined between a country and a family. Independent of a country, it consists of voluntary social members who want to protect and expand their interests and values. It possesses the right of autonomy when dealing with the country"[19].

It is indeed a nongovernmental organization defined by most U.S. political scholars. The civil society aid plan formulated by the USAID and the NED mainly aims to help an aided country to establish various civil social organizations which contain social or social-economic organizations such as churches and labor unions; social and cultural organizations such as sports clubs and nature clubs; informal organizations formed with social general characteristics, such as tribes, race associations and peasant associations. The U.S. helps an aided country to build a nongovernmental organization mainly through:

---

19 Christopher A. Sabatini, "Whom Do International Donors Support in the Name of Civil Society?" Development in Practice, Vol. 12, No. 1, 2002, p. 8.

1. Technical aid, wherein it provides training and consultations to nongovernmental organizations in terms of organizational development and management, capital collection, problem analysis and media relations.

2. Provision of economic support, wherein it directly supplies capital and equipment to nongovernmental organizations in aided counties or links the organizations up with U.S. foundations, and finds capital sources for it indirectly. The USAID, NED, Asia Foundation, Asia-Europe Foundation and so forth directly provide capital support in general. U.S. Peace Corps help organizations in some countries to build nongovernmental organizations and collect capital from the U.S. to build new nongovernmental organizations. For instance, volunteers of the Peace Corps in Latvia provided fifteen thousand dollars to the local nongovernmental-organization supporting center and also collected hundred thousand US dollars in the U.S. for it.[20]

III. Democratic aid and internal intervention by the U.S.

Since the late period of the Cold War, especially in the post-Cold War Era, the U.S. has been more and more enthusiastic to promote democratization in the developing countries and also provided different kinds of democratic to these countries. The new characteristic of the U.S. foreign aid reflects the U.S. politicians' superstition in political ideology and cultural values of the U.S.. In the meantime, under the new international situation, the U.S. employs its "hard power" and "soft power" more frequently to conduct international interventions with an attempt to oblige the aided countries develop according to the Western designed pattern.

In the post-Cold War era, the term "international interference" has been more and more frequently mentioned in international politics and international relations, to define an international political behavior.

Despite that there is no exact definition of it at present, international intervention shall at least contain the following aspects: interventions conducted by international relationship actors including sovereign states, international governmental organizations, and domestic and international nongovernmental organizations to internal affairs of other international relationship actors.

These behaviors contain political interventions, military interventions, and humanitarian interventions as well as fact investigation, election supervision and various interference behaviors which aim to promote domestic

---

20 Peace Corps, The United States Peace Corps Estonia Latvia Lithuania: The Legacy 1992-2002, Washington D.C., 2003, p. 36.

political, social and culture transformations in other countries. International interventions can be roughly divided into 2 types. The so-called "hard intervention" refers to the international intervention conducted to other international relationship actors which possess "hard power" such as political and economic manners, including military forces, while the "soft intervention" refers to an intervention conducted to other international relationship actors with "soft power" such as culture and values. The U.S. tries to promote the so-called "democratic aid" through "hard interventions" so as to force other countries to realize economic and political transformations by virtue of its strong economic power and the bait of economic aid. Moreover, the U.S. mainly conducts "soft interventions" in other countries by popularizing U.S. culture and values. In comparison with "hard interventions", U.S. "soft interventions" show very strong and more secret "altruism".

Both "hard interventions" and "soft interventions" have reflected the "missionary spirit" in the mainstream political culture of the U.S., namely the idea of "natural mission". In mainstream cultural traditions of the U.S., the idea of natural mission has a very special historical position. Most Americans firmly believe that the U.S. plays a unique role in human affairs and assumes an obligated mission. The U.S. is committed to the international community and assumes the obligatory responsibilities. U.S. historians Heald and Kaplan analyzed the idea in the introduction of the book Culture and Diplomacy that "the U.S. foreign affairs shall be checked based on the belief that the U.S. assumes a special mission towards its relations with the external world, which cannot be assumed by any other country."[21]

One important thing about this sense of mission is that the U.S. believes that its democratic political system is the unique and the best in the history of mankind. God had selected the U.S. as the model for all the other countries; and thus the U.S. is granted with sacred right and mission to propagate its political civilization and political system all around the world. Since the foundation of the U.S., politicians in history have continuously interpreted the "natural mission" of the U.S. in different forms. The first U.S. president George Washington viewed the U.S. as "a noble and novel government model which is always guided by justice and mercy for human beings"[22].

---

21 Morrell Heald and Lawrence S. Kaplan, Culture and Diplomacy: The American Experience, Connecticut: Greenwood Press, 1977, p. 4.
22 See, Washington's Farewell Address 1796," available at: http://www.yale.edu/lawweb/avalon/washing.htm.

President Woodrow Wilson firmly believed that "American people hold a kind of spiritual energy which can contribute to human's freedom, while any other nation cannot realize this...the U.S. is strongly and particularly capable of realizing destiny and saving the world."[23]

President John Kennedy also firmly believed in the missions of the U.S. and thought that the U.S. is the "nation aspiring to change the world...We are obligated to try our best to change everything around us...bring changes to Western world, the world assuming no obligation, the Soviet Union empire and other continents. In this way, we can bring more freedom to more people"[24].

In view of U.S. success in the Cold War, politicians and political ideologists further believed that the political system and ideologies of the U.S. were more superior to those of opponents in the Cold War. As strong "soft power", the political system and values of U.S. are indestructible and have become powerful weapons for the U.S. to incorporate global countries under current despotism, autocracy and power concentration into the big family of democracy. Missionary spirit or idea of "natural mission" and superstition in U.S. political values have laid a firm foundation for the contemporary U.S. to gradually strengthen its foreign democratic aid; and also become the best shield of U.S. foreign interventions – its responsibility for intervention implementation.

In the meantime, international interventions represented by "democratic aid" also conform to values and national interests of the U.S. After the Cold War, the governmental circle and the political school in the U.S. extensively argue that global democratization is conductive to maintaining national interests of the U.S., especially facilitating peace and safety in the U.S., eliminating terroristic threats and even maintaining economic interests.

After the Cold War, U.S. scholars proposed the "Democratic Peace Theory" after they have summarized the experience and lessons of the Cold War era, which is that global peace will be further guaranteed by higher degree of global democratization, there will not be conflicts and wars easily while revolutions or coups which overturn the current situations will not easily take place in democratic countries, thereby not threatening the interests of the U.S. and even the whole world. Therefore, the U.S. shall lead global waves of democratization and support global democratization movements.[25]

---

23 Arthur M. Schlesinger, The Cycles of American History, Boston: Houghton Mifflin, 1986, p. 16.
24 John F. Kennedy, "Are We Up to the Task," in The Strategy of Peace, New York: Harper&Brothers, 1960, p. 199.
25 See, relevant articles from Ted Galen Carpenter, "Democracy and War," The Independent Review, Vol. II (No.3, Spring, 1998); Rudolph J. Rummel, "Democracies Don't Fight Democracies," Peace (May-June 1999), etc.

Morton Halperin, senior assistant of the Carnegie Endowment for International Peace and was later assigned as Assistant Secretary of State by President Clinton, argued that "the U.S. shall serve as a leader during the process of democratization all over the world. Democratic governments prefer peace and rarely launch wars or violence. Countries which carry out constitutional democracy cannot start a war against the U.S. or other democratic countries and they prefer limiting weapon trade and encouraging, peaceful solution of disputes and promoting free trade. In this way, when a nation tries to hold a free election and establish the constitutional democracy system, the U.S. and the international community shall do a favor and ensure the result"[26].

Dobriansky also argued that the promotion of democracy can let the U.S. obtain other important interests all around the world, "Most immediately, it is an indispensable component of any viable strategy for winning the global war against terrorism, which poses a grave threat to international security in the 21st century. Democracy facilitates the establishment of legitimate and law-based political systems in states that may become sponsors or havens for terrorists, creates peaceful channels to reconcile grievances that can otherwise fuel bloody and destabilizing conflicts within nations, and instills hope, replacing the sense of powerlessness and despair that sometimes transform ordinary people into fully committed terrorist operatives."[27]

It is thus clear that both Halperin and Doriansky indeed deemed democratization as the manner to realize national interests of the U.S. In other words, democratic aid is used to promote democratization in developing countries, resolve various problems faced by U.S. diplomatic policies to the hilt and create a beneficial international environment for its diplomacy. Anthony Lake, national security consultant of the Clinton administration, analyzed it more clearly, "Propagation of democracy facilitates solution of other problems faced by U.S. diplomatic policies. Democratic countries will not infringe human rights, attack neighboring countries, employ restrictive trade policies, take terrorism actions or create refugees."[28]

The Democratic Peace Theory has become the theoretical basis for the U.S. to conduct international interventions in foreign countries through "democratic aid" after the Cold War.

26　Morton Halperin, "Guaranteeing Democracy," Foreign Policy, No.91 (Summer, 1993), p. 105.
27　Paula J. Dobriansky, "Democracy," The National Interest (Fall, 2004), p. 70.
28　Harry Harding," Asia Policy to the Brink," Foreign Policy, No.96 (Autumn, 1994), p. 61.

As a major mode of international interventions by U.S., "democratic aid" has strong ideological colors. For instance, the NED, which played an extremely important role in U.S. democratic aid, has shown very obvious anti-communist feature since its establishment. It initially targeted at communist countries, including the European socialist camp led by the Soviet Union as well as Vietnam and Burma in Asia, etc. Its missions are just what were handled by the CIA in the past. The only difference is that the CIA as a U.S. governmental organization exports democratic strategies secretly, while the NED as a non-governmental organization exports democratic activities legally and publicly.

When talking about the establishment of the NED, U.S. scholar William Blum said that the NED was established based on this concept: "the NED will publicly take actions which were always secretly done by the CIA in the past decades in order to get rid of the notoriety linked up with the CIA."[29]

Allen Weinstein, who once assisted in the NED establishment, bluntly said: "A lot of things being done by us today were just done by the CIA secretly 25 years ago."[30]

During the first 10 years since the NED's establishment, the most successful achievement was to provide various kinds of aid to the Polish Solidarity Union through its subordinate U.S. Congress organization and help the Solidarity Union to overturn socialist political power in Poland. After taking office, Walesa reciprocated and conducted the "democratic reform" expected by the U.S. with the assistance of the NED and USAID. After the Cold War, the NED paid more attention to the remaining few socialist countries. The 2004 action strategy formulated by the NED publicly announced that it would "go on concentrating its abundant resources in the existing socialist countries and centralized states like China, North Korea, Cuba, Serbia, Sudan and Burma"[31].

For instance, in 2007, the NED mainly funded Burma, China, North Korea and Pakistan, wherein funds of 3.114.560 dollars were provided to Burma's projects; funds of 6,110,486 dollars were provided to overseas opposition factions of China; funds of 1.518.780 dollars were provided to

---

29 William Blum, Rogue State: A Guide to the World's Only Superpower (Monroe: Common Courage Press, 2000, p. 179.
30 Gerald Sussman, "The Myths of 'Democracy Assistance': U.S. Political Intervention in Post-Soviet Eastern Europe," Monthly Review (December 2006), p. 15.
31 James M. Scott and Carie A. Steele, "Assisting Democrats or Resisting Dictators? The Nature and Impact of Democracy Support by the United States National Endowment for Democracy, 1990-99," Democratization, Vol.12, No.4, 2005, p. 453.

projects in North Korea. For projects in China, abundant funds were allocated: 430.000 million dollars for human right fights in China; 280.000 million dollars for Laogai Research Foundation, 240.000 dollars for Foundation for China in the 21st Century and Uyghur American Association (UAA), 136.000 million dollars for World Uyghur Congress, etc.[32]

Democratic aid and democratization in developing countries executed by the U.S. have influenced some countries and areas, but democratic aid of the U.S. brings principal interventions in international affairs of other countries. For instance, the American Center for International Labor Solidarity, International Republican Association and National Democrat International Affair Association funded by the U.S. NED brazenly promoted labor unions and opposition parties in some countries to conduct anti-governmental activities. The above organizations were also major external supporters of color revolutions in some Easter European and Central Asian countries in the past. They provided funds to anti-governmental dissident groups in the countries where color revolutions took place, and even made direct interventions to some countries and directly helped dissidents to formulate action strategies and plans. These actions certainly raised some countries' antipathy and query towards the U.S. Some countries in Russia and Central Asia announced that they never approved the above organizations. Some other countries even directly expelled some non-governmental organizations and those governmental organizations with the non-governmental nature which were sent by the U.S. to execute political activities.

Re-evaluating the experience and lessons of U.S.' promotion of democratization in foreign countries, some researchers of insight in the U.S. have argued that the U.S. when promoting its political values overseas or requiring other countries to accept its political and economic development modes "has neglected the cultural traditions and realistic conditions of other countries and mistakenly US has only insisted on its own criteria." Former U.S. President Nixon has also admitted that "The most frequent mistake made by the U.S. in its global communication is that it tends to measure all national governments by using Western democratic standards and evaluate cultures in various countries with Western European standards"[33].

---

32 NED, Annual Report, 2007, Washington D.C., 2008, pp. 48-61.
33 Richard Nixon, Leaders, translated by You Xie and Shi Yanhua, Beijing, World Affairs Press, 1983, pp. 394-395.

Kissinger, national security consultant of the Nixon administration, also pointed out that: "It is self-evident that the U.S. prefers democratic regimes to dictatorship regime. Obviously, the U.S. shall make mental preparations for paying certain price for such a preference. However, the Western democratic system was native-born and gradually developed from a small corner on Earth through hundreds of years. It is very dangerous if we forget this point. It was cultivated with some exclusive characteristics of Western civilization, while the same characteristics have not been presented in other kinds of civilization till now."[34]

The analyses of Nixon and Kissinger may enlighten U.S. politicians and political scholars who are now wild about implementing democratization all over the world, which deserve careful evaluation.

---

34 Los Angeles Times, November 22, 1987, quoted from American Culture and Diplomacy by Wang Xiaode, Beijing, World Affairs Press, 2000, p. 453.

On Western Neo-interventionism: The Libya War and the "Libyan Model"

Wang Lincong[1]

During about 42 years since Gaddafi governed Libya (from September 1969 to August 2011), Gaddafi regime stood against military strikes, embargoes and sanctions of Western countries and persistently followed a long-term confrontation policy against Western countries. Gaddafi "firmly" controlled the regime, becoming an "evergreen" in the Middle East political circle. However, in less than half a year since implementation of anti-government demonstrations by people of Benghazi of Libya which began on February 15, 2011, Gaddafi regime totally collapsed under domestic insurgency and heavy air strikes of NATO. The history of rise and fall of Gaddafi regime can be called as a history about relations between contemporary Libya and Western countries, which is full of confrontation and compromise. Survival and downfall of Gaddafi regime reflect the characteristics of era evolution and has also witnessed various changes in Western interventionism. Specifically, Western military interventions that were demonstrated in Libya War not only changed the development track of Libya, but also brought significant and profound influences to the international relations and international governance. The paper intends to analyze its main expressions, basic characteristics and influences of Western neo-interventionism in the 21st century based on the case of Libya War.

---

1 Researcher and director of International Relations Office of the Institute of West Asian and African Studies attached to CASS.

I. Premises and the roots of the Libya war

In the turbulent Middle East, Libya was once deemed as a relatively stable country. People often described Libya by three keywords – petroleum treasure, political strongman and tribal social life, which influenced social development of Libya. Under Gaddafi's rule, political integration of Libya was accelerated to a certain extent ("Third Universal Theory" was popularized while "Jamahiriya" practice was carried out domestically; in the initial phase of the new republic, internationally, "unification" of Arab world was promoted, later the "United States" of Africa slogan was advocated in order to emphasize African, Arab and Islamic attributes of Libya), but Libya's social structure did not change much. Instead, numerous tribes were still an important social form of Libya, while tribal traditions and concepts still continued. More importantly, dictatorship of Gaddafi regime and uneven distribution of petroleum incomes have intensified social contradictions. Therein, the tribe in Eastern Libya (rich in petroleum) was highly hostile against Gaddafi regime and had once launched large-scale protests in 1993 and 2006, while a lot of people were forced to exile, immigration or trialed for this reason. Hence, Libya was indeed trapped in the so-called "resource curse". Specifically speaking, despite having abundant petroleum wealth, unemployment rate of the country still reached up to 30%, while poor people still accounted for the 33% of the whole population.[2]

It is thus clear that uneven distribution of petroleum wealth, expansion of rich-poor polarization and the severe unemployment problem have undoubtedly weakened people's allegiance to Gaddafi regime, accelerating the trend of drifting off the regime, and also weakening and shaking the governance foundation.

However, Libya War broke out mainly because of the "Arab Spring" which had started by the end of 2010 and led the Arab world into an unusual historical period. Initiated in Tunisia, "Arab Spring" rapidly spread to various Arab countries, forming an upheaval tide which shook the seemingly strong Arab authoritarian regimes. Located between Egypt and Tunisia, Libya suffered from the direct impact of the sharp political changes in Tunisia and Egypt. In particular, collapse of Ben Arieh regime in Tunisia and quit of President Mubarak who was the political strongman of Egypt greatly stimulated both the domestic and foreign opposition factions of Libya and also nurtured general people's desire and will for an insurgency. As a result, people's social mentality has changed greatly, reflected mainly as the disappearance of fear from the torture of the Gaddafi regime, and rapid rise of resistance will.

---

2   See, CIA Factbook and EIU Country Report: Libya.

They mainly targeted at overthrowing the existing regime. It is fair to say that, the year of 2011 created a watershed in the historical development of Arab countries to a certain extent, indicating that the era of authoritarian regimes in the Arab world began declining. Hence, such a huge change with historical significance decided the destinies of strongman regimes like Gaddafi to a certain extent. Of course, the inevitability of the Libya War cannot be explained only from this grand era background. At initial stage of Libya crisis, domestic opposition faction was too weak to shake the Gaddafi regime. Libya crisis developed into a war due to internal factors as well as pushed by external forces and factors.

The isolated state of the Gaddafi regime in the Arab world has formed an important premise to push Libya into an international war. After coming into power, Gaddafi once energetically advocated Arab nationalism and deemed it and Islam as the foundation of his "Third Universal Theory",3 tried to surpass narrow national interests to a degree, strove for "grand Arab unification" in the Arab world and sought hegemony. He stated: "new world scale internationalism has been built, centering in Libya and has set its headquarters here. In Libya, it makes struggles to oppose USA and Judaism and defends Gulf of Sidra and Palestine".[4]

Unrealistically, Gaddafi pursued for Arab unity, leading to variable ups and downs in relations between Libya and other Arab countries. In particular, Gaddafi caused sharp contradictions between Libya and most of the Arab brother countries especially with those Arab gulf countries due to his own personality and foreign policies. As a result, conflicts were always there which formed a deep seated rancor. Estrangement and hostility between Gaddafi and the political leaders of countries like Saudi Arabia and Qatar appeared to be especially prominent. In the Arab world, the strange radical style of Gaddafi was deemed as a "threat" to regional stability by many countries.[5]

After running into brick walls and suffering a setback (after tiring futile efforts) in succession during pursuit of "Arab unity", Gaddafi had to shift his diplomatic focus from Arab world to African countries and saw the African Union (AU) as an important stage to perform his diplomatic strategies. At last, Gaddafi was deemed as the biggest "alien" in the huge Arab

---

3 Ronald Bruce St. John, Qaddafi's World Design: Libyan Foreign Policy, 1969-1987, London: Saqi Books, 1987, p. 21.
4 Ronald Bruce St. John, Qaddafi's World Design: Libyan Foreign Policy, 1969-1987, p. 69.
5 Mahmoud M. Ayoub, Islam and the Third Universal Theory: The Religious Thought of Mu'ammar al-Qadhdhafi, London: KPI Limited, 1987, p. 137.

world and highly isolated as he demonstrated no enthusiasm to deal with the Arab business world, made lots of enemies and even declared his wish to quit the organization of Arab League for many times.

For this reason, when Gaddafi regime ordered the military police to suppress domestic opposition faction which has caused a lot of bloody incidents, member states of Arab League did not make any effort to facilitate conciliation. Instead, they rapidly took a series of reverse actions. On February 22, 2011, Arab League criticized Libya and decided to suspend Libya's qualification to join conferences of the Arab League and all its subsidiary bodies till Libya responded to appeals made by its own people. After that, on March 12, member states of Arab League convened an urgent council meeting of foreign ministers in Cairo and made an important decision, which requested UN Security Council to take initiative in setting a no-fly zone in Libya through relevant procedure. Later, during international intervention wars against Gaddafi regime, Qatar and United Arab Emirates – as member states of Arab League directly sent troops to jointly fight with NATO forces, acting as interveners. On March 28, 2011, Qatar took the lead in recognizing the Libyan opposition faction "National Transitional Council" as the sole legal representative of the Libyan people, becoming the first Arab country which admitted Libyan opposition faction. It is thus clear that the long-term radical diplomatic policies of Gaddafi regime have made it a target of sharp criticism in many Arab countries.

Plot for Regime Change, "Strategy of the Union for the Mediterranean (UfM)"[6] and the Libya War

Domestic insurgency in Libya quickly evolved into an international war. As for the causes, internal reason – broad people's strong dissent has fueled the domestic rioting and crisis in Libya; while external reason – Western military intervention decided the direction and later evolution and severe results of the Libyan upheaval and change. The external factors have always been dominant. In other words, external forces have played a critical role during evolution of Libyan civil war into an international war, centering on Western great powers' strategic plot of "regime change" targeting Gaddafi rule. Such plot has been the profound root of Libya War.

As generally known, North Africa is adjoined to European continent and deemed as the backyard of EU. As one of the main petroleum sources of Europe, North Africa has a very important geostrategic position. However,

---

6 The Union for the Mediterranean (UfM) is an intergovernmental organization of 43 countries with Libya as an observer state.

for a long time, Gaddafi regime challenged the international order led by the Western countries and demonstrated a strong attitude of quarrelling towards them,[7] which naturally worsened the relations between Libya and major Western powers. Consequently, Libya had no real friendly relations with them, it was a hostile object and oppression target of Western great powers for long years, especially had hostile relations with the US and the UK. On April 15, 1986, the US initiated air strikes called as "prairie fire" and "golden gorge" targeting Tripoli and Benghazi with the pretext of explosion plotted by two Libyan citizens in a West Berlin nightclub which had killed some U.S. soldiers. Air strikes gave, disastrous losses to Libya, causing deaths of over 40 Libyans including the adopted daughter of Gaddafi. Later for 10 plus years, due to "Lockerbie Bombing" incident the relations between Libya and major Western powers were extremely awful.[8]

In April 1992, countries including the U.S. and Britain motioned UN Security Council to issue the Resolution No.748 which stipulated sanctions and restrictions of aviation, military affairs and diplomacy against Libya under the excuse that Libyan government refused to hand over 2 Libyans who were suspected of involvement in the "Lockerbie Bombing".

In November of the next year, the US and Britain again motioned UN Security Council to issue the Resolution No.883 concerning upgrading of former sanctions targeting Libya, which included forbidding the sales of oil refinery equipment and parts to Libyan petroleum and gas departments and freezing of overseas assets and bank accounts of Libyan banks and individuals and other restrictions.

In August 1996, the US Congress also passed the "D'Amato Bill" that would require the President to impose sanctions on foreign companies that invest heavily in Iran or Libya. The legislation require the U.S. President to impose sanctions against any foreign person, company or subsidy that invests $40 million or more in a year in Iran's or Libya's petroleum or natural gas sectors. The bill would also make sanctions applicable to those who sell goods or services to Libya that are covered by United Nations Resolutions 748 and 883.

---

7 Wang Lincong: Gaddafi's Diplomatic Ideas and Libyan Diplomacy, Journal of West Asia and Africa, 2004/6; Wang Lincong: On Diplomatic Relations between Libya and the US, Journal of Graduate School of Chinese Academy of Social Science, No.6, 2004.
8 On December 20013, Libyan government wrote to UN Security Council, declaring that it would bear the responsibility for "Lockerbie Bombing", and required that UN immediately removes the 11 years lasting sanctions, then reached an agreement with Britain and the US America, to pay a huge compensation amounting 2.7 billion dollars to relatives of Lockerbie Bombing victims in batches after UN would remove the sanctions.

The US also included Libya into its blacklist of "rogue states" those which "supported terrorism and tried to develop weapons of mass destruction". Gaddafi gradually turned to a concessive diplomatic line "concession" after the outburst of Iraq War in 2003.

On December 20013, Libyan government wrote to UN Security Council, declaring that it would bear the responsibility for "Lockerbie Bombing", and required that UN immediately removes the 11 years lasting sanctions, then reached an agreement with Britain and the US America, to pay a huge compensation amounting 2.7 billion dollars to relatives of Lockerbie Bombing victims in batches after UN would remove the sanctions.

With the settlement of the "Lockerbie Bombing" event and Gaddafi's announcement of giving up the development plan about weapons of mass destruction, Libya has managed to alleviate the fatigued relations with the Western countries and reestablished diplomatic relations in succession. After a long period of isolation from the international community, Libya had succeeded a comeback.[9]

Due to favorable atmosphere, determined by Gaddafi's concessive diplomatic line, for a period of time Western countries conducted a good cooperation with Libya on broad security issues—such as fight against terrorism, containment of Islamic extremism, and prevention of illegal immigration waves—and in other aspects, including oil and natural gas trade,

They tried to promote domestic reforms and rationalization of its foreign policies and pushed Libya to further distance itself from international terrorism. Additionally, EU countries tried to incorporate Libya into their regional security systems. In fact, since the middle period of 1990s, EU had devoted its efforts to promote the "Barcelona progress"[10].

The main idea behind this was to develop partnership between EU and Mediterranean riparian states which included Middle East countries such as Algeria, Morocco, Tunisia, Cyprus, Egypt, Israel, Jordan, Lebanon, Malta, Syria, Turkey and Palestinian National Authority—in the fields of economy,

---

9 On December 21, 1988, Pan American flight 103 flying from London Heathrow to JFK Airport in New York exploded over Lockerbie, Scotland, killing a total of 270, including 11 people on the ground and 188 US citizens. Following a three-year investigation, murder warrants were issued in November 1991 for two Libyans. Libyan leader Muammar Qaddafi eventually handed them over for trial in 1999 after protracted negotiations and UN sanctions.
10 In the end of November 1995, EU and Mediterranean South-bank countries proposed the "conception about EU-Mediterranean partnership" at the First Ministerial Conference and signed the Barcelona Declaration, "Barcelona Declaration", 1995, http://ec.europa.eu/external-relations/euromed/bd.htm.

energy, immigration and democratic system. At first, to promote regional peace and stability through common negotiations on political and security issues; secondly, to form a free trade zone including EU and Mediterranean south-bank countries, and achieve this goal before 2010 through economic and financial cooperation; thirdly, comprehensive cooperation between EU and Mediterranean countries should be promoted by strengthening communications and exchanges on social, cultural spheres and also staff exchanges among various countries.

Based on EU's needs for security and stability, EU has proposed clear ideas for domestic political reforms in the Barcelona Declaration, in the hope to ensure its security and stability by carrying forward democratization process of those countries located in North Africa.

Hence, "Barcelona progress" reflects EU's long-term goal and ideal of promoting the regional political reform, in order to generalize its values and promote European-style democracy, in the region. In 2004, after the UN removed the sanctions targeting Libya, in EU invited Libya to join the Barcelona progress and become a full member state. However, it failed to get positive response from Gaddafi; meanwhile Libya only acted as an observer country and did not see any real progress.[11]

In 2008, on behalf of EU, France took the lead in proposing the "Mediterranean Unity" plan – as the new phase of Barcelona process. French President Sarkozy set the initial conception to build this union into a highly integrated union like the EU, including convergence and integration in political field. However, in July 2008 when "Mediterranean Unity" was started, only limited goals including technological cooperation, energy source cooperation, environment, infrastructure construction was put forward. After the "Lisbon Treaty" of EU was ratified, implementation of the "Mediterranean Unity" process was accelerated.

However, Gaddafi publicly opposed to this process, saying: the Mediterranean Unity process intends to damage the unity between Arab world and African countries. Hence, the opposition by Gaddafi not only posited a big challenge for the EU to build the so-called regional security system, but also became the main obstacle for France to promote the Mediterranean Unity process and realize its own national strategic ambition.

As the initiator of this union, French President Sarkozy held the grudge

---

11 George Joffé, "Libya and the European Union: Shared Interests?", The Journal of North African Studies, vol.16, no.2, 2011, pp. 233-249.

to the dissenting voice of Gaddafi. Hence, it can be easily understood that when Western countries launched the military intervention in Libya, France took the lead in conducting air strikes. Nominally targeting at stopping the Libyan government forces "slaughtering common people" and in the name of supporting Libyan opposition, in fact these military actions aimed a regime change to topple the Gaddafi regime and ensure the smooth implementation of the Mediterranean Unity strategy. France has always deemed North Africa as its sphere of influence and tried to conduct the relations between France and North African countries via the platforms of "EU+-Mediterranean Unity Process" and "Summit of Francophone Countries" as well as other platforms.

Just for this reason, France took the lead in striking the Gaddafi regime in order to accelerate "Mediterranean Unity Process". In March 2011, French Foreign Minister Juppe pointed out: "French President Sarkozy's proposition of building the regional organization 'Mediterranean Unity Process' is a prospective suggestion. In view of changes in the world situation, today is the right time to rebuild such a regional organization".[12]

Hence, UN Security Council approved the Resolution No.1970 —putting arms embargo to Libya, preventing Gaddafi and his core family from travelling abroad, and freezing overseas assets of Gaddafi and relevant persons— on February 26, 2011 and approved the Resolution No.1973 on March 17, which stipulated setting a no-fly zone in Libya in order to protect Libyan civilians and civilian dwellings from the threat of armed attacks. On March 19 countries including the US, France, Britain, Italy and Canada immediately constituted a multinational joint military force to implement an air-attack operation called the "Odyssey Dawn" targeting Libya, wherein French fighter jets took the lead in the air strikes the targeting military bases of the Libyan government. Before that, France had announced that it had recognized the National Transitional Council founded by Libyan opposition. On March 31, NATO made continuous air strikes to the districts controlled by the Libyan governmental army after assuming the complete command of the military operation targeting Libya.

It is thus clear that Libya was quickly fell into an international war due to external force involvement. This war was also a major act with the aim of implementing the Mediterranean strategy by military means. France served as a daring vanguard in this war besides coveting abundant petroleum and natural gas resources in Libya. French Foreign Minister Alain Juppe once

---

12 New French Foreign Minister will take rebuilding of the Mediterranean as the major target in French diplomacy, March 2, 2011, http://gb.cri.cn.

announced in the public that France intervened in Libyan military conflict in order to "make a good investment for the future". Even when the intense fights were ongoing in Libya, France and Britain took the lead in visiting the temporary transitional council in Libya, for interest deals. On September 1, 2011, when the opposition faction just started to launch its attacks ed into capital Tripoli, France invited representatives of over 60 countries and international organizations to Paris to join the international conference called "Friends of Libya" and discuss post-war political and economic reconstruction in Libya. Hence, the development from "Barcelona progress" to "Mediterranean Unity strategy" clearly demonstrated European countries' long-term plot of implementing peaceful evolution in the Mediterranean-centered countries of North Africa; promoting democratic transformation through the means like economic aid, attached with political reforms and finally incorporating these countries into the EU system. It is fair to say that both "Barcelona progress" and the "Mediterranean Unity" have been soft and flexible "European-type" Middle East transformation schemes. Meanwhile, if we observe the frustration suffered in the Mediterranean Unity process and the following launching of the Libya War, they demonstrate that the France-led intention of accelerating Libyan regime change was pre-determined in order to further push the realization of Mediterranean Unity and political integration of the region to EU.

II. Western Neo-interventionism and the "Libyan Model"

Libya War has encountered 2 stages –civil war and the international war– wherein civil war lasted from the middle of February 2011 to March 19, and the international war under foreign military intervention lasted from March 19, 2011 to October 31, when the NATO announced the end of military actions. Libya War has lasted totally for over 8 months, transforming from a civil war to international war and intensively demonstrated the new changes and characteristics of the Western neo-interventionism.

The New Characteristics and the Essence of Western Neo-interventionism

Interventions often happen in international relations. During different periods, international interventions differ in their motivation, means employed and results. Intervention forms can be divided into direct intervention and indirect intervention, etc. The former is often expressed by launching of military operations like wars, while the latter is more complicated and expressed by the support or incentives given to opposition factions and nongovernmental organizations (NGOs) or implementing economic sanctions, public opinion manipulation and media encirclement, etc. Since the end of Cold War, neo-interventionism became a prominent phenomenon in the international arena. Kosovo War has created a new state for neo-interventionist military acts in the post-Cold War era. By then, neo-interventionism phenomena became one of the most controversial topics in the international relations. Libya War has been another typical case of neo-interventionism in the 21st century. By analyzing the Libya international war, we find that neo-interventionism mainly shows the following characteristics.

Firstly, "the concepts of responsibility to protect" and avoidance of "humanitarian crisis" are taken as the theoretical bases for implementation of interventions. These concepts insist on that "human rights should prevail over sovereignty", neo-interventionism emphasizes and holds the banner of "the responsibility to protect" in order to further negate the principle of "non-intervention in internal affairs" recognized by International Law.

But the connotations of "the responsibility to protect" have changed a lot since its appearance in 2001. In the World Summit Conference Results document which was passed at the 60th UN Conference on October 24, 2005, the Part 4 "Democracy and Rule by Law" does not directly adopt the wording of "the responsibility to protect", but defines those responsibilities such as "the responsibility to protect people from damages from genocide, war crime, ethnic cleansing and crimes against humanity".[13] However, what should be the criterion to allow an intervention by the international society including military intervention to a country which shows unwillingness or unable to protect basic rights of its people? Because, many complicated causes may lead to occurrence of turmoil's in countries. There always have been different understandings about how to judge whether government of a country is able or willing to protect its people. Hence, we can say that the "the responsibility to protect" document of 60th UN Conference supports selective implementation of interventions and concedes to neo-interventionism.

Secondly, neo-interventionism is characterized by selection and determination of intervention targets, also known as "selective intervention". The so-called "selective intervention" refers to that objects and targets of influence applying and intervention are selected according to the principle of bringing strategic benefits.[14]

---

13 2005 UN world summit, The responsibility to protect, 15 September 2005, p.31.
14 Wang Lincong: Research of Democratization in Middle East Countries, China Social Sciences Press, 2007, Beijing, p.314.

In 2011, military strikes by the multinational joint military forces and NATO targeting the Gaddafi regime can be seen as a typical case of "selective intervention". On the one side, Libya was highly isolated in the international society especially the Arab League, while long-term autocracy of Gaddafi has caused mass discontent and uprisings. Domestic and foreign dilemmas of the Gaddafi regime have driven the Western great powers to further isolate and trap Gaddafi regime. On the other side, by virtue of the historical "opportunity" that occurred by the "Arab Spring", Western countries have catered and coached a part of Libyan peoples' pursuit for "democracy" and opposition to "autocracy" and also made use of complicated relations and resentments among Arab countries to eliminate the Gaddafi regime which was famous for its obstinate and unruly style in many ways.

Thirdly, neo-interventionism is characterized by attempt of "legal" means for interventions.

Interventions in Libya War were authorized by the UN and supported by the regional Arab League. Hence, the intervention was cloaked by some legal forms. Meanwhile, as for the intervention means and methodology, the U.S. did not opt for the former unilateral action mode, but carried out the coordinated diplomacy and promoted group (NATO) action to include all the allies. In the whole Libya War, instead of standing on the cutting edge of war, the U.S. stayed at the backseat and opted to give full play to its role as a military ally.

Fourthly, neo-interventionism is characterized by "controllability" of interventions and "finiteness" of intervention modes.

On one side, multinational joint military forces and NATO realized accurate target clearing strikes through air attacks, which greatly weakened the strength of the Gaddafi forces, thus they avoided direct involvement of large-scale ground armed forces, in order to win the war at the minimum costs, wherein, multinational joint military forces and NATO forces nearly accounted no casualties in Libya War. Instead, they instigated, supported and armed those opposition factions in Libya. By expanding the strength of the opposition factions, they gradually changed the balance of strength between the two hostile warring parties in Libya. At last, the military power of the opposition faction completely gained the superiority, paving the way for Western countries violently overthrow the Gaddafi regime.

According to above facts, the "innovations" in neo-interventionism includes some major adjustments in the intervention means, modes and strategies. In comparison with the former pure gunboat policy and unilateral power politics, neo-interventionism is disguised by "righteous" and "legal" pretexts, employs more roundabout actions which hide interest pursuit behind humanistic and political motivations. In essence, it still bears the nature of intervention, and cannot be separated from it.

"Libya Model" and Its Connotations

"Model" refers to the standard form of an object or a standard pattern that can be imitated by people. The "model" is a relatively broad summarization, reflection, and demonstrative form or connotation. The Libya War was the specific demonstration of neo-interventionism. Specifically, it has overthrown the Gaddafi regime via "legal" means with the lowest cost. Hence, it was deemed as a "successful model" and labeled as the "Libyan Model" by Western countries. In summary, the connotations of the "Libyan Model" contain the following points.

(1) "Authorization" by the UN Security Council is the basic premise for "intervention" and the "Libyan Model". Passing of the Resolution No.1973 of the UN Security Council has stipulated that the Council "authorized" Multinational Joint Army and NATO to build a "No-fly Zone" in Libya, which provided a "justifiable and legal disguise" for them to conduct direct military strikes.

(2) "Support" given by the Arab League has been an important basis for "intervention" and "Libyan Model". As the highest authority and a prestigious regional organization which includes 22 Arab countries, the Arab League has demanded that UN Security Council should set a no-fly zone in Libya, which can be deemed as the expression of a "collective will" of most Arab countries. In the international intervention act, Arab League has played a pioneering role. Specifically, it provided an institutional basis and platform for the military intervention of Multinational Joint Forces and NATO, which endowed their operations with the impression of "a just act which conforms to the collective will" of Arabs. Hence, the support of Arab League became the most unique content of the Libya Model.[15]

(3) Concerted actions among the intervening subjects constituted the major aspect of implementation method of the "Libyan Model". After drawing a lesson from launching regime change in a unilaterally method in the Iraq War, the US made use of the influences of its allies especially European countries and some Arab countries bordering Libya, and promoted concerted

---

15 Alex Tiersky, "NATO's Libya Test", Turkish Policy Quarterly, Vol.10, No.3, 2011, pp. 63-64.

and collective actions among allies, in order to realize coordination of action among the intervention subjects and coordinated the division of work for the military tasks and responsibilities of the intervention.

(4) Supporting and arming the opposition factions has been the main content of "Libyan Model" and throughout the Libya War, internal and external attacks and encirclement tactics were conducted by the Western countries.

On the one side, external military forces conducted constant air strikes, to force Libya governmental military forces to give up resistance and hinder its military initiative. On the other side, Western countries politically recognized the provisional opposition government, favored and advertised for the activities of the opposition faction via media outlets and official government declarations, besides they provided economic support to the opposition faction, armed or even directly assisted their military operations by advisors. In this way, the forces around the opposition factions have gradually expanded and strengthened, finally gained the absolute superiority, overthrew and replaced the Gaddafi regime.

(5) Accurate air strikes and avoiding involvement of ground forces and wars were an important characteristic of the "Libyan Model". "Libyan Model" has been generated in the Libya War. In fact, Libya War was "a power struggle" between Western major powers and Gaddafi rather than a true war for democracy and humanity, thus became another "masterpiece" of Western neo-interventionism.

Here, it is necessary to distinguish two different "Libyan Models": the "Libyan Model" of 2003 and "Libyan Model" of 2011. The former refers to a positive attitude that Gaddafi regime voluntarily gave up its weapons of mass destruction development program meaning to exchange the said program for its security guarantee threatened by some Western countries, which has normalized its relations with Western countries and blended itself into the international society.

After the Iraq War in March 2003, Saddam regime was rapidly toppled. Consequently, the Libya leader Gaddafi had realized that it was necessary to give up research and development of weapons of mass destruction, in order to end Libya's isolated situation and return to the international society. For this purpose, Gaddafi terminated the long hard-line stand and opted for pragmatic approach and policies. On December 19, 2003, Libya government announced that it gave up the program of developing weapons of mass destruction and allowed controls and supervision by the experts from the US, Britain and International Atomic Energy Agency. Soon later, the government wrote a letter to UN Security Council, declaring that it was willing to accept the restrictions and rules of the Treaty on the Non-Proliferation of Nuclear Weapons, Comprehensive Nuclear Test Ban Treaty and other international disarmament treaties. Soon after that, UN Security Council passed a resolution to remove the sanctions targeting Libya. On January 26, 2004, Libya government transported relevant development documents and materials related to nuclear weapons and guided missiles as well equipment to Tennessee City in the USA. The equipment included centrifuges for uranium enrichment and guidance components for guided missiles, etc.

In March 2004, Libya government signed an additional protocol of Treaty on the Non-Proliferation of Nuclear Weapons, and ratified the Chemical Weapons Convention. Through the series of such positive measures, Gaddafi regime gradually normalized its relations with Western countries, surpassed its isolated situation and returned to the international society. Consequently, the international community has called such method of action as the Libyan Model in which a nuclear issue dispute was solved through peaceful negotiations in exchange of gaining security guarantees from Western countries. It has been an effective way to solve international issues or conflicts peacefully and maintain the international security system, reflecting an advance in the practice of international governance.

On the contrary, the "Libyan Model" of 2011 especially refers to a behavior pattern which finally overthrew Gaddafi regime by military interventions. In essence, it was deviated from the "Libyan Model" of 2003, also means that Western countries' have violated their "promise" of providing Gaddafi regime with security guarantee after Gaddafi voluntarily gave up developing weapons of mass destruction. Hence, we can see from Libya War especially from the differences of the two Libyan Models that Libya crisis and Libya regime change was retrogression situation of international governance.

III. Severe Challenges Brought by Neo-interventionism to International Governance

1. Influences of Neo-interventionism on Libya and International Relations

Libya War launched by Western neo-interventionists in the 21st century exerted significant and profound influences on international governance.

At first, military intervention operations of NATO posits severe challenges against the international governance. In particular, the sovereignty concept in international conduct codes is under threat. UNSC pointed out in the Resolution No. 1973 that dispatching ground forces to occupy Libya was not included among measures so as to protect Libyan civilians. Such a flawed stipulation initiated the precedent of quoting an international law (Treaty of Rome) in order to authorize armed interventions in the internal affairs of a sovereign state, which means superiority of human rights over sovereignty in international affairs.

More importantly, military intervention operations of NATO has far exceeded and violated the limit of UN-authorized No-fly Zone measure. Instead, NATO has realized a regime change by overthrowing the Gaddafi rule. UN has turned a blind eye and could not stop NATO operations which exceeded the authorization limit; this fat reflects the defects of the UN system and its role as one of the international governance subjects.

Secondly, military intervention operations of NATO demonstrate an obvious trend of "expansion to the South" after "its expansion to the East", which also reflects that the role and tasks of NATO are being expanded, its role and functions are gradually developing to include all the world regions, it tends to have a global strategic layout and action plan. All of these will exert profound influences to the global pattern.[16]

Thirdly, military interventions of NATO have caused numerous innocent civilian casualties and damaged civil infrastructure and dwellings. With uninterrupted bombings, NATO caused huge civil casualties in Libya and created new humanitarian disasters under the name of defending humanity. Meanwhile, due to the war, a refugees mass was created which rushed into surrounding countries including South Europe, also causing extensive attention and worries in the international community.

At last, collapse of the Gaddafi dictatorship marked the failure of the US "Libya Model" in solving the nuclear issues, which presents a negative after-effect example for the international community in solving nuclear issues, thus brought a brand-new challenge for the international governance. In the past 10-plus years, before the Libya war Gaddafi regime developed its relations with Western countries to a certain extent by criticizing the "9/11" event publicly, bearing the compensation responsibility for "Lockerbie Bombing" and voluntarily announcing that it gave up the development of weapons of mass destruction, etc.

---

16   See, Mostafa Dolatyar, "Sustainable Security in the Middle East: NATO's Role?", Turkish Policy Quarterly, Vol.10, No.3, 2011, pp.45-51.

In return, Western great powers recovered their relations with Libya and promised security guarantee to the Gaddafi regime.

Hence, when negotiating the solutions of nuclear issues—including those in North Korea and Iran—the international community deems the "Libya Model" as one example. However, the military action conducted by NATO to Libya has demonstrated that Gaddafi's compromises to Western countries did not bring Libya a real security guarantee. This fact as a result, triggers some countries to take an adventurous road and restart their nuclear weapon plans for self-security. In Middle East, the tide of nuclear capacity competition has already appeared and it has become more difficult for international community to solve nuclear issues.

It is thus clear that Libya War and Libyan Model has brought fundamental challenges to the capability and institutional design of future international governance.

2. Post-war Reconstruction in Libya and Importance of Strengthening International Governance

Flames of Libya War have gradually faded out, but Libya still has to bear long-term and arduous post-war reconstruction and political transformation which are full of uncertainty. Both Libya War and post-war reconstruction leaves us with a long-term introspection as the members of the international community, their lessons demonstrate the urgency and complexity of strengthening the international governance.

How to strengthen the international governance? On the one side, the principle of respecting and maintaining state sovereignty is still the basic premise of international governance. Improvement of international governance requires both the participation of sovereign states and the coordination by the international community. International governance subjects include both the sovereign states and international organizations such as the UN, World Bank, WTO and International Monetary Fund. International governance should never mean abandoning of state sovereignty. The sovereign states are still main subjects in the international governance and will play a leading role in international governance. Meanwhile, international governance does not refer to great power governance, in which the rights of developing countries are neglected or diminished.

On the other side, the maintenance of sovereignty and human right protection are of equal importance and have internal and external relations. A sovereignty state can establish its legitimacy of rule practically only by protecting human rights in order to realize and maintain its sovereignty.

Otherwise, maintaining sovereignty will become a flub dub and can hardly obtain support and response from its domestic people and internationally. Hence, maintaining sovereignty and human right protection are the two basic principles for strengthening international governance. The primary task for the current world is to strengthen the leading function of UN and perfect its international governance mechanisms and institutional design. UN is still an important platform to promote international governance at present.

Specifically speaking, post-war reconstruction of Libya involves fields like politics, economy and security. An important way to strengthen international governance lies in giving full play to UN's role and functions, and in paying attention to the secret deals of Western great powers in order to control and expanding their petroleum interests in Libya during its reconstruction and damage its sovereignty on its sources.

It is historically quite ironic that over 40 years ago, mainly with the inspirations of anti-colonialism and Arab nationalism, Gaddafi had launched a coup and overthrew the rule of pro-Western King Idris. That outstanding initiative taken by him drove away the Western petroleum companies and military bases in Libya. 40 plus years later, Gaddafi regime lost the power, replaced by the Libyan National Transitional Council came which paved the way to Western petroleum companies returning to Libya with ambitious plans as winners.

During the post-war Libya reconstruction, former Western colonialism which was once hardly beaten has appeared again with a new face. The plunder nature of Western petroleum companies will surely pose threats and challenges to sovereign independence of future Libya. This is an alarming reality.

In the meantime, construction of new regime, political integration and transition to democratic regime in Libya after the war all require creation of an inclusive political framework. The key for Libya's reconstruction also lies in: promoting and making use of the authority and governance capability of Libya's own government, as well as broad people's approval and allegiance and promoting of the support of local forces.

As the current representative of the new regime, the National Transitional Council has reached the peak of its power after overthrowing the Gaddafi regime during NATO's air strikes. Members of the National Transitional Council come from different factions the opposition. With extremely complicated internal relations, these members always hold different stands and tend to act autonomously in their own ways. With the elimination of the joint enemy – Gaddafi forces, there appeared obvious contradictions about power and interest distribution among members of the National Transitional Council.

It is a severe fact that during the anti-Gaddafi fights, some local armed forces grew rapidly, built their own armed forces and consolidated themselves, occupied respective regions, and refuse to take orders from the Transitional Council, and directly threaten the authority of the current regime.

Hence, Libya during this transitional stage demonstrates fragmented political situation full of various complicated internal and external factors.[17]

Under this situation, it is very difficult to establish a government authority. There is no charismatic figure or talent who can undertake state governance and financial management tasks among the members of National Transitional Council. In addition, Libya is a tribal society, in which people generally continue tribe consciousness and pledge more loyalty to their tribes than the state, while tribe interests and tribe consciousness can directly influence political identification of the state. Bloody conflicts and arbitrary revenge acts in Libya War have further deepened hostilities among tribes and the whole members of the society and also widened inter-regional and inter-tribal estrangement and cracks. On March 6, 2012, Cyrenaica – an eastern Libya region, bordered with Egypt, with rich petroleum announced it's "semi-autonomy" and called for implementing federalism in Libya.[18]

Deemed as an important signal, such an autonomy demand poses a huge problem to unity and territorial integrity of Libya and also directly challenges the authority of the Libyan government – the National Transitional Council, which posits huge risks faced by the Libya during re-construction and political transformation after collapse of the political strongman Gaddafi. What can be really brought by the "Libya Model" created by NATO's military intervention in Libya?

Libyan reconstruction is totally a different issue compared to NATO's overthrowing Gaddafi's autocracy by the military intervention. In history, when a strongman regime collapsed with a loud bang, another strongman regime has replaced it, otherwise the country fell into absolute anarchy. Under such social conditions like complicated divisions in the society or tribal relations, acute social problems and contradictions, advancing of e democracy will surely promote divisions – different ethnic groups or tribes

---

17 Wolfram Lacher, "Families, Tribes and Cities in the Libyan", Middle East Policy, Vol. XVIII, No. 4, Winter 2011.

18 Cyrenaica is the eastern coastal region of Libya. Also known as Pentapolis ("Five Cities") in antiquity, which formed a part of the Roman empire.

will opt for separation under the slogan of "autonomy". It is fair to say that NATO has to face this hard dilemma when creating a democratic regime attached to its "Libya Model".

Above facts and lessons exactly indicates that enhancement of democracy requires certain premises, and can be realized smoothly only through people's political identification and mutual cooperation among the leading political authorities. During the 6-plus months after collapse of Gaddafi regime, the "National Transitional Council" ruling Libya has not realized effective control in the difference regions of the country, meanwhile many regions act like "semi-independent" states. It is thus clear that National Transitional Council has not yet built its authority. Divisive effects of the recent bloody war and the old and new scores can hardly be forgotten and removed. After the war, revenge murders and revengeful acts have occurred frequently. The so-called "inclusiveness" in governance is still an extravagant hope, appearing to be a rhetoric written on ice. As for the decision of "semi-autonomy" announced by Cyrenaica, Mustafa Abdul Jalil – Chairman of National Transitional Council has responded publicly: "the Council will maintain unity by its "military forces", and our Libyan people will join hands to support federalism and oppose to autonomy." However, in post-war Libya, divisions have continuously deepened among different regions and social groups, and can hardly be surpassed by military means, at all. Amids the political contest about "semi-autonomy" and "federalism", post-war reconstruction and political transformation of Libya will be full of suspense and risks.

In such a period, Cyrenaica's announcement of autonomy is only surfacing of above mentioned seriousness of the problems and also strengthens our predictions of the partition of Libya, which suggests that the so-called "Libyan Model" created by neo-interventionism[19] is in fact a dangerous attempt and also a huge challenge to international governance and international relations.

19　Five years after Muammar Gaddafi's death, Anders Fogh Rasmussen, the former head of NATO and former Danish prime minister, have spoken about the 2011 Libyan intervention. He told Al-Jazeera: "It was really a model intervention". (http://www.news24.com/Africa/News/watch-ex-nato-chief-still-calls-libya-a-model-intervention-20161024-2)

The Military Intervention by EU in Libya

Wu Xian[1]

In the crisis of Libya, the U.S. together with its Western allies including France and U.K. made military interventions, which undoubtedly brought decisive influences to the development tendency of the event. On March 19, 2011, using the excuse of implementing UN Security Council Resolution 1973 and building a no-fly zone to protect Libyan citizens, countries including France, U.K. and the U.S. launched air strikes to the Gaddafi army. Afterwards, they built an effective no-fly zone within 1 week and the NATO completely took over the right to command and control wars. In order to keep the high-handed military manner, the NATO prolonged the action deadline and strengthened the attack to the governmental army while at the same time vigorously supporting the opposition faction in Libya, thereby causing fundamental changes in the domestic situation: in late August, the opposition faction attacked and occupied the capital Tripoli; in early September, the opposition faction controlled most regions in the country; after the Gaddafi regime collapsed, the "National Transitional Council" obtained a lawful seat in the UN Conference in mid Being expert at "economic integration" and "soft power", the EU countries changed the fixed mode of following U.S. military actions after the Cold War, and this time became the principal architects of the military interventions, and neglected military dilemmas until they realized the direct objectives. All these actions have undoubtedly attracted general attention of the international community. In

---

1   Researcher in the Institute of European Studies, Chinese Academy of Social Sciences.

fact, this was their first attempt to increase their own international position and realize long-term interest appeals after the Cold War and shall be further researched. EU countries led by France and U.K. tried to influence the surrounding world directly by military force with the support of the U.S. and the NATO on the premise of increasing defense independence in order to cope with situation changes. I will briefly introduce and analyze several important issues in this intervention respectively including its background and motivation, joint promotion of France and U.K. selection of organizational mechanism, and influences from the U.S. and the NATO, as is shown below.

I. Background and motivation

Countries such as France and U.K. launch military actions because they are deeply motivated and they attempt to promote "process of democratization" in the neighboring Arab countries by military interventions in order to satisfy European requirements about system, EU values and its long-term interests.

Briefly, the 3 key points of EU policies are as follows:

Firstly, in view of multiple aspects such as geopolitics, economy and safety, EU-Mediterranean countries led by France always argue that North Africa and Western Asia are related to many core interests of Europe and are very important. Hence, the "New Policy for Neighboring Countries" of the EU—including "Union for the Mediterranean" which is strongly advocated by France—adhered to the overriding core objective of maintaining long-term regional "stability" in order to meet the European demands for interests in other fields under this general premise.

The Economist wrote: "stability overrides everything for many reasons: to maintain the Arab-Israeli peace treaties; to fight pagan extremist terrorism; to curb the proliferation of large arms; to ensure oil and gas supply; to prevent large-scale Immigration, etc. These are not insignificant concerns."[2]

Secondly, in view of the strong impacts exerted by "Arab Spring" that began in the early 2011, various EU countries finally admitted that regional "stability" did not exist any longer, but they still firmly argued that the situation development had important "historical" significance, while the democratization process had started in the Arab world and would surely generate lasting influences especially to Europe. Hence, the EU adjusted

---

2 The Economist "Europe must do more to support Arab democracy, out of self-respect and self-interest", February 26, 2011, p. 48.

its political orientation and transformed the core objective of maintaining regional stability into vigorously promoting deep democratization so as to achieve lasting stability in the southern Mediterranean region and European requests for many interests at higher levels in the future.[3]

Thirdly, the EU argues that Libya's development has made it difficult to make directional strategic adjustments: previous "revolution" in Tunisia and Egypt have resulted as peaceful replacement of regimes there, while the Gaddafi regime suppressed the weak opposition faction by employing its own massive military force.

As a result, it would thoroughly overwhelm or even wipe out the latter and throttle democratization in Libya. What's more, once winning the war, Gaddafi would be a model to rulers of other countries, thus promote more violent oppressions and finally bring serious hinderance to the "Color Revolutions" in the Arab World. Hence, the EU required Gaddafi to "immediately give up the power in order to rapidly recover orders in Libya and then realize democratic transformation"[4].

It has also become a political objective with overall importance once and again which was firmly insisted by the EU. Due to the uncompromising attitude of the Libyan government, some military great powers in the EU tried to realize such an objective by their military forces.[5]

II. Libya intervention jointly promoted by France and UK: Its reasons and effects

Undoubtedly, France and UK played an irreplaceable important role in Libya interventions. It can be said that without joint acts made by these two countries, the Libya intervention would never happen, let alone continuous propulsion or current consequences, so we need to study the reasons and joint effects brought by these two countries. Associated Press News, Paris, article wrote on June 12th, "Some analysts pointed out that the military action against Libya is in France and UK-led".

---

3 European Commission & High Representative of the Union for Foreign Affairs and Security Policy, A Partnership for Democracy and Shared Prosperity with the Southern Mediterranean, Brussels, March 8, 2011, COM (2011) 200 final; European Commission & High Representative of the Union for Foreign Affairs and Security Policy, A New Response to a Changing Neighbourhood, Brussels, May 25, 2011, COM (2011) 303.
4 European Commission, "Developments in Libya: an overview of the EU's response," http://www.consilium.europa.eu; Catherine Ashton, "Statement by the High Representative following the London Conference on Libya," Brussels, March 29, 2011.
5 "The Libyan Crisis and EU Intervention," European Studies, 2011/3, pp. 15-18.

Another newspaper, The Economist published an article titled as: "France and Britain are leading the intervention in Libya. Rightly So."[6]

France and U.K. realized close cooperation mainly because of the following major factors:

At first, the two countries argued that the implementation of military interventions had satisfied their respective strategic interests, while both of them were able to take actions. Because of geopolitical, historical and realistic reasons, France always regarded "Africa especially North Africa" (the Mediterranean region) as its traditional sphere of influence, which became the major motivation for France to establish EU's New Policy of Neighboring Countries and the Union for the Mediterranean, but Gaddafi has opposed France's strategy: the Union for the Mediterranean.

Libya is located in the chief interest zone of France's defense strategy, so Libya's location and its political evolution has been directly related to many focuses of France.

The Sarkozy government established close relationships with the opposition faction in Libya—France was first to recognize the legal status of the opposition faction latter.

In order to show off its position as a great power and tried to gain a dominant position in the development of the situation in its major junctures, France, finally became the strongest supporter of the intervention.[7]

U.K. also emphasized that "North Africa is very important for the interests of U.K. and the EU", and "intervention in Libya is its urgent national interest"[8].

The Times pointed out that, in addition to strong humanitarian reasons, Libya's geographical location on the Mediterranean coast, its oil resources and trade potential have shown that intervention with Libya is in full compliance with British strategic interests.[9]

---

6   The Economist, March 26 , 2011, p.48.
7   "France's foreign-policy's woes,Nicolas Sarkozy's diplomatic troubles", The Economist, March 5, 2011, p. 53.
8   Nick Clegg, Transforming Europe's partnership with North Africa, March 2, 2011, http://www.libdems.org.uk/latest_news_detail.
9   See also, "Job done. It is time to get out of Afghanistan; The training must go on, but we should follow the US and withdraw combat troops this year," The Times, April 22, 2011.

Meanwhile, regarding their power and political influence, both France and UK possess the strongest military power among EU countries. Their defense expenditures respectively rank the 3rd and 4th places in world, while the sum occupies half of European defense budget. Both of them are capable of nuclear deterrence, and are permanent member states in the UN Security Council hoping to "get involved in the front edge of EU strategies" and deem themselves as "global great powers which are ready to independently invest military force when necessary."[10]

Secondly, more importantly, with the development and evolution of internal and external situations, French and British security appeals have become convergent and overlapped, and promoted both parties to strengthen bilateral defense cooperation. Both of them believed that "We do not see situations arising in which the vital interests of either nation could be threatened without the vital interests of the other also being threatened". This is the foundation upon which cooperation between the two countries rests.[11]

In recent years, France returned back to the NATO command organization. Meanwhile, the weakening of the demand of military power development among the EU member states, great cost increases of high-tech weapons, as well as other factors have also directly promoted this specific cooperation between U.K. and France.[12]

In November 2010, France and U.K. formally concluded the "Defense Cooperation Treaty". It is clearly stipulated in the Treaty that bilateral cooperation contains nuclear tests, aircraft carrier actions, establishment of "Joint Task Force" and vital supporting tasks.[13]

It is fair to say that current joint intervention is a part of an institutional arrangement. Meanwhile, both countries also admitted that action objectives could hardly be realized only by one country. Hence, some British critics said that "Mr. Sarkozy of course will not take actions alone. His alliance with British Prime Minister Cameron is of vital importance"; "British and French people know that they must help each other to expand influences". In addition, since the 20th century, Britain and France have a long tradition of alliances, such as the "Anglo-French Treaty of 1904", alliance during the two world wars, including the alliance in the 1956 Suez Canal war.[14]

10　Institute of Land Warfare, "The French-British Defense Treaty: Setting History Aside?"
11　Ibid.
12　The Economist, March 26, 2011, p. 48.
13　The Economist, March 26, 2011, p. 4; The Economist, June 18, 2011, p. 50.
14　The Economist, March 26, 2011, p. 48.

Thirdly, the complexity of the EU's security cooperation:

Security cooperation is an integrated high-end field of the EU, and it is always deemed as sensitive and complicated and can hardly reach a consensus. It also manifested the distinguished characteristics at that time. As everybody knows, since the Kosovo War, the EU has decided to accelerate the establishment of "joint security and defense policy". However, due to various reasons, such a strategy is currently limited in the field of peace keeping and humanitarian aid and can hardly obtain larger achievements.

Meanwhile, concerning how to cope with Libya's situation (the EU once discussed about this event at a special summit conference on March 11), all the members states consistently admitted that the Gaddafi regime was no longer legal and must quit the political stage and step down.[15] But, they could hardly reach a consensus in respect to the military force proposition of France and U.K. For instance, Germany clearly advocated solution by political means and opposed to military interventions (hence, it gave an abstention vote to Resolution 1973 and even "prohibited its warships from implementing arms embargo to Libya"). Italy also held a strong reserved attitude at the very beginning—especially Italy opposed to the implementation of military force under the NATO framework.[16]

EU member states located in the Central and Eastern Europe also took a "silent" attitude. Under these conditions, France and U.K. had to primarily depend on their bilateral coordination and cooperation for the intervention.[17]

Specific role played by the France and U.K. before and after interventions can be summarized as follows:

Firstly, France and U.K. both vigorously carried out multi-lateral diplomacy and tried to obtain "legality" for their intervention plan.. One characteristic of European security strategy executed since the end of the Cold War lies in that they emphasized "effective multilateralism" and functions of international organizations and regulations (all these contents are clearly described by the EU in documents (in respect to France and U.K. For example, the European Union "European Security Strategy Document (December 2003) clearly defines "effective multilateralism" as one of its three strategic objectives.[18]

---

15 European Commission, "Developments in Libya: an overview of the EU's response," http://www.consilium.europa.eu.
16 See, Li Miao's article "Italy and its position in the Libya issue," August 2011.
17 The Economist, March 26,2011, p.48; see also, Sun Yingwei'a article in July 2011 "Germany's Foreign Security and Defense Policy During the Libya Crisis"; besides see, Yan Jin's article in the Journal of European Studies, 2011/3 "Germany Libya crisis policy analysis".
18 See, "A Secure Europe in a Better World," European Security Strategy, Brussels, December 12, 2003, pp. 6-10.

In France, "Defense and National Security White Paper" (promulgated in June 2008, which is the first time in France's 14 years of its national defense strategy), it said: "the Sarkozy government will attach importance to the role of the United Nations", "support multi-lateralism, and reject unilateralism "as an important way to achieve national defense strategic goals.[19]

Also, UK's Strategic Defense and Security Assessment Report (October 2010) has highlighted, the following:"Will seek to directly strengthen the effectiveness of the multilateral institutions that are most important for the security interests of the United Kingdom and to take advantage of our leading role in the institutions that are the key to the global security and prosperity of the United Kingdom. The document defined the United Nations as the key to the global security and prosperity of the United Kingdom, and claimed that UK would use its position in the UN Security Council, which is another key institution with primary responsibility, for global peace and security."[20]

While making preparations for military intervention, France and UK, and they simultaneously, carried out active lobbying in order to obtain approval from the international community, which was crucial for their pre-war activities. Below we will present their lobbying activities:

Both countries emphasized the necessity and urgency of "humanitarian intervention". In the letter sent to Chairman of European Council dated March 10, 2001—this letter is very important to display the basic attitudes and propositions of both countries,

In this letter Sarkozy and Cameron highlighted that the Gaddafi regime deliberately launched military forces (including fighter planes and helicopters) to oppress Libyan civilians, which obviously formed a "crime against humanity". It was "completely unacceptable" and must be "condemned".

They urged the UN to pay close attention to Libya's "humanitarian situation" (and also supported "investigations" by the International Criminal Court). For these reasons, the joint letter pointed out that, in order to "immediately stop" the Gaddafi regime from using military forces to civilians, France and U.K. were willing to give support to Libyan people by establishing "a no-fly zone or other options to stop the humanitarian disaster caused by the air attacks"[21].

---

19 "The Security Strategy of France," November 2011.
20 Zhang Lei, "UK Security Strategy", August 2011, see also: http://www.direct.gov.uk/ prod_consum_dg/groups/dg_digitalassets/@dg/@en/documents/digitalasset/dg; David Cameron, "Securing Britain in an Age of Uncertainty: The Strategic Defence and Security Review," presented to Parliament by the Prime Minister by Command of Her Majesty, October 2010.
21 David Cameron and Nicolas Sarkozy, "Joint Letter from Prime Minister David Cameron MP and President Nicolas Sarkozy," March 10, 2011.

On this basis, both countries also highlighted the urgency for protecting civilians and implementing humanitarian interventions besides consideration of key points which should be contained when the UN Security Council approved a relevant resolution.

They tried to obtain recognition and support from involved parties, namely the Arab League and the UN.

In view of the extremely complex political situations and relations in the North Africa and Western Asia region, it was necessary to obtain recognition from the Arab countries. Besides, France and U.K. in order to show their difference from the US which launched a war in Iraq without UN approval, particularly emphasized to obtain "legitimacy" from the Arab region (Arab League Organization) "initiatively requested" intervention and finally obtained authorization from the UN Security Council. Here, the support of the Arab League Organization was critical in the UN negotiations.

To this end, France and U.K. implemented their diplomatic activities on three levels mentioned below:

Firstly, they pinpointed the Libyan government as the target party, and contacted the opposition. France had long maintained close contacts with the opposition faction for a long time. Under such a background, its leader Jalil (Chairman of National Transitional Council) clearly requested the establishment of a no-fly zone to the international community on March 8—which was deemed as "one of legal bases for France, U.S. and U.K. to launch sudden air strikes"[22].

Secondly, they tried to obtain the support of Arab countries.

This was particularly emphasized by France, and took the Arab League as its regional representative and the major lobbying target. With vigorous support from Sarkozy, on March 12 the Arab League formally suggested to UN that it should take measures to protect Libyan civilians (so French Foreign Minister Alain Juppe said that "Different from Suez Canal War, we have obtained support from Arabs this time").[23]

---

22 Digest, Vol. 2, distributed in September 6, 2011.
23 Financial Times "France backs Libyan opposition," news edited and produced by Peter Spiegel, James Blitz, and Peggy Holllingers, March 11, 2011, p. 5.

Thirdly, France and U.K. also jointly lobbied to persuade some members from the UN Security Council.

Thus the approval of UN SC Resolution 1973 was finally achieved, which stipulated the establishment of no-fly zones. In order to protect Libyan civilians, "all the necessary manners" (which were limited to air attacks and did not allow the use of ground forces[24].

This was the final stage of obtaining "legitimacy" and the "diplomatic success of France and U.K." EU made an official statement on the day of the adoption of the UN resolution and expressed its welcome, the statement called the international community to protect the Libyan civilians, which is based on a "clear legitimacy"[25].

French Foreign Minister Juppe said, "without the United Nations Security Council's clear mandate, we will not carry out any military intervention"[26].

The British government declared that the British intervention in Libya is the right decision because "there is a clear United Nations resolution and the support of the Arab League," ... "the intervention is carried out by the authorization of the United Nations it is is necessary, legal, and just"[27].

Secondly, France and U.K. promoted the establishment of the "coalition of the willing" and ensured timely execution of air strikes.

Intervention operations were implemented by volunteered participation of various states, to enable this participation, France and U.K. firstly needed to build the so-called "coalition of the willing". The key to the success of the war is to promote the United States to join.

On the premise that France and U.K. decided to make joint military actions, the necessary condition for launching a war lied in promoting the U.S. to get involved, because US contribution was vital, militarily. But in those days US still "held a cautious attitude towards military interventions". This issue, we will further discuss in the below.

---

24 The Security Council, (Paragraphs 6 and 8) UN, Resolution 1973 (2011), Adopted by the Security Council at its 6498th meeting, on March 17, 2011.
25 Joint statement by President of the European Council Herman Van Rompuy, and EU High Representative Catherine Ashton on UN Security Council resolution on Libya, Brussels, March 17, 2011, PCE 072/11, A 110/1.
26 See, the "Figaro", quoted from Peng Shiyi "the French government in the military before the statement", August 2011.
27 See, Zhang Lei's article, "British Security Strategy"; see also: http://www.direct.gov.uk/prod_consum_dg/groups/dg_digitalassets/@dg/@en/documents/digitalasset/dg. Besides see: "French and British Diplomacy", The Economist, March 26, 2011, p. 23.

For this reason, Cameron used the "special relationship" between U.K. and the U.S. and finally motivated the Obama administration to make a commitment for participation. As the Libyan opposition faction base camp already stayed on a razor's edge at that time, France, U.K. and the U.S. executed an air attack action (On March 19) within less than 48 hours after approval of the Resolution 1973, wherein France made direct air attacks to advanced troops of governmental army and timely stopped the Benghazi collapse. U.K. and the U.S. attacked air defense facilities of Libya, which promoted the effective establishment of the no-fly zone within a week[28].

Thirdly, France and U.K. have actively combined political and "hard power" during the intervention.

In order to realize their political objectives, France and U.K. have rallied and mobilized all the military potential forces that could be employed. Although, these countries are said to have reduced their defense budgets, the new reports displayed a contrast reality: U.K. still dispatched a dozen of fighter planes, several escort ships and a submarine. A senior commander of the British army said that "the military force they had employed had reached the limit. In the case of an eruption of a new crisis, they would have no military forces left."

France had mobilized more military forces compared to U.K., including Naval Air Force Group and Charles de Gaulle aircraft carrier (British media publications have commented that "but aircraft carrier, looked overstretched."[29]

After NATO undertook the command, France and U.K. have displayed the toughest stand among those eight states which launched air strikes, became the major pushers to maintain high-pressure military situation and finally bore important attack actions. After three months of air strikes, the commander-in-chief of the Army had even said, "I believe that in a few weeks, the military operations will end."[30]

Despite the fact that European countries have felt that they had insufficient financial resources and military power. For example, Norway decided to reduce action plans and completely quitted the intervention on August 1st.[31]

28　The Economist, March 26, 2011, pp.23-24; James Blitz, "And now for the hard part: three reasons to fear a stalemate,"Financial Times, March 27, 2011, p.8.
29　Philip Stephens, "Obama to Europe: Bon courage," Financial Times, March 25, p. 11 and also see, "Commander of the Western Generals in the Liberation of Libya", published in "Writers Digest" April 1, 2011/10.
30　Singapore newspaper, Lianhe Zaobao, March 26, 2011.
31　See, the news by Gerrit Wiesmann, James Blitz and Peggy Holllingers, "UK and France Became Isolated in the Acrion " Financial Times, April 15, p. 4; "Robert Gates' Parting Shot Exposes Europe's Military Failings," The Economist, June 18, 2011, p.50.

The French and British governments still declared clearly that "Gaddafi must quit the political stage immediately"; (military) actions for months were "valuable" and being "strengthened"; and they would not "set a final deadline". Afterwards, they even strengthened the attacks by intensifying the scale and frequency, continuously expanding the target scope, and using attack helicopters for the first time in order to attack ground targets more accurately. As reported, upon the "end" of the war in early September, the NATO had launched about 22 thousand attacks to Libya, of which 1/3 were carried out by British and French planes; about 5,000 military targets were destroyed, and 40% of these targets were hit by British and French fighter planes.[32]

Based on this, U.S. Ambassador to NATO admitted not long ago that U.K. and France played an "extraordinary" role in NATO's air attacks to Libya.[33]

General Secretary of the NATO also pointed out that air attacks reflected that, besides the U.S., Europe still "possesses the most advanced military capability in the world", and could "play a central role in a complex military intervention."[34]

Sarkozy, also underlined the historically significant military role of France and military forces of Europe. He also pointed out complacently: "For the first time, Europe has proved, that she is able to make decisive interventions to the conflicts in front of their gate, as Libya is directly connected to the Mediterranean, while Mediterranean affairs are firstly to the business of Europe and secondly that of the U.S."[35]

III. Selection of intervention methods and profound reasons behind them

France and U.K. decided to make joint military actions, but they could hardly reach their goals only by their military forces. Hence, they must obtain support from Western allies. For this reason, seeking for proper organization form and determination of uniform and effective commanding and coordination mechanism constituted basic conditions of action implementation and could surely become decision-making keys before and after

---
32 AFP, Brussels, 8 September, and see, "Reference News" September 9, 2011/2.
33 Ibid.
34 A.F. Rasmussen (NATO Secretary General),"The Atlantic Alliance in Austere Times," June 29, 2011, http://www.nato.int/cps/en/SID-0F54B199-D4926692/natolive/opinions_75836.htm.
35 "Reference News" September 9, 2011/2.

the interventions. With development and evolution of internal and external situations in Europe, strategic orientations of EU countries greatly vary especially between Europe and the U.S, while it was very difficult to reach a consensus. However, they have finally reached a consensus through continuous disputes and coordination. Situation development showed that due to many deep reasons, the U.S. or the NATO led by it was still indispensable and relied on which European countries launched military actions this time.

When designing an operation mechanism, European and U.S. allies firstly selected the form of the "coalition of the willing" and finally took the "NATO" as the action framework. This decision was made by various European countries and the U.S. with different strategic concerns and propositions through continuous coordination and compromises. In fact, as the prime initiators, France and U.K. held different opinions about it at the very beginning. U.K. believed that interventions could be implemented under the NATO framework and it even opposed to French implementation of arms embargo under EU navy force in August 2010. The famous French Admiral Philip Kendra as the EU anti-piracy commander, responsible for command and coordination was well received.[36]

France had opposed to this option because the NATO was viewed by the Arab world as a power political tool and should not show up directly any longer. However, France admitted that the U.S. played an inseparable role in intervention launching, so it initially adopted the form of the "coalition of the willing", which means that U.K. persuaded the U.S. to join them. Afterwards, 3 countries launched air attacks in alliance. However, the problem was that the U.S. government did not launch the intervention positively for the sake of its own interests, and further it was unwilling to continuously lead the actions because: at first, with the development and evolution of the situation after the Cold War, "security concerns of the U.S. have been changed from Europe to the Middle East and Southern Asia and finally focused on the rising China", while the U.S. argued that Libya was not a region which is vital for the U.S. interests, consequently Europe should handle its own security affairs alone.[37]

---

36 See, "The Western General Who Directs Libya Air Strikes," "The Digest of Writers," April 1, issue 2011/10.
37 The Economist, June 18, 2011, p. 50; Daniel Dombey and James Blitz, "Europe feels strain as US changes tack on Libya," Financial Times, April 6, 2011, p. 5.

Secondly, the U.S. was bogged down in Afghanistan and Iraq wars at the cost of huge military expenditures.

It keenly felt the difficulties of wars to be conducted in the Islamic world, and U.S. was also aware of the insufficient military power of European countries, and also it was worrisome about being so deeply involved that it would be difficult to quit when necessary.

Thirdly, disputes and doubts raised by the domestic political circles about the intervention and this situation has restrained the action space of the U.S. government.

As a result, although the U.S. agreed to participate the "coalition of the willing" at the initial stage of intervention and assumed commanding job and provide firepower support, the U.S. consistently insisted that the "command and control" of the operation should be transferred to the NATO as soon as possible, so that it could take and enjoy the back seat.

In the meantime, due to a lot of reasons, except for U.K., many member states of the EU and the member states of the NATO such as Italy, Luxembourg and Norway also supported the U.S.' position that the NATO should take the lead. The above differences of opinions caused heated debates in the NATO and have even led to the "most drastic diplomatic confrontation" since 2003 (the Iraq War). (The French Ambassador left the assembly site of NATO Council to make a protest). NATO Secretary General Rasmussen on March 21 at the Council, has criticized that France had hindered NATO involved and Germany is not actively involved in the operation, for this law, the two NATO ambassadors to NATO had angrily left the meeting venue.[38]

However, due to various reasons, France made a concession at last and approved that the NATO would take over all the command and control rights in actions. As per the agreements concluded by each party, on March 24 the NATO decided to join the action "coalition of the willing" and both parties also conducted necessary coordination. And the NATO Secretary General said in a statement: "NATO allies have now decided to establish a no-fly zone in Libya... We are taking action as part of the broad international effort to protect civilians against the attacks by the Gaddafi regime. We will cooperate with our partners in the region and welcome their contributions. All NATO allies are committed to fulfill their obligations under the UN resolution. That

---

38 For more information about NATO's internal debates, see, Peter Spiegel and Daniel Dombey, "Allies at odds over command," Financial Times, March 22, 2011, p. 3; Daniel Dombey and Peter Spiegel, "Coalition split over Libya action," Financial Times, March 22, 2011, p.1; Peter Spiegel and Peggy Holllinger, "NATO near to deal on control of military campaign," Financial Times, March 24, 2011, p. 3.

is why we have decided to assume responsibility for the no-fly zone. At this moment there will still be a coalition operation and a NATO operation but we are considering whether NATO should take on a broader responsibility in accordance with the UN Security Council resolution. But that decision has not been made yet. Through the chain of command NATO and the Coalition will ensure close coordination and de-confliction."[39]

On March 27, the NATO decided to take over the command of all the military actions" (called as "action of unified protector"), and declared that NATO "wills to protect the civilians and civilian districts under the threat of attack", in which Charles Bouchard, a Canadian air force Lieutenant General, would take charge of the joint command in the NATO's Allied Joint Force Command which is located in Naples, Italy.[40] On March 31, the NATO completed the full take-over of the command of the military operation.[41]

It shows that interventions conducted by France, U.K. and U.S. have been completely incorporated into the combat system of the NATO. According to statistics, among the 28 member states of the NATO, about half of them agreed to provide military support for the operations, but only 8 countries including the U.S., France, U.K, Canada, Italy, Denmark, Norway and Belgium directly joined the air strikes.[42]

As a matter of fact, the principle of voluntary participation was also implemented by the NATO.

The selection and situation development of the intervention mechanism showed that the U.S. and the NATO led by the US has played an irreplaceable role in this intervention. The main reasons are as follows:

NATO's role:

Firstly, NATO's own strategic adjustment.

As a collective defense organization for Europe and the U.S, the NATO has successively made three "new strategic concepts" in expansion focusing on the situation changes in the post-Cold War Era, as well as making adjustments and reform to objective orientations and manners of security strategies.

---

39 NATO Secretary General's statement on Libya no fly zone, March 24, 2011, http://www.nato.int/cps/en/natiolive/news_71763.htm, August 29, 2011.
40 See, news co-edited by James Blitz, Andrew England and Daniel Dombey, "NATO to take full control of Libya mission," Financial Times, March26/March27, 2011, p.2; NATO and Libya's Operation Unified Protector, http://www.nato.int/cps/en/natiolive/topics_71652.htm, 2011.7.15 and also see, NATO and Libya, Operational Media Update, 31 March 00.01-23.59, April1, JFC Naples, SHAPE, NATO HQ.
41 NATO and Libya, Operational Media Update, July 12-13 . JFC Naples, SHAPE, NATO HQ.
42 Reference News, September 9, 2011/2.

These adjustments are to a great extent related with interventions, as we will present below:

It shifted from restraining the Soviet Union by nuclear deterrence to preventing and handling regional crises and conflicts by relying on conventional forces; extended its activities beyond the territories of its member states; began to place greater emphasis on defending the common "interests" and "common values" of the member states.

Principle of consensus is applied at every committee level, which implies that all NATO decisions are collective decisions made by its member countries, but .when a member or group of members do not agree with the majority, they may "enter a voluntary alliance" and launch a joint operation, in this case members belonging to the majority will not obstruct the former group.[43]

The above adjustments as well as U.K's policy of following the footsteps of the U.S. in the NATO and thirdly France's return back to the NATO command structure in 2009, all these brought these three countries together, and provided a framework of conditions for the Libya intervention and the leadership of the US.[44]

Secondly, looking from the military level, due to three factors, France and U.K. needed to rely on the U.S. and the NATO.

Joint command-and-control factor: implementation of air strikes needed joint operations by the air forces of various countries which is one of NATO's major concepts. In order to avoid missing the targets during the air strikes, overlapping operations, or avoiding collisons occuring among the fighter planes belonging to alliance, an integrated command and control system needed to be determined to realize effective coordination among the participating countries, i.e their air forces.

Since France and U.K. had no experience in this regard, at all. Hence, at the initial stage of the "coalition of the willing", the U.S. government has promised that it would undertake the command-and-control task. (the "USS Mount Whitney" warship, which was deployed in the Mediterranean served

---

43 See, the book edited by Zhao Junjie, Gao Hua, "NATO's Strategic Adjustment and the EU's Common Defense and Its Impact on China's Security Environment," The first two chapters, Beijing, China Social Science Press, 2011.
44 The Economist, March 26, 2011, p.48; The Economist, March 5, 2011, p.54; "Pentagon welcomes Sarkozy's plan to bring France back to NATO's military structure," http://news.xinhuanet.com/english/2009-03/12/content_10996734.htm, 2011,9,21; see also, Hans Nichols, "Obama Welcomes France Back to NATO Command After 43-Year Hiatus," March 21, 2009, hnichols2@bloomberg.net.

as the command-and-control ship, which was equipped with a special operation system.[45]

After, the command was transferred to NATO, command-and-control was assumed by a special command organization of the NATO, (Combined Air Operations Centres (CAOC). but still the U.S. played an important role. According to a news by the Economist: " the outgoing American defence secretary, that most cruelly exposed Europe's shortcomings. At the outset Europeans relied on the Americans to lead the operation in Libya. Now under NATO control, they still depend on America to identify targets and provide air-to-air refuelling. American experts were rushed in to boost NATO's command centre in Naples."[46]

(2) The U.S. needed to directly participate in the military operations, because in many high-end technology and equipment, its role is still irreplaceable.

The U.S. ambassador to NATO highlighted that the U.S. "provided vital asset support and ensured success of air attacks", including 3/4 of tankers and surveillance aircrafts; high-precision target information provided by UAV; and key roles played by U.S. fighters and cruise missiles in destruction of the Libyan air defense system. The number of U.S. fighters' attacks was higher than those of other countries.[47]

The Pentagon stated on August 22 that since the action was launched by the NATO, the U.S. had carried out 5,316 flight tasks to Libya in total, which occupied about 27% of total actions of the NATO.[48]

(3) Maintenance of attack capacity and strength: after the in the post-Cold War era, the, European countries generally reduced the defense expenditures or maintained the expenditures at a low level. As a consequence, the proportion of total sum of various countries' expenditures in the total expenditures of the NATO reduced from 34% in 1991 to 21% currently.

Suffering from pressure from the financial crisis, the expenditures are still on the decline. At present, only U.K, France and Greece can meet NATO's requirements (The amount should not be lower than 2% of the country's GDP at least. However, the amounts of some countries are even

---

45 Peter Spiegel and Daniel Dombey, "Allies at odds over command," Financial Times, March 22, 2011, p.3.
46 Robert Gates's parting shot exposes Europe's military failings,"The Economist, June 18, 2011, p.50.
47 AFP, Brussels September 8th, and also see, "Reference News" September 9, 2011/2.
48 AFP, Brussels, August 22, and also see, "Reference News" August 24, 2011/2.

lower than 1%. This data is in a sharp contrast with the 5% defense budget allocated by the U.S.).[49]

Military expenditure cuts lead to lack of military power and failure to sustain the strength of actions for a longer time.[50]

Hence, in the 11th week of the air raids, the U.S. Defense Minister complained that "many allies are now short of firearms and again require the U.S. to make up for the deficiencies." ... "The underlying reason for these failings is no secret. Most Europeans spend too little on defence, and what they do is often wasted."[51]

For this, some critiques in Europe have pointed out that "Libya intervention has showed that NATO's "military power depends largely on how much the United States is going to put in, without the US support American people, "even the strongest" U.K. and France "can only conduct limited military operations ", and this "fact is disturbing."

All in all, France and U.K. were prime movers and participants, but the U.S. and the NATO led by the US still played a vital and irreplaceable role in supporting the whole action.

In view of that, European countries still require vigorous support from the U.S. due to their own insufficient military forces and insufficient defense industries. Consequently, the U.S. Defense Minister has showed strong dissatisfaction, and even showed deep concern about the NATO's future prospects.[52]

---

49 A.F. Rasmussen, "The Atlantic Alliance in Austere Times," (by NATO Secretary General Anders Fogh Rasmussen, Reprinted by permission of FOREIGN AFFAIRS, July/August 2011). Copyright (2011) by the Council on Foreign Relations,Inc.www.ForeignAffairs.com,http://www.nato.int/cps/en/SID-0F54B199-D4926692/natolive/opinions_75836.htm; "Robert Gates's parting shot exposes Europe's military failings," The Economist, June 18, 2011, p. 50.
50 See, co-edited by, Gerrit Wiesmann, James Blitz and Peggy Holllinger, "UK and France isolated inaction," Financial Times, April 15, 2011, p. 4.
51 See, Robert Gates's parting shot exposes Europe's military failings," The Economist, June 18,2011, p. 50.
52 Ibid.

IV. Political objectives and transcendence of the UN Security Council authorization limits

When proposing and pushing the establishment of a "no-fly zone", France and U.K. highlighted the necessity and urgency of humanitarian interventions. In fact, Resolution 1973 of UN Security Council affirmed the proposition and authorized that "all the necessary manners" could be used "in order to protect Libyan civilians and civilian areas from threats".

Hence, the European countries and the U.S. emphasized the "legitimacy" of use of force and launching military actions, stated that "the UN resolution allows all kind of military actions" thus built the "no-fly zone" for this reasoning. But, in the true sense, all actions taken in the framework this interventions should aim to protect civilians (rather than exceeding the limit). the NATO Secretary General also stated that: NATO-led forces are taking robust action to protect civilians and civilian-populated areas under threat of attack in Libya and enforcing the No-Fly Zone and arms embargo authorized by UNSCR 1973. We pay tribute to the skill, bravery and professionalism of our men and women in uniform carrying out this difficult task. We will continue to adapt our military actions to achieve maximum effect in discharging our mandate to protect civilians and civilian-populated areas. To this end, we are committed to provide all necessary resources and maximum operational flexibility within our mandate. A high operational tempo against legitimate targets will be maintained and we will exert this pressure as long as necessary and until the following objectives are achieved:

All attacks and threats of attack against civilians and civilian-populated areas have ended; the regime has verifiably withdrawn to bases all military forces, including snipers, mercenaries and other para-military forces, including from all populated areas they have forcibly entered, occupied or besieged throughout all of Libya, including Ajdabiyah, Brega, Jadu, al Jebal al Gharbiyah, Kikla, Misrata, Nalut, Raslanuf, Yefrin, Zawiyah, Zintan and Zuara; the regime must permit immediate, full, safe and unhindered humanitarian access to all the people in Libya in need of assistance.

We remain committed to the full implementation of UNSC Resolutions 1970 and 1973. In carrying out our mission, we reaffirm our support to the sovereignty, independence, territorial integrity and national unity of Libya.[53]

---

53 Statement on Libya "following the working lunch of NATO Ministers of Foreign Affairs with non-Nato contributors to Operation Unified Protector," April 14, 2011, http://www.nato.int/cps/en/natolive/official_texts_72544.htm?selectedLocale=en, 2011,7, 15.

However, due to definite political orientation, it became inevitable that the interventions exceeded the limits set by the UN authorization. As we have stated above, countries such as France and U.K. launched interventions for a short-term objective of urging Gaddafi to give up his rule as soon as possible. And their middle and long-term objectives of promoting the "democratization process" in Libya (even the whole Arab world).

The Libyan opposition faction was deemed as the political force to realize such objectives. Before intervention was launched, the situation in Libya was characterized by that the opposition faction organization with clear political objectives had been built (with "National Transitional Council" as the core, it firmly required Gaddafi to quit the scene and made a public promise that it would promote Libya's democratization process in the future.

Accordingly, it was reported that at the London International Conference on Libya, which was attended by circa 40 foreign ministers who supported the Libyan transformation (March 29), the National Transitional Council had actively sought to establish relations with the United States and its allies and announced its commitment to build a "civil society in Libya" also promised "to recognize ideological and political pluralism, to allow peaceful transfer of power through legitimate ways and institutions and ballot boxes."[54]

And the opposition took arms and fought violently against the Gaddafi regime in many regions. However, as for comparisons of military forces and strategic situations, the opposition faction obviously lagged behind and had almost been overwhelmed completely.

Hence, Europe and the U.S. further aimed to hit the governmental army by military actions to the hilt, support armed force of the opposition faction, improve its military force, change its strategic situation from defense to attack and finally force Gaddafi to give up the power by military force and let the opposition faction perform political promises. Fundamentally, their manners and implementation strength would surely exceed the authorization scope of Resolution 1973. In other words, the intervention was no longer limited to civilian protection and humanitarian aid implementation, but showed an obvious political tendency. Furthermore, to a great extent, this decided the final orientation of the Libyan Civil War.

The intervention actions of Europe and the U.S. exceeded the authorization at least in the following three aspects:

---

54 James Blitz, "Libya rebels expand relations," Financial Times, March 30, 2011, p. 2.

Firstly, the limits of the implementation of the "no-fly zone" resolution:

The so-called "no-fly zone" resolution of UN Security Council meant that any plane without special permission could not enter or fly over a specific territory, which could be explained that only fighters of the Libyan governmental army in the air were attacked, while ground objects were not involved (hence, at the EU council of foreign ministers, German Foreign Minister once questioned about whether ground attacks exceeded the authorization of UN Security Council and caused heated debates.[55]

Turkey has also opposed to NATO's implementation of such attacks.[56]

In addition, the NATO Military Commission also stated at the very beginning that the North Atlantic Council had never authorized it to plan tasks of attacking the ground targets or ground operation tasks.[57]

However, in view of that, Benghazi was nearly faced with complete siege of Gaddafi troops while it would collapse if no measure could be taken at once, and these countries vigorously promoted to approve Resolution 1973 and also launched air strikes within 48 hours. Of equal importance, French air forces directly took the lead in attacking governmental army's tanks and artillery forces army which marched into Benghazi.

U.K. and the U.S. took charge of attacking air defense facilities in Tripoli and other regions near. In this way they avoided the collapse of the opposition faction camp. US backed joint military actions obtained "major progresses" within a week, including preventing "advance of the governmental army", destroying Libya's air defense system and effectively build the no-fly zone.[58]

Since then, with the progress of the war, and as required by the war, they also employed attack helicopters and air-ground fighter bombers and so forth to carry out precise attacks to Gaddafi's tank and gun troops. In a nutshell, despite the Resolution 1973 which prohibited entry of foreign ground troops, direct air attacks to ground targets also, very effectively restrained the offense of the Libyan governmental army.

---

55 "Nato Near to deal on control of military campaign," co-edited by Peter Spiegel and Peggy Holllinger, Financial Times, March 24, 2011, p. 3.
56 The Economist, March 26, 2011, p. 24.
57 "Nato Near to deal on control of military campaign," co-edited by Peter Spiegel and Peggy Holllinger, Financial Times, March 24, 2011, p. 3.
58 James Blitz, "And now for the hard part: three reasons to fear a stalemate," Financial Times, March 27, 2011, p. 8.

Secondly, various means were employed to support the military operations of the opposition faction.

According to the true spirit of the UN Security Council resolution, interventions should not support any warring party of the Libyan civil war, or could not provide both parties with weapons or get involved in ground wars. In respect to equipment, training and organization conditions, the armed opposition faction obviously lagged behind the governmental army and stayed at a disadvantageous strategic position Before the air raids, the armed opposition faction once occupied several cities, but most of them were finally won back by the government army, and the last army barricade of Benghazi was almost re-captured back.[59]

Hence, intervention actions would surely support opposition factions' opposition against the governmental army to the hilt and make the battlefield situation (mainly concentrated on 2 battlefronts – the Mediterranean coast and Western mount region) gradually beneficial to the former. Besides the implementation of arms embargo, economic sanctions and financial support to the opposition faction, intervener countries also took measures in the following aspects.

They provided the opposition faction with a lot of weapons and equipment.

In view of the shabby equipment of the opposition faction (its leader pointed out that the quantity and quality of weapons should be strengthened in order to win the war and reduce casualties), in early June, 2011, Western countries once provided the opposition faction with military materials such as cannons, rocket propulsion grenades and ammunitions when the Western Nafusah mount area was encircled by the government army. In the end of the same month, France once again delivered a lot of weapons by planes to the southern mount area in Tripoli.[60]

They closely monitored and coordinated the combat operations and tactics of the opposition faction.

For instance, within one week before the air attacks launched by Europe and the U.S. bombers... Ajdabiya, an important eastern town with abundant petroleum, was captured by the opposition faction, which was considered as "first major success obtained by the revolutionary army" since issuance of the "no-fly" zone status. The opposition faction clearly said that "without

---
59 James Blitz, "And now for the hard part:three reasons to fear a stalemate," Financial Times, March 27,2011, p. 8.
60 Singapore newspaper, Lianhe Zaobao, July 1, 2011.

fighters of the coalition forces, we could never complete it. Gaddafi's weapons are much more advanced than ours", and also said that "with the assistance of the allied forces, the revolutionary army will go on marching into the capital Tripoli"[61].

In another prominent war, the opposition faction held fast to the key strategic town Misrata, which had an overall significant effect. Without long-term support provided by air attacks, the opposition faction could never repel fierce attacks from the governmental army.

They sent military consultants and various experts whose main tasks were to train and guide the operations of the opposition faction, provide them operational intelligence, help it to develop operational plans and various advice.[62]

(4) They carried out propaganda wars, psychological wars and information warfare through broadcasting, leaflets, internet and network. Purportedly, all these actions played an important role in propagating the West's military superiority, collapsing Gaddafi army's will to fight, disturbing its communication and command systems, and destroying its logistical support system and information collection. Russia's "Independent Military Review" wrote:"information operations and psychological warfare are an integral part of military operations in the world's major powers, and they have made important contributions to achieving the ultimate military goal. These operations similar to investigative espionage actions are one of the form of military operations, carried smoothly and covertly.

Successful information warfare and psychological warfare do not only enable the winning of the world public opinion to the back to attackers' side, but also can ensure that the battlefield to complete the specific battle and tactical tasks. NATO countries on Libya's military action 'joint protector' is no exception. ... In view of the recent experiences of US and NATO military operations, it can be concluded that (in Libya) the fourth US psychological war brigade, as well as the US military 193 special forces EC-130J psychological warfare aircraft the Fifteenth Brigade of Psychological Warfare of the UK, Italy's and other NATO countries" information and psychological warfare forces, have participated in this special warfare."[63]

---

61 Singapore newspaper, Lianhe Zaobao, March 27, 2011.
62 "Foreign troops helping for the downfall of the Libyan government", "Writer Digest" September 9, 2011/11.
63 "Reference News," September 3, 2011/5

In short, by the above means and methods, the opposition faction managed to reverse its declining tendency and made the stalemate situation possible and thus also created conditions so as to conduct final strategic counteroffensive.

Thirdly, they were closely involved in planning, organizing and directly dispatched troops to coordinate the Tripoli War.

As the capital and the center of Libyan politics, military affairs and economy, Tripoli was occupied by the opposition faction in late August. This fight has become a decisive battle in the Civil War, and symbolized the collapse of the Gaddafi regime and the victory by the opposition who won basic control of the whole country. It is worthy of mentioning that in this war the NATO "played an important role in controlling Tripoli" (said by an official belonging to opposition faction).

As early as May 2011, the NATO had begun planning and preparing for such action, centered on organization of various fight groups and dispatched them secretly to the capital. Once the order was issued, various groups were assigned with clear objectives, rapidly occupied important places and blocked relevant roads, which managed to take the governmental army off guard and timely mastered the strategic initiative. Meanwhile, despite the clear prohibition by the resolution of UN Security Council, countries such as U.K. still dispatched special airborne forces into Tripoli, assisted in and coordinated the military actions of the opposition faction on site and ensured its success.

NATO press speakers have publicly confirmed that some NATO member states might have sent their own ground troops or special forces to Libya. The so-called Tripoli victory of the opposition troops, cannot be understood without considering the role played by these special forces belonging to some NATO member states.[64]

According to a report by a Russian "business newspaper" on August 26, the Russian Foreign Ministry said that Moscow has identified that NATO used ground forces in Libya, including participation in the Tripoli battle. The newspaper said: the UN SC Resolution and its provisions to protect civilians were obviously and brutally trampled upon. The Resolution was used as the pretext of interfering the local civil war and intervention stood on the side of the rebels.

---

64   "Writer Digest," September 9, 2011/11.

Russia's NATO Ambassador D. Rogozin has argued that the findings about Western troops revealed by the "will hit NATO's reputation, and may even split NATO." He added: "in fact, it was an open-ended undeclared war, and besides France and UK ignored the spirit of the United Nation resolution, and decided to wage their own warfare at all costs, and not all NATO members have agreed to exceed the stipulations of the Resolution."[65]

All in all, in the Libyan crisis, France and the UK and other EU countries, displayed an initiative by not acting as a simple follower of the United States, launched an active military intervention, for the first time in the post-Cold War, although suffering financial crisis, and forced to reduce military spending to reduce the burden of this crisis. They have achieved the expected goals, by the help of various factors mentioned below:

The utilization of the geopolitical factors and considerations, the military autonomy of the EU in the post-Cold War era, relatively superior military capabilities of the France and UK and some other EU countries, defense arrangements between the Europe and the US, policy and strategic adjustments made by the US and NATO in the last decade, all of which have played an important role.

At the same time, this intervention has revealed a series of issues, such as the complexity and difficulty of developing security integration among the EU countries, problems in bilateral cooperation between member countries to develop a defense model for the EU, the issue of coordination of security strategy interests between the EU and the USA, adjustment of relations between the EU defense and the NATO alliance, all of which will affect the future development direction of the EU's security and defense integration, and which at the same time worthy of study and close attention in the future.

---

65 Quoted from, "Reference News," August 27, 2011/3.

International Interventions and International Governance in the Balkan Region: Bosnia and Herzegovina Case

Kong Tianping[1]

The Bosnian War has been the most horrifying war that took place in Europe since the end of the Second World War. Apart from mutual massacres of Serbians and Croatians inside Bosnia and Herzegovina as well as Muslim people in Bosnia and Herzegovina, the Bosnian War also included the involvement of Serbia, Croatia and Islamic countries to different extents. Under military interventions of the NATO, the Bosnian War was put into an end, while parties involved in the conflict signed the General Framework Agreement for Peace in Bosnia and Herzegovina (shortly the Dayton Agreement) which brought peace to Bosnia and Herzegovina again. After the war, Bosnia and Herzegovina was faced with numerous problems of governance. Due to weak governance power, disputes among ethnic groups and the complicated political structure formed after the implementation of the Dayton Agreement, effective governance cannot be realized in Bosnia and Herzegovina. As a result, the country had to rely on international governance. The paper will analyze international governance regarding Bosnia and Herzegovina, highlight discussions about the influences of High Representatives in international governance of Bosnia and Herzegovina and discuss on the preliminary experiences of international governance there.

---

1 Research Fellow, expert of Central and Eastern Europe issues, and Director of the Institute of European Studies attached to CASS.

I. The background of international interventions and governance in Bosnia and Herzegovina

Since the outbreak in 1992, the Bosnian War had lasted for over 3 years, causing 260,000 deaths and making 1.8 million people become destitute and homeless, and leading to economic losses of 45 billion dollars. On November 21th, 1995, under the mediation of the U.S., Milosevic, President of the Federal Republic of Yugoslavia (standing for Bosnian Serbs), Tudjman, President of the Republic of Croatia (standing for Bosnian Croats) and Izetbegovic, former President of the Republic of Bosnia and Herzegovina (standing for Bosnians) singed the Dayton Agreement in the U.S. Dayton Military Base, which formally put an end to the War of Bosnia and Herzegovina. The Dayton Agreement provided the legal basis for international governance in Bosnia and Herzegovina.

After signing the Dayton Agreement, Bosnia and Herzegovina in fact became a protectorate state in the international community. In accordance with the Dayton Agreement, the UN Security Council will dispatch High Representatives and specially-assigned police forces to Bosnia and Herzegovina, other international organizations will also be involved in the peace process of Bosnia and Herzegovina. As stipulated in the Dayton Agreement, principals of some important organizations are appointed by international organizations. For example, the temporary electoral committee consists of staff from the Organization for Security and Cooperation in Europe. European Court of Human Rights will dispatch staff to join the constitutional court and will assign the high court directors. President of the central bank is assigned by the International Monetary Fund. Committee of Ministers of Council of Europe will dispatch staff to join the commission on human rights and will assigns the chairman. European Court of Human Rights dispatches staff to join the Refugee Council and assigns the chairman; European Bank for Reconstruction assigns the chairman of Public Enterprises Leading Committee; the United Nations Educational, Scientific and Cultural Organization dispatches staff to join Committee for National Cultural Relics Protection and assigns the chairman. The NATO is dispatching stabilization forces (SFOR) to Bosnia and Herzegovina in order to further secure the implementation of the Dayton Agreement.

Most importantly, the Dayton Agreement has put an end to the war, and set up a preliminary framework for post-war governance in Bosnia and Herzegovina. After signing the Dayton Agreement, a complicated political structure was formed in Bosnia and Herzegovina: a state with two entities. Nominally, the (joint) state kept the power right, but actually power is shared between the two entities. The Federal government of Bosnia and Herzegovina stood for the alliance of Croat Nation and Bosnian Nation in Bosnia and Herzegovina. The Bosnian Serb Republic stood for the interests of Serbs. Both entities kept their own armed forces. The Dayton Agreement failed to deeply think about how to build Bosnia and Herzegovina into an effective state after the end of the conflict.

"The experiment that was hastily designed by the political engineering was based on an assumption: the more complicated will be the elected governing organs and the more layers there will be, the greater chance will be generated for the original rival groups to find it necessity to develop mutual cooperation."[2]

But based on the facts we have observed recently, it is obvious that a multi-layer decision-making structure cannot be conductive to encourage cooperation between irreconcilable rival parties. Instead, the multi-layer decision-making structure has made the governance more difficult.

II. High Representatives and international governance in Bosnia and Herzegovina

High Representatives organ forms the core part of the international governance in Bosnia and Herzegovina. Appendix 10 of theDayton Agreement, namely the Civil Execution Agreement, stipulates the authorization of High Representatives and its tasks.[3]

Major tasks of a High Representative include: supervising implementation of the peace agreement; keeping close contacts with agreement parties, promoting complete implementation of civil affairs of the peace agreement, maintaining senior-level cooperation between contracting parties and other relevant organizations and institutions in the implementation of civil affairs; seek to harmonize the activities of civil organizations and institutions in Bosnia and Herzegovina in order to effectively solve issues of civil affairs in the peace agreement.

High Representatives will respect the autonomous rights of civil organizations and institutions in their own activities and provide general guidance when necessary in view of influences brought about by their activities, especially those related to the implementation of the Dayton peace agreement. In addition, civil organizations are requested to provide relevant

---

2 Tom Gallagher, The Balkans in the New Millennium: In the Shadow of War and Peace, London: Routledge, 2005, p. 132.
3 See, http://www.ohr.int/dpa/default.asp?content_id=366.

information in respect to their activities to High Representatives and help High Representatives to perform its tasks. When deemed necessary, High Representatives will act to promote solution of difficult problems in the execution of civil issues. High Representatives will join the meetings about recovery and reconstruction held by those organizations in the donation donor countries. High Representatives will also periodically report on the accomplishment of the Dayton peace agreement to the UN, EU, U.S. and Russia, and some other. It will guide the work of specially assigned staff in the international specially-sent police troops.

From December 8 to December 9, 1995, the Peace Execution Meeting was held in London in order to increase the international support towards the implementation of the Dayton Agreement.

This meeting in London set up the Peace Execution Committee which constitutes 55 countries or organizations whic declared their support for the peace process in Bosnia and Herzegovina.

The meeting held in London also set up the Steering Committee of the Peace Execution Committee, which is an executive organization under the administration of the Peace Execution Committee. Wherein a High Representative is assigned as the chairman, and the organization is composed of Canada, France, Germany, Italy, Japan, Russia, Britain, the U.S., the EU and the Organization of the Islamic Conference (represented by Turkey).

The Steering Committee provides political guidance to High Representatives. In capital Sarajevo, every week, High Representatives hold a conference joined by ambassadors of member states of the Steering Committee. In late 1997, the powers of High Representatives was expanded, and the Peace Execution Committee which supervised High Representatives allowed High Representatives to make use of their maximum powers, when leading the civil affairs in stipulated in the Dayton Agreement.

In December 1997, the Bonn Meeting of Peace Execution Committee granted High Representatives with extensive powers of intervention, they were also allowed to remove the titles of officers or demote them including those elected ones. Based on the Bonn Principles agreed by the Peace Execution Committee, High Representatives are allowed to mandatorily practice law and remove titles of recalcitrant officers.

At the initial stage after signing the Dayton Agreement, the international community had estimated the situation in Bosnia and Herzegovina too optimistically, thinking that the situation would soon go better and even predicted that the stabilization forces of 60,000 troops led by the NATO would leave Bosnia and Herzegovina in 1996. As stipulated and hoped by the Dayton Agreement, people's free flow flourished, refugees returned to their hometowns and a balance of power was struck among the nationalities living in Bosnia and Herzegovina.

However, after the end of the conflict, the nationalist political forces still exerted very strong influences. In fact, national entities became shelter for nationalist forces, since nationalist political forces seemed unwilling to see normalization in Bosnia and Herzegovina. Due to the unique political arrangements in the Dayton Agreement, the national statehood attributes of Bosnia and Herzegovina have been very weak.

After signing of the Dayton Agreement, political arrangements did not prohibit politicians and political activists who were involved in the war, from working in custom offices, banks, telecom and tax offices, instead, they continued funding their political parties and continued their secret activities. Thus the governance in Bosnia and Herzegovina was faced with a difficult dilemma.

Carl Bildt, the first High Representative of the international Community in Bosnia and Herzegovina and Premier of Sweden, was assigned as the EU Special Representative in Yugoslavia in June 1995 and as the joint chairman of Dayton Peace Negotiation, and acted as the High Representative from December 1995 to June 1997. After signing the Dayton Agreement, Bosnia and Herzegovina mainly ensured the execution of the peace agreement. However, in terms of building a safe environment in Bosnia and Herzegovina, it was far from satisfactory. Within three months after the peace agreement was signed and became effective, the international community failed to ensure peaceful transfer of territory and population, while about 100,000 refugees that appeared suddenly made the political progress and refugees' returning more complicated. Further, the international Community failed also failed to guarantee that the capital Sarajevo would develop into a real multi-ethnic city.[4]

When assuming office, Carl Bildt was informed that all the work would be completed within a year. Obviously, the international community underestimated the complexity of problems in Bosnia and Herzegovina. In fact, High Representatives who assumed office after Bildt did not work more easily, either. During Bildt's tenure, power of a High Representative was not yet expanded, which limited his influences in politics of Bosnia and Herzegovina.

---

4 Carl Bildt, Peace after War, "Our Experience, The Tanner Lectures on Human Values," delivered at Cambridge University, March 2, 2005.

The second (1997-1999) High Representative was Carlos Westendorp from Spain. During his tenure, the title of High Representative was changed into a protectorate. After succeeding the position, Westendorp forced the nationalistic leaders in Bosnia and Herzegovina to give up the nationalism mark on the driving licenses and issued the uniform Bosnia and Herzegovina convertible Mark. He controlled TV stations of Bosnian Serb Republic and Federal of Bosnia and Herzegovina, and helped them get rid of parties' control. He forced the Federal of Bosnia and Herzegovina to approve the Real Estate Law, which laid a legal foundation for refugees to return to their hometown.

Wolfgang Petritsch from Austria was assigned as the third (1999-2002) High Representative. Continuing policies of his predecessor, he attempted to strengthen the central power in order to make up for administrative vacuum left by the Dayton Agreement. By using his power, he removed the positions of officers who were opposed to the establishment of effectively operated national organizations. In May 2000, the Peace Execution Committee determined a new agenda, and decided to strengthen national organizations which could make the joint country sustainable. The agenda contains national treasure, court system, special civil servant system, border policeman and other organizations which regulated the economic processes and standards. In July 2000, the Constitutional Court made a judgment that the constitution and other structures of an entity determined by the Dayton Agreement were unconstitutional as the entity constitution and other structures failed to stipulate all the entities which had equal national rights. The Constitutional Court commanded the Federal Republic of Bosnia and Herzegovina and the Bosnian Serb Republic to change the constitution. The Bosnian Serb Republic resisted to the command tenaciously. The Peace Execution Committee declared in 2000 that insular nationalistic and sectarian political interest groups had hindered the return of refugees, economic reform and operation of national organizations. The Peace Execution Committee required the High Representative to employ the power to carry out civil agreements faster and eliminate obstacles for the economic reform. During Petritsch's tenure, the international governance mechanism in Bosnia and Herzegovina did not change fundamentally, but the High Representative began paying attention to the constitutional reform. In early 2002, Petritsch tried his best to promote constitutional reform in Bosnia and Herzegovina. He highlighted that the Dayton Agreement should develop according to new challenges faced by Bosnia and Herzegovina. He argued that it was insufficient to merely execute the peace agreement; the peace agreement should be developed and the constitutional reform should be carried out to guarantee the equal status of three nations in Bosnia and Herzegovina. Under pressure from the High Representative, representatives of two entities in Bosnia and Herzegovina signed the Mrakovica-Sarajevo Agreement in late March 2002, indicating that leaders of the two entities in Bosnia and Herzegovina tried hard to make Bosnia and Herzegovina become a multi-ethnic country enjoying true democracy.

The two entities did not approve the constitutional amendment, so Petritsch, High Representative of the international community mandatorily carried out the constitutional reform in Bosnia and Herzegovina with two entities in April so as to ensure equal status of Muslims, Bosnian Croats and Bosnian Serbs. In order to ensure smooth implementation of the general election in October of the same year, Petritsch mandatorily modified election laws of the state and the two entities, and insisted that persons resigned by the High Representative could not campaign in general elections or local elections, or hold public posts. During the tenure of Petritsch as the High Representative, less than 264 laws which aimed to protect minority and strengthen democracy were approved, but a lot of laws were still forced out by the entities. Petritsch also made direct interventions in governance of Brcko. Brcko District is a long and narrow continent bridge which connects the East and West of the Bosnian Serb Republic. As stipulated in the Dayton Agreement, the Brcko District will be governed by international organizations. In 1999, Brcko arbitration made it into a neutral non-military area; the Brcko government was elected and accepted international supervision. Through the comprehensive judicial and legal reform, Brcko has formed an effective court structure and an independent judicial system. In March 2001, Ante Jelavic, a Croat member of the Presidency of Bosnia and Herzegovina, was resigned because he tried to build a third entity in Herzegovina. In May 2002, Petritsch was entitled to appoint judge and procurator from elected politicians; granted the power of appointment to a committee which was constituted of local and international experts in order to ensure independence of the judicature. When leaving his post, he pointed out that Bosnia had become a true state despite its weak power.

In May 2002, Paddy Ashdown from Britain replaced Petritsch and was assigned as the fourth High Representative of the international community in Bosnia and Herzegovina. Ashdown assumed office just after the 9/11 attacks, therefore the U.S. mainly focused its efforts on global counter-terrorism and paid less attention to Balkans. The Republican Party administration led by Bush doubted the intervention in Balkans. Rumsfeld, the National Defense Minister at that time, expressed the same idea.

In the face of severe challenges, Ashdown tried to strengthen central government organizations in order to prepare for the withdrawal of the international community from Bosnia and Herzegovina. With explicit understandings of governance problems in Bosnia and Herzegovina, Ashdown emphasized that he wanted "to build a state of Bosnia and Herzegovina which would be a free-standing state moving towards Europe, so that people of Bosnia and Herzegovina would enjoy full governance rights of their country."[5]

In August 2002, Ashdown, the High Representative of the international community, took measures to strengthen the judicial system in Bosnia and Herzegovina. These measures included constructing a special committee constituted by international and local officers which would nominate and supervise judges and public prosecutors. The measure aimed to eliminate corruption, low efficiency and ethnic discrimation and prejudice in the judicial system of Bosnia and Herzegovina.

In December of the same year, Ashdown, the High Representative of the international community using his authority issued a new law which aimed to simplify the central government organizations of Bosnia and Herzegovina and expanded their powers. According to the new law, Bosnia and Herzegovina would build two new departments, the Ministry of State Security and the Ministry of Justice, in which the premier tenure would be four years rather than eight months taken in turn by the three national representatives.

Ashdown has also emphasized the participation of Bosnia and Herzegovina people in the governance. He planned to gradually transfer certain powers to the elected organs, but the pace of power transfer would depend on the pace of reform progress which aimed to develop Bosnia and Herzegovina into an effectively working state.

On 16 July 2003, Marcus Cox (ESI Senior Editor) and Gerald Knaus (ESI President) sent an open letter to Lord Paddy Ashdown, the High Representative in Bosnia and Herzegovina. Published by IWPR, the letter put forward a concrete proposal.

It argued that the OHRs powers to dismiss public officials should be dispensed with; that the powers to impose legislation should be defined and limited to a publicly declared agenda; and that at the latest by the summer of 2004 there should be no further need for the Bonn powers at all.

---

5 "Interview with Paddy Ashdown, the High Representative for BiH," BIH Radio 1,Mirsad Bajtarevic, Wednesday, July 16,2003.

In the face of obstacles to the peace process, Ashdown undertook "Bonn Powers", dismissed the recalcitrant officers, with his authority practiced the laws and issued administrative decrees.

Till July 2003, 11 decisions or decrees were issued each month, compared to four decisions in 1999.

In 2004, the High Representative Ashdown put forward four reform agendas, including strengthening the rule of law, economic reforms, strengthening construction of governmental organs, state courts as well as reforms regarding national defense (Joint General Staff) and the intelligence agency of the state. In early 2004, Bosnia and Herzegovina passed a law to build a common intelligence agency and form a new defense structure and a Joint General Staff based on the people's control over civil officers. But without personnel resources or financial budgets, the new Ministry of Justice and the Ministry of State Security were still hollow and weak government organs.

With the stabilization of the situation in Bosnia and Herzegovina, the country demonstrated a will of joining the EU and NATO which was also coached by Western forces.

However, since the Bosnian Serbs—a stake holder Bosnia and Herzegovina—failed to realize smooth cooperation with the International Criminal Court in the Yugoslavia Trial Issue, which posed an obstacle against Bosnia and Herzegovina's participation process into the EU.

In late 2004, the number of peacekeeping force soldiers was decreased from over 60,000 to 7,000, the leadership of the peacekeeping forces which were deployed in Kosovo was transferred from the NATO to the EU. The EU led military (called as the EUFOR) replaced the stabilazation force which was led by NATO (SFOR).

The High Representative representing the international community in the BIH (Bosnia & Herzegovina) issue was thus enforced by EU's higher commitment, consequently the EU Special Representative for BiH assumed a key role in the process.[6]

---

6 The European Union Special Representative (EUSR) is mandated by the Council of the European Union to reinforce the EU's political support for its policy objectives in BiH (Bosnia & Herzegovina): 'BIH's progress in the Stabilisation and Association Process, with the aim of seeing a stable, viable, peaceful, multi-ethnic BiH, co-operating fully and peacefully with its neighbours in the region'. The EUSR offers advice and facilitation support in the political process to institutions at all levels, aimed at ensuring greater consistency and coherence of all political, economic and European priorities – particularly in the areas of the rule of law and security sector reform. The EUSR is responsible for the co-ordination of the

In 2005, the High Representative further strengthened its cooperation with local organizations in Bosnia and Herzegovina, which helped Bosnia and Herzegovina leaders to conduct suggestions in the EU integration feasibility study reports, helped Bosnia and Herzegovina to satisfy NATO's requirements of Partnership for Peace strategy and implement the its defense reform. In fact, the High Representative Office led by Ashdown has become the major actor to promote participation of Bosnia and Herzegovina into the EU and NATO.

On November 25, 2005, the EU and Bosnia and Herzegovina formally started negotiations about signing the Stabilisation and Association Agreement.

This was a turning point in the history of Bosnia and Herzegovina, which showed that Bosnia and Herzegovina had made a solid start in Europeanization. The negotiations for signing the Stabilisation and Association Agreement has been beneficial to stabilizing politics in Bosnia and Herzegovina and facilitated the evolvement of Bosnia and Herzegovina into a normalized European country.

In January 2006, Ashdown left his position. At that moment, the statehood attributes of Bosnia and Herzegovina were strengthened by the implementation value-added tax and establishment of a uniform indirect tax system, building uniform first-class state organizations for frontier defense, customs and intelligence agencies, establishment of a uniform judicial system, the formation of an effective Council of Ministers and stipulating that the position of premier no longer existed, this post was later replaced by Chairman of Council of Ministers.

Bosnia and Herzegovina also made progress in Europeanization by starting to negotiate with the EU for signing the Stabilisation and Association Agreement. The initial framework of a modern European country was formed in Bosnia and Herzegovina, but effective state operation has not yet been realized, besides lacked inter-ethnic harmony. Moreover, important state organizations such as joint police forces have not been yet formed.[7]

EU's public communication in Bosnia and Herzegovina, and for contributing to the further development of respect for human rights and for fundamental freedoms. The EUSR reports to the Council of the European Union, the inter-governmental body representing the 28 EU member states, through the High Representative for Common Foreign and Security Policy/Vice President of the Commission. The Delegation of the European Union to Bosnia and Herzegovina also has regional offices in Banja Luka, Mostar and Brcko.

7 Beth Kampschror, "2006: A decisive year for the Balkans," The Christian Science Monitor, February 1, 2006.

Soon after the 10th anniversary of signing of the Dayton Agreement, Christian Schwarz-Schilling from Germany was assigned as the High Representative (OHR) in January 2006. Besides, he was also assigned as the EU Special Representative for Bosnia and Herzegovina. Since then, international governance of Bosnia and Herzegovina has become a task assumed by the international community and the EU.

Schilling has argued that after experiencing bloody ethnic wars, all parties in Bosnia and Herzegovina ahould have the courage to hope a bright future and strive to normalize their country. He argued that the international protectorate is coming to a close. "Bosnia now will have 'the opportunity to be a fully independent sovereign state', with responsibility for its own political reform and economic development. Schilling urged the international community to 'stand back and allow the Bosnian authorities to take decisions', in order to allow a sustainable democratic culture to develop. He added: "after 10 years of living under an international protectorate, it would be a good thing if the people of Bosnia were to be free to determine their own political future and develop into a true state enjoying independent sovereignty."

Schilling hoped that Bosnia and Herzegovina could obtain true independence in 2007. After the signing of the Dayton Agreement, Bosnia and Herzegovina was in fact under an international protectorate , therefore this protectorate represented by Office of High Representatives, appointed international officers to govern it in some way, and it leads political process in Bosnia and Herzegovina.

The Dayton Agreement has put an end to the bloody war in Bosnia and Herzegovina which had lasted for 3.5 years, and laid the initial foundation for peace, stabilization and development in Bosnia and Herzegovina. However, at present, the agreement can no longer satisfy Bosnia and Herzegovina's demand for entering the EU and the NATO or the demand for realization of long-term peace and order. Weak central state power and overly strong powers enjoyed by the stakeholder nations have been important negative factors influencing the political development. Hence, the constitutional reform which would transcend the Dayton Agreement was put in the agenda of development.

Since 2005, supported by the U.S., EU, and representatives of the eight major political parties, constitutional, reform negotiations were started in Bosnia and Herzegovina, and reached some preliminary agreements regarding the issues such as "reducing the powers of two entities", "replacement of three-person presidium by a single presidency system" and "status and tasks of Council of Ministers".

On March 18, 2006, major political parties in Bosnia and Herzegovina reached an agreement on some governance issues, i.e. simplifying the political structure and strengthening the central government. On April 27, 2006, the above constitutional reform agreement was submitted to the parliament for approval and voting, but rejected by the parliament, fell two votes short of the required .

In the second half of 2006 and the first quarter of 2007, people in Bosnia and Herzegovina were busy with the general elections and the formation of the new Council. The election held on October 1 had completely proceeded in a peaceful and orderly manner. However, government (Council of Ministers) could not be established very smoothly. By the end of 2006, only the Bosnian Serb Republic could manage to form a new government. Finally, a state-level government formation started in February 2007 and formed in March. Worse still, 6 months after the election, 3 cantons states among a total of 10 cantons still had no new governments.

During and after the elections, the Bosnian Serb Republic called for a referendum of independence, while the central state called for cancelling stake-holder partnership (entities) system, which made people worry about the future of the joint state of Bosnia and Herzegovina.

Power of nationalist-oriented parties such as the Party of Democratic Action of Bosnia and Herzegovina, the Democratic Party of Serbia and the Croatian Democratic Union of Bosnia and Herzegovina had weakened during the 2006 general elections, but political influence of nationalist forces had not disappeared yet.

In June 2006, the Peace Execution Committee decided to start the power transition from Office of High Representative to the EU Special Representative, which paved the way for the dismissal of the High Representative in June 2007. But in February 2007, the Peace Execution Committee decided to keep the High Representative Office in view of adverse factors occurring in the region and domestic situations of Bosnia and Herzegovina and due to continuous disputes in respect to constitutional reforms, police forces reform and other issues among the three partner nations of Bosnia and Herzegovina. (Croats, Serbs and Bosnians.)

In July 2007, Slovakian Foreign Minister Miroslav Laják was assigned as the sixth High Representative of the international community in Bosnia and Herzegovina as well as the EU Special Representative in Bosnia and Herzegovina. Two months after his taking office, Laják highlighted that the problem facing Bosnia and Herzegovina was that the establishment of

Bosnia and Herzegovina state lacked a consensus about the national strategic targets and manners, and some of them even doubted the existence of the state and its organs and partner entities. The police forces reform was stagnant while the constitutional reform showed a lack of consensus. In October, Laják presented reform measures in order to strengthen the functions of central state organizations. One of the reform measures was to modify the provision about quorum of parliament voting with the purpose of preventing either of the 3 ethnic groups representative from blocking the new law enactments by quitting or boycotting the parliament.

The reform proposed by Laják aimed to accelerate the decision-making process of the joint parliament and the government in Bosnia and Herzegovina and promote necessary reforms. Laják asked the parliament of Bosnia and Herzegovina to approve relevant law bills before December 1, or he would use his authority to implement these measures. But people of Bosnian Serbs, believed that Laják's reform measures would damage their interests. The Bosnian Serb Premier Špirić showed his dissatisfaction by resignation on November 1.

Laják criticized that Špirić had done an irresponsible act. He said: "It is greatly ironic that a Council Premier has resigned due to measures that could make the government more efficient."

On October 31, the Peace Execution Committee meeting ended, the statement of the Peace Execution Committee highlighted that the High Representative Laják's will and decision should be respected, and any behavior that violated the High Representative's decision would be deemed as a violation of the Dayton Agreement. The statement said: "the International community will stick to necessary policies that can reverse those intentions of violating the Dayton Agreement."[8]

The Steering Committee of the Peace Execution Committee also highlighted that it would take proper measures to punish political leaders and organizations in Bosnia and Herzegovina, who or which contravene the policies of High Representative and the Steering Committee of Peace Execution Committee.

Laják continued his reform attempt to simplify the decision making process, yet opposed by Bosnian Serb politicians, who thought that their interests would be damaged and they predicted that they could expand their political influence by resisting the said reform. After 13 years of governance

---

8 Press Conference by the High Representative Miroslav Laják, following the PIC meeting, http://www.ohr.int/ohr-dept/presso/pressb/default.asp?content_id=40767.

of Bosnia and Herzegovina by the international community, the task to strengthen the state organs was still far from completion. Under the pressure from the international community, Bosnia and Herzegovina reached an agreement about the joint police force reform in 2008, meanwhile major political powers in Bosnia and Herzegovina finally reached an agreement for starting constitutional reforms at the end of the same year.

In June 2008, Bosnia and Herzegovina signed the Stabilisation and Association Agreement with the EU, which marked a major progress in the Europeanization of Bosnia and Herzegovina. The EU also took into account the changes in the international governance mechanism in Bosnia and Herzegovina, and hoped to end the mission of High Representative Office in mid 2009.

On October 31, 2008, Solana, EU's High Representative for diplomacy and security policies, and Ryan, specialist for the EU's expansion, suggested that the High Representative's governance in Bosnia and Herzegovina should be ended. Ryan has commented: "in the short-term and long-term levels, the EU needs to maximize its influence in Bosnia and Herzegovina."[9]

The two figures have argued that the EU needed to re-think about the effect of power transition from the governance led by a High Representative to that led by the EU. On March 13, 2009, the Steering Committee of the Execution Council for Peace Agreement of Bosnia and Herzegovina assigned Austrian diplomat Valentin Inzko as the seventh High Representative for Bosnia and Herzegovina, as suggested by the international community. Inzko was also assigned as the EU Special Representative in Bosnia and Herzegovina. In the days, when Inzko took office, the political atmosphere of Bosnia and Herzegovina tended to deteriorate.

In October 2010, a general election was held in Bosnia and Herzegovina, but the new government could not be built soon and the state organs could not operated normally due to serious political divergences. There were obvious surge of nationalism and separatism inside the Federation of Bosnia and Herzegovina and among the the Bosnian Serbs, and the Croatian party was dissatisfied with its status in the Federation, and proposed to build a third entity. And as a seperatist act the National Assembly of the Bosnian Serb Republic also decided to hold a referendum in order to determine whether or not the Court of Bosnia and Herzegovina, the Prosecutor Office and the High Representative Office of Bosnia and Herzegovina would be were authoritative. Under the pressure of the international community, the

---

9   EU Proposes Taking Over Bosnia Role In 2009, http://www.javno.com/en/world/clanak.php?id=200904.

Bosnian Serb Republic cancelled the referendum plan, and Valentin Inzko frankly admitted that Bosnia and Herzegovina was faced with the most serious challenge in the 15 years after the signing of the Dayton Agreement.

The EU's attention to Bosnia and Herzegovina has increased steadily. On May 30, 2011, Ashton, EU's High Representative for diplomacy and security affairs, nominated Peter Sorensen as the Head of EU Delegation to Bosnia and Herzegovina and the EU Special Representative in Bosnia and Herzegovina. By August 31, 2011, Valentin Inzko's post, was replaced Peter Sorensen. Having 15 years of working experience in Western Balkans, Sorensen had once worked in EU departments in Kosovo, Serbia and Macedonia. Due to his rich working experience in Western Balkans, the EU could deeply intervene in the governance of Bosnia and Herzegovina. It was predicted that he would conduct close cooperation with Valentin Inzko as the—international community's High Representative—in order to promote stabilization, development and prosperity in Bosnia and Herzegovina, boost its European integration process and prepare for the future withdrawal of the High Representative from Bosnia and Herzegovina, that would mean independence.

All in all, after 16 years of international governance in Bosnia and Herzegovina, the task for strengthening of state organs is far from completion, meanwhile major political parties in the country still cannot reach an agreement about the constitutional reforms.

III. Lessons and experiences of international governance of Bosnia and Herzegovina

In general, internal governance of a country is its own business and does not require external interventions. However, under specific conditions especially when a country has weak or no governance capability, external forces will intervene in the country's governance, consequently we will be faced with the question of a proper and benevolent international governance.

In Balkans, intensification of conflicts between countries or inside a country have caused international interventions which have put an end to the conflicts, and international powers—which have employed different intervention ways—have taken part in the country's governance, till the end of conflicts. International governance in Bosnia and Herzegovina which was conducted by the High Representative Office after the signing of the Dayton Agreement was a typical case for post-conflict regional international governance. The case in Bosnia and Herzegovina demonstrates that as for a "weak state" which cannot maintain domestic peace, the international community will make interventions in it through different ways. Allowing a post-conflict country alone and out of control will threaten international peace and also directly damage the interests of the local citizens.

Despite numerous problems, it has been a great achievement to maintain the peace in Bosnia and Herzegovina under the governance of the High Representative Office. During 16 years since the signing of the Dayton Agreement, three nations of Bosnia and Herzegovina failed to heal the wounds of the past conflicts, and nationalist political forces have been able to cause frequent uproars. However, peace was kept and number of conflicts reduced, and people gradually began to live a normal life. In view of unique historical heritage, its conflict history and political ecology, a civil war would likely take place again in the absence of international governance and people living in this country, can be put into a hopeless situation once again in Bosnia and Herzegovina. As a civil coordinating body to supervise execution of the Dayton Agreement, the Office of High Representative (OHR) has played a constructive role in keeping peace in Bosnia and Herzegovina.

With efforts made by successive High Representatives, Bosnia and Herzegovina has managed to restore order, and the central state organs have been strengthened. The power was gradually transferred from the two entities to the central government, and statehood attributes of the stata were also consolidated gradually. Bosnia and Herzegovina has built such important organs as the national frontier defense, a uniform intelligence department, Ministry of State Security, Ministry of National Defense, Ministry of Justice, National Court and Procuratorate, it has implemented uniform value-added tax, approved the criminal law and the criminal procedure law; and set up the Committee of Civil Servants.

The most important progress has been that in 2007 the EU and BiH have signed the Stabilisation and Association Agreement. For Bosnia and Herzegovina the Europeanization prospect has become a major factor for its stabilization.

In 1997, the High Representative was granted with the "Bonn Powers" policy which became one of the main strategic means employed by the High Representative in the international governance. With "Bonn Powers" policy, High Representatives have been able to use their mandates to carry out the reforms which were conductive to improving people's life standards in Bosnia and Herzegovina.

For example, implementation of a uniform car license registration system all over the country has helped people to travel freely and they need not to disclose their national identities when travelling. The implementation of value-added tax has promoted an increase in social welfare expenditures, issuance of the regulations about residence has allowed nearly 1 million people returning to their hometowns. The "Bonn Powers" policy was also the major support for by the High Representative to resist nationalists forces and fight against corrupted officers, and promotion of electing trustworthy officers. The High Representative can fire nationalistic-oriented officers who violate the Dayton Agreement, which has reduced the damage caused by nationalist political forces and helped to develop the political stability in the country. Such results reflects the constructive significance of the "Bonn Powers" policy, but we cannot say this policy fully democratic. In particular, with this policy tool the democratically elected officers have faced extreme practices including dismissal which went against the "democratization" slogan raised by the international community. In one occasion, in late June 2004, Ashdown had dismissed 60 officers, which caused liberal criticism from both inside and outside Bosnia and Herzegovina.

Besides the "Bonn Powers" policy, the High Representative is supported by the weight and effect of the peacekeeping forces. After the signing of the Dayton Agreement, the stabilization force of the NATO marched into Bosnia and Herzegovina, while the army only had 60,000-plus troops at the initial phase. In December 2004, peace-keeping task in Bosnia and Herzegovina was transferred to EU from the NATO, which marked that the multinational stabilization force led by the EU formally replaced the military mission of the NATO. Without the support from the peacekeeping force deployed in BiH, the High Representative's decisions would hardly be implemented, when conflicts occur, national government organs can demand security support from the international peacekeeping forces.

As the core organ of the international governance in BiH, the High Representative can directly intervene in the political process, but there are other international actors and organizations which participate in the governance of Bosnia and Herzegovina, besides the agendas they have and their priorities are not completely the same.

Hence, it is difficult to harmonize activities among all international participants. International organizations in Bosnia and Herzegovina include the UN, the Organization for Security and Co-operation of Europe, the NATO and the EU, Organization of the Islamic Conference, etc.

Each participant organization will report its work to its headquarters, while we see both competition and coordination co-existing among these different organizations. International organizations which play a part in the peace process of Bosnia and Herzegovina have different agendas and different degrees of openness, besides the cross-organizational communication and coordination is not quite smooth, therefore some tasks assumed by them is repeated or overlap.

Frequent leadership changes of the High Representative post and the Office of High Representative organization hinder the implementation of long-term strategies set by the international community. Since the Office of High Representative was established, there have been eight High Representatives taking office with the average tenure of two years. As Gillard Knaus pointed out in the Proposition for European Stability Mechanism "the so-called system construction and democratization attempts in the whole region are quite improperly designed and inefficient. In a protectorate state, due to changes of leaders and personnel who govern the international organizations, we see changes taking place in basic strategies in most fields in every two years (or less)".[10]

Personnel working in the Office of High Representative come from the local governmental departments or state departments of foreign signatories. Temporarily hired employees are very young or so old which will retire soon. Employee turnover is too fast which hinders the smoth continuity of work.

High representatives try to strengthen statehood attributes of Bosnia and Herzegovina and construction of leading national institutions and departments, and increase decision-making efficiency to facilitate Bosnia and Herzegovina's entry into the Euro-Atlantic structures.

However, governance of High Representatives cannot completely control and design the local political process in Bosnia and Herzegovina, it cannot completely promote the national reconciliation among various nations in Bosnia and Herzegovina, cannot restrict the growth of nationalism in the ideological and political spheres, it does not possess the sole power to promote the strengthening of the statehood character of the BiH, as well as the constitutional reform process, in fact all these developments ultimately depend on the evolvement in the domestic politics. All in all high representatives can promote the domestic reforms in BiH, but cannot completely monitor and replace the local subjects active on the ground in this country.

---

10 Tom Gallagher, The Balkans in the New Millennium, in: The Shadow of War and Peace, London: Routledge, 2005, p. 142.

The experience of Bosnia and Herzegovina, has revealed that, though 16 years of painstaking efforts by the international community, it hasn't achieved to become a self-reliant state, yet. This also reflects the limitations of international governance. Since 2007, the international community has often discussed the possibility of withdrawing the control of the High Representatives in Bosnia and Herzegovina, but till today there is no explicit timetable for such a withdrawal. Taking into account the Europeanization prospect of Bosnia and Herzegovina, the EU Special Representative for BiH will be undertaking greater responsibility in the governance of Bosnia and Herzegovina, which will mean that the current protectorate by the international community over this country will gradually pass to the protectorate of the EU, but there is still a long way to go, before it becomes a normal country.

External Religious Intervention: The Case of Kosovo Conflict

Zhang Yuan[1]

The religions develop and coexist with human civilization, and the beliefs, as a source of spiritual relief provide peace to people's misery and confusion. The religions provide social cohesion among their believers and provides a goal and purpose of life for people who believe they need one.

After the end of Cold War, the religions have revitalized and surged up. With the International Religious Freedom Act of 1998 which was passed in the US, more and more international actors pay attention to or even directly intervene in problems about religious freedom and religious human rights violations in other countries and regions. The above law was passed to promote religious freedom as a foreign policy of the United States. As a result, the topic of religion has gradually transcended the secular prejudice and began to exert continuous influences on the international politics.

The Kosovo issue constitutes an important research object in the field of international relations after the Cold War.

Whether the Kosovo independence was declared under the pretext of humanitarian intervention or under the trusteeship of foreign powers, each significant event that occurred in Kosovo often infringed and challenged the existing international conventions.

---
1 Assistant researcher at Politics Research Institute of East China University of Political Science and Law, researcher at postdoctoral research department of East China University of Political Science and Law.

Therein, challenges arising from the religious field have their origins from special historical background of Balkans. In the eyes of Europeans, the Ottoman Empire brought "a backward governance to the region by alien race" to the Balkan region, contrarily the Byzantine Empire was the basis for self-identification.[2]

The Serbians deem Orthodox Eastern churches and monasteries in the Kosovo region which were built in the Byzantine Empire age, as the cultural signs standing for Kosovo's importance and also as the demonstration of subordinate position of Kosovo in the history of Serbia.

The nations have a more modern concept than that of the religions, the initial shapers of nations have always blended and adapted pre-modern values and symbolism into this modern nation concept.[3]

The religions form one of the main sources in the identity of various nations in Balkans. Serbia is an Eastern Orthodox nation which took the lead in building an independent national church – archbishop area. Hence, the Eastern Orthodox Church in Serbia is often deemed to have close political relations with the state since its establishment.[4]

During the reign of Ottoman Empire, a lot of Albanian residents in Kosovo who originally believed in Christianity were converted to Islam.

Nowadays, the Albanians in Kosovo prefer to highlight their national identity more than religious identity in the public, but the Albanians still deem religious symbols as their important national characteristic. The humanitarian crisis caused by long-term confrontations among religious groups in Kosovo drove international powers to carry out external religious intervention in Kosovo Conflict. Based on the case of Kosovo Conflict, this paper will discuss specific connotations of external religious intervention; expound three sources which motivate external religious intervention; and analyze influences and consequences brought by external religious intervention to regional security issues. The paper believes that external religious intervention is the trans-national manifestation pattern of religious intervention under a crisis situation. In essence, external religious intervention can be classified as a non-traditional security issue, and its belief-based three sources are respectively: belief protection for maintaining religious

---

2 Mark Mazower: Balkans: Misinterpreted "European Powder Magazine", translated by Liu Huiliang, Tianjin Peoples Publishing House, 2007, p.18.
3 Ger Duijzings, Religion and Politics of Identity in Kosovo, London: C. Hurst and Co. Publishers Ltd., 2000, pp.157-158.
4 Iwan Borichi et al.:History of Yugoslavia, translated by Zhao Naibin, Beijing, Commercial Press, 1984, p.91.

power; missionarial pursuit for developing religious power; and suppression of heresies which are deemed to seriously threaten a major institutional religion (mainstream). External religious intervention is one supplementary option of the intervention policy. It is also an important mediator which may promote intervention by political and military entities and will thus further influence and complicate the direction of regional security issues.

I. External Religious Intervention and Religious Involvement

With the "global religious revival and upsurge"[5], religions have also embraced the secular world during social development and have entered into political communication. On the levels of practice of godliness and worshipping concepts, modern religious life has an ideological analysis dimension; and on the levels of religious etiquette norms, religious titles and congregation, it is the object of behavioral mechanism analysis.[6]

On one side, religious concepts and religious consciousness influence men's world view and their values; on the other side, by virtue of institutionalized organizations and externalized behaviors, religions affect the regional security issues which have political significance and constitute social structural dimension.

Orientation of the concept of external religious intervention also follows the analysis mode of coexistence of both the traditional religious intangible ideas and tangible organizational behaviors.

A. Scope of External Religious Intervention

Religious intervention starts from intervention in domestic politics of a country or the state. It is generally acknowledged by the outside world that religious intervention into secular politics is conducted mainly because of negative effects of secular intervention.[7]

---

5 See, Xu Yihua, "Religious Revival and Upsurge " under Current International Relations, published in Religion and American Society (Volume 4), Editor-in-chief: Xu Yihua, Current Affairs Press Beijing,, 2007, pp.2-12.
6 For analysis framework of religious influences on national security with its intangible and tangible dimensions, see article, "Discussion about Paths and Forms of Religious Influences on Chinese National Security", by Xu Yihua and Zhang Yuan, Journal of Fudan University (Section of Social Sciences), No.4, 2009, pp.109-116.
7 Pavlos Hatzopoulos and Fabio Petito (eds), Religion in International Relations: The Return from Exile, New York: Palgrave, 2003, p.1.

For example, religious conservatives suppress believers and suppress the survival space of alien religious groups in accordance with strict religious doctrines; by virtue of certain religious beliefs, terrorism obtains theological legality; religions have potential extremism tendency or they even trigger clash of civilizations. As for religious authorities, despite its negative consequences, intervention in politics always has the basic intention of maintaining and increasing religious interests. External religious intervention is the trans-national manifestation pattern of religious intervention, under crisis situations, while the latter part has the connotation of political power's intervention into other countries' religious affairs.

Due to duality of the subject, external religious intervention is not limited with pure religious interests, in value judgment.

On one side, religious intervention into politics refers to that religious groups conduct lobbying activities among political leaders and political organizations, and guide political powers to select public policies which can better satisfy religious demands; on the other side, it indicates that religious leaders implement substantial political actions with the aim of influencing state's domestic and foreign affairs.[8]

As an example of the history, American religious right-wing groups pressed on believing senators and recalled religious responsibilities in order to pass decrees of limiting abortion, such as the 1976 Hyde Amendment. As an another example, the American "Rescue Operation" took place in 1987, wherein people attacked clinics in order to stop abortions as well. A necessary premise for religious intervention into politics requires a religious belief that holds an important social status inside a country. For instance, various Western European countries have a high level of secularization, while the US has relatively low level of secularization. In the US right-wing Evangelical Christians are very active and powerful, thus religious intervention into the US politics obtains better result than that in politics of Western European countries.

In comparison with religious intervention, general significance of the external religious intervention is characterized by following aspects. Firstly, external religious intervention has more extensive actors. Not limited to religious interest groups, these actors also include trans-national religious and political organizations which try to change religious situations in other countries. Secondly, external religious intervention involves in more diversified topics that religions care about such as education, charity and medical service, as well as political

---

[8] Allen D. Hertzke: God in Washington – Role of Religious Lobbying in American Political System, translated by Xu Yihua et al., Shanghai People's Publishing House, 2003, pp.3-6.

topics containing religious factors like stabilizing regional security situation and preventing the outburst and upsurge of religious conflicts.

Thirdly, external religious interventions rather target international objects including religious people and deal with political and religious situations in other countries. For example, independent involvement by American Christian community to rescue Christians suffering in South Sudan can be understood from the religious intervention perspective, which demonstrates that a religious institution of a western country has infringed the treaty system of inter-state sovereignty in order to protect brothers of the same religion; and intervened in the human rights situation of another sovereign country in a religion-oriented manner. It was a case of external religious intervention.[9]

In comparison with traditional political intervention, external religious intervention is characterized by the following aspects. Firstly, external religious intervention coexists with strong moral temptation, while its legality is authorized by sacred classical text and religious beliefs. On the subject of protecting the historical and cultural symbols of the weak groups and saving the religious victims in power struggle, external religious intervention shows more obvious moral characteristics. Religious intervention tests the loyalty of various parties to the religion, while all the parties are also restrained by the religious doctrine and thus distinguished from other kinds of political intervention.

Secondly, major institutional religions in the world possess mature transnational organizational systems, thus the external religious intervention can directly influence religious affairs of a region by its powerful organizational arms. On the contrary, there is no sacredly-authorized ultimate power possessed by a sovereign state, and a sovereign state has limited powers compared to an institutional religion with stronger executive forces. Hence, practically and organizationally, any legality of political intervention is weaker than that of an intervention implemented by an institutionalized religions.

Thirdly, as one supplementary option of intervention by great powers, external religious intervention may not have enough powerful political support to achieve its subsequent implementation.

However, political intervention is determined by the requirements or demands of a domestic political-system of a major world state actor, on the other side the religious intervention conducted by religious organizations has higher flexibility compared to that of political intervention.

---

9 Xu Yihua: Religion and US Diplomatic Policies after The Cold War – with "Sudan Campaign" of American Religious Groups as Case, Journal of Social Sciences in China , Issue 5, 2011.

B. Research status quo related to external religious intervention

"Religious intervention" involves abundant personal private spheres in western literature, such as marriage counseling, spiritual tutorship and palliative care. Religious intervention and religious interference in public spheres and state affairs are mainly studied from the aspect of politics-religion relationships, wherein "the principle of freedom of religious belief" and "the principle of separation of church and state" in civil society are discussed.

As for the research of religious intervention from the perspective of international relations, Jeffery Haynes – a British scholar has made a comprehensive summarization in the following aspects in the Introduction to International Relationship and Religion.

Firstly, paradoxes and conflicts are generated from globalization and human's technological achievements, while religions are revitalized in a large scale and extensively engage in every sphere of human life.

Secondly, due to unbalanced development between different regions of the world, and development gaps between them have gradually increased to an unprecedented degree, therefore many victims as certain interest actors of this process generate negative emotions of dissatisfaction against secular values which support traditional international relations system and turn to seek an alternative, replaceable, complete and rigorous value order system.

Religious fundamentalism emphasizes returning to those original holy texts such as Torah and Koran and to doctrines which are explicit and forcible, which are taught they can satisfy the demands of the dissatisfied people. As a result, religious fundamentalism has managed to spread widely in the world.

Thirdly, trans-national religious actors cause diversified influences on the global political system. With the Roman Catholic Church as the most influential one and spreading religious creeds as its major mission, trans-national non-state actors have incomparable advantages with their organizational network. Their involvement and influences to the issues like human rights and democratization can even threaten the existing international system.

Fourthly, religious terrorism sharpens the differences of religious identities and agitates religious conflicts in order to protect its own belief.

Fifthly, religious actors intervene in international conflict reconciliations by universal religious ethical-value norms in order to realize final peace among men.[10]

---

10 Jeffrey Haynes, Introduction to International Relations and Religion, New York: Palgrave Macmillan, 2007, pp.63-331.

Haynes highlights the necessity to increase religions' status in international relations, but his analytical assessment, to a certain extent, underestimates the spiritual nature of religious influences when comparing them with other secular political powers; and he also fails to analyze multiple and complex motive forces behind external religious interventions which constitute intertwined spiritual and material pursuits.

At present, the researches on religious intervention into international politics are limited by three factors. Firstly, there is no theoretical framework about existing international relations which can fully explain religious intervention. Secondly, the analyses of external religious intervention are often confused withan analysis of "soft power" which is known more common. Thirdly, western academic schools discuss religious intervention mainly from three aspects including religious fundamentalism, religious terrorism and "clash of civilizations"[11]. However, external religious intervention is not equal to the participation of religions in a religious conflict or a peace reconstruction process.[12] Without all parts, discussion on external religious intervention will be incomprehensive.

The intervention of great powers in Kosovo conflict is an important topic in studies of international politics. Existing literature mainly involve hegemonism, unilateralism, geopolitics and neo-interventionism. All of the researches admit that the universal values embraced in western countries are the major reasons for the intervention of great Powers in Kosovo. However, nearly none of them incorporate the religious factors into the analysis of intervention policies.[13] This is different from the Sudan researches which pay attention to religious factors. To a great extent, researches incorporate the religious revival, the strengthening of social mobilization capability of international religious human right organizations and American Evangelism. Analysis of external religious intervention in Kosovo conflict can be deemed as contemporary supplement for researches on Kosovo to demonstrate the tracks of religious revival in the international political field.

---

11 See the book by M. Gopin, Between Eden and Armageddon, New York: Oxford University Press, 2000; Scott R. Appleby, The Ambivalence of the Sacred: Religion, Violence, and Reconciliation, Lanham, MD: Rowman and Littlefield Publisher, Inc., 2000; Mark Juergensmeyer, Terror in the Mind of God: The Global Rise of Religious Violence, Berkley: University of California Press, 2000; quoted from Jeffrey Haynes, Introduction to International Relations and Religion, London: Longman, 2007, pp.160-161.
12 David R. Smock, Religious Perspective on War: Christian, Muslim, and Jewish Attitudes toward Force After the Gulf War, Washington, D. C.: US Institute of Peace Press, 2002, pp. 33-46.
13 For more detailed research, overview about western intervention in Kosovo, see, Zhang Yuan, Research Overview of Western Academic Circle about Topics Concerning Religious Factors and Regional Conflicts – with Religious Conflict in Kosovo Case, published in the European Studies, No.6, 2009.

C. Types and Forms of External Religious Intervention

According to intervention objects, types of external religious intervention can be approximately divided into two part; intervention aiming at specific religious objects and intervention aiming at specific religious affairs. According to intervention subjects, it can be approximately divided into two parts; religious intervention subjects and non-religious intervention subjects. According to two dimensions of religious ideology and organizational etiquette, external religious intervention is implemented respectively in forms of propaganda and education, missionization, preaching as well as organizational management and carry out specific religious activities. The intervention of a political power in religious affairs also basically respects the two core religious dimensions. In Kosovo conflict, all the aforementioned intervention types and intervention forms appeared. External religious intervention aiming at specific religious objects: the interventions specially aim at a specific religious existence – religious building which is accepted as the belief center of believers. After the Kosovo War, Serbian Eastern Orthodox monasteries in Kosovo were faced with a harder situation.

Different from Albanian groups in Kosovo who were longing for withdrawal of NATO forces and realization of real independency and autonomy, monks and friars in Eastern Orthodox monasteries of Kosovo were quite unwilling to see any possibility of NATO's withdrawal, unless there is greatly improved security situation in Kosovo.[14] Many monks and friars who still stay in Serbian Eastern Orthodoxy churches and monasteries which were under attack in Kosovo believed that they needed powers inside Kosovo to protect their lives, security and basic rights, and to punish severely Albanian Muslims which often attacked monasteries and friars. Bishop Teodosije – director of Kosovo Decani Monastery, a world cultural heritage of UN–once formally thanked for the proposal suggested by Italian senators and humanists that Italian government should maintain their garrison of Kosovo peace-keeping force in order to protect Decani Monastery.[15]

External religious intervention targeting special religious affairs:

This kind of intervention aims at religious events or a religious situation during a certain period. After 1999, according to Resolution Nr. 305 of the UN Security Council, Organization for Security and Co-operation in

---

[14] Glass Kosova I Metohije (The Herald of Kosovo and Metohija), "Interview with Fr. Sava: Forgive Them, Father, for They Know Not What They De," official published by the Serbian Orthodox Diocese of Raska-Prizren, March 15th, 2002, http://www.glaskim.co.yu/; KDN, March 14, 2002, http://groups.yahoo.com/group/decani/message/65518.

[15] ERPKIM Info-Sevice, "Abbot Teodosije of Decani: Protection of Monastery is Our Priority Task," Kosovo.net, March 19, 2003, http://www.kosovo.net/news20.html.

Europe was authorized to "monitor and report human rights situation and promote human rights training in Kosovo".[16]

OSCE Mission would also involve in contents concerning the group interests of Serbian Eastern Orthodox community in Kosovo. The Mission has included protecting the Serbian Eastern Orthodox churches and monasteries, paying attention to living conditions of Serbians in Kosovo and Metohija, as well as returning of and security guarantee of Serbian refugees"[17]. In 2004, UN Interim Administration Mission in Kosovo and OSCE Mission in Kosovo drafted a law on Freedom of Religion. According to this draft law, residents who were not born in Kosovo cannot take important posts in churches. Including the diocesan bishop of Kosovo, many Eastern Orthodox bishops and monastery directors staying in Kosovo were born in Serbia, therefore new draft bill does not fit to their conditons, they will lose their posts[18]. If this draft law is passed in parliament, these bishops will be dismissed from Kosovo religious communities, while it will be very difficult to find another Eastern Orthodox bishop who can be dispatched to Kosovo and who is born in Kosovo as well. Due to this draft religious law, the Eastern Orthodox belief in Kosovo will be further weakened.

Intervention by religious organizations: hierarchically superior religious leading organs inside the same religion or religious organizations of other countries attempt interventions for moral concern or religious obligation in coordination with international political intervention, regarding unstable religious regions. There are over 6,000 dioceses of Serbian Eastern Orthodox Church in Balkans.[19] In principle, organizations that are subordinate to the church shall obey decisions made by the superior church. Teodosije Bishop, the monastery director mentioned before, was dismissed by Bishop Artemije of the superior church – Diocese of Raska-Prizren and Kosovo-Metohija. For this, the diocese wrote in an official statement that "since 2004, Teodosije Bishop had opposed to all the activities conducted by the diocese bishop to fight against injustice. In fact, the diocese bishop did these things in order to protect our people and our temple. Teodosije clique in his own monastery opposed

---

16 Helmut Kramer, Vedran Rixiqi: Kosovo Issue, translated by Yuan Jianhua et al., Beijing, Central Compilation and Translation Press, 2007, p.20.
17 Information Service of the Serbian Orthodox Church, "Press Conference on the Occasion of the Return of the SOC Delegation from The USA," Serbian Orthodox Church, March 28, 2006, http://www.spc.rs/Vesti-2006/03/29-03-06-e.html.
18 Felix Corley, "Kosovo: 'Religious Freedom will be Seriously Hindered' by Draft Law," Forum 18 News Service, November 19, 2004, http://www.forum18.org/Archive.php?article_id=457.
19 Information Service of the Serbian Orthodox Church, "Press Conference on the Occasion of the Return of the SOC Delegation from The USA," Serbian Orthodox Church, March 28, 2006, http://www.spc.rs/Vesti-2006/03/29-03-06-e.html.

to the diocese's propositions. Hence, he can no longer implement blessing on behalf of us. They choose a shameful road and they are exiled from the monastery."[20] Russian Eastern Orthodox Church is equal to the seniority of the Serbian Eastern Orthodox Church in Kosovo. The Eastern Orthodox circle in Russia has always motivated Russians believing in Eastern Orthodoxy to provide humanitarian aid to believers of Serbian Eastern Orthodoxy in Kosovo; and transport humanitarian aid materials to Serbians in Kosovo. The Solojindu Bishop (Archbishop Pitirim) in Russia called Kosovo as "bleeding wound of Europe" and encouraged "Russians to provide generous aid to religious brothers in Kosovo" in order to show their brotherly love.[21]

D. Intervention by non-religious organizations

In comparison with external intervention of religious organizations, intervention implemented by nonreligious organizations to specific religious issues is always taken as a component of overall political intervention. During democratization process under international society's supervision in Kosovo: on one side, UN Interim Administration Mission in Kosovo (UNMIK) mastered major governmental and administrative authorities after Kosovo War. Meanwhile, international society actively supported Albanian residents in Kosovo to build modern democratic structure and cultivate foundation for political autonomy;[22] on the other side, in order to avoid excessive power in one ethnic group in the future political structure of Kosovo. UNMIK deliberately and mandatorily blended some Serbians in government, judiciary, police and political parties of Kosovo. However, a Serbian priest in Kosovo once pointed out that real authorities of these Serbian civil servants in Kosovo were only limited in Serbian neighborhood, while they had very distant relations with Albanian colleagues.[23] Kosovan governmental organs which have ethnic proportion set by international organizations failed to stop Albanians' attack to Serbians and there occurred a serious chaos in Eastern Orthodox churches in March 2004.[24]

---

20   Diocese of Ras-Prizren and Kosovo-Metohija, "Announcements of Diocese and Text about Kosovo-Metohija: Insurrection in Visoki Decani, The Official Note," August 24, 2008, http://www.eparhija-prizren.com/defaultE.asp?s=vesti&idvestep=3191.
21   ИТАР-ТАС/Православие. Russian, "МОСКВА НАПРАВИЛА ГУМАНИТАРНУЮ ПОМОЩЬСЕРБСКОМУ НАСЕЛЕНИЮ КОСОВА И МЕТОХИИ," Pravoslavie.ru, October 16, 2002, http://www.pravoslavie.ru/news/021014/12.htm.
22   Mark Malloch Brown, "Only Voting is not Democracy" International Herald Tribune, July 1, 2004.
23   Fr. Sava Janjic, "Comment: Are Kosovo Serbs Really Making Progress, Mr Haselock?" ERP KIM Info-Service, October 20, 2002, http://www.kosovo.net/rep201002.html#sava.
24   U.S. Department of State, Bureau of Democracy, Human Rights, and Labor, "International Religious Freedom Report 2004: Serbia and Montenegro," State.gov, 2004, http://www.state.gov/g/drl/rls/irf/2004/35482.htm.

Worse still, violence incidents like the attack to local UN Mission Office in Kosovo took place.[25]

In November 2011, the event of an Albanian's shooting at a Serbian policeman in Kosovo once again verified the priest's previous concerns about the situation in public affair departments of Kosovo.

Form of external religious intervention on ideological dimension:

Intervention derived from inside of religions often shows very strong spiritual colors. In an interview on the 10th Anniversary of The Rebirth of The Brotherhood of Visoki Decani Monastery published in the Orthodoxy – the newspaper of Serbian Patriarchate, a lot of non-secular transcendent words were conveyed to believers in order to pass on religious ideas to them. "If we are spiritually strong, the shrines of Kosovo and Metohija will survive"[26].

"Our message to them is that we Orthodox Christians must not rely on anything of this world. We cannot rely on the idea that we can create a paradise on earth by wise politics, strong armies, and economic welfare. It is all transient and temporary. We must not seek the peace of this world but the peace which can only be given to us by Christ. We must not become careless in our material prosperity and become easily deceived by the spirit of modern heresies and secularization, but should on the contrary stick to our tradition canons, and the teachings of the Holy Fathers. Only the Truth can set us free.[27] This type of religious intervention advocates Serbian Eastern Orthodox believers in Kosovo to protect their beliefs, believe in miracle and let Kosovo obtain final rescue by praying.

Form of external religious intervention on organizational etiquette dimension:

Religious etiquette is an important part in religious life. More than externalizing religious experience, religious etiquette modifies and shapes religious experience further. According to the view of Anthony Giddens – a sociology scholar, all the religious ritual behaviors held periodically at special sites target at "religious symbolic significance."[28]

---

25 International Crisis Group, "Collapse in Kosovo," ICG Europe Report No.155, April 22, 2004, p.19.
26 Jelena Tasic, translated by Snezana Lazovic, "On the 10th Anniversary of the Rebirth of the Brotherhood of Visoki Decani Monastery," Pravoslavlje, March 20th, 2002, http://groups.yahoo.com/group/decani/message/65950. Serbian Version: http://www.spc.rs/Pravoslavlje/840/teodosije_c.html.
27 St.Herman of Alaska Press, "Interview with Abbot Theodosios," from Orthodox Word, Nos. 193-4, Kosovo.net, December 8, 2011, http://www.kosovo.net/theodos.html.
28 Anthony Giddens: Sociology (Edition 4), translated by Zhao Xudong et al., Peking University Press, 2003, p.507.

For example, "Decani Monastery Relief Fund" (DMRF) – a religious charity organization in Idaho (a state in US)-declares that its patron saint is St. Sava of Serbia, while the Fund is in fact a non-profit organization subordinated to the Greek Orthodox Archdiocese of America, and tax exemption is provided to donations. Except for economic aid, DMRF also often calls on American Christian groups to come to the churches and hold rites for brothers and sisters of Eastern Orthodoxy in Kosovo so that they can obtain more care and support from western countries under the god's love, in order to "unite American Christians and Serbian Christians together."[29]

II. Faith Based Belief Power: Sources of External Religious Intervention

External religious intervention involves in securitization of religious conflicts, while its internal sources lie in religious obligations and loyalty to belief. Based on the perspective of belief and according to dimensions in trying to change the current religious power structure, power sources of external religious intervention can be divided into three parts respectively: belief protection for maintaining religious power; missionarial pursuit for developing religious power; and suppression of heresies which are deemed to threaten a serious rivalry.

A. Belief Protection for Maintaing Religious Power:

Traditional religious belief protection on theological level indicates that believers have the religious responsibility for bowing to god's divine will and maintaining belief immortalization. A religious group is a social community with very high emotional affinity degree among its members. When a particular religious group faces a direct attack, external groups within the same religion tend to believe that the attack targets at the whole belief system, and they try to seek positive intervention and interference in order to protect their own religion and tend to fight against the possibility of incessant damages to the belief. Being in a close geographical distance or religious affinity to the direct victim, or closer distance to the perpetrator group, the external religious group will instigate a deeper frustration and worries for the decline of their belief and will be motivated further to change the current status. Trans-national analogous religious groups are united within the religion due to the tradition of belief protection.

---

29 See from official introduction of DMRF Rev. Archimandrite Nektarios Serfes, "Missionary Support: Decani Monastery Relief Fund: A Non Profit Organization," DMRF, Dec. 9, 2011, http://fr-d-serfes.org/missionary/charter.htm.

Religious volunteers are radical activists who join religious confrontations in a conflict region due to the tradition of belief protection.

Islamic "Mujahideen" have taken active role in the wars of Bosnia and Kosovo. They usually stem from those countries like Afghanistan, Saudi Arabia, Iran and Pakistan, recruited by certain organizations. In addition to provide economic and technological support, they also directly act as belief-protecting soldiers and participate inter-religious conflicts. We cannot affirm whether these volunteers who autonomously join the fighting groups could decide the development of the situation, but we feel certain about that the interventions driven by the passion of belief protection intensifies local conflicts and make the situation more severe and complicated.

Belief protection demands are closely related to the religious group's cognition of its own religious status. Warren Treadgold once discussed the intimacy between Eastern Orthodox world and Christendom in the Concise History of Byzantium. Comparing the historical relations between Eastern and Western European Christendom, he argued that Eastern and Western Europe was "union of Roman Empire's Christian successors", while "there still exists the split between Eastern Orthodox Church and Roman Catholic Church, but their doctrinal differences are much less than those between Roman Catholic Church and Protestantism."[30]

Perhaps, just because of the consanguinity ties permeated into religious bloodline, when the clerical delegation of Serbian Eastern Orthodoxy visited Vatican and talked to Pope John Paul II – Pope of Roman Catholic Church. He has emphasized that Europe should strengthen religious protection in Kosovo – as the spiritual and cultural homeland of Serbia. Similarly, in the field of belief protection, Roman Catholic Church can give up condemning Serbian government in Kosovo issue and get along well with Serbians who follow the Eastern Orthodox Church.

As a basis of external religious intervention, the tradition of belief protection is in the essence of a conservative defense and closely connected to certain religious suffering consciousness. For the Christians, suffering is evident in God's creation and the whole human experience and one part of the apostolic mission is to be a witness to Christ's suffering as a community.

With the description of Kosovo War in 1389 as the case, folk tales of Serbia mainly praised Archduke Lazar who died in this war, for hundreds of years. Basic image of Lazar Archduke is depicted as a noble prince who

---

30   Warren Treadgold: Brief History of Byzantium, translated by Cui Yanhong, Shanghai People's Publishing House, 2008, p.270.

devoted himself to build the Kingdom of Heaven. However, with incursion of Serbian nationalism in the 20th century, Kosovo War is granted with more theological connotations: martyrdom of Lazar Archduke was analogized to the crucifixion of Jesus, while his sacrifice was also deemed as the God's choice – beginning of the whole Serbian nation's suffers. At this time, enemies of Serbia were no longer limited with the aggressor Ottoman Turkey, but extended and included all the Muslim people. They were all deemed as anti-Christ heretics. Serbian Eastern Orthodox churches, nationalist politicians and intellectuals jointly reconstructed such a history in Serbia in order to unite more pro-Serbia Christians by using the consciousness of suffer, thusurge to let them to fight against Islamization of Kosovo.

B. Obligation of Mission Work

The obligation of missionary refers to believers' responsibility to preach the gospel, and to spread the doctrine and practice of a certain religion propagandizing spiritual ideas and striving for a betterworld. Believers are commissioned for such an obligation by religious texts. By spreading their beliefs, religious powers expand alliance and seek for more protection to strength other parties.

It will also build spiritual links by describing the religion in order to realize closer internal integration and accumulate power for confrontation. Starting from religious texts, religious practice, religious traditions and theological ideas, the external religious intervention seeks for concurrent space between politics and religion. As thought by believers and idealists, the external religious intervention driven from the obligation of missionization shall be called as "diplomacy based on belief". The external religious intervention driven from the obligation of missionization often gently and gradually infuse religious beliefs with value connotations of the local country to target groups by providing theological education, mending belief etiquettes and taking other manners with the aim of improving social conditions of religious survival.

Subject of the external religious intervention with the obligation of missionization as the power source may not be a great political power. Religious people and religious organizations with special identities can conduct an intervention with religious significance, while such an intervention is not limited with the national power of their country. Vuk Draskovic – Foreign Minister of Serbia and the originally an extreme nationalist said that he saw the hope of peace in Yugoslavia and felt confident about putting an end to the war after seeing by Patrijarh Pavle – patriarch of Serbian Eastern

Orthodoxy Church and Franjo Kuharic – cardinal of Croatia praying hand in hand. I will list another instance for religious intervention: Only 5% of Albanians in Kosovo believed in Catholicism, but the group photo of Rugova and religious authorities was especially hung in the presidential office of Ibrahim Rugova – the deceased "President of Kosovo". "West-following" Albanian politicians in Kosovo paid deliberate attention to the Catholics in Kosovo, caused dissatisfaction of traditional Muslim society in Kosovo. Muslims thought that politicians empowered Catholicism which was originally unimportant and held no status in Kosovo, while the actual existence of Islam in Kosovo were underestimated or even betrayed by politicians. Religious leaders of Muslim society in Kosovo deliberately ignored government's supportive policies to Catholicism in Kosovo, while the devout Albanian Muslims in Kosovo were densely dissatisfied about this situation. However muftis and imams in Kosovo had still kept silent even when they heard that the Catholic bishop in Kosovo excitedly said that "whole Kosovo is accepting the 'cultural baptism.'"[31]

C. Contemporary Transformation of Just War Theory

There is no monopoly of authority beyond various religions.[32] In the case of competitive relationship among religions, each party will deem itself as the moral and just party and believe that only theirs is the true God. According to Just War Theory, if religious confrontation breaks out between two parties, being a party in it will be considered as defense of justice and embodiment of love, while it is not contradictory to peace. In order to strike possible threats, an action to oppress the religious competitor is also acceptable. To a certain extent, neo-interventionism highlighting humanitarian intervention is the modern political follower of the just war concept of religious history. Understanding of divinity seems to obtain greater ultimate meaning in punishment of heresies, while in this way, the principle of righteousness can be realized. A lot of leaders of religions like Christianism, Judaism and Islam all approve that it is acceptable to abolish the principle of non-violence under special circumstances when religious justice is damaged.[33]

---

31 Besnik Sinani, "The Politics of Religion in Kosovo," New Kosova Report, March 3, 2008.
32 Tom Gallagher, Glasgow, The Uneasy Peace: Religious Tension in Modern Scotland, 1819-1914, Manchester: Manchester University, 1987, p. 3.
33 Mark Juergensmeyer, The New Cold War? Religious Nationalism Confronts the Secular State, Berkley: University of California Press, 1993, p. 164.

In the areas lack of normative systems and with frequent outburst of violence, some non-religious circles also hope that the religious circle "does not stand by as the war is not a 'religious war'"[34], and they initially can require the external religious intervention to defend justice. In comparison with the external religious intervention driven from the tradition of belief protection, the external religious intervention driven from modernized just war concept is more aggressive.

During the War of Bosnia and Herzegovina, Bosnian Muslims, Croatian Catholics and Serbians Eastern Orthodoxes fought against each other and all conducted certain ethnic cleansing actions. During 1991-1992, Atanasije Jevti, a theologian who served as the bishop of Servet Banat Diocese (The Eparchy of Banat) and once served as director of Belgrade Eastern Orthodoxy Divinity School, published a lot of articles to highlight that Serbian Eastern Orthodoxes under administration of Albanians, Croatians and Bosnians in Kosovo where is inside the territory of Yugoslavia and outside Serbia were faced with "unique" ethnic massacre. The Eastern Orthodoxy (Pravoslavlje)– a magazine of Serbian Orthodox published articles to reveal Serbians' solemn and tragic sacrifice history since the earlier stage of 1980s.[35]

In order to support Serbian independence from Bosnia and Herzegovina, in 1993, Priest Dragomir Ubiparipovic wrote "the God personally sends them to save Serbians."[36]

In addition, Roman Curia, and Croatia Cardinal and Archbishop all explicitly supported Croatians under the identity of Catholicism. A lot of religious symbols such as rose and cross were decorated soldiers' costumes, weapons and chariots during the war. When talking about contradictory future outlooks, Bishop Dubrovnik and Bishop Zelimir Puljic said that "fighting for Croatians is equal to fighting for Catholicism"[37]. The Catholic circle in Croatia was once excited about splitting in Yugoslavia and "Croatian

---

34 Peter Palmer, "The Churches and Conflict in Former Yugoslavia," in K. R. Dark, ed., Religion and International Relations, New York: Palgrave Macmillan, 2000, p. 98.
35 David A Steele, "Christianity in Bosnia-Herzegovina and Kosovo: From Ethnic Captive to Reconciling Agent," in Douglas Johnston, ed., Faith-Based Diplomacy: Trumping Realpolitik, New York: Oxford University Press, 2003, p. 131.
36 Dragomir-Ubiparipovic, "At the Dusk of War in Bosnia and Herzegovina," printed in both Svecanik, Nos. 1-2, 1993, and Hriscanska Misao, No. 608, 1993, quoted in Radic, "Serbian Orthdox Church and the War in Bosnia and Herzegovina," in Paul Mojzes, ed., Religion and War in Bosnia, Atlanta: Scholar Press, 1998, pp. 176-177.
37 Gabriel Patros (Southeast Europe Analyst with the BBC Service), "Religion and The Balkan Wars," Institute for War and Peace Reporting, 1996, http://www.demon.co.uk/iwpr/partos40.htm; David A Steele, "Christianity in Bosnia-Herzegovina and Kosovo: From Ethnic Captive to Reconciling Agent," in Douglas Johnston, ed.,Faith-Based Diplomacy: Trumping Realpolitik, p. 139.

liberation"[38], but turned a blind eye to atrocities conducted by Croatian army against Serbian civilians. Religious wars and religious punishments are ways to amend the unsatisfying reality for interveners, wherein they take the belief as the symbol of internal unity, encourage confrontation and finally cause tension that is revealed in dislocation and reorganization of the nation and the state.

Despite of being called by religious spirit, a source of power based on a belief is not enough to inevitably cause external religious intervention. For a long time, Serbian government has broadcasted that Kosovo Liberation Army (KLA) that is devoted to achieve independence in Kosovo is a typical Islamic extreme religious organization. However, Dayton Peace Agreement has become a successful precedent. Additionally, ideal conditions for building a new sovereign Islamic state – Kosovo – in Europe have not matured. Hence, religious radical militants from Iran and Arab world are not so willing to help Kosovo Liberation Army like what they did to support Bosnian Muslim during 1992-1995. Thus it is clear that religious intervention which exceeds territorial limits and means to protect Islam from being damaged in order to praise it in the brother states is not the same with knee-jerk response that is spurred when the state interests are damaged. Religious intervention is merely an optional value that can be used to satisfy political interests. From the perspective of the military intervention, the sanction conducted by Western Christian countries to the Eastern Orthodox Serbia which is also Christian is another example of preferring political interests in case of a conflict between religious interests and political interests.

III. Various Cases and Influences of External Religious Intervention

In 1999, NATO carried out "a humanitarian intervention" to Kosovo by bombing Federal Republic of Yugoslavia. After the war, Kosovo coexisted with Serbia and Republic of Montenegro under a special autonomous identity under trusteeship of UN and NATO. On February 18, 2008, Kosovo unilaterally declared its independence and separation from the Federation. In 2010, the International Court of Justice declared that independence of Kosovo did not violate International Law. During turbulent development of Kosovo, the external religious intervention has influenced circles of group interests, peace reconstruction process and violence which have made an impact on the security situation in Kosovo.

---

38 David A. Steele, "Christianity in Bosnia-Herzegovina and Kosovo: From Ethnic Captive to Reconciling Agent," in: Douglas Johnston, ed., Faith-Based Diplomacy: Trumping Realpolitik, p.140.

A. Divergence between External Religious Intervention and Group Interests

First of all, the external religious intervention always oppresses inter-religious interests which directly threatens religious security. As for Kosovo issue, such confrontation refers to the interest divergence between Christendom and Islamic world. Since 1999, external intervention has completely changed balance of power among religions, so that interest differences among different religions are no longer the major cause for instability in Kosovo. However, the new negative influences generated there from cause dissimilar interests among denominations and different religious groups or even within them. Divergence of interests within the same religion will become the new unstabilizing factor for later political developments.

At first, external religious intervention disorganized interest requirements inside Serbian Eastern Orthodox groups. Serbian Eastern Orthodox believers in Kosovo who stayed at the forefront of ethnic confrontation, such as friars in Eastern Orthodoxy monasteries of Muslim communities, were not so aggressive any longer at opposing to Western Countries about what they did at initial stage of Kosovo War. Serbians outside Kosovo were unwilling to see such "retrogressing". After Kosovo's independence, America hoped that Serbian Christians in Kosovo could still peacefully live under the new regime led by Muslim. In 2009, American Vice President Biden visited Kosovo while treating it as an independent country. Biden's visit caused huge diversity within Serbian Eastern Orthodoxy as Biden had firmly supported Kosovo's independence and condemned atrocities in Serbia during 1990s. During visit to Kosovo in 2009, Biden got the "Golden Medal for Freedom" – highest honor of Kosovo government.[39] Nevertheless, Decani Monastery in Kosovo still hosted Biden enthusiastically.[40] As for monasteries, they hoped to host American Vice President friendly in order to obtain more external protection for Eastern Orthodox heritages and Kosovan Serbians.[41] However, the diocesan bishop Artemio has strongly opposed to the reception of Decani Monastery. The bishop called for actual operations for Kosovo's

---

39 Agence France-Presse, "Biden ends Balkans Tour, Heads to Lebanon," AFP, May 21, 2009, http://www.google.com/hostednews/afp/article/ALeqM5jtMFK8wLcamElXQlmEBh0CEBE9dQ.
40 David Lienemann, "The Vice President's Trip to the Balkans and Lebanon," Whitehouse.gov, May 21, 2009, http://www.whitehouse.gov/photogallery/The-Vice-Presidents-Trip-to-the-Balkans-and-Lebanon.
41 Adam Tanner, "Biden's Visit to Kosovo Monastery Splits Serbian Orthodox Church," Reuters, May 22, 2009, http://blogs.reuters.com/faithworld/2009/05/22/biden-visit-to-kosovo-monastery-splits-serbian-orthodox-church/.

status to strengthen Serbia. Using drastic words, the bishop called Biden as a "racist mob" and reminded Decani Monastery that it should not become a "new Kosovo base of America".[42] Some Serbians residing abroad in western countries deemed Bishop Artemio as a tragic hero of Serbia and nowadays they have likened the bishop as the real "St. Mark of Ephesus".[43]

Interest divergence within Islamic groups is the new form of security threats brought by external religious intervention to the stability of Kosovo. Albanian Muslims in Kosovo tried to get rid of influences of Turkey and tried to shape and retain Islamic culture with Albanian characteristics. After Kosovo War, Albanians failed to restore numerous mosques that were damaged in the war due to their backward economy. Turkey – a great power of Islamic culture – initiated to build many Albanian mosques. However, during repair and reconstruction, disputes were generated between Turks and Albanian Muslims in Kosovo. Albanians thought that, after Ottoman Empire left Kosovo, a lot of cemeteries in Albanian style were built in mosques left by the original Ottoman Empire. However, temple repairers from Turkey and other Islamic countries thought that these styles did not suit Islamic etiquettes and rules. They refused to repair these Albanian cemeteries and rebuilt those with Ottoman Empire styles, turning a blind eye to Albanian Islamic culture valued by Albanians. Rexhep Boja, a mufti in Kosovo, condemned the support in construction: "our Albanians have acted as Muslims for over 500 years, and we do not need to learn what the Islam is from you."[44]

Contributers from Turkey and other Islamic countries and the aided could hardly reach a consensus. Worse still, Albanian Muslims even beat Turks violently in front of those mosques which were built under Turkey's assistance in this period. Under this dilemma, Islamic groups in Kosovo often required imams from these mosques to negotiate with local governments and international organizations; and tried to realize peaceful cooperation between two kinds of Islamic culture by replacing the construction aiding organizations.[45]

---

42 Diocese of Ras-Prizren and Kosovo-Metohija, "Deani and Bondsteel," Press Department Diocese of Ras and Prizren, May 20, 2009, http://www.eparhija-prizren.com/print.asp?idvest=3692.
43 In the 15th century, Bishop St. Mark in Ephesus was finally poisoned because he turned down Florence Alliance uniting Eastern Orthodoxy with Roman Catholic Church, which was promoted by Byzantine Empire under approaching of Turkey aggressors. See from comment part in news of Reuters about "Biden visits Decani Monastery", May 22, 2009, http://blogs.reuters.com/faithworld/2009/05/22/biden-visit-to-kosovo-monastery-splits-serbian-orthodox-church/.
44 Christopher Deliso, The Coming Balkan Caliphate: The Threat of Radical Islam to Europe and the West, Westport, Conn.: Greenwood Publishing Group, Inc., 2007, p.54.
45 International Crisis Group, "Religion in Kosovo," p. 5.

B. External Religious Intervention and Post-conflict Reconstruction

If the external religious intervention could effectively collect religious resources into reshaping of damaged confidence of belief and reconstruct destroyed belief temples, reconstruction after conflicts could be carried out more smoothly. In areas with large population of religious people, some external interventions required for diversified local religious education, while others built religious places for normalized religious activities. All these measures facilitated the comforting of mental damages as soon as possible. A priest who was pleased by the restoration of Prizren Saint George Church by international intervention once said that "even if we are discriminated and abandoned by people around, our lord and numerous honorable Christians who are serving God here still stay with us."[46]

In general, premise of humanitarian aid from Arab countries lies in the local construction of a mosque at first. After this, the capital for building hospitals, residents and schools are provided. At present, there are about ten Islamic non-governmental organizations working in Kosovo, wherein the largest one is Saudi Arabia Joint Rescue Committee in Kosovo (SJRCK) which belongs to radical Wahhabi Islamic sect. SJRCK aided Kosovo mainly by giving a lot of Quran books including Albanian-Arabian comparison,[47] and assisted in repairing 190 mosques which were damaged in conflicts and building new mosques including a pro-Bin Laden Mosque.[48] A retired soldier of Kosovo Peace-keeping Force (KFOR) led by NATO once said: "villagers in Kosovo need new water supply equipment rather than new mosques."[49]

Nevertheless, Islamic groups were willing to give economic aid in religious renaissance as the premise of economic aid. Such an aid includes training of imams and expansion of Islamic literature.

Some international religious charity organizations did not opt the traditional way of monastery repairing, instead they have provided the poor civilians with economic and material aid. "International Eastern Orthodoxy

---

46 KIM Info-Service, "DMRF Donations Distributed to Prizren Serbs: Bishop Teodosije Visits Church of St. George and Remaining Serbs in Prizren," *Kosovo.net*, March 16, 2007, http://www.kosovo.net/news/archive/2007/March_16/3.html.
47 Frank Brown, "Islam Builds a Future in Kosovo, One Mosque at a Time," Religious News Service, September 12, 2000.
48 Gary Leupp, "'Threatening the Foundation of a Word Order': The Independence of Kosovo," Counter Punch, February 19, 2008.
49 Christopher Deliso, The Coming Balkan Caliphate: The Threat of Radical Islam to Europe and the West, p.54

Charitable Community" (IOCC) from Baltimore helped Kosovan monasteries for repairing and expanding a wine making workshop that have been maintained for 600 years, and provided a lot of local employment. More importantly, it "encourages more mutual cooperation between Serbian and Albanian communities in Kosovo".[50]

Priest Marko Diklic once learned about wine making techniques in France and Italy, while he would love to share grape planting techniques with Albanian farmers in Kosovo. For this reason, this priest thought that at least "Albanian grape planters are very close to our wineries and monasteries".[51]

Priest Marko believed that cooperation with IOCC in Decani wineries could improve inter-ethnic relations within Albanian communities.

International society has argued that their garrison was primarily aimed at protecting the security and human rights of religious and national minorities in Kosovo and Metohija, such as Decani Monastery, indiscriminately respecting religious rights of the groups with different beliefs in the same region. A group of Kosovan Eastern Orthodox thought that these external interventions indeed could protect Christians who had become minority to a certain extent, but "in fact, all official organizations of Serbian government have been mandatorily expelled from Kosovo and Metohija territories, so we can only rely on Kosovo Peace-keeping Force, UN Integrated Mission of Temporary Administration in Kosovo and many other international non-governmental organizations. We have no choice and have no reason to refuse them. After all, they are not aggressors who occupied this place. They are only people who want to help us"[52]. However, the root cause for the current unsafe situation in Decani Monastery region is exactly the international society which has expelled or hindered the Serbian government establishment here, which originally could prevent the monasteries from encroachment.[53]

---

50 IOCC, "IOCC Expands Community Development Projects in Kosovo," IOCC, February 22, 2008, http://www.iocc.org/news/2-22-08kosovo.aspx.
51 Nenad Prelevic, "Medieval Monastery Cultivates Good Will in Kosovo," International Orthodox Christian Charities News and Needs, Vol.10, No.3, 2007.
52 See, ERPKIM Info-sevice, "Abbot Teodosije of Decani: Protection of Monastery is Our Priority Task.
53 Martin Hall, "Blackbirds and Black Buttflies," in Carolyn Hamilton, et al., Refiguring the Arcive, Cape Town: David Philip, 2002, pp.341-342.

C. External Religious Intervention and the Vicious Circle of Violence

Any tendentious and short-sighted religious interventions lacking strategic ideas cannot build justice and security necessary for maintaining state running.[54] Vicious circle of violence is a politicized side-effect product brought by radical and prejudiced external religious interventions. Violence may be an intensified response cause by the oppressed party to resist intervention or may be a new political military intervention generated from dissatisfaction from regional status quo.

Before the Kosovo War, international society accused that Serbian Eastern Orthodox Church the only patriotic institution which had not betrayed Serbian national state.[55] In the earlier stages of 1980s, Serbian Eastern Orthodox Church was persistent in cultivating the remembrance of the victimazation of the Serbian people by focusing on the situation in Kosovo. Serbian Eastern Orthodox Church, was especially disturbed by the exodus of Serbian people from Kosova and by the destruction of Church property and shrines, such phenomena which in fact increased after 1981. In 1982, twenty-one Serbian Orthodoxy priests, including three bishops signed an appeal to the church hierarchy asking it to raise its voice "protect spiritual and physical existence of Serbians in Kosovo and Metohija…and to write about the destructions, arsons and sacrilege of the holy shrines Serbian religious temples in Kosovo"[56]. All the appeals made by the Serbian Orthodox Church for violence in Kosovo were downplayed by the international society under the excuse of insufficient evidence. External political powers preferred to believe that these complaints about the Kosovan situation made by Eastern Orthodox Church were exaggerated. However, the church's complaints were enough to motivate Eastern Orthodox believers' tense feelings and hostile awareness against the Kosovan heresy forces; or even supported religious legality of radical nationalists.

---

54 Giovanna Bono, "Explaining Failures in Security and Justice," in Aidan Hehir, ed., Kosovo, Intervention and State building: The International Community and the Transition to Independence, London: Routledge, 2010, p.145.
55 Qemajl Morina & Sava Janjic, "Religion in Kosovo: A Christian and A Muslim View," Decani Listserve, October 22, 1998, pp.4-7, www.egroups.com/list.decani.
56 As for English translation edition of Petition, see from South Slav Journal 5, No. 3, 1982, pp. 49-54, quoted from David A Steele, "Christianity in Bosnia-Herzegovina and Kosovo: From Ethnic Captive to Reconciling Agent," in Douglas Johnston, ed., Faith-Based Diplomacy: Trumping Realpolitik, p.147.

In another word, western countries, neighboring countries, countries with similar religions and various religious organizations may attempt to external religious intervention into regional conflicts. External religious intervention involves religious factors in non-traditional security, so that it is greatly different from political military intervention which pays attention to traditional security on spiritual and organization levels. Generally speaking, the external religious intervention is still a supplementary option in interventionist policies of great powers. Religious traditions and religious obligations including belief protection, missionization and heresy suppression may all become power sources for implementation of external religious intervention. In comparison with an ordinary religious intervention, external religious intervention is mainly the staged trans-national combination or alliance between religious power and political power after occurrence of an international political crisis. By religious intervention, an external force may be able to change group interests that are implemented in an intervened region or directly take a part in peace construction in this region. Nevertheless, it may still intensify vicious circle of violence with the motivation of revenge. Western countries hope to popularize and promote the principle of separation between politics and church (religion) in those countries and regions which face frequent religious conflicts. Albanian Muslims in the newly emerged independent Kosovo try to dilute their Islamic religious colors in order to obtain EU's approval and satisfy western expectations. International organizations and western countries also hope that the Serbian Orthodox citizens of Kosovo can break away their relations with Serbian politicians. However, in the modern politics, the principles of "religious tolerance" and "religious freedom" also coexist with the principle of "politics-religion separation". We think it would be both unrealistic and irrational to ignore religious characteristics of a region and attempt to enforce detachment or isolation between religion and politics. Considering the manifestations and concrete effects of external religious intervention in the Kosovo conflict, we can say that the general premise of properly dealing with religious affairs and conflicts lies in treating religious beliefs rationally and realistically, respecting the objective existence of religious powers, and avoiding religious extremism and religious discrimination.

www.ingramcontent.com/pod-product-compliance
Lightning Source LLC
Chambersburg PA
CBHW050841040426
42333CB00058B/116